Guy G. Stroumsa

Barbarian Philosophy

The Religious Revolution
of Early Christianitiy

Mohr Siebeck

GUY G. STROUMSA, born 1948; 1969 B.A. Hebrew University of Jerusalem; 1978 Ph.D. Harvard University; since 1991 Martin Buber Professor of Comparative Religion at the Hebrew University of Jerusalem.

Die Deutsche Bibliothek – CIP-Einheitsaufnahme

Sṭrûmzā, Gai' G.:
Barbarian philosophy : the religious revolution of early Christianity /
Guy G. Stroumsa. – Tübingen : Mohr Siebeck, 1999
  (Wissenschaftliche Untersuchungen zum Neuen Testament ; 112)
  ISBN 3-16-147105-9

© 1999 by J.C.B. Mohr (Paul Siebeck), P.O. Box 2040, D-72010 Tübingen.

The book was typeset by Gulde-Druck in Tübingen using Times typeface, printed by Gulde-Druck in Tübingen on non-aging paper from Papierfabrik Niefern and bound by Heinr. Koch in Tübingen.

Printed in Germany.

ISSN 0512-1604

Wissenschaftliche Untersuchungen
zum Neuen Testament

Herausgegeben von
Martin Hengel und Otfried Hofius

112

For Shaul Shaked
and R.J. Zwi Werblowsky

and in memory
of Shlomo Pines

Contents

Part IV: Radical dualism

Envoi

Acknowledgments

Most chapters in this book have been written over the last few years, and reflect problems and questions that I have been tackling with the help of many friends and colleagues, both formally and informally. Invitations to speak on a given theme, in Israel, in Europe and in the United States, have often provided the impetus for presenting ideas. Versions of various chapters were presented at the Israel National Academy of Sciences and Humanities, and at the universities of Cambridge, Utrecht, Bologna, Pisa, Turin, Frankfurt, Tübingen, Heidelberg, Princeton, Chicago, Virginia, and the Free University in Berlin, at the Ecole Pratique des Hautes Etudes (Paris), and at various conferences and workshops.

The Department of Comparative Religion at the Hebrew University of Jerusalem has been my institutional home for the last twenty years. Its congenial atmosphere, and the intensive exchange of ideas with colleagues from various fields in the university, has provided an intellectual environment for which I am grateful. Over the years, almost daily contacts with David Satran and David Shulman have led to the finding of rather unexpected links between the Greek and Latin Fathers and Tamil and Telugu poets.

Thirty years ago, I was privileged to meet three impressive scholars and remarkable persons, who encouraged a highly underqualified and underprepared student to swim in high and turbulent waters. I have neither learned to crawl in style, nor ever reached shore, but I still enjoy the effort. The dedication of this book acknowledges my thanks for their trust and friendship. It does not repay my debt.

During the last few years, a research project on "Religious Anthropology and its Transformations in the Ancient and Late Antique Near East," undertaken together with Jan Assmann of Heidelberg University, and funded by the Germany-Israel Foundation for Scientific Research (GIF), has provided a stimulating context for a comparative study of the anthropological transformations precipitated by Early Christianity. I wish to thank, together with Jan Assmann, our collaborators in this enterprise, Serge Ruzer and Brouria Biton-Ashkelony (both of the Department of Comparative Religion at the Hebrew University of Jerusalem), and Robert Meyer (of the Institut für Ägyptologie, Heidelberg).

Thanks are also due, for their invitations, suggestions, answers to queries, and fruitful discussions, to many people. Among them, I must mention at least Jean Robert Armogathe, Albert Baumgarten, Rémi Brague, Hans Dieter Betz, Hubert Cancik, Hildegard Cancik-Lindemaier, Harold Drake, Giovanni Filoramo, Cristiano Grottanelli, Ithamar Gruenwald, Moshe Halbertal, Pieter van der Horst, Moshe Idel, Maurice Olender, Evelyne Patlagean, Lorenzo Perrone, Arieh Kofsky, Mark Silk, and Laurence Vianès.

I am grateful to Ms. Alifa Saadya, who edited the final text with wisdom and alacrity, and to Ms. Ronit Nikolsky for readily agreeing to compile the indices despite her many other duties.

I should als like to thank Mr. Georg Siebeck and Professor Martin Hengel, for inviting me to publish this book in WUNT, as well as Mr. Matthias Spitzner, for the high quality and impressive celerity of the production process.

As always, Sarah Stroumsa has been an incorruptible censor. Without her, this book would not only have been longer and illegible. It would not have been.

Guy G. Stroumsa   Jerusalem, November 1998

List of Abbreviations

An Bol	*Analecta Bollandiana*
ANRW	Aufstieg und Niedergang der Römischen Welt
ARW	*Archiv für Religionswissenschaft*
BZNW	Beihefte der Zeitschrift für Neutestamentliche Wissenschaft
CBQ	*Catholic Biblical Quarterly*
CG	Cairoensis Gnosticus
CMC	*Cologne Mani Codex*
CR	*Classical Review*
CRINT	Compendium Rerum Iudaicarum ad Novum Testamentum
DACL	*Dictionnaire d'Archéologie Chrétienne et de Liturgie*
DOP	*Dumbarton Oaks Papers*
DS	*Dictionnaire de Spiritualité*
EDNT	*Exegetical Dictionary of the New Testament*
EEC	*Encyclopedia of the Early Church*
EI	*Encyclopedia of Islam (2nd ed.)*
EJ	*Encyclopedia Judaica*
ER	*Encyclopedia of Religion*
HLB	*Harvard Library Bulletin*
HrwG	*Handbuch religionswissenschaftlicher Grundbegriffe*
HSCP	*Harvard Studies in Classical Philology*
HTR	*Harvard Theological Review*
HUCA	*Hebrew Union College Annual*
IEJ	*Israel Exploration Journal*
JAC	*Jahrbuch für Antike und Christentum*
JAOS	*Journal of the American Oriental Society*
JBL	*Journal of Biblical Literature*
JEH	*Journal of Ecclesiastical History*
JES	*Journal of Ecumenical Studies*
JHS	*Journal of Hellenic Studies*
JJS	*Journal of Jewish Studies*
JNES	*Journal of Near Eastern Studies*
JR	*Journal of Religion*
JRS	*Journal of Roman Studies*
JSAI	*Jerusalem Studies in Arabic and Islam*
JSSR	*Journal for the Scientific Study of Religion*
JTS	*Journal of Theological Studies*
LCL	Loeb Classical Library
NHC	Nag Hammadi Codex
NHS	Nag Hammadi Studies
NT	*Novum Testamentum*
NTS	*New Testament Studies*
PG	Patrologia Graeca
PGM	Papyri Graecae Magicae

PL	Patrologia Latina
PO	Patrologia Orientalis
PS	Patrologia Syriaca
PW	*Pauly-Wissowa Realenzyklopädie der klassischen Wissenschaften*
RAC	*Reallexikon für Antike und Christentum*
RB	*Revue Biblique*
REA	*Revue des Etudes Augustiniennes*
REJ	*Revue des Etudes Juives*
REL	*Revue des Etudes Latines*
RGG	*Religion in Geschichte und Gegenwart*
RHR	*Revue de l'Histoire des Religions*
RMM	*Revue de Métaphysique et de Morale*
ROC	*Revue de l'Orient Chrétien*
RSPT	*Revue des Sciences Philosophiques et Théologiques*
RSR	*Recherches de Sciences Religieuses*
SHR	Studies in the History of Religions
TDNT	*Theological Dictionary of the New Testament*
TDOT	*Theological Dictionary of the Old Testament*
TRE	*Theologische Realenzyklopädie*
TUGAL	Texte und Untersuchungen zur Geschichte der Altchristlichen Literatur
VG	*Vigiliae Christianae*
VT	*Vetus Testamentum*
YCS	*Yale Classical Studies*
ZDMG	*Zeitschrift der Deutschen Morgenländischen Gesellschaft*
ZfR	*Zeitschrift für Religionswissenschaft*
ZPE	*Zeitschrift für Papyrologie und Epigraphik*

Introduction

Early Christianity as Religious Revolution

> ... one should say that which appears
> to be plausible, looking upon the
> readiness to do so as evidence of
> modesty rather than of temerity, pro-
> vided that one rests content with but a
> little success in matters that cause us
> great perplexity.
>
> Aristotle, *De Caelo* II.12.291b 24ff.

For a number of years, I have sought to tackle from various angles the complex transformation of religion in the Roman Empire, from approximately the first to the fourth centuries, or, if one wishes, from the revolution of Paul to that of Constantine. To be sure, these two revolutions are quite different, but both deal with the nature and status of religion, and both define, or redefine, a new religion, of a new kind: Christianity. For the historian of religious phenomena, it makes sense to study them together. Quite consciously, then, this volume opts for the *longue durée*. What this approach loses in detailed analysis of the specific differences between the different stages, situations, texts, and tendencies, I hope it will gain in contextual vision of the major transformations that I seek to detect.

From the first to at least the fifth century, Early Christianity represents an extremely complex set of religious phenomena. In recent years, it has become common practice to speak, in the plural, of early Christianities, as a convenient way to emphasize this complexity. The sources are written in many different languages, and stem from various cultural and religious backgrounds. Their baffling richness, combined with various theoretical difficulties, concur in complicating the scholar's task. Rather than attempting a grand synthesis, I have preferred to tackle different but related problems, aspects of what I call the religious revolution of early Christianity. In so doing, however, I have constantly kept in mind my overall goal of understanding better a major transformation in the religious history of humankind and its mechanism. The student of ancient cultures and societies must attempt to decipher their internal logic, or grammar, to crack their code, as it were. If this can be done at all, it is through a process of trial and error. I have sought to approach early Christianity from as many different angles as possible. In a sense, this process may be compared to a kaleidoscope, where a different but somewhat similar structure obtains from the same materials, each time one turns the lenses.

In a world which valued most ancestral traditions, *patrioi nomoi,* the basic intuitions and assumptions of Christianity were novel to Jews and gentiles alike. The religious revolution that it launched was not limited to the birth of new theological concepts, such as the (single) Incarnation or Trinitarianism, previously unknown to both Jews and gentiles. Powerful as these religious ideas may be, their greatest impact lies in their anthropological or psychological implications. A different theology entails not only a new conception of the Divinity, but also a new anthropology, a fresh perception of the human person, of its components and of its unity. New theological ideas, moreover, also have the power to transform, sometimes in radical fashion, conceptions of society and attitudes to outsiders. My approach throughout remains that of the historian of religious ideas. Rather than focusing on their social context, this inquiry attempts to locate and emphasize the paramount power of concepts, beliefs, and theologoumena.

There are four main parts to the present volume, which seek to understand (1) the radical nature of some of the early Christian beliefs and their dialectical transformations in the first centuries, (2) attitudes to the other and the growth of intolerance in late antiquity, (3) the birth and development of new anthropological conceptions, and (4) the extreme character of dualist trends, the role of which can be compared to "a revolution within the revolution."

Part I, Radical religion, seeks to delineate the new and radical character of early Christianity, from its beginnings as *religio illicita* to the Constantinian revolution and the self-transformation of Christianity into a state religion. In the first chapters, I investigate various aspects of this radical character and of its evolution from the first to the fourth century.

As I try to show, much of the later tensions within Christianity are better understood in the light of two opposite tendencies, irenic and eristic, both found in the earliest stages of Christianity, indeed in the New Testament itself.

The dual structure of the new Scriptures of Christianity permitted the development of a series of religious equivalences and cultural translations, in ways previously unknown in Jewish or Hellenic culture, and thus permitted the dramatic hermeneutical revolution achieved by late antique Christian intellectuals. This revolution only began with the dialectical relationships between the two Testaments. A new *paideia,* perhaps the most decisive single step toward the formation of European culture, was developed in late antiquity, in which the Greek and Latin classics were studied together with the Christian Bible.

Before this new cultural synthesis was achieved, however, pagan and Christian intellectuals had been unable to understand that they held vastly different conceptions of religion. To hallowed traditions the Christians were opposing a new and highly dynamic form of piety, which encouraged rather than feared religious change. This profound cultural misunderstanding highlights the vastly different presuppositions about the individual and society held by pagans and Christians. The latter had soon come to perceive themselves as neither Jews nor gentiles, but as a third kind of people, a *triton genos,* or *tertium genus.* They were proud to offer a new, "barbarian" wisdom, foreign to the Hellenic world.

Part II, Living with the Other, attempts to isolate some of the more salient factors which brought about that most puzzling fact of early Christian history, namely, the transformation of the religion of love into an intolerant religion, unable to accept competing visions and patterns of behavior. Indeed, before the end of the fourth century, all forms of religious expression, except for Orthodox Christianity, had become prohibited. There is no denying the painful fact that after the victory of Christianity, late antique society is strikingly less open, less pluralistic, less tolerant (although the modern concept of tolerance might be rather inadequate for ancient societies).

The first aspect to be emphasized in this context is the paradox of internalization and the new emphasis on conviction as a major factor of religious identity. The world of the cities around the Mediterranean in which the Christians lived in the second and third centuries offered what has been called "a market place of religions." The new religious pluralism forced the Christians as well as the Jews to live in close daily contact with what was for them a variety of intolerable phenomena. Idolatry, the worst of all sins, was everywhere: statues of the idols adorned the streets; meat from pagan sacrifices was sold at the butcher shop; various forms of magic and divination were practiced. Far from fostering religious tolerance, this symbiosis encouraged the erection of strong inner boundaries.

Palestine offers a particularly interesting case in point. Tensions of various kinds were mounting between Jews, Christians, Samaritans, Manichaeans, Hellenized pagans, Arabs. In their daily religious life, however, these vastly different populations often behaved in similar ways, or even shared the same beliefs, unconsciously following the same syntax of religious behavior. One can indeed speak here of a religious *koinè* of sorts.

One of the clearest examples of the radicalization of Christian attitudes toward non-Christians in late antiquity is, of course, the development of anti-Jewish attitudes on the part of the Church Fathers. While anti-Judaism is inherent in Christianity from its very beginnings, one can discern a shift for the worse in late antique Christian discourse on Jews and Judaism, in a sense, a *praeparatio antisemitica.* The history of Christian discourse reveals the progressive demonization of the Jews, together with the transformation of religiosity in the fourth century.

Part III, Shaping the Person, seeks to follow the transformations of the concept of the person, and the new anthropological perceptions developed in early

Christianity. These transformations represent a major chapter in the intellectual history of the West. In various ways, early Christian beliefs and theology propounded new conceptions of the self and attitudes to the human person quite unknown in antiquity.

A clear example of this transformation can be seen in the passage from repentance to penance. The ritualization of repentance encouraged the public expression of deeply intimate transformations of the self. Various rituals of public expiation of sins and penance developed in the first Christian centuries emphasize the passage from an ethic of shame to an ethic of guilt as Christianity grew: public humiliation is the best warrant of the Christian reversal of values.

The bodily as well as spiritual expressions of repentance and sorrow reflect the new attitudes to the body and the whole person. Augustine's *Confessions* is not only a book sui generis reflecting Augustine's great originality. It also represents the emergence of a new subject, the acme of a major process in the history of western consciousness, which would have momentous implications for the future. The work is the logical consequence of a series of beliefs and attitudes developed in the first centuries in Christian theological literature. It also reflects a new sensitivity among early Christian intellectuals, directly related to some fundamental Christian theologoumena. The idea of *homo imago Dei,* of the unity between body and soul, and of resurrection, were all quite simply unthinkable for pagan philosophers. With his great psychological sensitivity, Augustine was able to reach dramatic conclusions based on the Christian theological premises, but he was certainly not the first or only thinker to insist on a new Christian concept of the person.

In contradistinction to Hellenic thinkers, Christian intellectuals did not locate the great divide between soul and body, or between the higher firmaments and the sublunar world. Rather, they insisted on the rift between the created cosmos and the transcendent God. The passage between the divine and the created world, although it was never completely blocked, had now become much more difficult to traverse than ever before. In their successful bid to redefine the borders of the self, and to restructure religious experience, the Church Fathers limited the experience of dreaming, or rather, the experience of discussing dreams, in a drastic way. In the Christian *imaginaire,* most dreams no longer announce the future, but rather reflect the state of the soul. In a sense, then, the Freudian revolution can be said to have begun with the early Christian *Entzauberung der Welt.*

Part IV is devoted to *Radical dualism*. If Christianity effected a revolution in patterns of religiosity, Gnosticism and Manichaeism were even more radical movements. The importance of dualist trends in early Christian history can hardly be overemphasized. In a sense, Basilides, Marcion, Valentinus, and Mani were all following to their radical consequences some of the deeper intuitions and choices of the various writings of the New Testament itself. Second-century Gnosis, however, cannot be said to have been on the margins of the Christian movement. To describe it as such is anachronistic, applying criteria of fourth-century orthodoxy. Ernst Troeltsch showed that it was precisely the revolutionary character of the dualist tendency within early Christianity, which explained how it lost the battle for ultimate self-definition of Christianity to the less radical trends. These had neutralized rather than emphasized some characteristics inherent in the earliest expressions of the new religion. The study of dualist trends (and Manichaeism is here as important as the various Gnostic schools) remains essential for any full understanding of the early Christian phenomenon. Encratism and antinomianism, for instance, are notoriously difficult to disentangle from one another. And we now know that the early monastic movement, with its demand of radical behavior, seems to have been dangerously close to various dualist theologies.

The *Envoi* deals with the tragic city in which Christianity was born two thousand years ago, and where this book was written. It offers a reflection on what the French call the *imaginaire* of Jerusalem in western Christian consciousness. Both the idea of a heavenly or mystical New Jerusalem, and the multiple *translatio* of the Anastasis, the Christian *omphalos,* reflect the radical transformation of geography and history, of memory and expectations, all effected by early Christianity: nothing less than a revolution in patterns of religious thought and behavior.

Part I

Radical Religion

Chapter 1

Early Christianity as Radical Religion

> Also in the case of evils the end or actuality must be worse than the potentiality; for that which is capable is capable alike of both contraries.
>
> Aristotle, *Metaphysics* IX. 9. 3, 1051 a 16–18

An intense interest in religious radicalism is being forced upon us by puzzling contemporary developments, including religious revolutions, which seem to threaten the very texture of our social and intellectual life.[1] Even the ancient historian cannot quite hide from today's threats behind the heavy drapes of antiquarianism. Exclusivity, violence, intolerance, fundamentalism: these are some of the key concepts used, together with radicalism, in order to describe the multiple mischiefs of religion in our world. The following pages cannot attempt to sort out the overlapping semantic fields of these various concepts. Yet, by focusing on some paradoxical aspects of Christianity in its early history, they may shed some light on the process through which a dynamic religious movement can become threatening towards outsiders. Namely, can we account for the ways in which a persecuted religion became a persecuting religion, and the believers in the religion of love were able to invent new patterns of religious violence and intolerance, until then unknown in the ancient world?

Sociologists, indeed, seem to refer to religious radicalism in a rather restrictive sense. According to a recent definition, it is "a mode of thought and action that entails, first of all, the rejection of those surrounding cultural forms and values perceived as non-indigenous (or inauthentic) to the religious tradition."[2] Such a definition may well be valid in the case of contemporary trends in traditional religions; it is obviously off the mark when we seek to analyze new religious movements, often exhibiting a character of protest against the tradition from which

---

[1] A French version of this chapter, "Le radicalisme religieux du christianisme ancien: contexte et implications," appeared in *Retours aux Ecritures,* eds. A. Le Boulluec and E. Patlagean (Bibliothèque de l'Ecole Pratique des Hautes Etudes, Section des Sciences Religieuses; Louvain 1993), 347–74.

[2] E. Sivan, in *Religious Radicalism and Politics in the Middle East,* eds. Sivan and M. Friedman (Albany, N.Y. 1990), 1, referring to C. S. Liebman, "Extremism as a Religious Norm," *JSSR* 22 (1983).

they stem. Such is the case, for instance, with early Christianity. Although the radical or revolutionary character of nascent Christianity has been recognized, it is my distinct impression that it has not been analyzed carefully enough. This is due, probably, to the fact that this character is perceived only *in bonam partem,* while deep ambiguities or tensions in the overall structure of the new religion are usually ignored. An *unpartheilich* study of Early Christianity, such as nineteenth-century scholars sought to establish, seems to remain a matter for the future. Thus, Christian radicalism, since it stems from love, can be defined in direct opposition to extremism,[3] or else, as Gerd Theissen has recently claimed, Christianity in its earliest stages represents a revolution in values *(Wertrevolution),* essentially different from a revolution seeking power, hence entailing violence.[4]

The present investigation seeks to call attention to some theological structures of early Christianity, embedded in its foundational texts, and in their transformation during the first Christian centuries. It represents a study of intellectual, rather than social history, but is predicated upon the idea, best emphasized recently by Michel Foucault, that the discourse of a religion or culture is closely related to the practice of power. The late Foucault, as is well known, developed a deep interest in early Christianity, although his research in this area remained unfinished.[5] It should, of course, be noted from the outset that the correlation between theological conceptions (or even legislation) and practice is far from being direct and total. The social historian can show how behavior can be significantly different from proclaimed principles. Hence, a shrinking margin of theoretical toleration of outsiders in the Christianized society of late antiquity does not necessarily mean exclusion in the daily business of common life.[6] Yet, the trends are there, which explain how the new, unstable, and precarious equilibrium can degenerate, as it did indeed.

To be sure, such an investigation runs the risk of anachronism: when we speak of religious tolerance and intolerance, are we forcing modern categories upon a society in which they are rather meaningless? The greatest caution is *de rigueur,* but the fact remains that ancient societies could afford, according to their evolution, more, or less, religious freedom – both individual and collective – or freedom of religious expression. In this matter, there is no doubt that the emergence of Christianity made a major difference. A. D. Nock had shown in his seminal study of conversion how in the Hellenistic world a new possibility of religious

---

[3] See A. Rich, " Was heisst christliche Radikalität?" *Reformatio* 25 (1976): 278–88.

[4] See G. Theissen, "Jesusbewegung als charismatische Wertrevolution," *NTS* 35 (1989): 343–60.

[5] For an analysis of Foucault's impact, see the perceptive remarks of Averil Cameron, "Redrawing the Map: Early Christian Territory after Foucault," *JRS* 76 (1986): 266–71. Cameron insists that "Foucault was interested in Christianity as the provider of a totalizing and therefore repressive discourse, which spread a different kind of power relation" (266).

[6] See P. Brown, *Authority and the Sacred: Aspects of the Christianisation of the Roman World* (Cambridge 1995).

expression arose, established upon the choice of the individual rather than upon the secure and recognized boundaries of ethnos and tradition, the polymorphic exclusivity of archaic religions, that of Israel included. [7] Christianity, as Nock well saw, presented the main example of the new attitude; predicated as it was upon the need to convert, the choice of faith in each individual, irrespective of ethnic identity, social class, or sex. As John North has most recently argued, the Mediterranean world in the first centuries of the common era exhibited a "supermarket" of religions.[8] In a sense, the victory of Christianity represents that of the fittest in the new world of religious pluralism. As North understood, the transformation of religious life "established a system of interactive competing religions," hence fostering, together with great religious creativity, great religious conflict. Not the least puzzling aspect of a Christian victory achieved in a world of religious pluralism, is the fact that the new ecumenical faith left so little place for difference and dissent. Late antiquity, indeed, shows the final transformation of religious exclusivity, through religious pluralism, into religious intolerance.[9] Religious violence is not necessarily more common in the emerging world, but it can draw new theological justification, or at least latent encouragement, from a religion claiming a new, total, and universal grasp on truth.

1. Ambiguities of Earliest Christianity

The coexistence, in the New Testament, of both "irenic" and "eristic," or "peaceful" and "aggressive" tendencies is well-known. The context and implications of these opposite trends, which represent, as it were, a fundamental antinomic couple, are still in need of some clarification. This deep-seated ambiguity is directly related to the radical nature of earliest Christianity, a movement born within the chiliastic context of Jewish apocalypticism.[10]

---

[7] A. D. Nock, *Conversion: the Old and the New in Religion from Alexander to Constantine* (Oxford 1933).

[8] J. North, " The Development of Religious Pluralism," in *The Jews among Pagans and Christians in the Roman Empire,* eds. J. Lieu, J. North, and T. Rajak (London and New York 1992), 174–93.

[9] For a classification of the different kinds of intolerance, see A. J. Ayer, "Sources of Intolerance," in *On Toleration,* eds. Susan Mendus and David Edwards (Oxford 1987), 82–100. On tolerance and intolerance in late antiquity, see for instance A. H. Armstrong, "The Way and the Ways: Tolerance and Intolerance in the Fourth Century A.D.," *Vigiliae Christianae* 38 (1984): 1–17, and especially K.-L. Noethlichs, *Die gesetzgeberischen Massnahmen der christlichen Kaiser des vierten Jahrhunderts gegen Häretiker, Heiden und Juden* (Ph.D. diss., Köln 1971), and also Lellia Cracco Ruggini, "Pregiudici razziali, ostilita' politica e culturale, intolleranza religiosa nell'impero romano," *Athenaeum* 5 (1968): 139–52.

[10] For bibliographical references, see for instance D. E. Aune, *Prophecy in Early Christianity and the Ancient Mediterranean World* (Grand Rapids, Mich. 1983), 126–29.

Love of the enemy

Let us listen to the Gospels:

> You have heard that it was said, "You shall love your neighbor and hate your enemy."
> But I say to you, Love your enemies and pray for those who persecute you, so that you
> may be children of your Father in heaven; for he makes his sun rise on the evil and on
> the good, and sends rain on the righteous and on the unrighteous. For if you love those
> who love you, what reward do you have? Do not even the tax collectors do the same?
> And if you greet only your brothers and sisters, what more are you doing than others?
> Do not even the Gentiles do the same? Be perfect therefore, as your heavenly father is
> perfect. (Matt. 5: 43–48)

Thus spoke Jesus in the Sermon on the Mount. In the parallel passage in Luke,
we read:

> But I say to you that listen, Love your enemies, do good to those who hate you, bless
> those who curse you, pray for those who abuse you. If anyone strikes you on the cheek,
> offer the other also; and from anyone who takes away your coat do not withhold even
> your shirt. Give to everyone who begs from you; and if anyone takes away your goods,
> do not ask for them again. Do to others as you would have them do to you. If you love
> those who love you, what credit is that to you? For even sinners love those who love
> them. If you do good to those who do good to you, what credit is that to you? For even
> sinners do the same. (Luke 6: 27–33).

The demand put forward in the Sermon on the Mount would seem on first sight
to be at the antipode of any violent or intolerant attitude. Christian tradition has
always seen in such verses the quintessence of Jesus' message, the clearest mark
of its originality and of its power. It is only recently that the literary and doctrinal
Jewish and classical context of the Beatitudes have been studied in depth.[11]

The same intuition is picked up in lapidary fashion by I John; "God is love (*ho
theos agapè estin,* I John 4: 16). These words, which represent for the Christian
mind the very model of human relationships, above all within the community of
the faithful, will vibrate throughout Christian history. To be sure, the attempt to
retrieve the *ipsissima verba* of Jesus reflects an epic but probably illusory effort.
In our present context, however, what is important is that since the Patristic
period, these verses have been perceived in Christian consciousness as faithfully
representing the very words of the Lord, and hence modeling the Christian ideal
of interhuman relations established upon *imitatio Christi.*

We are probably too well-acquainted with such verses, which impregnate
Western culture as a whole, to read them carefully. "Love your enemies": we
ought to be puzzled by such a sentence, according to which the order of love, a

---

[11] The studies of the Sermon on the Mount are too numerous to be referred to here. One
should at least mention H.D. Betz, *The Sermon on the Mount* (*Hermeneia;* Minneapolis, Minn.
1995). On our passage, Betz is able to produce many parallel texts from various literatures of
antiquity, Jewish and pagan. The sheer number of such parallels sheds light on the original context of the passage, without denying its strength and originality.

paradox in itself, is carried ad absurdum. To answer hatred with love: here lies, according to common opinion, Jesus' fundamental intuition, and the very genius of Christianity. One can find the classical expression of this pattern of thought, for instance, in Günther Bornkamm's *Jesus of Nazareth,* a work that reflects a remarkable effort to grasp the historical figure of Jesus.[12] More recently, Gerd Theissen has offered a seminal sociological study of the *Jesusbewegung* in first-century Palestine – a movement he defines as "radical-theocratic."[13] Theissen aptly points out that the origin of the idea of love of the enemy remains an enigma, which the various analyses have not really succeeded in explaining in a convincing way. We shall seek here to recall the cultural and religious context of this idea.[14]

"You have learned that it was said: you will love your neighbor and hate your enemy. ..." This double injunction, of course, is found nowhere in the Hebrew Bible. Leviticus 19: 18 refers only to loving one's neighbor, not to hating one's enemy. Traditionally, however, Christian hermeneutics has set the Gospel's dictum in opposition to the attitude supposedly implicit in the Old Testament. According to this fundamentally exclusionist attitude, not only the love of the enemy was inconceivable, but also the hatred of the enemy would have been a natural, unavoidable consequence of the order to love one's neighbor (understood to mean *only* one's neighbor) in Leviticus.[15]

The "eristic" attitude

The pattern of thought reflected in the above-quoted verses forms what one might call the "irenic" trend of earliest Christianity. It is not, however, the only trend to be found in the Gospels. This might seem to be stating the obvious, but sometimes the obvious needs to be spelled out. Indeed, in the study of early Christianity more perhaps than in any other field, historical and theological stances seem to be inextricably entwined. A recent work, such as Robert Hamerton-Kelly's *Sacred Violence,* which applies René Girard's sweeping theory about religion and violence to Paul's thought, is a case in point. The book is

---

[12] G. Bornkamm, *Jesus von Nazareth* (Stuttgart 1956); English tr., *Jesus of Nazareth* (San Francisco 1960).

[13] G. Theissen, *Soziologie der Jesusbewegung* (Munich 1977). English tr., *Sociology of Early Palestinian Christianity* (Philadelphia 1978), 110. See also his article on "Wanderradikalismus," *ZTK* 70 (1973): 245–71, a thesis which he has maintained; G. Theisssen, *Lokalkolorit und Zeitgeschichte in der Evangelien: ein Beitrag zur Geschichte der synoptischen Tradition* (NTOA 8; Fribourg, Göttingen 1989), 61, n. 84; quoted by H. D. Betz, "Wellhausen's Dictum: 'Jesus was a Jew, not a Christian,'" *Studia Theologica* 45 (1991): 110, n. 85.

[14] For an authoritative study on the Palestinian Jewish context of Jesus' teaching, see E. P. Sanders, *Jesus and Judaism* (Philadelphia 1985).

[15] Such an exegesis reflects of course the deep anti-Judaism of traditional Christian thought and its ambivalence towards the Old Testament.

fraught with simplistic assumptions, perceiving for instance non-violence and the teaching of love as the only dimensions of the New Testament.[16] This approach entails some frightening implications, which, however, cannot be dealt with here. Although this chapter does not deal with Paul, my approach should be seen in radical opposition to that represented by Girard and Hamerton-Kelly.

Other verses quote certain words of Jesus which run a very different direction, which one might qualify as violent, or eristic. Let us examine here one instance:

> Do not think that I have come to bring peace to the earth; I have not come to bring peace, but a sword *(ouk elthon balein eirènèn alla makhairan)*. (Matt. 10: 34).[17]

This logion is reflected in Luke 12: 49–51:

> I came to bring fire to the earth, and how I wish it were already kindled!... Do you think that I have come to bring peace to the earth? No, I tell you, but rather division *(diamerismon)*.[18]

Theissen, following many other exegetes, interprets this verse as "alluding to a conflict within the family." The importance granted by Jesus to the sword appears also in the famous passage of Luke on "the two swords: (Luke 22: 35–38), where Jesus advises his disciples to acquire weapons.[19]

The simultaneous existence of these two languages in the synoptic Gospels seems to leave most exegetes, who are often also Christian theologians, per-

---

[16] R. G. Hamerton-Kelly, *Sacred Violence: Paul's Hermeneutic of the Cross* (Minneapolis, Minn. 1992); passim, and for instance, 14, 179. On p. 11, thesis 12, Hamerton-Kelly calls the Jews who claim innocence (of the death of Jesus) "the mimetic doubles of the Christian antisemites" [*sic!*]. Hamerton-Kelly is quite entitled to believe that "all the human race is responsible of the death of Jesus in its violence against the divine," although this theological stance can hardly be of any use to the historian.

It is embarrassing to have to remind one that throughout history, Christian antisemites have perceived the Jews of their own day as being responsible for the supposed action of the High Priest and his colleagues in first-century Jerusalem. To write that a Jewish claim of innocence is "the mimetic double" of antisemitism is not only utterly distasteful; it also reveals a disturbingly mixed-up mind. A claim of innocence of Jesus' death, after all, has never induced Jews to kill Christians. On Christian antisemitism, see now G. I. Langmuir's companion volumes, *History, Religion and Antisemitism* and *Toward a Definition of Antisemitism*, both published the same year (Berkeley, Los Angeles, and Oxford 1991). For a careful appraisal of Girard's theory and its bearing upon biblical matters, see R. North, S.J., "Violence and the Bible: the Girard Connection," *CBQ* 47 (1985): 1–27. See also chapter 8 of this volume.

[17] On this verse, see for instance Matthew Black, "No Peace but a Sword, Matt 10:34ff, Luke 12:51ff," in *Jesus and the Politics of this Day*, eds. E. Bammel and C. F. D. Moule (Cambridge 1984), 287–94.

[18] The word "division," in fact, appears to be an interpretation of "the sword" in Matthew, which softens the impact of the *lectio difficilior theologica,* as it reads the verse in the light of Matt. 10: 35–36 (Cf. Luke 12: 52–53).

[19] The Origenian interpretation of this passage, incidentally, would be crucial for the medieval conception of the relationships between the two powers, the spiritual and the temporal. This was demonstrated by Gérard Caspary in his *Politics and Exegesis: Origen and the Two Swords* (Berkeley 1979).

plexed.[20] The "eristic" evangelical tradition goes manifestly against the "irenic" tradition, usually considered to reflect the essence of the Gospels' kerygma. One is under the distinct impression that even the greatest scholars seek to avoid direct confrontation with such verses. Thus Rudolph Bultmann spoke of "embarrassing verses," while Adolph von Harnack explained away the passage on the two swords as a metaphor: the sword would represent the passionate defense of the Church under persecution.[21] Today, Theissen, too, seems to shun the confrontation between the two traditions. For him, the new vision proclaimed by Jesus is all love and reconciliation, a vision in which the many tensions of Palestinian society are internalized. Theissen refers here, in a rather cursory way, to the psychoanalytical term "introjection"; psychologists are indeed able to notice the complex links between introversion and repressed aggressiveness.[22]

The "eristic" verses, for their part, have been used by many scholars, from Reimarus to R. Eisler and S. G. F. Brandon, who see in Jesus a disciple of the Zealots, or at least their ally.[23] Hence, according to these scholars, Jesus would have been tainted by the Zealots' use of violence. The main textual basis for this opinion is, of course, the reference to a "Zealot," Simon, among Jesus' disciples (Luke 6: 15; Acts 1: 13). Both Mark (3: 9) and Matthew (10: 4) refer to him as *kananaios,* a transliteration of the Hebrew *qannay,* itself the origin of *zèlotès* in the LXX. According to Brandon's radical thesis, it is above all in the context of the revolt against Rome that one should understand the figure of Jesus. The many refutations and polemics to which this thesis gave birth have insisted on the selectivity of such a reading, which ignores too many texts to be convincing.[24] "Terrible simplifiers": thus Oscar Cullmann called these scholars in search of a thesis on Christian origins. Indeed, they choose to emphasize some dimensions of the earliest Christian movement while ignoring other dimensions just as important.[25]

---

[20] For a comprehensive collection of the New Testament texts, see M. Desjardins, *Peace, Violence, and the New Testament* (Biblical Seminar 46; Sheffield 1997). It should be pointed out that most studies do not recognize this double heritage of the New Testament. See for instance W. Klassen, *Love of Enemies* (Philadelphia 1984), for whom the only trend in the New Testament is the "irenic" one.

[21] A. von Harnack, *Militia Christi: die christliche Religion und der Soldatenstand in der ersten drei Jahrhunderten* ([Tübingen 1905], 4; English tr., Philadelphia 1981). See also C. John Cadoux, *The Early Christian Attitude to War* (London 1919), 39.

[22] Theissen, *Sociology,* 105.

[23] See esp. S. G. F. Brandon, *Jesus and the Zealots: a Study of the Political Factor in Primitive Christianity* (New York 1967).

[24] See the works referred to n. 16 above.

[25] O. Cullmann, *Jesus und die Revolutionäre seiner Zeit* (Tübingen 1970); English tr., *Jesus and the Revolutionaries* (New York 1970). See also R. Horsley, *Jesus and the Spiral of Violence: Popular Jewish Resistance in Roman Palestine* (San Francisco 1987).

Qumran: the hidden hatred

Let us go back to the teaching of hatred referred to in Matthew 5:43. The discovery of the Qumran manuscripts has made available a very interesting parallel.[26]

The *Community Rule* found at Qumran mentions the rules to be followed by the Master, or Instructor *(ha-mevaqer)* in his relationships with members of the sect:

> He shall judge every man according to his spirit ... and he shall love and hate likewise *(ken ahavato 'im sin'ato).*

> He shall not rebuke the men of the Pit nor dispute with them.

> He shall conceal the teaching of the Law from men of falsehood *(anshei ha-'avel),* but shall impart true knowledge and righteous judgment to those who have chosen the Way.

> He shall guide them all in knowledge according to the spirit of each and according to the rule of the age, and shall thus instruct them in the mysteries of marvelous truth *(be-razei pele ve-emet).* ...

> Everlasting hatred in a spirit of secrecy for the men of perdition *(sin'at 'olam 'im anshei shahat be-ruah haster)*!

> He shall be a man zealous for the Precept whose time is for the Day of Revenge *(ve-li-hyot ish meqane hoq le-yom naqam).*[27]

This text reflects a paradoxical attitude that must be underlined. On the one hand, it preaches hatred towards all those who are not members of the sect, while on the other hand, it claims that this hatred must remain secret. The members of the sect must not reveal their true feelings towards outsiders, in their dealings with the "men of the Pit" – i.e., with the rest of humanity, including the other members of the Jewish people.[28] This text, preaching a passive, or quietist attitude in front of the enemy, is remarkably violent.[29] As is well known, the Essenes were considered to be pacifists. Josephus calls them "ministers of peace,"[30] while Philo describes their peaceful way of life and the pacific character of their relationships with their neighbors.[31] This peaceful behavior of the Essenes with

---

[26] This parallel is already analyzed by M. Smith, "Mt 4: 43: "Hate thine Enemy," *HTR* 45 (1952): 71–73.

[27] P. IX. I quote according to G. Vermes, *The Dead Sea Scrolls in English* (Hardmondsworth 1962), 88. For the text, I follow Y. Licht, *Megillat ha-Serakhim* (Jerusalem 1965).

[28] See E. P. Sanders, *Paul, the Law and the Jewish People* (Philadelphia 1983), 174: "The Dead Sea Scrolls offer some help in understanding substantial adoption by Paul of the concept of 'true Israel' and the unwillingness to call the members of the new group simply 'Israel.'"

[29] References in G. Theissen, *The Social Setting of Pauline Christianity* (Philadelphia 1982). 193 and n. 34. P. Alfaric, for instance, referred to the Essenes as "quietists."

[30] *Bellum iudaicum*, II. 135; cf. Todd S. Ball, *Josephus' Description of the Essenes Illustrated by the Dead Sea Scrolls* (Cambridge 1988).

[31] *Quod omnis probus liber sit*, 76. On the ancient sources on the Essenes, see G. Vermes and M. Goodman, eds., *The Essenes: according to the Classical Sources* (Sheffield: 1988).

the surrounding world appears now to have been only a mask hiding a bellicose theology.

Indeed, the text quoted above clearly indicates the esoteric dimension of Essene theology. Truth is to be taught only to members of the sect – Sons of Light at war until the final struggle with the Sons of Darkness. For Essene consciousness, this fight opposes the members of the sect to the rest of humanity, perverted in its ways. It is their sectarian radicalism that helps the Essenes develope such an esoteric theology: one does not reveal strategic secrets to the enemy. Thus we find, within the framework of a utopian community, what is to my knowledge the first expression of the attitude which will find its classical expression in the Shi'ite theory of *taqiyya*.[32] This attitude crystallizes in an introverted religious community, which lives very intensely the active preparation for a cosmic redemption. In their indispensable relationships with the outside world, the Essenes must keep secret the tenets of a theology that will be justified only through its eschatological dimensions. The hatred must thus remain secret until the *Endzeit*. Despite the recent attention devoted to the Qumran scrolls, the implications of the esoteric character of hatred in Essene thought for the history of religions in general, and for earliest Christianity in particular, do not seem to have been investigated in earnest.[33] One must emphasize here that more than Rabbinic Judaism, early Christianity seems to have inherited in some respects radical or marginal trends from second Commonwealth Judaism.[34]

Holy war, as developed in particular in the *War Scroll,* forms an integral part of Essene eschatology. The roots of this idea are of course biblical, although the concept "holy war" itself does not appear in the Hebrew Bible.[35] The Essene

---

[32] For an effort to interpret the social context of some basic theological tenets of Jewish, Gnostic, and Christian radical groups, see Alan F. Segal, "The Ruler of this World," in his *The Other Judaisms of Late Antiquity* (Brown Judaic Series 127; Atlanta 1987), 41–77. Utopian themes in Essene thought have been studied by Doron Mendels, "Hellenistic Utopia and the Essenes," *HTR* 72 (1979): 207–22. On *taqiyya*, see for instance Etan Kohlberg, "Taqqiya in Shî'î Theology and Religion," in *Secrecy and Concealment: Studies in the History of Mediterranean and Near Eastern Religions,* ed. H. G. Kipperberg and G. G. Stroumsa (SHR 65; Leiden 1995), 345–80.

[33] On Qumran in general, see Geza Vermes, *The Dead Sea Scrolls: Qumran in Perspective* (Philadelphia 1977), esp. 163–98. On hatred in Qumranian theology, see esp. E. F. Sutcliffe, "Hatred at Qumran," *Revue de Qumrân* 2 (1959–1960), 345–56, as well as Krister Stendahl, "Hate, Non-Retaliation, and Love: 1QS X, 17–20 and Rom 12: 19–21," *HTR* 55 (1962): 343–55. The most recent comparative study of the problem of esotericism in Mediterranean and Near Eastern religions, H. Kippenberg, *Die vorasiatischen Erlösungsreligionen in ihrem Zusammenhang mit der antiken Stadtherrschaft: Heidelberger Max-Weber-Vorlesungen 1988* (Frankfurt 1991), does not discuss Qumranian theology.

[34] See, for instance, the recent research of E. H. Pagels, *The Origin of Satan* (New York 1995).

[35] Although the term itself is not to be found in the Bible, one should note the single reference (Numbers 21: 14) to a lost "Book of the wars of the Lord" *(sefer milḥemot YHWH),* which

case, which highlights the dramatic importance accorded to apocalyptic warfare in sectarian theology, tends to strengthen Walzer's approach. But this case also permits us to emphasize the new conditions that transform the holy war into an apocalyptic war, of a somewhat abstract or unreal (although not metaphorical) character. It is in this context that one can understand the violence advocated by John's *Revelation*.[36]

But it is also in the same context that one should read the Gospel verses quoted above. Does Jesus allude to Essene doctrines when he refers to the teaching about hating the enemy? This stands to reason, as Morton Smith argued long ago.[37] In any case, the Dead Sea Scrolls reflect, at least in part, the natural context in which the new Christian movement was born. It is to a great extent in opposition to the political radicalism of the Zealots that the movement launched by Jesus defined itself in its early days. Before the Great Revolt of the sixties, the term "Zealots" should probably be understood in the generic sense of nationalist thugs, without a precise reference to a concrete political and military group.[38] But to political radicalism, Jesus and his disciples oppose another form of radicalism, eschatological and itinerant in nature.[39] The expression of this eschatological radicalism picks up certain themes found also in Essene literature, in particular that of apocalyptic violence. Jesus' eristic words should be understood in this context. As Otto Betz has argued, such eristic words do refer

---

seems to have contained lyrical texts on the wars of Israel; see Sh. Talmon's article (in Hebrew) in *Encyclopedia Biblica*, 4: 1065–1066, and in particular F. Stolz, *Jahwes und Israels Kriege: Kriegstheorien und Kriegserfahrungen im Glauben des alten Israels* (Zürich 1972).

On religious intolerance in ancient Israel, see for instance Bernhard Lang, "Segregation and Intolerance," in *What the Bible Really Says*, eds. M. Smith and R. J. Hoffmann (Buffalo 1989), 115–35. Lang, however, commits a serious methodological mistake when he identifies intolerance and exclusivity. On this, see below.

[36] On the Book of Revelation, see, e.g., Adela Yarbro Collins, *The Combat Myth in the Book of Revelation* (Harvard Dissertations in Religion; Missoula, Mont. 1976).

[37] See n. 26 above.

[38] On the Zealots, the classical study is that of Martin Hengel, *Die Zeloten: Untersuchungen zur jüdischen Freiheitsbewegung in der Zeit von Herodes I bis 70 n. Chr.* (AGSU 1; Leiden-Köln 1961), see esp. 384–86 on the relationships between Zealotism and earliest Christianity. Hengel rightly points out the various links between Zealots and Christians, but he ignores the eristic dimension of the New Testament. Hence he can write: "Die Bedeutung des uneingeschränkten Liebesgebots als Grundlage der urchristlichen Ethik steht in absolutem Gegensatz zu dem in NT noch am Rande erscheinenden 'Eifer für Gott' im Sinne der Gewaltanwendung" (p. 386). Eng. tr., *The Zealots:* (Edinburgh 1989). See also M. Smith, "Zealots and Sicarii: their Origins and Relation," *HTR* 64 (1971): 1–19. On the concept of *zèlos*, see G. Kittel, ed., *TDNT*, 2: 877–88. R. A. Horsley, "Popular Messianic Movements around the Time of Jesus," *CBQ* 46 (1984): 471–95, raises some methodological doubts on the legitimacy of using the term before the second year of the great revolt (472). For the kind of literature produced by such nationalistic groups, see M. Hengel, *The Pre-Christian Paul* (London and Philadelphia 1991), 131, n. 224. This work was originally published in German in *Paulus und das antike Judentum*, eds. M. Hengel and U. Heckel (Tübingen 1991).

[39] See n. 13 above.

to a holy war, but one of an apocalyptic nature, to be waged against demonic forces and cosmic powers of evil rather than against the Romans.[40] It is here that we must search for the roots of the military metaphors that are so predominant throughout Christian literature and consciousness, from the martyrs and ascetics of the first centuries to the Jesuits and the Salvation Army.

Although Jesus and his disciples did not prepare the revolt against Rome, they were conscious of living the trials and the violence predicted for the eschatological times. As much as that of the Essenes, their attitude can be called radical. But instead of the Essenes' hidden hatred, they offer an even newer attitude, both anarchist and utopian: to return love for hatred. Within the frame of the interpretations of the eristic trend in Early Christianity, I shall also point out the psychological implications of such a paradoxical attitude.

2. Interpretations

Alternative interpretations of Christian intolerance

"I have described the triumph of barbarism and religion." Thus did Edward Gibbon summarize the goal of his *Decline and Fall of the Roman Empire*.[41] The strength of this short sentence lies in the innuendo: Gibbon does not mean to speak only of barbarism and of religion, but of the joint efforts of barbarians and Christians who, together, destroyed the ancient world. For Gibbon, it is above all thanks to their religious zeal, inherited from Jewish monotheism and quite unknown to the pagans, that the Christians had won their major battle against paganism in the Roman Empire. In the famous Chapter fifteen of his magnum opus, Gibbon lists intolerant zeal as the first among the five causes that made the Christian victory possible. In other words, the historical strength of Christianity stems from its innate fanaticism. Gibbon's approach is the prototype of an attitude that one can call "paganophile," and which reflects a trend of research that is deeply anti-Christian. This trend, sometimes compounded by anti-Judaism, ultimately stems from the "pagan reaction" of the Enlightenment. The overly simplifying opposition between pagan and Christian behavior can be too easily manipulated by this pattern of thought. Such opposition is reflected, in particular, in Robin Lane Fox's *Pagans and Christians*.[42] It can also be found, on another level, in the multi-volume *Kriminalgeschichte des Christentums* being published

---

[40] "Jesu heiliger Krieg," *NT* 2 (1958): 116–37.

[41] E. Gibbon, *Decline and Fall*, chapter 71(the conclusion of the whole work).

[42] On Lane Fox's *Pagans and Christians* (Harmondsworth 1986), see the remarks of Averil Cameron, *Christianity and the Rhetoric of Empire* (Berkeley 1991), 20–21: according to her, the use of binary oppositions has the paradoxical effect of reversing the Gibbonian perspective and of leading towards a Christian triumphalism.

by Karl-Heinz Deschner, a former journalist, Nietzschean epigone, and Catholic apostate, and which has quickly become, at least in Germany, a *succès de scandale*.[43]

Against such presentations of the evils transmitted by Christianity to Europe, there is a position that can be described as apologetic. This position has traditionally been developed particularly by Protestant thinkers and historians, among enemies of Caesaro-papism inclined to present an opposition between a mythical apostolic community, living according to the pure word of the Lord and between the decadence of the Catholic *ecclesia triumphans*. This alternative "model" views the Constantinian revolution as the capital sin of Christianity. The mixture of religion in the *saeculum*, its politicization, were bound to bring catastrophic results and transform in its very nature the message of peace taught by the prophet of Nazareth. These thinkers thus oppose the original kerygma, unblemished by any intolerance or violence, to what they considered degenerate Christianity.

Such an apologetic approach, however, is not restricted to Protestant theologians. The French historian Jean Delumeau, for instance, has devoted much thought to the possible Christian roots of modern totalitarianism. In a certain sense, his answer follows the "apologetic" line:

> Because Christianity was in power and had become merged with the state, it became totalitarian and persecuted all those who dissented from official doctrine.[44]

Moreover, Delumeau insists, like Jacob Talmon, upon the utopian character of modern totalitarian movements, and notes that millenarian movements and revolutionary totalitarianism are both established upon utopia.[45] One could have expected Delumeau to reflect upon Christian origins and upon the implications of theological conceptions for the much later birth of some social or political attitudes. But Delumeau is not a historian of the ancient world, and the many examples he brings to support his thesis are not earlier than the middle ages. One should here at least refer to Arnaldo Momigliano's rejection of the "political" conception of the roots of Christian intolerance. In an important study of the political implications of theology, he was able to point out the ambivalent attitude of Christian universalism toward the concept of the state.[46]

Karl Mannheim, who established the Sociology of Knowledge as a discipline, has also contributed some very interesting thoughts on the deep and dialectical

---

[43] K. H. Deschner, *Kriminalgeschichte des Christentums* (Frankfurt 1986). When completed, the whole work is to include ten volumes.

[44] J. Delumeau, *Le christianisme va-t-il mourir?* (Paris 1977), 55. See also J. Delumeau, "Religion et totalitarisme," *Les temps modernes* 410 (1980): 462–68.

[45] J. Talmon, *The Origins of Totalitarian Democracy* (London 1952).

[46] A. Momigliano, "The Disadvantages of Monotheism for a Universal State," *Classical Philology* 81 (1986): 285–97, reprinted in his *Ottavo contributo alla storia degli studi classici e del mondo antico* (Rome 1987), 313–28.

influence of utopian ideas upon society. In his *Ideology and Utopia,* he alludes to the tension existing in ancient Christianity between the command of love and life in an unredeemed world. But Mannheim is too interested by the modern world to pursue his analysis of the deep religious roots of contemporary political and ideological utopias.[47]

I have briefly presented here two essentially opposed approaches to the roots of Christian intolerance:

1. Gibbon's "paganophile" approach: Christian intolerance stems from its monotheistic character. This intolerance is intrinsically linked to the "religious zeal" inherited by the Christians from the Jews. The worst consequences of this zeal were revealed only after the religious transformation of the empire. This approach does not take into account the following fact: it is precisely after the transformation of Christianity, under pervasive pagan influence, in the Roman Empire of the third and fourth centuries, into a *qualified* monotheism, that the violence and intolerance come to the fore.

2. The "apologetic" approach: Jesus' original message would in no way represent a danger for religious tolerance. Fourth-century politicization of Christianity bears the full responsibility for its degradation.

In the first of these approaches, Christianity corrupted the state. In the second, the state corrupted Christianity.

For the historian of religion, the major weakness of these two approaches lies precisely in their static, a-historical character. Everything is either decided in the first century, or one can see no threat before the fourth century. Neither of these two patterns of thought provides a satisfying historical "model" which would take into account the evolution of Christianity, from the first to the fourth century, as well as the impact of earliest Christianity on the later development of intolerance within Christian milieus. The obvious ideological and theological overtones of both approaches leave us confronted with a false dilemma. The two abovementioned approaches insist on a single aspect of Christianity, either innate or acquired, and avoid both the polysemy of what one can call the "foundational" texts and the historical dimension of their transformation. In other words, in both cases it is the lack of a dialectical dimension, the inability to interpret the transformation of some characters from the first to the fourth century, that renders these two approaches inadequate for understanding the complex phenomenon of Christian violence and intolerance.

A true understanding of the complex transformation of Christianity in the first centuries must overcome this fictitious opposition, and study religious phenomena in their historical and sociological dimensions. The approaches of Max

---

[47] I quote the English edition, K. Mannheim, *Ideology and Utopia: an Introduction to the Sociology of Knowledge* (New York 1964; first ed.1936). *Ideologie und Utopie* was first published in Bonn in 1929.

Weber and Ernst Troeltsch, in particular, seem to offer a useful departure for a new study of the roots of Christian intolerance.

Troeltsch and Weber: dialectical tensions and Entpolitisierung

Probably more than any other thinker, Ernst Troeltsch was able to offer, in the first quarter of this century, a fundamental reflection on the relationships between theology and social thought in Christianity. In contradistinction to Max Weber, who did not dedicate a full-fledged synthetic study to early Christianity, Troeltsch begins his analyses with its earliest stages. In his seminal *Social Teachings of the Christian Churches*, Troeltsch insists on the transformation of Christianity in the Roman Empire.[48] According to him, it was originally a radical and eschatological movement, actively awaiting the return of Christ and cosmic salvation. With time, and the waning of this hope, Christian faith accommodated itself to the world. It assimilated to a certain extent the patterns of thought and of life prevalent in the Roman world, and developed a new, conservative approach which permitted the integration of the Church in the Empire. Troeltsch's great originality does not lie in the idea of a deep transformation of Christianity in the Roman world, but in his identification of the conditions which made this transformation possible. First among these: the embryonic coexistence of opposite tendencies since the very first stages of the new religion. Thus Troeltsch is able to point out the existence of both "conservative" and "revolutionary" elements in Pauline thought.[49] Troeltsch himself was close to those biblical scholars, mainly from Göttingen, identified in the early years of this century as the *religionsgeschichtliche Schule*, and was a major figure in Protestant liberal theology. In Weberian terms, one could describe his interpretation of ancient Christianity as a community of individuals defined above all as innerworldly, a community functioning upon earth but keeping its head in the heavens. The sociologist Louis Dumont enthusiastically adopted the Troeltschian analysis. According to him, with the victory of the otherworldly element in ancient Christianity, it is the extremist tendencies of the Jewish rebels, the apocalyptic authors, the Gnostics, and the Manichaeans who are defeated.[50]

---

[48] E. Troeltsch, *Die Soziallehren der christlichen Kirchen und Gruppen* forms the first volume of his *Gesammelte Werke*, published in 1912. See the reprint of the 1922 edition (Aalen 1961). See also the English tr., *The Social Teachings of the Christian Churches* (New York 1960).

[49] E. Troeltsch, *Gesammelte Werke,* vol. 1, 72–78. For some comparative studies of Weber and Troeltsch, see W. Schluchter, ed., *Max Webers Sicht des okzidentalen Christentums: Interpretation und Kritik* (Frankfurt a.M. 1988), esp. the contributions of K.V. Selge, R. E. Lerner, and C. W. Bynum.

For an anthropological analysis, which also insists on the dialectical character of opposite tendencies in early Christianity, see Edmund Leach, "Melchisedech and the Emperor: Icons of Subversion and Orthodoxy," *Proceedings of the Royal Anthropological Institute*, 1972 (London 1973), 5–14.

[50] L. Dumont, "De l'individu hors-du-monde à l'individu-dans-le-monde," reprinted in his

Although it has some advantages, this view does not explain the fact that it is precisely with the victory of the "reasonable," "bourgeois" tendency of Christianity in the Roman Empire that religious intolerance was unleashed, with a quite unprecedented violence. If Christianity had really succeeded in freeing itself from the radical and extremist tendencies of its origins, how can one explain that some aspects of these tendencies, far from disappearing, flourished after the fourth century?

According to Max Weber, religious movements in the Mediterranean and the Near East during Hellenistic and Roman times had been born within groups of what he calls "depoliticized intellectuals." These intellectuals, rejected by the leading classes and outside the corridors of power, developed new forms of religious expression that insisted upon the idea of salvation, a rather peripheral idea in archaic and classical religions. *Entpolitisierung:* this important Weberian concept has not been used very much in order to understand the formation of new religious attitudes towards the end of antiquity. The first major study devoted to the concept, written by Hans Kippenberg, was published in 1991.[51] Yet, the idea of *Entpolitisierung* seems remarkably useful for describing the interest developed in Jewish and Early Christian apocalyptic in the eschatological war between the forces of good and evil. Indeed, the bellicose and violent vocabulary of apocalyptic writings becomes clearer when one postulates that these writings were redacted and read in communities that stood rather far from the center of political power. In the case of Qumran and of early Christian communities, this hypothesis is clearly confirmed by the evidence. Thus, the exclusivity and the violence reflected in such texts are conditioned by the very milieu in which they were conceived. Exclusivity is indeed present in marginal social forms, while violence usually remains only verbal. The interest proclaimed by small sectarian groups for the salvation or the damnation of all mankind is surprising only when one forgets that the attitudes expressed in these texts are more often than not very removed from any concrete political program. One may hence speak of the "neutralisation" of eristic conceptions in "depoliticized" religious movements.[52]

With the Constantinian revolution and its accession to power, Christianity abandoned its former privilege of political irresponsibility, a privilege granted only to movements thriving far from political power circles. "Foundational" texts, however, retained the major influence that they had previously exerted on the development of Christian doctrines and attitudes. Some of their ideas could now be translated into political reality. It is in this simplistic transformation of an

---

Essais sur l'individualisme: une perspective anthropologique sur l'idéologie moderne (Paris 1983), 33–67.

[51] H. Kippenberg, *Die vorderasiatischen Erlösungsreligionen,* (quoted in n. 33 above).

[52] Gershom Scholem refers to "neutralization" in reference to the (Husserlian) *epochè* of Jewish messianism in Hassidism.

entpolitisiert ethic into the vocabulary of political activism that lie the gravest dangers of the preference, and then of the monopoly, granted to Christianity by Constantine and his direct successors. It is this process that gave birth to an active intolerance, which meant, too often, the persecution of Jews, pagans, and heretics. The naive reading of texts transformed into a program of radical action injunctions which had until then remained lucubrations free of any concrete application. It is indeed an anachronistic reading of the texts in a new cultural and political context.

Freud: love and intolerance

I have here called attention to the influence exerted by eristic tendencies in New Testament texts. One must now go further, and insist also on the following paradox. The absolute and unconditional command of love cannot be considered to be "irenic." Indeed, the hiatus between the attitude dictated by the command of love and social and psychological reality entails a deep and irradicable tension, usually referred to as "cognitive dissonance." As John Gager has shown, the cognitive dissonance between messianic expectations and the disappointment caused by Jesus' crucifixion is fundamental for understanding the development of first- and second-century Christianity.[53] Anthropologists make use of the term "rituals of reversal" in order to describe the peculiar phenomena observed in some societies in times of particularly intense tensions due to chiliastic expectations.[54] The term might be useful in reference to the command of love for the enemies. The new attitude is perceived as radical and paradoxical by its proponents. It is opposed to any legitimate expectation; in other words, it is utopian. We have seen how this command is linked to the idea of secret hatred in Essene theology. Hence, some links between this command and the esoteric trends in early Christian doctrine (trends ignored by most scholars) cannot be excluded.[55]

Theissen, who speaks of an "introjective aggressiveness turned into self-acceptance," offers a first attempt at a psychoanalytical interpretation of the com-

---

[53] J. Gager, *Kingdom and Community: the Social World of Early Christianity* (Englewood Cliffs, N.J. 1975). In his analysis, Gager refers to the "cargo cults" in twentieth-century Polynesia. The term "cognitive dissonance" seems to have been coined by Leon Festinger. See Festinger, H. Riecken, and S. Schachter, *When Prophecy Fails: A Social and Psychological Study of a Modern Group that Predicted the Destruction of the World* (New York 1965). For the application of the term on early Christianity, see A. F. Segal, *Rebbeca's Children: Judaism and Christianity in the Roman World* (Cambridge, Mass. and London 1986), 99–105, and notes, pp. 191–92. Segal developed his ideas on Paul's conversion in his *Paul the Convert* (New Haven and London 1990).

[54] Bibliographical references in H. Kippenberg, "Apokalyptik, Messianismus, Chiliasmus," *HrwG*, 2: 9–26, esp. 12.

[55] See G. G. Stroumsa, *Savoir et salut* (Paris 1992), ch. 7, 127–43, and idem, *Hidden Wisdom: Esoteric Traditions and the Roots of Christian Mysticism* (SHR 70; Leiden 1996), ch. 6, 92–108.

mand of love.[56] Freud himself, however, had already pointed out with great clarity the tragic paradox of this command. In a striking, yet generally unnoticed passage of *Civilisation and its Discontents,* Freud emphasized the direct relationship between the idea of love of mankind and that of intolerance.

> After the apostle Paul made general love of mankind *(die allgemeine Menschenliebe)* the foundation of his Christian community, the greatest intolerance towards those who remained outside this community *(die äusserte Intoleranz gegen die draussen Verbliebenen)* became the unavoidable consequence. The Romans, who had not established their political collectivity upon love, did not know religious intolerance, although religion was a state matter for them, and the state imbibed with religion.[57]

To be sure, the lack of historical precision of this passage, as well as its rather sweeping generalization, do weaken the statement made by Freud. Indeed, we cannot ignore the limits of Roman religious toleration. Even before their ferocious fight against Christianity, the Romans reacted violently, in the second century B.C.E., to the development of the Bacchic cult in *Magna Graecia,* and to the Druidic cult in first-century C.E. Gaul.[58] One must also insist upon the deep ambiguity and the limits of any conception of tolerance in antiquity, be it religious or political. We might perhaps refer here to the idea developed by Paul Veyne concerning belief in the gods in ancient Greece.[59] In order to explain the double attitude of belief and skepticism among Greek intellectuals up to Plutarch, Veyne appeals to what he calls "truth programs" *(programmes de vérité).* The same person can show signs of faith and disbelief at different levels. In this way, it seems to me, one can refer without oversimplification to the complex relationships between tolerance and intolerance in the first Christian centuries. There are no *Idealtypen* in historical reality. It is the specific equilibrium, in each case, between tolerance and rejection of the other, which distinguishes between the different attitudes.

These remarks however should not overshadow Freud's original intuition (who seems here to extrapolate on I Cor. 13). He does not say, like Gibbon – what would be only partly true – that Christian monotheism, confronted with Roman polytheism, shows clear signs of intolerance. The roots of Christian intolerance, according to Freud, should not be found in the idea of a single God,

---

[56] Theissen, *Sociology of Early Palestinian Christianity*, 105.

[57] S. Freud, *Das Unbehagen in der Kultur* (Studienaufgabe, vol. 5, Gesellschaft/ Religion), 243. For a summary treatment of Freud's views on religion in general, and of Christianity in particular, see M. S. Bergmann, *In the Shadow of Moloch* (New York 1992), 219–43, esp. 241–43.

[58] See for instance A. Momigliano, "Roman Religion," *ER, s.v.*, reprinted in *Religions of Antiquity,* ed. R. M. Seltzer (New York and London 1989), 230–33. Cf. Albrecht Dihle's claim: "Ein Motiv der Intoleranz freilich fehlte dieser Gesellschaft vollkommen, nämlich der Absolutheitsanspruch irgendeiner Religion oder Weltanschauung," *Die griechische und lateinische Literatur der Kaiserzeit* (Munich 1989), 26.

[59] P. Veyne, *Les grecs ont-ils cru en leurs dieux?* (Paris 1983). Eng. tr., *Did the Greeks believe in their Gods?* (Chicago 1988).

but in the totalitarian character of a universal command of love. In other words, it is the very universalism of Christianity that is shown here to be threatening. By right, the Christian community must include all mankind. A refusal to join the community of believers reflects a perverse and shocking vice. While ethnic or religious particularism tends to turn rather fast into exclusivity that ignores or despises outsiders, ecumenical inclusiveness entails the illegitimization of the other's existence, and hence generates tensions and violent intolerance. For Arnaldo Momigliano, the roots of religious intolerance in the western world are to be found to a large extent in Christian universalism.[60] Here Momigliano comes close to the conclusions of Paul Hacker's analysis of what he called Indian "inclusivism," an attitude to be strongly distinguished, Hacker argues, from true religious tolerance.[61]

One should also note that the duty of perfection central to Jesus' teaching ("Be perfect as your Father in heaven is perfect") entails the highest ethical and spiritual standards, and hence the harsh disappointment upon the inevitable failure in meeting these standards. In other words, it is the *combination* of the idea of love – and the duty of love – and the universalist nature of Christianity that Freud finds to be so threatening, almost totalitarian in its unattainable expectations.

Last not least, Freud's intuition about the deep-seated ambiguity of the Christian idea of total love refutes a central thesis of René Girard, according to which only Christianity avoids, through the love sacrifice of Jesus, the violence intrinsic to any other form of expression of the sacred.[62]

The letter and the spirit

"The letter kills, but the spirit gives life." Paul's lapidary dictum (II Cor. 3:6) soon became a cornerstone of Christian thought and sensitivity. Prima facie, it would seem to preempt the danger of "fundamentalism" (in the broader sense of a literal reading of the Scriptures) within Christianity. Paul's words, indeed, have always been understood as referring to the Old Testament, while the New Testament, reflecting the teaching and actions of Jesus, means for Christian consciousness, above all, an *exemplum,* to follow in the *imitatio Christi.*[63] But the imitation of Christ entails an activist attitude. When the reading of the Gospels

---

[60] See A. Momigliano, "Empieta ed eresia nel mondo antico," in his *Sesto contributo alla storia degli studi classici e del mondo antico*, vol. 2 (Rome 1980), 437–58. See also Momigliano, "Freedom of Speech and Religious Tolerance in the Ancient World," in *Anthropology and the Greeks,* ed. S. C. Humphreys (London 1978), 179–93.

[61] This concept is discussed by Wilhelm Halbfass, *India and Europe: an Essay in Understanding* (Albany, N.Y. 1988), 403–18 and notes.

[62] See n. 15 above, for a discussion of R. Hammerton-Kelly, *Sacred Violence,* who applies it to Paul Girard's ideas.

[63] See P. Brown, "The Saint as Exemplar in Late Antiquity," *Representations* 2 (1983): 1–25.

became politicized, as was the case in the fourth century, the ambiguities, the tensions, and the contradictions in the figure of Jesus would soon be reflected in Christian life. Side by side with the ascetical and mystical *imitatio Christi,* one would find the *zèlos* of religious activists in late antiquity, these monks whom Gibbon, although he avoided the term, considered to be fanatics.[64]

The tragedy of ancient Christianity is not directly dependent upon the cognitive dissonance created by the delay sine die of the Second Coming. Rather, this tragedy reflects the Christians' lack of sensitivity to the dissonance caused by the reading of utopian texts in a new political context and of their new power to activate them. I wish to insist here on the importance of *actualization,* a concept opposite to "neutralization," in order to understand various phenomena in the history of religions.

Christian utopia lies at the very heart of New Testament kerygma.[65] The French ancient historian Fustel de Coulanges could say how, together with Christianity, "the spirit of propaganda replaced the law of exclusion." The problem here stems from the very fact that Christianity is a religion of conviction, based on the spirit rather than on the letter, in contradistinction with the religions of the ancient world, and even to some extent with Judaism. Conviction, indeed, entails the duty to convince, and too often the wish to conquer. The strength of the Christian message is a naturally ambiguous force, which is also at the root of an ineluctable, though spiritual, will to power.

---

[64] For a bibliography and a definition of fanaticism, see Hildegard Cancik-Lindemaier, "Fanatismus," *HrwG* 1: 414–20.

[65] One may point out that Jewish scholars often seem to have problems with the Sermon on the Mount. In front of this sublime ethics, Rabbinic ideas appear somewhat pale. For Solomon Zeitlin, the weakness of Jesus' love commands lies precisely in their utopian character, since it is only in a utopian world that a utopian ethics can be applied. See his "Prolegomenon" to Gerald Friedlander, *The Jewish Sources of the Sermon on the Mount* (New York 1969), xxv.

Chapter 2

The Christian Hermeneutical Revolution
and Its Double Helix

Throughout the Mediterranean and the Near East, the creation of the Roman Empire meant a radical transformation of the cultural and religious scene no less than of the political conditions. This transformation was compounded by the multiplicity of religious and cultural systems. One might perhaps start by stressing the obvious: the very concept of Scriptures is embedded in the idea of a Divine revelation, and hence, in the Hellenistic world, remains almost exclusively a Jewish reality. Although much has been written on Jews in the Hellenistic world, surprisingly little has been said concerning the fate of their revealed Scriptures in a civilization to which the concept of a transcendent God having revealed Himself once and for all remained essentially foreign.[1] As a matter of fact, the Greeks knew very little of the Jewish writings. But despite the radical difference between the Jewish Scriptures and any Greek literary corpus, some striking similarities have been noticed between the status of the Bible in the Hellenized Jewish world and that of Homer in Hellenistic culture. The *Letter of Aristeas,* in that respect, is a case in point.[2]

Just like the Hebrew Bible, the Homeric writings underwent a process of canonization during Hellenistic times. Like the Bible, again, they were subjected to commentaries, throughout antiquity and beyond it. The canonization of the Homeric writings and their interpretation were as central to Greek culture as the canonization and interpretation of the Bible was important for the Jews, and later, for the Christians. This parallel status of the two *corpora,* which needs

---

[1] See for instance N. Belayche, "Sem et Japhet, ou la rencontre du monde gréco-romain et des livres sacrés des juifs," *Dialogues d'histoire ancienne* 23 (1997): 55–75, who underlines the very small number of quotations from the Septuagint in the Hellenistic world. Belayche recalls Momigliano's remark that the failure of the LXX to attract interest on the part of pagan intellectuals is parallel to the end of the myth of the Jew as philosopher.

[2] On the place of Homer in Greek culture, see for instance F. Buffière, *Les mythes d'Homère et la pensée grecque* (Paris 1956), and H. I. Marrou, *Histoire de l'éducation dans l'antiquité* (Paris 1948), ch. 1. On the canonization of the Homeric epics, see G. Nagy, *Poetry as Performance: Homer and Beyond* (Cambridge 1996), ch. 7. See also F. Kermode, "The Canon," in *The Literary Guide to the Bible,* eds. R. Alter and F. Kermode (Cambridge, Mass. 1987), 600–10, and M. Greenberg, "The Stabilization of the Text of the Hebrew Bible," *JAOS* 76 (1956), reprinted in *Canon and Masorah of the Hebrew Bible: An Introductory Reader,* ed. S. Z. Leiman. (New York 1974), 317–18 and 325–26.

no elaboration here, is underlined by the fact that when Friedrich August Wolf published in 1795 his *Prolegomena ad Homerum,* the models he used for searching the ways in which the Homeric writings were canonized were precisely those developed by contemporary scholars of the Old Testament, and in particular by his Göttingen colleagues.[3] It is surprising that to this day, no one has yet carried out the comparative study of Masoretes and Alexandrians that Wolf called for.

Such similarities between Homer and the Bible should lead us to question the traditional definition of Scriptures. A comparative cultural analysis needs to refer not only to revealed texts, but also to texts written, edited, read, and preserved in cultural and religious contexts rather different from those in which the Hebrew Bible was formed. Such texts may nonetheless show clear similarities to the biblical texts in terms of their place and function in their own culture and society. In other words, at least in our present search, perhaps the most important criterion for what constitutes a Scripture, should be what one may call the *foundational status* of a text – or a body of texts – for cultural or religious identity. Such a foundational status is easily discerned by the attitude of respect toward the texts involved and by the significance given to them. In particular, Scriptures are canonized, i.e., defined, delimited, and given a special, lofty, and hallowed status. Scriptures, moreover, undergo a constant process of interpretation and reactualization. Indeed, there can be no Scriptures without hermeneutics, which seek to overcome the constantly threatening cognitive dissonance, the distance and tension between conceptions reflected in the Scriptures of old and in present perceptions.

1. A sense of belatedness

While the Christians basically adopted the Jewish Bible, the *concept* of Scriptures underwent some radical transformations in the first Christian centuries[4]. It is with the changing status of Scriptures under the Roman Empire that I shall deal here. In the Christianized Empire of late antiquity, from the Cappadocian Fathers and Augustine to Cassiodorus and John of Damascus, we witness the birth of Christian culture. This birth can be understood only by reference to the new status of Scriptures.[5]

---

[3] Friedrich August Wolf, *Prolegomena to Homer,* tr. with introduction by A. Grafton, G. W. Most, and J. Zetzel (Princeton 1985).

[4] For an introductory study of Scriptures, see for instance W. A. Graham, "Scripture," *ER* 13: 133–45 (with bibliography). See further M. Levering, ed., *Rethinking Scripture: Essays from a Comparative Perspective* (Albany, N.Y. 1989), and W. A. Graham, *Beyond the Written Word: Oral Aspects of Scripture in the History of Religions* (Cambridge 1987).

[5] See F. M. Young, *Biblical Exegesis and the Formulation of Christian Culture* (Cambridge 1997), esp. ch. 2.

It is already in the first centuries of the (still pagan) Roman Empire that we can witness a radical and multiple transformation of the various Scriptural traditions. The greatest novelty is the major cross-cultural interaction that eventually brought about the formation of what is often called the Western canon. To a great extent, this interaction was achieved thanks to the decision of patrician families in the Eastern Empire in the fourth century not to create a new, Christian, educational system, but to establish their sons' education upon the best classical cultural tradition, with the addition, of course, of the Gospel. The new, Christianized *paideia* born in late antiquity was perhaps the most decisive single step toward the formation of European culture.

In the ancient world, where tradition *(patrioi nomoi, mos maiorum)* was highly valued, the radical newness of Christian religiosity was bound to draw sarcastic remarks. Christianity presented itself as a religious revolution on various accounts.[6] As I shall contend here, this revolution is also reflected in the attitude to Scriptures developed by Christian thinkers of the first centuries. These thinkers developed a radically new conception of Scriptures, different both in terms of content and structure from what was known by Jews and Greeks alike. In so doing, the Church Fathers were to reshape in various ways the concept of Scriptures and of their uses. Not only the scope of the canon, but also its very idea was defined anew, while the attitude to language and to cultural memory underwent some drastic changes. These changes reflect what can be called the Christian hermeneutical revolution – a revolution that has not received the interest it deserves.[7] It is a banality to repeat the double foundation of European culture, its Greek and Biblical aspects, between Athens and Jerusalem. Yet, the mechanisms through which some central elements of Greek culture functioned in parallel with the Christian Bible are still in need of clarification. These two scriptural bodies created what I call a "double helix," using Crick and Watson's metaphor for describing the structure of the DNA. Together, they formed the backbone of the cultural memory of the Christian world in the Middle Ages.

When Tertullian, in a lapidary and pregnant formulation, opposed Athens to Jerusalem, however, he was using a double shortcut.[8] "Athens" was in fact Rome, and by "Jerusalem" he meant the heavenly city, or the Church, rather than the earthly one. More precisely, Greek culture (Tertullian was thinking essentially of philosophy) had been translated into Latin, and Christians did not read the Bible in the original Hebrew, but in Greek, with the addition of the New Testament. In other words, we are dealing with a later stage of cultural and relig-

---

[6] See for instance, chapter 1 of this volume.

[7] See nonetheless, A. Le Boulluec, "L'apport des chrétiens au langage symbolique de l'antiquité," in *Les Pères de l'Eglise au XXe siècle* (Paris 1997), 225–49, who refers to Clement of Alexandria's "parabolic revolution" of symbolic language.

[8] Tertullian, *De Praescriptione Haereticorum,* 7.

ious history, clearly secondary and reacting, or responding to an earlier, original stage.

Belatedness is no doubt a typical trait of Greco-Roman intellectual culture in the Empire. One can think in this respect of the very long chain of tradition in the philosophical schools, like Platonism, or of the various attempts, during the Second Sophistic movement, to use archaizing language in order to reclaim the cultural heritage. Cicero and Quintillian had successfully attempted to re-canonize and translate the Greek classical tradition. Cicero's main cultural achievement lies in his translation into Latin of Greek philosophical language. The typical ambivalent attitudes of the Romans toward Greek culture (the culture of the political and military losers) brought them to recognize, in a very clear way, their own "secondary" character vis-à-vis their illustrious predecessors. The Romans could never forget that they came after the Greeks. Culturally, they felt strongly inadequate, condemned by their belatedness to interpret their former enemies' superior culture. It is in this context that we can follow the growth, in Rome of the second century C.E., of the idea of a "classic." The Roman world, hence, lived in what we can call a fundamental cultural diglossia.

The modeling of Roman cultural identity is perhaps best reflected in Virgil's *Aeneid*. The Homeric epic was something the Romans could not simply translate and use. They had to recreate it and suit it to their own needs. It is significant that for the Christians, too, the same Homer (the closest the Greeks had to a Scripture) would remain the most questionable item in Greek literature, the hardest to assimilate. Tertullian could say "Seneca saepe noster."[9] Neither Clement nor Origen could ever have adopted Homer in similar fashion. But the Christians' efforts to recapture the best in Greco-Roman culture, i.e., philosophy, which was least contaminated by the pagan gods, came to the fore only later. The original Christian sense of belatedness was vis-à-vis Israel. In order to show, to themselves as well as to their opponents, that they were legitimate heirs to a long cultural and religious tradition, the Christians soon insisted on perceiving themselves as *verus Israel*. Hence, they consistently and systematically refused to deny Israel's de facto and de jure primacy, despite strong pressures to do so, mainly, but not only, from Marcion's quarter.

For the Christians, the past was not simply idealized, depicted as golden and by nature superior to what came later. On the contrary, for them, it was essentially thanks to what came *after* the Hebrew Scriptures, and which the Scriptures were supposed to announce, clearly or in veiled fashion, that these Scriptures were valued. The Messiah has already come. During the first centuries, Christian intellectuals of various shades developed highly sophisticated hermeneutical rules in order to read the Jewish Scriptures in the light of this coming, which represented a radical caesura in world history. Most Jews, of course, hotly con-

---

[9] Tertullian, *De Anima* 20.1.

tested this vision of history, and strove to establish competing scriptural hermeneutics. The past, hence, was no longer universally and axiomatically assumed to
be better than the present. Christian hermeneutical behavior thus reflects a
radical change of attitude toward the past, and quite a new approach to Scriptures. This change of attitude is tantamount to a revolution.

The deepest difference between traditional views of belatedness and that developed by the Christians, and which would prove to be their most powerful advantage, was their perception of their own belatedness as a force, rather than as
a weakness. Such a perception was predicated upon a radically new attitude to
time and history: in sharp contradistinction to then-current conceptions of the
past golden age, among both Jews and pagans, the Christians, who knew they
lived in the messianic age, could think of themselves as knowing better, understanding more deeply, being closer to the full truth, than previous generations.
Mutatis mutandis, the description of the early Christian attitude to the Scriptures as a hermeneutical revolution is also true of Rabbinic Judaism after Yavneh. To some extent, the Rabbis, like the Church Fathers, propounded a religious revolution. Like the Fathers, they had to invent a complex hermeneutical
system meant to salvage the Bible in radically new conditions. Prima facie, the
situation of the Rabbis vis-à-vis their Scriptures seems different from that of
their Christian counterparts. No doubt with much historical simplification, they
considered themselves to be the direct spiritual inheritors of the Pharisees. Yet
they could never forget that they were acting in a radically new, latter-days, post-
classical situation: no sacrifices could be offered since the Temple had been destroyed and prophecy had ended. This was indeed a less than perfect world,
which imposed a cult significantly different from the one advocated by the Bible.
The Talmudic classical problem of the respective priority of the prophet or the
sage reflects the Rabbis' self-affirmation, their intense sense of responsibility in
re-modeling the Biblical heritage. Hence, the Rabbis had to find new, sophisticated ways of relating to the Scriptures of old, those texts pertaining to the
Temple, to the inheritance of a lost land, and to past prophecy. Like Roman culture, Talmudic culture starts from a perspective of belatedness: the Sages consider their main task to lie in new interpretations of Scriptures revealed to previous, worthier generations. They are, however, careful to hide the novelty of
these interpretations. The Rabbis, then, were thinkers functioning in a rather
special system, using an almost private language, and should also be considered
as late antique intellectuals.

2. Secondary canonization

The canonization process in Christianity is established directly upon the corpus
of the Jewish Scripture, which it broadens, ipso facto drastically transforming

both its structure and status. Hence, the Christian Scriptures exhibit some specific characteristics which, I suggest, stem from this process of "secondary canonization," or the filiation of canons, to use a term coined by Carsten Colpe.[10]

Much has been written about the canonization of the books of the New Testament, a process which essentially took place in the last decades of the second century (the very concept of "New Testament" seems to appear for the first time in Irenaeus's writings, around 180).[11] What is essential in our context is the fact that this process was directly triggered by the challenge provided by Marcion and his claim to reject the Old Testament as irrelevant to the Christian *kerygma*.[12] This well-known fact underlines the dialectical connection between canon and heresy. Marcion had emphasized the radical newness of Christianity. According to him, the religion of Jesus Christ had no use for the old Jewish Scriptures, which belonged to a quite different religious world. Marcion's radical attitude had a logic of its own. To some extent, his rejection of the Hebrew Bible and his demand for wholly new Scriptures fitting the newness of Christian identity is reflected in other heretical movements, such as various Gnostic trends and Manichaeism. Before Muhammad, actually, Mani himself decided to write wholly new Scriptures for the new religion he was founding.

More generally, however, the fact that Marcion's challenge triggered the crystallisation of the Christian Scriptures highlights the direct relationships between canonization processes and social realities. Discussions of the canon reflect arguments on the social boundaries: who are the insiders and who are the outsiders. In other words, canonization processes reflect another aspect of questions of identity: texts are excluded from the canon and defined as "apocryphal" just as contenders are defined as "heretics" and excluded from the Christian Church.[13]

---

[10] See C. Colpe, "Sakralisierung von Texten und Filiationen von Kanons," in *Kanon und Zensur: Archäologie der literarischen Kommunikation*, 2., eds. A. Assmann and J. Assmann (Paderborn 1987), 80–92. For Colpe, there are only three major filiations of canons in the history of religions, the Jewish, the Hindu, and the Buddhist. See further L. L. Patton, ed., *Authority, Anxiety, and Canon: Essays in Vedic Interpretation* (Albany, N.Y. 1994).

[11] For a classical study, see H. von Campenhausen, *Die Entstehung der christlichen Bibel* (Tübingen 1968), as well as B. S. Child, *The New Testament as Canon: An Introduction* (Philadelphia 1985) and B. M. Metzger, *The Canon of the New Testament: its Origin, Development, and Significance* (Oxford 1987). On the idea of canon, see B. Lang, "Kanon," *HrgG*, 3: 332–35; W. Künneth, "Kanon," *TRE*, 17: 562–72; W. Schneemelcher, "Bibel III: Die Entstehung des Kanon des Neuen Testaments," *TRE* 6: 22–48.

[12] For a recent study, see H. D. Betz, "Le canon néotestamentaire fonde-t-il une Eglise en morceaux?" *Concilium* 271 (1997): 51–63.

[13] Incidentally, the central importance of Scriptures in conflicts of identities within a given tradition is also reflected in the status of the Scriptures in the Rabbanite-Karaite controversy. See B. Chiesa, "Judentum und Heilige Schrift von der Antike zum Mittelalter: von der Kreativität zur Hermeneutik" (forthcoming). On earlier movements, see J. Fossum, "Social and Institutional Conditions for Early Jewish and Christian Interpretation of the Hebrew Bible with Special Regard to Religious Groups and Sects," in *Hebrew Bible/Old Testament: The History of Its Interpretation*, ed. M. Saebo (Göttingen 1996), 1: 239–54.

The very idea of canonization entails closure. As a body of texts is defined, it becomes closed to further additions; moreover, it is defined in opposition to other texts that are excluded from the canonical body of writings. Hence, canonization is in itself, by nature, a late process, which follows a previous stage of opening up, of redaction or successive additions of texts to the cultural memory of a society. The canonization process, indeed, is intended to put an end to such a natural creation of collective memory, to regulate and limit it. In that sense, canonization processes reflect the will of a society, a clear decision about what to remember and what to forget, what to upgrade and what to reject. In Jan Assmann's terms, "Kanon ist die *mémoire volontaire* einer Gesellschaft."[14] Or, as Ernst Robert Curtius put it, "If we resume our historical consideration, we find that forgetting is just as necessary as remembering. Much must be forgotten if the essential is to be preserved."[15] In that sense, opening up and closing, enlarging and limiting, are fit metaphors for describing what takes place in canonization processes.

There is no canon without exclusion from that canon. Like "sacred," "canon" is meaningful only in context, alongside the realm of the "profane," which of course remains outside. Canon, in other words, can only be understood as a comparative term. In legal context, for instance, not all laws can have the same status. If fundamental laws can be called canonical, it is in contradistinction to regular laws.[16] The study of canon is thus ipso facto a study of exclusion and loss. This insistence on the oblivial side of religious memory is certainly applicable to the Christian Scriptures. But because of the secondary and dual nature of these Scriptures, the Christian canon is endowed with some peculiar characteristics.

Above all, the canonization process reflects a given society's decision to choose various texts as belonging to what eventually becomes the foundational corpus for that society. At the same time, this process excludes as much as it includes. In the case of early Christianity, the main texts rejected from the canon are obviously the apocryphal Gospels and Acts, while in Rabbinic Judaism, mention should be made of the *beraitot*, literally, the "exterior" texts, excluded from the Mishnaic corpus. The main difference between the apocryphal writings of the New Testament and *beraitot* lies, of course, in the fact that the latter are in no way considered to be heretical or to threaten orthodoxy-in-the-making.

One should point out here that Christian canonization occurred in what we may call an "enclave society," i.e., a protected minority enclosed within the society at large, a counter-culture obeying rules of its own, often encouraging or

---

[14] J. Assmann, *Das kulturelle Gedächtnis: Schrift, Erinnerung und politische Identität in frühen Hochkulturen* (Munich 1992), 18.

[15] E. Curtius, *European Literature in the Latin Middle Ages,* tr. W. R. Trask (Bollingen Series 36; New York 1953), 396.

[16] See D. Conrad, "Zum Normcharakter von "Kanon" in rechtswissenschaftlicher Perspektive," in *Kanon und Zensur,* above, n. 10, 47–61.

permitting few relationships with outsiders. Literary decisions to include texts in a canon and exclude others from it cannot be discussed in isolation from the social context. Can we identify some elements in the doctrine of canonical Scriptures that make them more easily acceptable to those within the "theological main stream" – however we define it? And did the apocryphal writings seem more palatable to those whose theological views were marginalized, and who soon become identified as heretics? We know, indeed, various Gnostic groups and the Manichaeans to have been avid readers of apocryphal literature, from the Old as well as from the New Testament. I shall not ask here the reasons for such literary preferences. Nor shall I speculate on the question of chronological precedence, of what comes first, the radical views expressed by some texts, which shape the perceptions of those who adopt them, or rather the redaction of these texts within marginal groups. What should be emphasized here is the correspondence of the canonization process and the question of social and cultural (or theological) identity, which is always asked in reference to the outsider. The first outsider, here, is the heretic. "Tell me what you read, and I shall tell you who you are." Hence, the process of textual inclusion/exclusion directly reflects a social situation and the groups' boundaries.[17]

The hoard of literary documents discovered fifty years ago in Nag Hammadi has revealed that various trends within the earliest stages of early Christianity offered highly diversified interpretations of the nature and message of Jesus Christ. Most of these interpretations were eventually rejected by the intellectual and religious leadership of what became main trend Christianity. These writings, usually referred to as dualist, or "Gnostic," were excluded from the canon, and defined as apocryphal *in malam partem:* they were propounding heretical views, inspired by the Devil. Important aspects of early Christian speculation, which in some cases seem to have been rather central at the time in the spectrum of possible views, were later excluded, censored, and condemned to oblivion. Were it not for the hubris of the heresiographers, who dwelled upon the details of loathed heretical views, and the fortunes of modern discoveries, we would ignore the nature of most of these views to this day.

3. Two-tiered Scriptures

The context in which the writings of the New Testament are added in Christian communities to those of the Septuagint remains in need of further investigation. In the first two centuries, Jews and Christians, in search of their own identity, were in a state of fierce competition with one another. At the same time, they

---

[17] See R. Grant, *Heresy and Criticism: The Search for Authenticity in Early Christian Literature* (Philadelphia 1987).

were arguing within their own communities and polemicizing against the pagan majority culture. The canonization of the Mishna and that of the New Testament both seem to have taken place at the same time, toward the end of the second century. Despite the enormous amount of research done on the canonization of the New Testament, and to a lesser extent on that of the Mishna, this striking simultaneity does not seem to have elicited any attention. As I have argued elsewhere, it may reflect the competition between the two communities on the hermeneutical key to the proper understanding of their common Scriptures. For the Jews, the Mishna, or *deuterosis,* is the proper key. For the Christians, this key is offered by the New Testament, their own *deuterosis*.[18]

This parallelism between Mishna and New Testament, however, is far from being absolute. Although the Mishna (and later on the Talmud) is indeed presented as the key to the correct understanding of the Scriptures, it does not become part of these Scriptures. The very term "oral Torah," attributed to Talmudic literature distinguishes it from the Scriptures proper, the "written Torah." The oral Torah can be described as a different kind of canon, normative or legal in essence, which complements the Scriptural, revealed canon. The fact that the Mishna does not become part of the Scriptural canon implies that despite the respect it commands, it remains second in importance to the Bible.[19] A very different development occurred in early Christianity, where the quite novel conception of the canonical Scriptures entails the equal – or even superior – status soon granted to the new layer of Scriptures, the New Testament, with its *ipsissima verba* of Jesus, over the Old Testament.

As soon as the status of the New Testament became formalized, then the Christian Scriptures were established upon two layers, clearly defined and differentiated from one another, and which must each be read in the light of the other. What should be noted is the fact that the intertextuality is built into the system, which includes a time element: the whole dual corpus of the Scriptures includes both an earlier and a later layer, each either announcing, reflecting, or completing the other. These two layers have to be read together, each is the key to the proper understanding of the other. But the way of reading them is essentially different.

The New Testament not only became an integral part of the Christian Scriptures. It was also clearly felt to be higher in status than the Old Testament. The latter was only, as it were, its prefiguration, presenting the *typos,* or *figura,* a *sacramentum futuri,* of what would be more clearly repeated, developed, and fully exposed, in the final and perfect revelation, the New Testament, the Scripture par excellence, which preserved the *ipsissima verba* of the Savior. Such a percep-

---

[18] G. G. Stroumsa, *Hidden Wisdom: Esoteric Traditions and the Roots of Christian Mysticism* (SHR 70; Leiden 1996), 79–91

[19] On the various kinds of canon in Rabbinic Judaism, see M. Halbertal, *People of the Book: Canon, Meaning, and Authority* (Cambridge, Mass. 1997).

tion further encouraged some devaluation of the Old Testament in Christian religious memory: its deepest significance lay in what happened later on. It is the redeeming suffering of Christ that the Christians must constantly actualize, not its hints in the Old Testament, hallowed as it may be, which only announced it.

It is in this light, I think, that we must see the development of another kind of canon in early Christianity, like the Mishna a normative and regulating canon, but non-literary in nature, the *kanôn tès alètheias (regula veritatis)*. The nature of this *regula veritatis* is best understood if we recognize its identity with the *regula fidei*. This rule presents the criteria according to which one should understand the right meaning of the Scriptural text and distinguish orthodoxy from heresy.[20] In other words, both in the case of Rabbinic Judaism and of early Christianity, another canon, of a different nature, is needed on the side of, and as a complement to, the Scriptural canon. The Scriptures are not their own criterion of truth. Although the Christians had developed a two-tiered system of Scriptures, they still needed another canon, exterior to the scriptural one and established upon ecclesiastical tradition – and of course endowed with a lower status.[21]

The two-tiered structure of Christian Scriptures underlines the fundamental differentiation of Christian identity from Jewish identity.[22] The Christian way of reading the common Scriptures (the LXX) entails an expropriation of the Jewish reading of these texts: without the key of the New Testament, claim the early Christian writers, the Jews are unable to decode their own texts properly. They have become blind to their own revelation, and the Christians, *verus Israel,* have received the spiritual inheritance of the Jews, now Israel only in the flesh.[23]

One of the most powerful expressions of this well-known Christian claim is found in a striking passage of Origen's *Commentary on John:*

> Then, one should not eat raw the kid's flesh, as do the slaves of the letter, who are like dumb *(alogôn)* animals and like wild beasts compared to men. The latter are truly intelligent, and desire to know spiritual realities through the logos. The former, on the other hand, partake the life of the wild beasts. Whoever takes the raw flesh of the Scripture to cook it must take care not to transform the text into something rather flabby, wet, soft, as do those who, "as their ears itch them, turn them away from truth" (II Tim 4: 2–3), giving to their explanations the inconsistent and wet character of their way of life.

---

[20] See R. A. Greer in *Early Biblical Interpretation* (Philadelphia 1986), by J. L. Kugel and R. A. Greer, 112ff. On the *regula veritatis,* see E. Lanne, "La règle de vérité: aux sources d'une expression de saint Irénée," in *Lex Orandi, Lex Credendi, in onore di P. Cipriano Vagaggini* (Studia Anselmiana 79; Rome 1980), 57–70.

[21] On the different meanings of *kanon* in Christian parlance, see H. Cancik, "Kanon, Ritus, Ritual: Religionsgeschichtliche Anmerkungen zu einem literaturwissenschaftlichen Diskurs," in *Kanon* (Heidelberg 1997), ed. M. Moog-Grünewald, 1–19.

[22] See G. G. Stroumsa, "Herméneutique et identité: l'exemple d'Isaac," *RB* 99 (1992): 529–43.

[23] On the early history of the Christian polemics against Judaism, see chapter 8 of this volume.

As to us, with the boiling Spirit and the burning word given by God, similar to those that Jeremiah received from He who told him: "Lo I have put my words like fire into your mouth." (Jer 5: 14), let us roast the kid's meat. ... One must roast the kid's meat.[24]

The Christians know how to roast the Biblical text, through its correct, i.e., Christological interpretation, while the Jews, as it were, eat the text "raw" when they understand it literally, or else overcook it into a flabby, indigestible dish when they misinterpret it. Note that this graphic description of the raw and the roasted, which strikes one as if coming from a work of Claude Lévi-Strauss, is also, of course, one of the traditional oppositions between nature and culture.

To be sure, the decision of Christian intellectuals, such as Irenaeus, to oppose Marcion and retain the Jewish Scriptures may have been in part prompted by arguments of practical political wisdom and advisability. In the ancient world, religion was to a great extent identified with following the *patrioi nomoi,* ancestral tradition, and not to be heir to such a tradition was to cast oneself outside the pale of *religio licita.* But the Church Fathers' insistence on keeping the Jewish Scriptures also entailed some logical difficulties. Origen's *Contra Celsum* is a witness to these difficulties: the Christian position on the nature and use of Scriptures was barely understandable to a Roman intellectual in the second century. The Christians claimed the Jewish Scriptures as their own. Yet, for Celsus, these Scriptures were either legal or historical in nature. As such, they were meant to be read *au pied de la lettre*, and *not* interpreted. Hence, the Christians, in particular the intellectuals among them, were betraying the spirit of their own Scriptures, when illegitimately reading them through allegory, a hermeneutical method developed for mythical texts, such as the Homeric writings. As I argue below, Celsus and Origen are here practicing what the French call "un dialogue de sourds."[25]

4. Translated Scriptures

In their appropriation of the Jewish Scriptures, the Christians had given up one element of Scripture that until then had been universally considered to be essential, namely their language. In ancient cultures, it had been a postulate, and as such in no need of written and specific legitimization, that foundational texts such as the Homeric epics or the Torah had been preserved in the very language in which they had been first written. This language was considered hallowed, endowed with a divine quality. Its heavenly source was reflected in its own, inherent nobility. This language could not be equaled, and remained inimitable – a

---

[24] *Com. Joh.* X. 103–105; Origène, *Commentaire sur saint Jean,* ed. and tr. C. Blanc (SC 157; Paris 1970), 444–45; M. Olender, "Dans la cuisine d'Origène," in *Proceedings of the Conference on Paradise in the History of Religions* (Jerusalem, April 1997), M. Idel, ed. (forthcoming).

[25] See chapter 3 of this volume.

conception later reflected in the Islamic concept of the *i'jâz al-Qur'ân*. In other words, the Scriptural text was characterized by its sublime and superior quality. Even more than the quality of poetic language, it was recognized as having some numinous aura. In the Jewish conception of biblical language, indeed, every word in the Bible has been revealed. But in the Greek conception, Homeric language, and more generally, early poetic language, was endowed with a sublime quality. This conception remained a common postulate even among later Greek intellectuals, for whom language only later developed prosaic qualities, as they were learning to give up all decorative and festive aspects, learning, in a sense, "to go on foot," in Plutarch's words.[26]

A canonical text should be preserved, read, memorized in the original tongue in which it had been redacted or revealed. But the divine inspiration attributed to the Septuagint was enough for the Christians, and dispensed them from going back to the original text. The fact that the Jews read the revealed text of the Old Testament in the original language was in no way considered by Christian intellectuals to be an advantage, a warrant of its correct understanding. Even a biblical scholar such as Origen, living in Palestine and in relatively close contact with the Rabbis, did not feel embarrassed by his ignorance of Hebrew. Indeed, the Hieronymian search for *hebraica veritas* remained an oddity among the Church Fathers.[27] The most eloquent testimony to this fact, perhaps, is found in Jerome's exchange of letters with Augustine, where the latter expresses his complete lack of understanding for his correspondent's obstinate efforts to learn Hebrew and to seek the original text of the Scriptures. To go back to the logic implicit in Origen's *Commentary on John,* the Hebrew Scriptures, the original text itself, is "raw" and needs to be processed, or "roasted" before it can become a legitimate spiritual food. It is not only the spiritual blindness of the Jews that prevents them from developing a proper understanding of their own Scriptures. One can even go as far as saying that according to this logic, Scriptures *must* be translated.

In the ancient world, this attitude to Scriptural language, developed by the Church Fathers, or at least implicit in their writings, was quite revolutionary. The very translation of the Hebrew Bible, the Septuagint, had reflected a belief in the translatability of Scriptures which did not have its parallel in Greek and Hellenistic culture. As Arnaldo Momigliano has reminded us in his *Alien Wisdom,* Greek intellectuals did not express any significant linguistic curiosity. For most Christians, the very idea of a sacred tongue, in which Divine revelation was couched, had become obsolete. They often did not even understand it, and the idea of a privileged tongue ran counter to their ecumenical ethos, to the missionary character of their faith. The idea of translatability of the Scriptures was in-

---

[26] See Stroumsa, *Hidden Wisdom,* 11–26.

[27] To be sure, the ignorance of Hebrew did not mean ignorance of Jewish exegetical traditions. See for instance G. Stemberger, "Exegetical Contacts between Christians and Jews in the Roman Empire," in *Hebrew Bible/Old Testament,* 1: 569–86.

deed an essential element of Christian theology: the revelation first offered to Israel, in it own language, had now been opened up to the whole of mankind. All peoples, civilized and barbarians, within and without the Roman Empire, were invited to hear the new message of hope, each in his own language, of course. The Christians, in a word, appealed to the barbarians as much as to the Greeks.[28]

Although the Christian Scriptures soon became translated into various languages, such as Syriac, Coptic, Latin, or Armenian, they had first circulated in Greek. Those Greco-Roman intellectuals who were first introduced to Christian writings (and to the New Testament in particular), found them insipid, unpleasant, and absurd on various accounts. One of the main arguments against the New Testament was the low, popular language in which the Gospels were written: this was a language of fishermen, not of philosophers, said Celsus, for instance, a reliable witness to the general intellectual reaction to Christianity in the second century. In order to be true, and respected as such, a divine revelation, a text of supreme wisdom, should be couched in high, not low language. Preferably, it should be put in poetry, not in prose. Two centuries later, Julian's *Kata tôn Galilaiôn* would reflect a similar attitude.

To the accusation of being uncouth, the Christians replied, in essence: "We wear your scorn as a badge of honor!" More precisely, they claimed that the low language of the Gospels was the direct reflection of an essential characteristic of the Christian message of salvation. It was equally offered to all mankind, barbarians as well as Greeks, and to the simple, uneducated masses as well as the literati. Hence, it should be equally understandable by all. This answer complements the conception of *philosophia barbarum,* i.e., the Christians' proud acceptance of the Greco-Roman intellectuals' claim that Christian thought was foreign to the Hellenic tradition. Christian intellectuals were thus able to transform weakness into strength and to assert their specific intellectual identity within the society at large.

As we have seen, the canonization of the New Testament had stemmed from internal polemics, while the two-tiered structure of Christian Scriptures must be understood in contradistinction to the simpler structure of the Jewish Scriptures. At the same time rose the consciousness of a specific Christian language and voice, what Augustine would call *sermo humilis*. The nature of this *sermo humilis* has been remarkably analyzed by Erich Auerbach, who has emphasized its long-term implications for the representation of reality in European literature.[29] Of more direct relevance for us here is the personal relationship to Scriptures which it immediately entailed, the development of an intense closeness to the Scriptures among Christians. Hence the wide and natural use of

---

[28] See chapter 4 of this volume.
[29] E. Auerbach, *Literary Language and its Public in Late Antiquity and the Middle Ages* (London 1965), chapter 1.

Scriptures as *exempla* for daily life and as direct inspiration for action. "Tolle, lege!" does not only reflect the use of Scriptures in the magical way of divination and *sortes*. It also emphasizes the status of Scriptures as intimation to personal ethical and supererogatory behavior.[30] Such a personal, open relationship to the Scriptures was rendered possible by the Christian radical rejection of the ancient belief in the esoteric dimensions in Scriptures, a rejection that brought them to their drastic "demoticization."[31]

5. Religious and cultural memory

In the Hellenistic world born from Alexander's conquests, cultural identity disentangled itself from ethnic and religious identity. Whoever could speak, or rather, write and read Greek, was entitled to a Hellenic cultural identity. Then, in another dramatic transformation, which took place during the first centuries of the Roman Empire, various criteria of cultural identity progressively became criteria of religious identity. One can note a correlative passage from cultural to religious memory. This civilizational process was brought to its acme with the Christianization of the Empire throughout the fourth century.

The Constantinian revolution represents the end result of a long and complex process of religious transformation, through which perceptions and attitudes, no less than beliefs, were profoundly changed. As Ernst Troeltsch showed long ago, Christianity itself also passed through a deep mutation as it converted the Roman Empire, and as a former Jewish radical sect became a world religion.[32] While the very fact of this revolution is broadly acknowledged, its implications for the status of Scriptures are still in need of clarification. Constantine's revolution finalized the transformation of identity parameters. In the fourth century C.E., religion, rather than culture and language, would become the main criterium of identity. The consequences of this drastic change would be in some ways ominous for the future of tolerance, or rather the lack thereof, in the Christian empire, and then in European history. But it is with its significance for the attitude toward Scripture that we are concerned here.

In his seminal *Das kulturelle Gedächtnis*, Jan Assmann has analyzed the concept of cultural memory in ancient societies such as Egypt, Israel, and Greece, as well as the concept of canon in these societies. It may be useful to pursue his investigation in the Christianized Roman Empire. One may first point out the cardinal importance of memory in early Christianity. The very heart of Christian cult, the Eucharist, is conceived as the actualization, or re-presentation, *anam-*

---

[30] See D. Burton-Christie, *The Word in the Desert: Scripture and the Quest for Holiness in Early Christian Monasticism* (New York and Oxford 1993). See also J. Kirchmeyer, "Ecriture sainte et vie spirituelle," *DS* 4: 127–69.

[31] See Stroumsa, *Hidden Wisdom,* 132–46.

[32] See chapter 1 of this volume.

nèsis, of Jesus Christ and of his saving sacrifice. Christian memory, of course, was rather different from what is expressed by the verb *zakhor* in Jewish cult and culture. This difference stemmed, mainly, from a different attitude to the past, and from the Christians' complex, or even ambivalent, attitude to the Old Testament. The Christians, indeed, reclaimed these writings for the cultural memory of European culture. But they read them in translation, and mainly in reference to the New Testament. They had adopted the Jewish Scriptures as their own, but at the price, as it were, of neutralizing their autonomous power. Jewish religious memory, from now on, could now only be deciphered as on a palimpsest in the expropriated *Tanakh.*[33]

At the same time, early Christian intellectuals were soon brought to propose a radical reinterpretation of Greco-Roman cultural memory. Mention has been made of the scornful perception of the Christians as barbarian proponents of an "alien wisdom," both because their "philosophy" was not originally Greek, and because when they did write in Greek, it was in a low language reflecting their lack of culture. I have also alluded to the Christians' proud acceptance of such a designation. Yet, if they wanted to convince the authorities to tolerate them, Christian intellectuals could not really refuse to "play the game"; they could not appear as radical cultural rejectionists within imperial society. Apologetic literature from the second and third centuries reflects their obstinate attempts to force dialogue upon their recalcitrant Hellenic opponents. In the quid pro quo, Christian intellectuals were brought to accept Hellenic culture, at least to a point. As is well known, they did that willingly, insofar as philosophy was concerned.

From Justin Martyr to Eusebius and Augustine, the Church Fathers recognized what they considered to be the more spiritual aspects of Greek philosophy (especially Platonism) as a parallel revelation of sorts. According to this view of things, God would have inspired the best among the pagans with some seeds of divine wisdom, which Justin calls *sperma pneumatikon,* thus helping to prepare the Gentiles for the Gospel. In a sense, then, according to the logic of this theory, one could follow throughout history the traces of a double system through which God had revealed His Wisdom to mankind, until the incarnation of Jesus Christ: the Scriptures to Israel, and philosophy to the Greeks – as well as to the other peoples: Indians, the people of the mythical Seres (the Chinese), the Babylonians, the Persians, or the Egyptians. In our context, Justin's theory should be seen as more sophisticated than, but essentially parallel to the "theft theory" propounded, in particular, by Clement of Alexandria, according to which there is only one divine revelation in human history, and any true or just idea to be found in pagan, i.e., Hellenic literature must reflect a plagiarism from Moses.

What remained a major unresolved problem in this conception was the status

---

[33] In a different historical context, Jan Assmann speaks about a "structural amnesia" as the reverse side of any cultural memory; see his *Das kulturelle Gedächtnis,* 72.

of the Homeric writings. As we have seen, they had become Scriptures of a sort in Greek culture: foundational texts endowed with a particular status, distinguished and higher than other writings, framed in a hermeneutical construct of commentaries and interpretive methods. Of all of Greek literature, however, the Homeric epics created an insurmountable problem for the Christians: it is not about the search of wisdom that they spoke, but about idols which could not even be said to really exist. When pagan intellectuals accused the Christians of atheism because they did not respect the gods, the Church Fathers could return the accusation of atheism to their opponents, whose so-called gods were in fact lower and evanescent demons.

Early Christian intellectuals succeeded to a great extent in integrating the mainstream culture of the Greco-Roman world, and in transforming its cultural memory. But just as canonization processes entail the exclusion of various texts, the most dramatic aspect of this transformation, perhaps, was the exclusion from this memory of texts which had had quasi-Scriptural status in that culture, namely the Homeric epics. To be sure, in Christian hands the Homeric texts underwent no complete *damnatio memoriae*. As Hugo Rahner has amply shown, some central Homeric myths and stories were echoed in Patristic literature.[34] All in all, however, such echoes remained rather faint, and the Church Fathers never attributed to Homer the importance that became his at the hands of pagan intellectuals in late antiquity. There is no doubt that we witness in this a process of de-canonization. This process is parallel to the process of secondary canonization. There is a tendency, when dealing with canonization processes, to ignore the importance of the converse phenomenon of de-canonization. The radical shift in late antique cultural and religious identity brought with it a need to choose anew, to re-evaluate, to adjust. The process of promotion was at the same time one of demotion, of renewal of memory and forgetfulness. In order to fully understand the religious revolution of early Christianity and its drastic transformation of classical culture, we should perceive canonization as only one aspect of a complex reshuffling of the status of texts and of the relationships between them.

6. Conclusion: the double helix of late antique culture

Philo had applied to "barbarian philosophy," i.e., to the Hebrew Torah, hermeneutical methods, in particular allegory, first developed by Greek grammarians in order to interpret embarrassing passages in Homer. Philo's approach then became the model for much of Patristic hermeneutics. In applying his rules to their Scriptures, the Church Fathers insisted on the intertextuality between the two Testaments as an essential element of Biblical hermeneutics.

---

[34] H. Rahner, *Griechische Mythen in christlicher Deutung* (Freiburg 1992 [1984]), esp. Part 3: "Heiliger Homer."

A fundamental difference between the Bible and Homer consisted in the fact that the first was read as a revealed religious text, while the other was perceived originally as a literary and cultural monument. There were gods in Homer, and there was poetry in the Bible, but the basic viewpoint for the appreciation of the nature and role of these two kinds of Scriptures was strikingly different. In the Roman Empire, the structural difference between the approach of Homer and that of the Bible was progressively blurred. This highly significant phenomenon does not seem to have elicited the attention it deserves. On the one hand, the instances of the *Chaldean Oracles* in the second century, and later of the religious longings of the Neo-Platonist philosophers, show the extent to which later Hellenic intellectuals, perhaps under Christian influence, craved for Scriptures of their own.[35] Like the Christian Scriptures, these would exhibit a religious or even revelatory character then felt to be lacking in their own tradition. On the other hand, the birth of a Christian *culture* in late antiquity, a culture whose parameters Augustine defines so clearly in his *De Doctrina Christiana,* reflects, through hermeneutics, the transformation of the Bible into a *cultural* monument.

What I have called the double helix is the parallel establishment of two series of texts as the double backbone of the emerging culture: the new Scriptures (Old and New Testaments) on the one hand, and what could be salvaged of Greek and Latin culture on the other hand, i.e., mainly Platonic and Stoic philosophy, valued primarily for (respectively) their lofty metaphysics and ethics. One could perhaps speak of a double translation process: the Hebrew Scriptures appear now in Greek garb, while Greco-Roman culture is subsumed to the Bible. The Old and the New Testaments, in a sense like philosophy, represented what had been salvaged, since the Jewish interpretation of Scriptures, as well as the Apocryphal writings of both Testaments, were not recognized as authentic. Perhaps one of the main intellectual contributions of Christian intellectuals in late antiquity was their weaving a web of links and relations between these two scriptural systems. This web was based both upon the wish to retain, at least metaphorically, Israelite identity, and the feeling that Christianity needed to develop a system of relationships and equivalencies with the best of Greek and Roman literatures. It is this web which permitted, at the end of our period, the preservation of much in classical culture and its integration into Christian culture-in-the-making, which would become, in the East as well as well as in the West, the core of European medieval and early modern culture.[36]

---

[35] This development is well analyzed in R. Lamberton, *Homer the Theologian* (Chicago 1984).

[36] As late as the seventeenth century, Homer and the Bible are often seen as parallel. See for instance Joshua Barnes' *Susias* (London 1629), written on the story of Esther in close imitation of the Iliad. In the first line, "Haman son of Amalek" takes the place of "Achilles son of Peleus"; in the second "Hebrew" supplants "Achaeans"; in the third "mighty heads of Persians" stands for "many mighty souls," and so on.

Chapter 3

Celsus, Origen, and the Nature of Religion

1. A dialogue of the deaf

Both in scope and intellectual power, Origen's monumental *Contra Celsum* can be compared only to Augustine's *De Civitate Dei* within Patristic literature. The *Contra Celsum* is usually perceived as exemplifying "the conflict between paganism and Christianity." From an epistemological point of view, such an approach is not only simplistic, but also profoundly misleading. Rather, I shall contend, it reflects the passage from the Roman to the Christian understanding of religion – a major transformation that remains singularly understudied.

Indeed, some of the ways the book has traditionally been perceived prevent us from finding the key to its correct understanding, from cracking its code, as it were. In order to do so, we must question these perceptions. First, the *Contra Celsum* is not a polemic between the great Origen and an otherwise unknown, and hence supposedly mediocre, Middle Platonist philosopher. There is no reason to consider Celsus as a mediocre mind, intellectually (or spiritually) inferior to the Christianity he addresses. This Christianity, one should remember, is not that of Origen. Rather, the development of Alexandrian Christian thought was made possible, in a way, by Celsus's arguments against earlier, less intellectualized expressions of Christianity. Secondly, one cannot speak of a real confrontation between Celsus and Origen, since the latter wrote about eighty years after the former. As Carl Andresen was able to show in his *Logos und Nomos*, Celsus should be seen in the context of mid-second century Hellenic and Christian thought.[1] When Origen answers Celsus's argumentation in the mid-third century, Christian thinkers had had time to develop a cogent refutation of their intellectual opponents' objections to what the latter perceived as a new and uncouth school of thought. In many ways, Clement of Alexandria reflects the Christian response to Celsus. In the *Contra Celsum* we are dealing with two excellent minds, but they cannot be said to be involved in any kind of dialogue. What we have is a *dialogue de sourds*. It is not even a religious polemic of the kind we know between Jews, Christians, and Muslims, for instance. Celsus and

---

[1] C. Andresen, *Logos und Nomos: Die Polemik des Kelsos wider das Christentum* [Arbeiten zur Kirchengeschichte 30] (Berlin 1955). On this most influential study, see especially the review of H. Dörrie in *Gnomon* 29 (1957): 185–96; see also K. Pichler, *Streit um das Christentum: der Angriff des Kelsos und die Antwort des Origenes* (Frankfurt a.M 1980).

Origen are both deeply religious minds, but their respective understanding of what religion means puts them poles apart from one another. Hence, neither one of them considers the other as having different religious ideas. For Celsus, the Christians are fundamentally irreligious, "atheists." Origen returns the compliment, and accuses Celsus, too, of atheism.[2] This fundamental misunderstanding on the very nature of religion forms the core of the *Contra Celsum*'s historical importance.

Another epistemological fallacy stems from the mistaken perception of the *Contra Celsum* as reflecting the conflict between paganism and Christianity. This fallacy focuses upon "pagan religions" in the text, while ignoring Judaism. Analyzing the grand clash between paganism and Christianity as the main focus of the whole work, for instance, Michel Fédou ignores the Jewish dimension.[3] Such an approach, which reflects the Harnack legacy of studying the growth of Christianity only within the background of Hellenism, is basically flawed, and misses the main point of the *Auseinandersetzung*. The presence of Judaism is in fact essential for a proper understanding of the work. Both for Celsus and for Origen, the Jewish dimension is essential for any definition of Christian identity. In that sense, one can speak of a "hidden closeness" between Judaism and Christianity.[4] Celsus notes that the polemics between Jews and Christians remind him of a dispute about the shadow of an ass.[5] But in order to buttress his arguments against Christianity, he introduces a Jew who spells out various claims and slanders against the followers of Jesus. Indeed, we are dealing with a triangle: the complex relationships between philosophy, Judaism, and Christianity can only be understood in their full context.

Celsus is not a representative of "paganism," whatever the term may cover, but of philosophy. He is a conservative intellectual, insisting on the importance of tradition in human cultures.[6] In many ways, he is as much a monotheist as

---

[2] Justin Martyr, *Apol.*, I.46, is already aware of pagan accusations of Christian atheism. A few decades later, Tertullian answers by refusing the name of religion to paganism, which offers a cult to idols, not to real gods (*Apologeticus*, 24). See further A. von Harnack, *Der Vorwurf des Atheismus in den drei ersten Jahrhunderten*, [*Texte und Untersuchungen* 28.4] (Leipzig 1905).

[3] M. Fédou, *Christianisme et religions païennes dans le Contre Celse d'Origène* (Théologie historique 81; Paris 1988).

[4] See G. G. Stroumsa, "The Hidden Closeness" (in Hebrew), *Jerusalem Studies in Jewish Thought* 2 (1982): 70–75.

[5] L. Rougier, tr., *Celse, Contre les chrétiens* (Paris 1963), II.33, p. 65. See also idem, *Celse contre les chrétiens: la réaction païenne sous l'empire romain* (Paris 1977; 1st. ed. 1926). One might point out that this work of a typical anti-Christian rationalist is reprinted in a series edited by Alain de Benoist, one of the intellectual leaders of the neo-pagan movement in Western Europe after the Second World War, a movement also notorious for its revisionist attitudes regarding the Nazis and their deeds. For the last translation of Celsus's *Alèthes Logos*, see R. J. Hoffmann, *Celsus, On the True Doctrine: A Discourse Against the Christians* (New York and Oxford 1987).

[6] See R. L. Wilken, *The Christians as the Pagans Saw Them* (New Haven and London 1984), ch. 5: "Celsus: a Conservative Intellectual."

Origen.[7] There is only one supreme power ruling this universe. And it is this same, unique God that all peoples address while calling Him by different names. Celsus's eyes, we are told, are turned away from the flesh in order to reach the *visio dei* (VIII.36). It is less upon the nature of God that Celsus and Origen argue than upon the nature of God's relationship to mankind and of what He demands, or expects of men, i.e., upon the nature of religion.

Celsus, it seems, wrote his *Alethes Logos* in the 70s of the second century. The very title of his work, *Alethes Logos*, reflects an expression used first by Justin Martyr.[8] His polemics, the first sustained discourse against the new, outlawed religion, should be seen in the context of views expressed by contemporaries such as Marcus Aurelius and Galen. Since the late nineteenth century, rationalists and free thinkers have seen in Celsus an enlightened hero, fighting against the intellectual shadow of Christian barbarism.[9] One has even called him "a second century Voltaire" seeking to "écraser l'infâme." But "Celsus is no second-century Voltaire," as Henry Chadwick notes;[10] he does not want to transform society, but to preserve its culture from an exogenous threat of an unknown kind. He fights with the arguments and intellectual tools at his disposal, but remains unable to clearly identify the nature of the threat. His intellectual and political ideals both reflect a deep desire of stability, hierarchy, continuity, and the acceptance of various cultures and religious traditions within a single political unit. Christianity, for him, threatens to overthrow all that. But it seems that he remains unable to perceive correctly the origin and nature of the Christians' strength and dynamism. This lack of understanding is Celsus's main weakness, and it seems to reflect the fundamental inability of Hellenic thinkers under the Empire to argue convincingly against Christianity.

Werner Jaeger argued that philosophy had prepared the Roman Empire for Christianity.[11] In an obvious sense, this is true, but it is no less important to point out that philosophers – and Celsus is an excellent case in point – remained blind to the true nature of Christianity as a new spiritual force. This new force was to

---

[7] This was first shown by A. Miura-Stange, *Celsus und Origenes: Das Gemeinsame ihrer Weltanschauung nach den acht Büchern des Origenes gegen Celsus; eine Studie zur Religions- und Geistesgeschichte des 2. und 3. Jahrhunderts* (Giessen 1926), esp. 113–19. See also Fédou, *Christianisme et religions païennes,* 222: "On sera alors en mesure de conclure le chapitre, et l'ensemble de cette première partie, en montrant que le 'conflit des croyances' s'éclaire par un débat sur la nature même d'un véritable monothéisme."

[8] Andresen sought to show that Celsus was actually responding directly to Justin's idea of *alèthès logos*. Dörrie expressed serious doubts about this thesis. See further, H. D. Saffrey, "Les débuts de la théologie comme science (IIIe-VIe siècle)," *Revue des Science philosophiques et théologiques* 80 (1996): 201–20, esp. 205.

[9] This is for instance the case of Rougier, n.5 above.

[10] H. Chadwick, tr., *Origen, Contra Celsum* (Cambridge 1953), Introduction, xxii. Throughout this article, I am quoting Chadwick's masterly translation of the *Contra Celsum*.

[11] W. Jaeger, *Humanism and Theology* (Milwaukee 1943), n. 65, quoted by R. Walzer, *Galen on Jews and Christians* (Oxford 1949), 5, n.1.

be fought on its own turf, as it were, or with its own weapons. As a religion, Christianity was outlawed: the first pagan witnesses report on it as a *superstitio*, not as a *religio*.[12] Hence, in order to acquire intellectual respectability, Christian intellectuals presented their movement, or *hairesis,* as a philosophical school rather than as a Jewish sect, searching – and finding, better than other schools – the *alethes logos.* This is the thrust of Justin Martyr's writing, in his *Apology*, but especially in the first eight chapters of his *Dialogue with Trypho,* where he wanders in his search for truth from one philosophical school to another. The Christians, aware of the new character of their sect, claimed to represent a "barbarian philosophy," stemming from outside the cultural boundaries of Hellenic traditional wisdom.[13]

The Christian self-perception as members of a "barbarian philosophy," however, reflected their perception by Hellenic thinkers as a particularly weak school of thought. By the mid-second century, some Greek and Roman intellectuals had begun to acknowledge the existence of Christianity and to reflect upon this strange movement. Among them, Galen, a contemporary of Celsus, was the first to refer to the Christians as to a philosophical school. In antiquity, members of such schools were as much united by their way of life as by their method in the search for truth, their *logos.* As a philosophical school, however, the Christians strike him as being particularly weak, since their teaching – as well as that of the Jews – puts so much emphasis upon faith, *pistis*, rather than upon reason.[14]

A different direction in the attitude toward Christians is reflected in another contemporary, the Emperor Marcus Aurelius, who calls the Christians "a radical opposition" (*psilè paratasis*, XI.3). In contradistinction to Galen, and as befits an emperor, Marcus Aurelius refers to the Christians' perceived political and cultural threat to Roman state and society rather than to the nature of their philosophical views. The radical nature of the Christian threat is reflected in speaking of Christian "atheism." In a sense, then, it seems that Galen and Marcus Aurelius insist upon different aspects of Christianity as perceived by outsiders, as a philosophical school or as a religious sect. In both cases, the diagnosis is strongly negative, but the viewpoint and the argumentation are essentially different. Celsus's perception of Christianity, we should note, combines both argumentations. In the first extent detailed criticism of Christianity, Celsus attacks the new move-

---

[12] On *religio* and *superstitio,* see P. Stockmeier, "Christlicher Glaube und antike Religiosität," in *ANRW,* II.23.2 (1980): 871–909, esp. 888–89; also R. Muth, "Vom Wesen römischer 'religio,'" in *ANRW* II.16.1 (1978): 290–354. See especially H. Bouillard, "La formation du concept de religion en occident," in *Humanisme et foi chrétienne,* eds. Ch. Kannengiesser and Y. Marchasson, (Paris 1976), 451–61, which refers to Arnobius, Lactantius, and especially Augustine, but ignores Origen; see further M. Sachot, "Comment le christianisme est-il devenu *religio?,*" *RSR* 59 (1985): 95–118, and idem, "'*Religio/superstitio:*' Historique d'une subversion et d'un retournement," *RHR* 208 (1991): 355–94.
[13] See chapter 4 of this volume.
[14] See Walzer, n.11 above.

ment both as a philosophical school and a religious sect, and finds it guilty on both accounts. This double trend in Celsus's discourse is well noted by Marta Sordi.[15] In the following pages, I shall first seek to analyze some of Celsus's presuppositions, which bring him to misinterpret the nature of Christianity. Then, I shall look at Origen's fundamental misunderstanding of Celsus's religiosity.

2 Alethes logos and palaios logos

The obvious should be stated first: neither "paganism" or philosophy, nor Christianity can be approached as monolithic entities in the second and third century. In that sense, one should be careful of moving too fast from the textual evidence to sweeping generalizations. We may however postulate, at least as a working hypothesis, that the religious transformation which would find its eventual conclusion in the religious revolution heralded by Constantine, entails a passage from *to theion* to *ho theos,* in other words a clear personalization of the divine.[16] Maurice Sachot has recently analyzed the semantic transformation which occurred in our period in the couple *superstitio/religio,* transformation which reflects directly the passage from the Roman to the Christian understanding of religion.[17]

For Celsus, religion is first and foremost a matter of tradition. In that sense, the religion of the Jews is a legitimate one, an intellectual fact reflected in its legal status as *religio licita.* By rejecting the traditional ways of expression of Jewish religiosity, the Christians undermine their own position, and give up on their only possible justification. Some of the more intellectually-minded Christians, of course, claim to offer a spiritualized, deeper interpretation of the fundamental truths of Jewish religion. But in doing so, says Celsus, they betray the very nature of Judaism. Celsus reveals here his own perception of religion, and his basic misunderstanding of Judaism, which does not fit his cultural presuppositions. And it is through his own argumentation with Celsus that Origen is brought, like a latter-day Balaam, to sing the praise of Judaism.

Celsus considers the "doctrine of old," the *palaios logos* which teaches the fundamental unity of God, to be partaken by all religions except by that of the

---

[15] M. Sordi, *The Christians and the Roman Empire* (Engl. transl.) (London 1994), 160–61: "Christianity comes under fire from both the fideists and the rationalists; the first see the Christians as guilty of bringing down the wrath of the gods by teaching atheism and impiety, the second accuse them of being irrationally dogmatic. Occasionally, the two positions become confused, as when Celsus blames the Christians for their fideistic outlook in the name of rationality, but then reveals that he himself believes in oracles and prodigious signs."

[16] This is well described by H.-I. Marrou, *L'Eglise de l'antiquité tardive* (Paris 1963), 161.

[17] See Sachot, n.12 above. For studies of the various terms in the semantic field of religion in the Roman Empire, see M. Despland, *La religion en Occident: évolution des idées et du vécu* (Montréal 1979), ch.4: "L'idée de religion chez les Pères." See also L. Koep, "'Religio' und 'ritus' als Problem des frühen Christentums," *JAC* 5 (1962): 43–59.

Jews. In his words: "There is an ancient doctrine which has existed from the beginning, which has always been maintained by the wisest nations and cities and wise men...." such as "the Egyptians, Assyrians, Indians, Persians, Odrysians, Samothracians, and Eleusinians." (I.14). The absence of the Jews in this list is indeed striking, and, as Origen is fast to point out, stands in radical opposition to the attitude of Numenius of Apamea, another second-century intellectual, who includes the Jews among the wise nations which conceive of God as incorporeal (I.15).[18]

Celsus's exclusion of the Jews from the list of wise nations, and of Moses from that of wise men, finds its explanation in his conception of the *palaios logos*.[19] For him, this true doctrine about the divinity is nothing less than obvious. It is not a doctrine that can be understood by simple people, who are unable to conceive of a single, incorporeal God, and imagine representations of a multiplicity of gods and of their adventures, in the various mythologies of the nations of the earth. It is precisely these mythical texts that the wise men of the various nations strive to interpret, by means of allegory, seeking to offer spiritual interpretations of a sometimes embarrassing literal meaning of the text. Now Celsus points out the radical difference between mythological literature and the writings of the Bible. For him, the Bible (i.e., essentially, the books of Moses) is a book of laws and of history (the historians being the prophets) and as such should be understood according to its literal sense, but not according to a spiritual meaning. The Bible is no collection of myths, and hence should not be interpreted in an allegorical way. For Celsus, only myths, i.e., stories about the gods that cannot be read literally, need an allegorical interpretation. Laws one should simply obey, and history one should understand at the textual level. In a sense, one can say, Celsus recognizes the original character of Biblical revelation and the vast difference between it and the various mythological literatures of the ancient Near East and of Antiquity. The whole Alexandrian tradition (best exemplified by Philo) of allegorical interpretation of the Biblical texts strikes him as fundamentally flawed. Moses asks us to obey the laws he gives, and the prophets tell us the history of their people. Neither lawgivers nor prophets should be called philosophers, since the latter's task is to reveal the deeper meaning of traditional tales (myths), thus retrieving the *philosophia perennis,* the *palaios logos.* Incidentally, a similar conception of the illegitimacy of Biblical allegorical interpretation will be offered in the third century by Porphyry.[20]

---

[18] On Numenius on Judaism, see M. Stern, *Greek and Latin Authors on Jews and Judaism,* vol. 2 (Jerusalem 1980), 206–16.

[19] In the mid-1450s, Marsilio Ficino would be a latter-day proponent of this "ancient theology," see J. Hankins, *Ancient Theology: Plato in the Italian Renaissance* (Columbia Studies in the Classical Tradition 17; Leiden 1991), 282–86.

[20] See G. G. Stroumsa, *Hidden Wisdom: Esoteric Traditions and the Roots of Christian Mysticism* (SHR 70; Leiden 1996), 11–26.

The Jews, therefore, (and hence the Christians) are not entitled to hermeneutics of their religious texts, and are kept out of the list of wise religions. For
Celsus, there is no such thing as a true religion: all religions are wrong if their
mythologies are understood *au pied de la lettre*. Or, more precisely, all mythologies need to be interpreted in order to express clearly their deeper meaning
about the divinity. Hence, religion is essentially practice, respecting and keeping
the tradition. Such an attitude is based upon the idea of the divinity of the
kosmos: the divinity *(to theion)*, is everywhere. In this respect, Celsus criticizes
the Jews for worshipping heaven while forbidding the worship of the sun, the
moon or the stars, "as though it were possible for the whole to be God but its
parts not divine" (V.7). This tradition lies in all traditions, which are equally respectable, and under the various names by which different peoples have called
the same supreme God: "It makes no difference whether one calls the supreme
God by the name used among the Greeks, or by that, for example, used among
the Indians, or by that among the Egyptians" (I.24), or elsewhere: "It makes no
difference whether we call Zeus the Most High, or Zen, or Adonai, or Sabaoth."
(V.56).[21]

This attitude also permits the development of what one could perhaps call a
comparative reflection on religion: different peoples hold different conceptions
of God, and different attitudes to the question of iconic representations of the
divinity: the various religions of the Scythians, the Nomads of Lybia, and the
Persians, for instance, are strictly aniconic (VII.62). Such a comparative interest
in religious practices, however, does not remain Celsus's privilege. Origen on his
side points out that prima facie similar cultic practices stem from different theological conceptions. For instance, circumcision is practiced by different peoples,
but for different theological reasons. Hence, the circumcision practiced by the
Egyptians or by the Colchians should not be perceived as identical to that of the
Jews (V.47). Origen's assessment of Celsus's views on that matter strikes one as
correct:

> According to his [i.e., Celsus's] view, piety will not be divine by nature, but a matter of
> arbitrary arrangement and opinion; for among some people it is pious to worship the
> crocodile and to eat some animal worshipped by others, and among others it is pious to
> worship the calf, and among others to regard the goat as a god. Thus the same person
> will be making things to be pious by the standard of one set of laws and impious by an-
> other, which is the most monstrous thing of all. (V.28)

This paragraph strikes one as taken verbatim from Montaigne's "Essay on the
Cannibals." "Indeed," says Celsus, "among the Scythians cannibalism is a good

---

[21] Celsus stands here in a long tradition of Greek reflection upon foreign religions; see for
instance J. Rudhardt, "De l'attitude des Grecs à l'égard des religions étrangères," *RHR* 209
(1992): 219–38.

thing; and there are acting piously when they eat even their fathers" (V.34).[22] For Celsus, "piety and holiness are reckoned to be relative," as Origen is fast to point out. *Cujus rex, ejus religio*: "Probably, however, the reply would be made to this that the man who observes the traditional customs is pious and not at all impious provided that he does not keep those of other people as well" (V.29). If religion is relative, as argued by Celsus, then religion is not the area of truth, but only of ethnic traditions. In Celsus's terms, "Pindar seems to me to have been right when he said that custom is king of all" (V.34). According to Celsus, in other words, the very conception of God is different in different religions: like the Christians, the Scythians, the nomads of Lybia, and the Seres, "who believe in no gods," have aniconic religions; "they cannot bear to see temples and altars and images."[23]

No wonder, then, that Origen's rejection of such views is radical: they undermine both fundamental attitudes of Christianity regarding the idea of religious truth (religion should show the path to salvation) and that of universality (the same saving truth is offered to all mankind: "Where there is neither Greek not Jew, circumcision nor uncircumcision, Barbarian, Scythian, bond nor free: but Christ is all, and in all." (Col. 3:11).[24]

Celsus's conception of religion is characterized on the one hand by its conservatism and traditionalism, and on the other hand by its radical relativism. Such a conception makes perfect sense. If it surprises us, this is because we have come to perceive a relativist attitude to things religious as directly connected to a revolt against Christian tradition. This, however, should not necessarily be the case. For instance, it is precisely Montaigne's relativism which will permit him to remain a loyal Catholic in a time of religious upheaval.

Such a position reflects Celsus's deep mistrust of religious change: various views on the sacred are expressed in the different ethnic traditions. One should not foster a transformation of these traditions; the structure of the religious world should remain static. This mistrust of religious change prevents him from understanding correctly the nature of Christian religiosity. For instance, he remains blind to the ethical dimension of Christianity

The demand to follow one's own ethnic traditions, or *patrioi nomoi*, entails the pre-eminence of tradition over faith.[25] Religion, indeed, is no matter of

---

[22] On attitudes to human sacrifice in the Roman Empire, see J. Rives, "Human Sacrifice among Pagans and Christians," *JRS* 85 (1995): 65–85. Rives shows that the motif of human sacrifice moved from discussions about civilization and barbarism (in early and classical Greece) to discussions on good and bad religion, with the progressive emergence of religion as an autonomous area of discourse.

[23] VII.62; on Christianity as aniconic religion, see VIII.17, 20. See further C. Ginzburg, "Idols and Likenesses: Origen, *Homilies on Exodus* VIII.3, and its reception," in *Sight and Insight: Esssays on Art and Culture in honour of E. H. Gombrich at 85*, ed. J. Onians (London 1994), 55–72.

[24] See chapter 4 of this volume.

[25] On *patrioi nomoi*, see. H. G. Kippenberg, "Die jüdischen Überlieferungen als *patrioi no-*

faith, and this for two reasons. First, because tradition tells us already how we should worship. Secondly, because of the lack of rationality involved in faith. This is developed at the beginning of Origen's work: "But if they will not consent but say, as they usually do, 'Do not ask questions,' and so on ... (I.12). Such a preponderance of 'faith' permits the emergence and success of various dubious religious cults, like those of Cybele, of Mithras, of Sabazius, of Hecate, etc..." (I.9).

Christianity is a particularly bad religion, since it stems from a revolt against tradition. It is revolutionary in essence, encouraging change and rejection of time-hallowed behavior and beliefs. Just as they rejected the traditions of their Jewish forefathers, the Christians do not respect any tradition on which social order is established. Indeed, the very language of their religious texts, the mean style of the Gospels, reflects their lowly origin. The apostles should be regarded as seditious people, as "infamous men" (I.63). Their fundamental impiety consists precisely in their abandoning religious customs. The first Christians were Jews debasing their own religion, thus behaving impiously (V.52, cf. VII.44). This reflects a traditional Roman argument against Christianity, one of the most potent reasons for defining Christianity as *religio illicita,* a dangerous *superstitio,* that threatened the basis of society. We see here how Celsus's argument offers a synthesis of both Galen's and Marcus Aurelius's perception of Christianity. If Christianity is dangerous for the welfare of the state, it is precisely because of its intellectual illegitimacy and misconception of the nature of religion. Celsus ends his argument with a plea to the Christians, asking them to start behaving as responsible citizens, and to accept their share in the burden of protecting the commonwealth by serving in the Imperial army (VIII.73).

3. Religion as personal conviction

Origen does not hesitate to define Celsus's religious affiliation. For him, Celsus is a pagan, and his arguments against Christianity are void, since pagans do not understand the nature of real religion. Those who send Christians to their death "have no notion of what piety is" (VII.44). How could they, when "the worship of the supposed gods is also a worship of demons"?[26] Origen's conception of religion is radically new. What was considered as piety by the pagans has become impiety, whereas what they called superstition has now become the core of the new religion. There is no middle ground between the two conceptions.

---

moi," in *Die Restauration der Götter: Antike Religion und Neo-Paganismus,* eds. R. Faber and R. Schlesier (Würzburg 1986), 45–60.

[26] VII.69. For a discussion of impiety, see also IV.97.

Origen confronts Celsus on so many issues that it is hard to find a major axis of his argument. At the end of book IV, he has a paragraph that has been described as an abstract of his whole theology:

> but He inflicts judgment and punishment upon men, seeing that they have gone against the impulses of nature. And He threatens them through prophets and through the Saviour who came to visit the whole human race, in order that by means of the threat those who hear may be converted, whole those who neglect the words aimed at their conversion pay penalties according to their deserts. It is right that God should impose these according to His will to the advantage of the whole world upon people who need healing and correction of this kind and of such severity (IV.99).

Personal conviction, as a prerequisite for a religion of conversion, is here essential.[27] Sin, repentance, moral progress, all these are direct implications of Origen's conception of religion. In a sense, one could speak, following Robert Wilken, of Origen's attempt to "privatize religion." In the new perspective, what is central is the will and the ability of the person to accept a radical change of identity, following a call from heaven. Obeying divine will is very different from following traditions. On the other hand, the decision to abandon previous behavior and beliefs and to change one's life, is typical of the new approach. Hence, pagans who oppose Christianity have no notion of what piety is, since for them religion is not a matter of personal decision (VII. 44).

In a highly original development which does not seem to have elicited much interest, Origen notes that like philosophers, who are expected to abandon pagan rituals or superstitions practiced among the people they belong to, so it is the Christians' duty to abandon Jewish religious practices. Like other philosophers, Christians are not only permitted to abandon traditional religion, but also encouraged to do so. A philosopher who would insist on keeping traditional customs "would be a ridiculous philosopher because he would be acting unphilosophically,... not wanting to advance in devotion to the Creator" (V.35). Similarly, Christians retaining Jewish practice are ridiculous, like the Ebionites, whose name comes from the poverty of their mind, states Origen elsewhere.[28] Indeed, the Christians should be considered as the best among the Jews, or the philosophers among them, just as the Brahmans are the philosophers among the Indians, and as the Jews themselves were sometimes considered as the philosophers of the Syrian race. The Christians offer a deep, spiritual understanding of the Biblical texts, while "the Jews, on the other hand, have not looked deeply into them, but read them superficially and only as stories *(muthoi)*" (II.4). In

---

[27] See for instance H. Crouzel, "Conviction intérieure et aspects extérieurs de la religion chez Celse et Origène," *Bulletin de Littérature Ecclésiastique* 77 (1976): 81–98. For a broader perspective on the concept of faith in the early Roman Empire, see A. Momigliano, "Religion in Athens, Rome, and Jerusalem in the First Century," reprinted in his *On Pagans, Jews and Christians* (Middletown, Conn. 1987), 74–91.

[28] *De Principiis* IV.3.8; cf Chadwick, n.3 on *Contra Celsum* II.1, p. 66.

pointing this out, Origen answers Celsus's critique of the Hebrew writings, namely that they cannot be considered as mythical texts, i.e., as texts requiring spiritual hermeneutics. In the light of Origen's understanding,

> all the doctrines of the Jews living now are myths and trash (for they have not the light of the knowledge of the Scriptures), whereas the Christian doctrines are true, and are able to lift and raise up the soul and mind of man and convince him that he has a certain citizenship, not like the earthly Jews, somewhere down here on earth, but in heaven. (II.5)

While he argues against the limited and misleading understanding of the Jews, Origen also rejects Celsus's conception of the Hebrew Scriptures as not worthy of spiritual interpretation. Jewish wisdom is thus higher than philosophy:

> Though Celsus will not agree, the Jews do possess some deeper wisdom, not only more than the multitude, but also than those who seem to be philosophers, because the philosophers in spite of their impressive philosophical teachings fall down to idols and daemons, while even the lowest Jew looks only to the supreme God. (V.43)

Jewish wisdom is not only deeper than that of the philosophers, but also older: Moses is far earlier than even the Geek alphabet (VII.28). Origen accuses Celsus of applying to the Biblical texts hermeneutical methods different from those he applies to Greek mythology (VIII.45). But for Origen, the real problem with the Greeks is not that they did not know the single God. Referring to Romans 1:19–21, he points out that the Apostle himself recognized that the Greeks could know God. Despite their correct understanding of the notion of divinity, however, they remained unable to offer God a correct worship (III.47). In contradistinction, the Christians are characterized by their "simple and pure worship of God" (IV.22). This simple and pure worship, however, can have some drastic consequences: for both Christians and Jews, their radical rejection of idolatry entails intolerance of images and idols, and also readiness for martyrdom (VII.64).

The Christian conception of piety stands at the antipode of the traditional conception accepted by Celsus. Origen's conception of piety is essentially dynamic; whereas religious change was feared or despised by Celsus, it is encouraged by Origen. The whole fourth Book of the *Contra Celsum* is devoted to the idea of religious and ethical reformation. Christ's message was a message of moral reformation. The new religion is a religion of personal conviction.[29] We should remember that Origen is a religious activist. For him, the new conception of religion propounded by the Christians, to which one should convert, offers new vistas: true religion is identical to moral reformation: the man whose life and teachings are on a par is able to enter in a direct relationship with the supreme God. This, for Origen, is real religious cult *(threskeia)* (I.30). Religious

---

[29] Koep, *Religio und ritus,* 49.

change, conversion, should be perceived as a merit, not as a sign of one's former lowly life. Hence Celsus is not entitled to reproach Christ's disciples because of their life prior to their conversion. Their conversion and their simple language, only reflect their religious qualities. Here lies, also, the difference between Jesus and various sorcerers. His miracles are not meant, like theirs, to show his own power, but rather to offer the believers the path to moral reformation (I.68). The same, incidentally, is true of Moses: he too is a pious man, a lawmaker dedicated to the God of the universe, and not a sorcerer, despite his miracles (III.5).

If the Christians' piety is so powerful, then Celsus's argument against them, namely that by refusing to serve in the army, they weaken the state, should be rejected: it is the Christians' piety and their prayers, more than the soldiers, which protect the state: "Indeed, the more pious a man is, the more effective he is in helping the emperors – more so than the soldiers who go out into the lines and kill all the enemy troops that they can" (VIII.73). And so, answers Origen, the Christians, far from representing a fifth column in the Empire, should be seen as responsible citizens, as the true patriots.

In this context, moreover, Christian universalist monotheism can also be perceived as offering the only possible unity of opinion among the various peoples in the Empire; or at least, such a unity can be aspired for after the soul is separated from the body (VIII.72). We touch here the essence of the deep change of identity in the Empire: more than cultural, it is of a religious nature.[30]

Conclusion

Can the Christians become responsible citizens? This was the question asked by Celsus, who could not foresee that they would, one day, rule the Empire. Neither was he able to perceive the forces of change that would soon rock the boat of traditional religion. For him, indeed, the world was a static scene on which the different personae played a role fixed in advance. He could not have predicted the deep crisis into which the Empire would soon be thrown, and which would touch upon all realms of life and belief for most of the third century.[31] It is this great crisis which permitted the transformation of a well-spread anxiety to phenomena of mass conversion.

In a seminal book, E. R. Dodds has brilliantly described the maelstrom of spiritual tensions into which all were thrown.[32] But he failed to emphasize the

---

[30] See A. Momigliano, "Some Preliminary Remarks on the 'Religious Opposition' to the Roman Empire," in *Opposition et résistances à l'empire d'Auguste à Trajan* (Entretiens Hardt sur l'Antiquité 33; Vandoeuvres-Genève 1968), 124.

[31] See P. Brown, "Approaches to the Religious Crisis of the Third Century A.D." in his *Religion and Society in the Age of Saint Augustine* (London 1977), 74–93.

[32] E. R. Dodds, *Pagan and Christian in an Age of Anxiety* (London 1967).

crucial fact that pagans and Christians had vastly different presuppositions about individual and society.[33] The Christians were better equipped to confront the crisis. Their insistence that the essence of religion lies in personal conviction rather than in tradition explains their success. Perhaps, however, one should not overly rely upon the metaphor of a "privatized religion" used by Robert Wilken to describe Christianity in the Roman world. Privatization, in the sense that religion is first and foremost the domain of the individual, and of all individuals, irrespective of social, economic, ethnic background, or even gender, but not in the sense that there are no social or political direct implications of religious belief and practice.[34]

More than a century after Origen, Augustine too would seek to define proper religion. His *De vera religione* begins with a sentence on God being known only by the purest piety. But Augustine was not arguing against Celsus anymore. Rather than with Hellenic philosophy, it was with Manichaeism that he was polemicizing. The fight with ancient religiosity had already been won. By then, however, Christianity had also been changed in the great quid pro quo. To refer to only one phenomenon hotly discussed in the *Contra Celsum,* the Christians were now serving without any qualms in the Imperial army.

---

[33] See R. C. Smith and J. Lounibos, eds., *Pagan and Christian Anxiety: a Response to E. R. Dodds* (Lanham, Mich., New York, and London 1984), J. G. Gager, "Introduction."

[34] See A.-J. Festugière, *L'idéal religieux des grecs et l'Evangile,* 2nd. ed. (Paris 1981), 32, on Greek religion and aristocratic perceptions. Origen is a better spiritual director than a pagan philosopher like Celsus could ever be.

Chapter 4

Philosophy of the Barbarians:
On Early Christian Ethnological Representations

The early Christians sought to convince all and sundry, outside as well as inside the Roman Empire, to believe in the one God who had sent His Son and sacrificed Him for the salvation of mankind. In this, they were following the injunction of the resurrected Jesus in the Gospel: "Go to all nations, baptizing them and bringing them instruction."[1] The new religious movement born in Palestine soon developed a real ecumenical consciousness. As a rule, the Romans did not express a strong need to explore or understand the world outside the borders of their empire. Indeed, they had at times the impression that the Empire was more or less identical with the civilized world.[2] Appian, for instance, points out in the preface to his *History* that the Roman Empire has conquered all that it needs.[3] As the conscious bearers of a world religion, Christian thinkers, on the other hand, appealed in the first centuries to men and women from all ethnic groups. Reaching to the ends of the *oikoumenè*, Christian missionaries made often successful efforts to convert various exotic, barbarian peoples to the new faith. In the early fifth century, the Christian impact was felt far beyond the borders of the Roman Empire, among the Armenians, the Ethiopians, and the Georgians. In such conditions, the Jewish stubborn refusal to recognize the Messiah who had come from amongst Israel, and who was being accepted the world over, was felt as a painful paradox by Christian thinkers.

In the Roman Empire, the Christians themselves were considered by pagan intellectuals as uncouth followers of a barbarian faith, unable to establish their beliefs in rational argumentation and to express them in polished language, reflecting a proper education. Christian thinkers soon adopted this perception as their own, and saw themselves as the proud possessors of a *barbaros philosophia,* different, older than and superior to the Hellenic philosophical tradition. Is there a relationship between the Christians' strong interest in propagating the

---

[1] Mt 28: 18–20; cf. the parallel text in Mk 16: 15, quoted by Rufinus at the beginning of his discussion of the expansion of Christianity among the barbarian peoples outside the Roman Empire. This text is quoted and discussed in F. Thélamon, *Païens et chrétiens au IVe siècle: l'apport de l' "Histoire ecclésiastique" de Rufin d'Aquilée* (Paris 1981), 33.

[2] See M. Goodman, *Mission and Conversion* (Oxford 1994), 12.

[3] This text is referred to by F. Millar, "Byzantium, Persia and Islam: the Origin of Imperialist Monotheism," *Journal of Roman Archaeology* 7 (1994): 509–11.

new faith to barbarian peoples and their self-identification as "barbarian philosophers"? Can we perceive in early Christian literature (roughly, from the second
to the fifth century), the development of some kind of ethnological curiosity, or
interest in exotic peoples? Oddly enough, such questions do not seem to have
been addressed, at least directly, by modern scholarship. What Arnaldo Momigliano did splendidly for the Hellenistic world in *Alien Wisdom* has not been
pursued for the early Christian mind.[4]

In the following pages, I shall first offer some remarks on identity and ethnological categories in early Christianity. I shall then propose an analysis of some
early Patristic texts on the concept of *barbaros philosophia,* arguing that these
texts remodeled in significant fashion a topic that they inherited from Hellenistic literature. In a third step, I shall compare some early Christian views of two
"barbarian" peoples from the East, the Arabs and the Indians, and ask whether
they reflect a specific Christian sensitivity. Finally, I shall reflect on some structural similarities and differences between two intensely missionary religions of
late antiquity, Christianity and Manichaeism, in their approach to foreign cultures.

1. Early Christian identity and ethnological categories

Paul, the Apostle to the Gentiles, put into action the evangelical command of
Jesus quoted above:

> There is neither Jew nor Greek, there is neither bond nor free, there is neither male nor
> female: for ye are all one in Christ Jesus (Gal 3: 28).

Indeed, Christianity sought from its very origins to erase the cultural and religious boundaries between the peoples of the world. From now on, all men and
women, from all nations, had the same claim for salvation. Elsewhere, Paul develops his ethnological categories slightly more explicitly:

> I am debtor both to the Greeks, and to the Barbarians; both to the wise, and to the un-
> wise. So, as much as in me is, I am ready to preach the gospel to you that are at Rome
> also. For I am not ashamed of the gospel of Christ: for it is the power of God unto salva-
> tion to every one that believeth; to the Jew first, and also to the Greek. (Rom. 1:
> 14–16).

It is important to note that in these verses Paul seems to conflate two different,
although in many ways similar ethnological taxonomies, both very loaded. According to the Greek taxonomy the *barbaroi* are those who do not speak Greek,
and therefore can have no part in Hellenic culture, while the Jewish taxonomy
posits a basic dichotomy between Jews and Gentiles (*goyyim,* lit. "peoples").

---

[4] A. Momigliano, *Alien Wisdom: The Limits of Hellenization* (Cambridge 1975).

Paul possibly means here the Jews when he speaks about "barbarians," although in the Deutero-Pauline literature, *barbaros* is understood *in malam partem*, in the common Hellenic generic sense:

> Where there is neither Greek nor Jew, circumcision nor uncircumcision, Barbarian, Scythian, bond nor free: but Christ is all, and in all. (Col 3: 11)

The idea that ethnological terms are inadequate in order to express Christian identity is reflected best, perhaps, in a famous passage of the *Epistle to Diognetus*, an anonymous text belonging to second century Apostolic literature.

> For the distinction between Christians and other men, is neither in country nor language nor customs. For they do not dwell in cities in some place of their own, nor do they use any strange variety of dialect, nor practise an extraordinary kind of life. ... Yet while living in Greek and barbarian cities, according as each obtained his lot, and following the local customs, both in clothing and food and in the rest of life, they show forth the wonderful and confessedly strange character of their own citizenship. They dwell in their own fatherlands, but as if sojourners in them; they share all things as citizens, and suffer all things as strangers. Every foreign country is their fatherland, and every fatherland is a foreign country. (5.1–5).

The quotations from Paul and the *Epistle to Diognetus* are enough to underline the fact that the early Christians thought about nations and cultures according to new parameters. Since early Christianity did not form a culture of its own, and did not claim to represent an ethnic entity of any kind, the Christians had to invent new parameters according to which they could fashion their own identity.[5] As the quotation from the *Epistle to Diognetus* shows, they were quite aware of their specificity in this regard. This awareness encouraged them to seek new ways of expressing their own identity amid the nations of the earth. It remains to be seen whether it also lured them into developing a new ethnological interest in peoples and cultures with whom they entered in contact.

This important question, however, should be recognized as bearing directly upon Christian self-definition. The early Christians understood in a new fashion the unity of humanity, since all peoples *(ta ethnè)* had been created by the one God.[6] They recognized the inadequacy of current ethnological vocabulary for the definition of their identity. They were not a nation *among* the nations, but "a nation *from* the nations ['*ama de-'amamei*']," as Aphrahat, the Persian Sage, would say in the fourth century.

---

[5] On this issue, see F. Millar, *The Roman Near East, 31 BC-AD 337* (Cambridge, Mass. and London 1993), which deals at length with the problem of ethnicity and cultural identity in the Near East, of the impact of Hellenism (he deals with Porphyry, for instance, and denies him a "Semitic" identity), the progress of Christianity, and insists on the plurality of identities. On Tatian, for instance, see ch. 6. See esp. the first half of the epilogue, "East?," 489–523.

[6] J. Waszink, "Some Observations on the Appreciation of the 'Philosophy of the Barbarians' in Early Christian Literature," in *Mélanges offerts à Mlle Christine Mohrmann* (Utrecht and Antwerp 1963), 41–56, esp. 46.

Indeed, when the Christians first sought to define their identity, they recognized as inadequate the two existing dichotomies that they knew, the Jewish and the Greek ones. The Greek dichotomy differentiated in radical fashion between Greeks and Barbarians. In many ways, insisted the Christians, they themselves should be called barbarians, and their religious thought a barbarian philosophy. Here, as we shall see later, they adopted an already existing concept, deeply transforming it.

When confronted with the Jewish dichotomy between Jews and non-Jews, they argued that it too was inadequate, insisting on defining themselves as a "third race" *(triton genos, tertium genus),*[7] In the metaphorical terms of the *Epistle to Diognetus,* the Christians are not, like all peoples, a clearly delineated limb in the body of humankind, but are everywhere in this body, infusing it with its very living power: what the soul is in the body, that the Christians are in the world (6.1).

As one follows the transformation of the main criteria of identity in the Roman Empire, the crucial role of the Christians in this transformation appears clearly. It has often been pointed out that in the Hellenistic and Roman world the main criteria of identity moved first from ethnicity to culture, and then to religion. Thus John North could recently speak of a "supermarket of religions" under the early Empire in order to describe the open competition between the different cults and religions to win hearts and minds.[8] It is in this context that one can also speak about the "religious revolution of late antiquity," an expression by which one means the new, central importance of religious factors among the criteria of identity. To be sure, the Christians were not the only group to recognize or foster this transformation, but they seem to have been able to profit from it more directly and more deeply than other religious groups.

2. Christianity as barbaros philosophia

In order to understand the origin and evolving semantics of the expression *barbaros philosophia,* one has to remember that since the days of Herodotus – who could be called *philobarbaros* – many Greeks admired the old wisdom of certain

---

[7] As Harnack points out, the expression is very rare in early Christian literature, where it appears in the *Kerygmata Petrou* and in pseudo-Cyprian, *de pascha computus* (a text from the mid-third century). See A. Harnack, *The Expansion of Christianity in the First Three Centuries,* vol. 1 (London and New York 1904), 313–14. See also J. Jüthner, "Barbar," *RAC* I, 1175: "...wird die Gegenüberstellung Juden-Heiden durch des Hinzukommen des "dritten Geschlechts" der Christen au einer Dreiteilung ergänzt. In ihr ist für den Begriff "Barbar" kein Platz mehr. ..."

[8] J. North, "The Development of Religious Pluralism" in *The Jews among Pagans and Christians in the Roman Empire,* eds. J. Lieu, J. North, and T. Rajak (London and New York 1992), 174–93.

barbarian peoples. Pythagoras, for instance, was said to have gone to the Thracian Zalmoxis in order to be initiated, and to have been under Jewish influence. Throughout Greek history, this trend existed side by side with the traditional denigration of the non-Greeks as culturally and intellectually inferior to the Hellenes. Epicurus, for instance, did not want to hear about barbarian philosophy.[9]

This is not the place to offer even a brief summary of the history of Greek representations of foreigners – the topic, most recently, of an excellent study by Albrecht Dihle[10] – nor of the evolution of the idea of a "barbarian philosophy" in the Greek world. I should perhaps only point out that the attitudes towards barbarians evolved radically in the Hellenistic world, with the huge expansion of the boundaries of Hellenic culture and the spread of the Greek language, and of intense contacts between the peoples within and without the Hellenistic world. Alexander's Asian campaigns, in particular, left a legacy of attraction to the ancient cultures of the East. This legacy is reflected, for instance, in the new image of India, which became topical throughout the Hellenistic and the Roman period, and to which we shall return. Broadly, one can say that the semantics of *barbaros* evolved from denoting a person who cannot speak Greek to the ethnic "non-Greek" and later on, to somebody devoid of Greek or Hellenic culture.[11] A similar semantic evolution occurred in Greek attitudes to the wisdom of the barbarians. In the Hellenistic period, H. Dörrie has argued, the Platonic philosophers developed a methodical interest in universal themes, transforming the earlier dichotomy between Greeks and barbarians into a synthesis of human knowledge.[12]

Among other Oriental peoples, the Jews were perceived in some trends of Greek literature as the bearers of an ancient wisdom (something broader than what is commonly called Wisdom literature, and different from it) in a foreign tongue, i.e., of a barbarian philosophy. In the oldest Greek traditions about them, the Jews seem to have been perceived as a race of philosophers. Such views range from Theophrastus, Aristotle's disciple, to Posidonius, who reflects the origins of the antisemitic movement at the end of the second century B.C.E.[13]

---

[9] This is reported by Clement, *Strom.*, 1.15.67.1.

[10] A. Dihle, *Die Griechen und die Fremden* (Munich 1994). See also E. Fascher, "Fremder," *RAC* 8 (1972): 306–48, and W. Nippel, *Griechen, Barbaren und "Wilden": alte Geschichte und Sozialanthropologie* (Frankfurt 1990), esp. 1–29.

[11] See Windisch, "*barbaros*," in *TDNT*, ed. G. Kittel, 1: 546–53, Jüthner, "Barbar," I. Opelt/ W. Speyer, "Barbar," *Nachträge zum RAC, JAC* 10 (1967): 251–90, and E. Lévy, "Naissance du concept de barbare," *Ktèma* 9 (1984): 5–14.

[12] See H. Dörrie, "Die Wertung der Barbaren im Urteil der Griechen," in *Antike und Universalgeschichte: Festschrift H. E. Stier* (Münster 1967), 146–75.

[13] These traditions are conveniently presented and discussed by M. Hengel, *Judaism and Hellenism: Studies in their Encounter in Palestine during the Early Hellenistic Period* (Philadelphia 1974), vol. 1, 255–61.

The first significant figure in that tradition is Hecataeus of Abdera (late fourth cent. B.C.E.), who praises the wisdom of the legislator of the Jews and of his law. After him, the most important figure is Megasthenes, ambassador of Seleucus I Nicator to India. In his *Indica* (written around 290 B.C.E.), Megasthenes speaks admiringly of the Jews, whom he says to be to the Syrians what the Brahmans are to the Indians, that is, a sect of philosophers, the elite of the people, entrusted with the traditions of old dealing with the nature of the Divinity:

> Everything that was taught among the ancients about nature is also said among the philosophers outside Greece, first among the Indians by the Brahmans, and then in Syria by the so-called Jews.[14]

Clearchus of Soli, a pupil of Aristotle, depends on Megasthenes when he considers the Jews to be offspring of the Brahmans, and their wisdom as a "legitimate inheritance" from the Indians. This tradition, which had become a literary *topos,* was apparently accepted by the Jews, since both Philo and Josephus refer to it.[15] For Philo, who follows Megasthenes too, "barbarian philosophy" represents the original reproduction of truth and wisdom, expressed in Hebrew, rather than in Greek. This is identical with the Torah, a book of perfect wisdom. For Philo, the Essenes, in particular, are the possessors of a barbarian wisdom. They are, in a sense, the Jews' Brahmans, the elite among the elite. Philo does not hide that for him barbarian philosophy is of higher value than Greek philosophy.[16]

> We may fairly say that mankind from east to west, every country and every nation and state, shew aversion to foreign institutions, and think that they will enhance the respect for their own by shewing disrespect for those of other countries. It is not so with ours. They attract and win the attention of all, of barbarians, of Greeks, of dwellers on the mainland and on islands, of nations of the east and the west, of Europe and Asia, of the whole inhabited world from end to end.[17]

For Philo, then, Jewish laws unite where the laws of other peoples divide. It is the destiny of the Jewish religion to overcome the differences between Hellenes and barbarians and thus to become the universal religion. Josephus inherits the same tradition, and his final source is probably Megasthenes when he compares between Jews and Indians.[18] As we shall presently see, this Hellenistic fascination

---

[14] See text and translation in Hengel, *Judaism and Hellenism*, vol. 1, 257. See also M. Stern, *Greek and Latin Authors on Jews and Judaism*, vol. 1 (Jerusalem 1974), 45–46.

[15] For Josephus, see *Contra Apionem*, 1. 176–182. For Philo, see *Quod omnis probus liber sit*, 72–94; see also *de Vita Mosis*, 2.19–20. Cf. *de Abr.,* 181; *Spec. Leg.,* 2.165). See also Clement, *Strom.*, 1.71.3.

[16] See F. H. Colson, Philo, *Works* IX (LCL), 52, n.1.

[17] *Vita Mosis*, 2.19–20, transl. Coulson, Philo, *Works* VI (LCL), 459..

[18] See F. Schmidt, "Entre juifs et grecs: le modèle indien," *Purusartha* 11 (1988): 33–47. When Josephus refers to *hellènes kai barbaroi*, moreover, he thinks only about the Gentiles, and does not include the Jews. On the relatively rare use of *barbar* in Rabbinic literature, see

with eastern wisdom is reflected among various intellectuals in the Roman Empire, in particular from the eastern provinces.

Numenius was a second century eclectic Platonist, born in Apamea, a Syrian city which was under the Empire a crossroad of cultures and a center of cultural and religious syncretism. In a seminal study, H. C. Puech mentions both Cerdo, Marcion's teacher, and the Elchasaites as linked to Apamea or its surroundings.[19] Numenius's interest in *barbaros philosophia* is best understood in this background and within the romantic trend of *Drang nach Osten* among Platonist philosophers – a trend fought by Plotinus.[20] His case reflects the fact that the concept of *barbaros philosophia* had become a commonplace of philosophical doxography. The phrase, perhaps, for which he is most widely known is his remark on Plato as a Greek-speaking Moses: *Ti gar esti Platôn è Môusès attikizôn*.[21] Note, says Puech, that Numenius says "Moses," not, for instance, "Zoroaster," adding that it may not be pure chance if this text is preserved by Clement, a Christian writer.[22]

The first book of Numenius's lost work *Peri tagathou* [On the good], of which Clement preserves some excerpts, seemed indeed to include a "call to the East," a clearly syncretistic program, according to which some famous nations possessed a traditional wisdom compatible with Platonism. Among these nations, he mentioned the Brahmans, the Magians, the Egyptians, and the Jews (*brachmanes kai ioudaioi kai magoi kai aigyptoi*).[23]

We owe to Jan Waszink what is probably the most sustained study of the concept of "barbarian philosophy" and its evolution in early Christian literature.[24] In this study, Waszink argues that it is possible to discern a certain evolution in the appreciation of the "philosophy of the barbarians" by the early Christians. One of his most significant finds is that the major semantic shift occured first among Near Eastern Platonist thinkers, and that this shift was accepted by the Christian authors. More precisely, Waszink claims that the roots of the idealization of "the philosophy of the barbarians" among early Christian thinkers such

---

Strack and Billerbeck, *Kommentar zum Neuen Testament aus Talmud und Midrasch*, 2.27ff. See also S. Liebermann, *Tossefta Ki-peshuta*, on Jerusalem Talmud, *Baba Metsi'a* 56a (p. 48, commentary p. 135); I wish to thank Moshe Halbertal for calling my attention to this text. Porphyry, *de Abstinentia* 4 repeats what Bardaisan says on the Indians; the latter repeats Josephus.

[19] H.-C. Puech, "Numénius d'Apamée et les théologies orientales au second siècle," in *En quête de la gnose* (Paris 1978) (written in 1934), vol. 1, 29–30. One could add that various other Neo-Pythagorean and Platonist philosophers, the most prominent among them Porphyry, were also of oriental origin.

[20] Dörrie, "Die Wertung der Barbaren," 168.

[21] Fragment 8, in E. Des Places, *Numénius, Fragments* (Paris 1973), 50–51; same expression in *Eusebius, Praep. Evang.* XI. 10. 12–14.

[22] In *Strom.* 1.22.150.4. See Puech, "Numénius d'Apamée," 31.

[23] Fragment 1 (41 Des Places). On Numenius, see M. Stern, *Greek and Latin Authors on Jews and Judaism*, vol. 2 (Jerusalem 1980), 206–16.

[24] Waszink, "Philosophy of the Barbarians."

as Tatian and Clement of Alexandria are to be found among Greco-Roman philosophers of the later Hellenistic period, from Posidonius to Philo and
Numenius.

Waszink's study, however, seems to ignore some important elements bearing
directly upon the Christian attitude to the concept of *barbaros philosophia,* an
attitude which can be characterized by its complexity. While they were in search
of their identity, the Christians in the first centuries carried their efforts in two
different, almost opposite directions.

On the one hand, the early Christian thinkers had naturally little sympathy for
most religious cults and philosophical doctrines they encountered in the Empire. Members of a *religio illicita,* the Christians were accused of stemming from
a foreign, or barbarian doctrine (that of the Jews). As they were rejecting pagan
behavior and values in a radical way, claiming to be "spiritually barbarians," the
Christians came to develop a certain curiosity for the traditions of "real" barbarian peoples outside the empire. These peoples they sometimes considered to
carry from time immemorial, hidden under various mythical garbs, a *philosophia perennis* of sorts. This reflected the tradition of a single truth scattered
among them, and which could be understood as a *praeparatio evangelica.* Justin
Martyr's doctrine of the spiritual seed *(sperma pneumatikon)* scattered by God
amidst the nations, stands at the origins of this conception. This curiosity for
exotic cultures was buttressed by the Christian missions and communities beyond the boundaries of the empire. As they were outlawed in the Empire, they
soon prided themselves in being the proponents of a *barbaros philosophia,* of a
teaching originally not taught in Greek, and which did not belong to the Hellenic cultural world. The idea of *barbaros philosophia,* which had a long history
in Greek culture, soon took a new turn and became part of Christian self-definition.

On the other hand, there were some parameters of Christian identity which
did not encourage ethnological curiosity. In the first centuries, the Christians
identified themselves as foreigners, as *peregrini* in the Roman Empire. "Our
politeia is in heaven": the words of the *Epistle to the Phillipians* (3:20) are reflected in a long tradition from the *Epistle to Diognetes* up to Augustine. This
self-definition prevented them from developing a real interest in other barbarians. Since the only criterium of Christian identity was religious, opposing idolatry to monotheism, ethnic terms were not really deemed relevant by the Christians. In Cyprian's lapidary formula: "extra ecclesiam nulla salus:" no salvation
outside the Church.[25]

The main reason, however, which militated against the development of a real
Christian ethnological consciousness lies elsewhere. With more and more con-

---

[25] *Ep.,* 73.21; *de cath. eccl. unitate,* 6; cf. Augustine, *de baptismo,* 4.17 (24); references in M.
Goodman, *Mission and Conversion,* 98.

viction and energy, the Christians sought to become accepted and recognized in
the Roman Empire, intellectually as well as legally. When they eventually succeeded, they soon Christianized the Empire, identifying themselves as Romans,
and coming to perceive the "barbarians" as in traditional Roman eyes. We shall
see how the Christian attitude toward the barbarians, as had been the case in the
Hellenistic and Roman intellectual tradition, developed ambiguous characteristics. It is precisely when "the barbarians" threaten the Empire from within and
without, in the late fourth and in the early fifth century, that the Christians
ceased to see themselves as "barbarians", or *peregrini*, and identified, for the
first time unambiguously, as Romans.

Augustine's decision to write the *De Civitate Dei,* for instance, is a point in
case. It is precisely because Alaric's sack of Rome had so deeply shaken the
Christians that Augustine felt he had to argue at length against the identification
of the Christians with Rome and its fate. But his own attitude reflects a minority
position. When the Romans became Christians, the Christians had become Romans.

Albrecht Dihle has probably spent more efforts than any other classicist on
the question of the relationships between Christianity and the East in late antiquity.[26] He has recently provided a fresh survey of the problem, pointing out the
new meaning of the "barbarian philosophy" as applied to the Christians.[27] In his
reflections on the relationships between the inhabitants of the civilized world
and the barbarians outside the boundaries of the Empire, Dihle points out the
importance of the Christian mission in the East and of the Christian communities outside the Empire from the second to the fifth century. In conclusion,
Dihle notes that "the new Christian *Romidee* ... brought with it new criteria of
the difference between barbarism and civilization." I shall presently seek to delineate more precisely the steps of this process.

As Harnack pointed out long ago, their early self-identification as belonging
to a "barbarian philosophy" permitted the Christians to conceive of themselves
not as members of a religion, which could be despised or dishonored, but as a
philosophical school.[28] They could therefore expect to benefit from the toleration, if not the respect, granted to philosophies. This toleration extended to philosophical schools explains why Celsus, the first pagan thinker to have polemicized against Christianity, rejects the Christians' pretension to be, like the
Jews, representatives of a "barbarian philosophy".[29] The evaluation of the Jews
as "barbarian philosophers" seems to have been recognized only progressively
in early Christian literature. Justin Martyr, for instance, argues that the *ioudaioi*

---

[26] See the studies reprinted in A. Dihle, *Antike und Orient.*
[27] In the last chapter of Dihle, *Die Griechen und die Fremden,* "Von der fremden Sekte zur
Staatsreligion," which is devoted to early Christianity.
[28] Harnack, *Expansion of Christianity,* 319–20.
[29] See esp. Origen, *Contra Celsum,* 1.14–16.

are indeed *barbaroi*, but he does not seem to acknowledge a special wisdom of the barbarians. [30] The same identification of *ioudaioi* as *barbaroi* is also found in Melito of Sardis.[31]

In the conclusions of his study, Waszink singled out the influence upon the Christian thinkers of a semantic transformation that had occurred in the Hellenic period. Waszink's argument, however, ignores the specificity of the Christian point of view. It is certainly true that Patristic literature shows few points of intellectual originality as to problems dealt with in the Hellenic tradition, and it is obvious that the Fathers' knowledge of classical literature is most often derivative in nature, usually stemming from epitomes. So, for instance, Waszink notes that Tertullian's knowledge of Plato is derived mainly from Albinus's *Didaskalikos*. But this derivative nature in terms of knowledge does not mean that Christian intellectuals were unable to raise new questions, or to phrase old problems anew, upon the premises of their faith. In that context, for instance, Glen Bowersock is justified in calling for a greater sensitivity to the importance of the Christian representations when we seek to analyze the deep intellectual changes under the Empire. In his words: "Christianity had a powerful influence on the paganism that prospered in the late antique world to a degree...no less important than the influence – much more frequently remarked – of paganism on Christianity."[32]

The semantic evolution of the term *philosophia* itself is well known. It had always reflected a way of life *(politeia)* as well as patterns of thought. With time, it became more and more endowed with religious connotations. Indeed, *philosophia,* which could already mean *eusebeia*, piety, in II Maccabees, eventually came to signify martyrdom. In late antique Christian literature, the term becomes almost identical with the practice of Christian orthodoxy.[33] Eusebius calls Constantine a *philosophos,* and the desert monks are also called *philosophoi,* since they were followers of Christ, who had been the first real *philosophos.* Monasticism, then, came to be identified as the *vera philosophia,* in opposition to the false philosophy of the Hellenic thinkers, which might have developed legitimate teachings but did not recognize the importance of ethical behavior, or praxis on the side of its followers. The monks, on the other side, are not content in understanding the world, but insist on practicing what they teach.

In the introduction to his *Address to the Greeks*, written in Greek around 152, the encratite Apologist Tatian (author of the *Diatessaron,* the famous "Harmony" of the four Gospels) attacks the Greeks' claim to cultural supremacy:

---

[30] *Apology*, 1.5.4; 1.7.3.
[31] See Eusebius, *H.E.*, 4.26.7.
[32] G. W. Bowersock, *Hellenism in Late Antiquity* (Ann Arbor 1990), 26.
[33] A.-M. Malingrey, *"Philosophia": Etude d'un groupe de mots dans la littérature grecque, des présocratiques au 4e siècle après J.-C. (Etudes et documents* XL; Paris 1961).

Do not maintain a totally hostile attitude to foreigners, men of Greece, nor resent their beliefs. For which of your own practices did not have a foreign origin? The most famous of Telmessians invented divination through dreams; Carians foreknowledge through stars; Phrygians and the most ancient of the Isaurians the lore of bird-flights, Cyprians a cult of sacrifices; Babylonians astronomy, Persians magic, Egyptians geometry, Phoenicians education through the letters of the alphabet. Therefore, stop calling imitations inventions. It was Orpheus who taught you the practice of poetry and singing, also initiation in the mysteries; the Etruscans taught sculpture, Egyptian chronological records taught the composition of history.[34]

So in practically all fields of culture, the Greeks only copy the original contributions of the most varied nations. The Greeks, however, although willing to admit barbarian primacy in many fields, usually believed that they themselves were able to improve on what they had received. Tatian echoes here a long tradition in Greek self-perception, from Plato to his contemporary Celsus.[35] In such a scheme these nations are barbarians: they don't speak Greek. But even here, argues Tatian, the Greeks' claims of supremacy are vain. They do not speak a single language, but a series of dialects:

> The speech of the Dorians is not the same as that of men from Attica and Aeolians do not speak like Ionians.

This lack of linguistic unity raises a serious question as to the very concept of a Greek identity. According to Tatian, moreover, Greek is now contaminated by the presence of too many foreign words. In such conditions, why should one remain attracted by Greek philosophy? Indeed, Tatian announces that he has left Greek wisdom, "even though I was myself very distinguished in it."[36]

In the following chapters, Tatian develops two main arguments against Greek philosophy. He presents Christianity as the newest form of the "wisdom of the barbarians." He first points to the moral supremacy of Christian (or "barbarian") philosophy over pagan licentiousness and the immorality of Greek teachings, in particular of mythology, which corrupts the youth (*Oratio,* 31–35). He then develops what is often called the "chronological argument": while all Greek philosophical teachings eventually go back to Homer, the Christian teachings have their source in the wisdom of Moses, who is older than Homer (*Or.,* 36–41).

Tatian tells us about himself that he comes "from the land of the Assyrians" (*Or.,* 42), a term which might mean Mesopotamia proper, but more probably

---

[34] Tatian, *Or.,* 1; I quote M. Whittaker's translation, in Tatian, *Oratio ad Graecos* (Oxford Early Christian Texts; Oxford 1982), 3.

[35] For Plato, see *Epinomis,* 987d. On his side, Celsus says: "Barbarians can discover things, but the Greeks know to interpret them better," in Origen, *Contra Celsum,* 1.2.

[36] *Or.,* 29. This biographical remark alludes to what he will develop later, namely that it is after all kinds of journeys and wanderings (*Or.,* 35), like Justin Martyr before him, that he converted to Christianity. Incidentally, the pattern of Tatian's conversion may reflect the influence of Justin, whom he admired (*Or.,* 18.2).

refers to Syria. His provenance from the Syrian Orient, at the linguistic, cultural, political, and also religious borderline between East and West, is a matter of some significance. Like Numenius, and like Mani after him, he lived in a state of cultural diglossia, feeling in a most concrete way the complex intercourse of cultures – which does not necessarily entail syncretism – and sought to deal with their conflicting claims. At the crossroad of cultures, Tatian can at ease reflect on the multiplicity of ethical codes. The Greeks don't encourage intercourse with one's mother, while the Persians do so. On the other side, pederasty, which is considered to be criminal by the barbarians, is legitimate for the Romans. Unlike pagan thinkers, however, Tatian does not use this multiplicity of behavioral patterns, however, as an argument in favor of the ethical and legal relativism. Celsus, for instance, "thinks that it is impossible for the inhabitants of Asia, Europe, and Lybia, both Greeks and barbarians, to be agreed."[37]

> All should have one common way of life, but as it is there are as many codes of law as there are types of cities, so that things which among some are shameful are good among others." (*Or.,* 28).

Tatian uses the plurality of mores in order to promote an *interpretatio christiana* of the argument already encountered in Philo, namely that the Torah alone represents a universal law. The message of the Gospels, or *kerygma,* seems here to be the heir of the Torah: it can be accepted by all, Greeks and barbarians alike. In order to denigrate the intellectual value of Christianity, the Greeks often used to point out the low level of linguistic and intellectual sophistication of Christian Scriptures. The counter-argument developed by Tatian, which will reappear later in Origen's *Contra Celsum,* considers this artlessness of the Christian writings, their lack of arrogance, their intelligibility to all, and not only to a thin layer of highly sophisticated intellectuals, and finally the doctrine of a single ruler of the universe, to be strong arguments in favor of their truthfulness. According to Tatian, it is this simplicity which convinced him to accept Christianity (*Or.,* 29).

It is important to note that for Tatian, the claim of monotheism to truth lies as much in its social and ethical implications as in its metaphysical arguments. The unity of mankind, as much as the unity of the creator, is at stake here. Because of both the ethical weaknesses of paganism and of the irradicable dichotomy between Greeks and barbarians inherent in Hellenic culture, the Greeks had been unable to provide a convincing model of universality. Such a model was provided to men and women of East and West by the best "barbarian philosophy," i.e., the Law of Moses in its *interpretatio christiana.*

Although Tatian praises the "barbarian philosophy" in the course of his virulent polemic against Hellenic culture, he does not remain uncritical of the beliefs

---

[37] Origen, *Contra Celsum,* 8.72 *in finem.*

or practices of the various barbarian peoples. When, for instance, he mentions that "there is no cannibalism among us" (*Or.*, 25.3), he implies that this is practiced among some barbarian peoples. At approximately the same time, the Syriac writer Bardaisan also shows some ethnological interest in the mores of various eastern peoples in his *Book of the Laws of Countries*.[38] Like Tatian, Bardaisan shows a critical ability. After having reviewed the immoral laws of peoples as different from one another as the Indians, the Persians, the Bactrians (i. e., the Kushans), the Parthians, the Medes, the Gauls, the Amazones and others, he concludes: "in all these countries, the disciples of Christ do not practice the morally condemnable habits of these pagan peoples." Bardaisan primarily seeks to bring down the Greeks from the pedestal on which they think they stand, rather than to argue for a superiority of the barbarians.[39]

Such a criticism of barbarian mores (before conversion to Christianity) is rather common in Patristic literature. When the Christian Apologists sought to convince the pagan Romans to accept them, they showed no interest in barbarians, repeating the prejudices about them common in ancient literature. Eusebius, for instance, a writer close to the main stream of Greek culture – and to the corridors of power in the Empire – writes:

> the customs of all nations are now set aright, even those customs which before were savage and barbarous; so that Persians who have become His disciples no longer marry their mothers, nor Scythians feed on human flesh, because of Christ's Word which has come even to them, nor other races of barbarians have incestuous union with daughters and sisters.[40]

Here as in many other instances, the references to the barbarians do not reflect a genuine intellectual interest, but rather are part of the effort of Christian intellectuals to become acceptable in Roman eyes. Hence one can often detect in them an apologetic sound. Tertullian, to take an instance from the Latin West, insists on the fact that the Christians' beliefs do not make them less human than their pagan neighbors – using expressions echoed, as it were, by Shakespeare's Shylock:

> We are of a different nature, I suppose! Are we Cyropennae of Sciapodes? Have we different teeth, different organs of incestuous lust? ... Nay, a Christian too is a man, he is whatever you are.[41]

Or else:

> Christian men live beside you, share your food, your dress, your customs, the same necessities of life as you do. For we are neither Brahmins nor Indian gymnosophists, in-

[38] For an excellent *status quaestionis* and bibliography, see H. J. W. Drijvers, "Bardesanes," *TRE* 5, 206–12.

[39] See Bardesanes, *Liber legum regionum* in *Patrologia Syriaca* I, 2, 606–607.

[40] *P.E.*, 1.4, 11b-c.

[41] *Apol. ad Nationes*, 8.

habiting the woods, and exiles from existence.... If I do not attend your religious ceremonies, none the less am I a human being.[42]

From his native Africa, Tertullian has no reason to express any interest in the
peoples of the East. For him, like for many of his pagan contemporaries, humanity is more or less correlate of the *oikoumenè* as defined, more or less, by
the Empire's boundaries. For a Rufinus, too, the Roman Empire is equivalent
to the *orbis terrarum,* the *oikoumenè.* As a Christian, however, his representation of the world is broader than the traditional Roman political and cultural
vision.[43] Let us note, then, that even for Christian writers uninterested in oriental wisdom, what counts most is not to offer a defense of a "Western culture"
about which Tertullian does not care much, but to preserve the unity of humanity.[44]

At the turn of the third century, Clement of Alexandria would develop with
great enthusiasm the Christian self-fashioning as a barbarian philosophy, which
had begun to take shape with Tatian. According to Clement, the barbarian philosophers were older than the Greeks. In what may be his most important statement on the topic, he says that the teachers of the Greeks were the barbarian
philosophers.[45] But Clement does not only repeat this old *topos.* Rather, he
transforms it into a new argument for the derivative character of Greek philosophy, which he calls "stolen." It is from the barbarians that the Greeks stole their
knowledge; the stolen arguments of philosophy they then adorned by Greek
speech. The Greeks are not only imitators of the barbarians, as Tatian had accused them of being. They are also thieves of ideas,[46] as well as of literary styles.
Clement concludes a chapter on Egyptian and Indian wisdom with the following
sentence: "And that the Greeks are called pilferers of all manner of writing, it is,
I think, sufficiently demonstrated by abundant proofs."[47]

The Jews are for Clement the oldest barbarian nation to have had a formative
– though unrecognized – influence upon Greek culture, and Moses is the first
philosopher. It is in this context that Clement, quoting Numenius, claims Moses
to have been Plato's model.[48] The institutions and the laws of the Jews are far
older than the philosophy of the Greeks.[49] It is from the Jews that the Greeks
learned the main truths of philosophy, although they sought to hide their origin
through the artificial ornaments of Greek language:

---

[42] *Apol.,* 42.
[43] See Thélamon, *Païens et chrétiens,* 34.
[44] See the discussion of Tertullian's texts in Harnack, *The Expansion of Christianity,* 341.
[45] *Strom.,* 6.7.57, 2–3.
[46] See also *Strom.,* 1.17.
[47] *Strom.,* 6.4.
[48] *Strom.,* 1.25.
[49] *Strom.,* 1.21.

> Of all these [barbarian peoples], by far the oldest is the Jewish race; and that their philosophy committed to writing has the precedence of philosophy among the Greeks, Philo shows at large.[50]

But the Greeks were not only the Jews' pupils. They were also influenced by the philosophy of other barbarian peoples, bearers of ancient traditions, such as the Egyptians, the Magians, and the Brahmans. So Clement can also state that "the Greeks drew many of their philosophical tenets from the Egyptian and Indian gymnosophists.".[51] These peoples, however, came only after the Hebrews; each of them reached only a partial truth:

> Similarly to the Bacchae who tore Pentheus's limbs, so the sects of barbarian and of Greek philosophy each take pride in what they have reached, as if they were in possession of the whole truth.[52]

For Clement, then, barbarian philosophy par excellence is the Bible: he can speak of "the devil about which barbarian philosophy tells us so much" or about "the Writings of barbarian philosophy."[53] What the Greeks acquired illegitimately, the Christians reached legitimately, receiving even the key for a perfect, spiritual understanding of the Law of Moses. Thus Clement perceives both Jews and Christians to represent, together, barbarian philosophy.[54] The Christians are of course the direct heirs of the Jews, but since the coming of Christ is the last step of divine revelation in history, only Christian barbarian philosophy, received from Jesus Christ, is at once true, complete, and perfect.[55]

It should be pointed out that the scheme of the revelation of truth to mankind summarized here is not quite spelled out by Clement, who seeks to retain some esoteric character to his *Stromateis*. Clement does nowhere argue for a direct connection between the wisdom of the Magians, the Egyptians, or the Brahmans on the one hand, and divine revelation to the Jewish prophets on the other hand. Therefore, there must be two independent chains of transmission of philosophical ideas, a diachronic one, of course, but also a synchronic one, as it were, which distributes wisdom to different nations. Clement's view of things does not seem to reflect any idiosyncrasy on his part. On the contrary, it may have been rather widespread, since it is echoed by Augustine:

---

[50] *Strom.*, 1.16

[51] *Strom.*, 6.4.

[52] *Strom.*, 1.13.57.

[53] Respectively *Strom.*, 5.4.92 and *Strom.*, 5.9.56.

[54] See G. G. Stroumsa, *Hidden Wisdom: Esoteric Traditions and the Roots of Christian Mysticism* (SHR 70; Leiden 1996), ch. 7, 109–31.

[55] *Strom.*, 2.2.25; 1.18.90. Gustave Bardy suggests that Clement might have been the first author to clearly fix the transposition into Christian vocabulary of the meaning of *philosophia*, while the term usually keeps with Origen its traditional meaning; see G. Bardy, "'Philosophie' et 'philosophe' dans le vocabulaire chrétien des premiers siècles", *Revue d'Ascétique et de Mystique* 25 (1949): 97–108, esp. 106. This, however, is not precise, since Origen also speaks about the "true philosophy of Christ" (*Hom. Gen.,* 111.2) and identifies philosophy with ascetical life.

Those who were esteemed as sages of philosophers in other nations: Lybians of Atlas, Egyptians, Indians, Persians, Chaldeans, Scythians, Gauls, Spaniards...: we rank such thinkers above all others and acknowledge them as representing the closest approximation to our Christian position.[56]

3. Indians and Arabs

We have heard different Church Fathers mention the names of various barbarian nations, sometimes with great emphasis, but usually with little detail on the contents of their hailed wisdom. Let us now come back to the question raised at the beginning of this inquiry. How did Christian intellectuals in the first centuries construct their own identity, in contradistinction or opposition to others? Can we discern certain specifically Christian ways of approaching peoples of the East and their traditional cultures? In order to formulate the question more concretely, I propose to compare the Christian appreciation of two eastern peoples in Late Antiquity, Indians and Arabs.

Although both Indians and Arabs were considered in the ancient world to be barbarians, they were barbarians of different kinds. Throughout Antiquity, the Indians were perceived as bearers of a respectable cultural tradition. They were, in other words, a *Kulturvolk* par excellence. The Arabs, on the other hand, or Saracens, as they were usually called, were consistently described in ancient literature as tent-dwellers, inhabitants of the desert, a *Naturvolk*, in other words, barbarians *in malam partem*. Do early Christian representations of Indians and Arabs show some distinctive traits, which differentiate them from their image in pagan literature?

Although Christian authors did not usually develop very daring or original anthropological perceptions, neither did they feel themselves quite bound by Hellenistic literary traditions on foreign peoples. It is this relative freedom which permitted them to propose a somewhat fresh understanding of Indian wisdom, and also of the Arabs. It should be pointed out, however, that the willingness to recognize the presence of important truths among the barbarians was not self-evident for early Christian theologians. To some extent, it was harder for them than for contemporary pagan thinkers, who did not believe in divine revelation, to accept the idea that different religious traditions could have a legitimate claim to the knowledge of truth. These barbarians, after all, were pagans, remaining as such outside the pale of divine revelation.

But what might seem difficult to accept from an abstract theological viewpoint was rendered possible both by the Christians' new awareness of the unity of mankind and by their dissociation from classical culture and from Roman in-

---

[56] *De Civitate Dei*, 8.9.

tellectual representations. It is thanks to his strong belief in the unity of mankind that Justin Martyr, in the mid-second century, was able to develop his theory of the *spermatikos logos* infiltrating all cultures as a kind of parallel, implicit revelation. This same attempt to 'recuperate,' as it were, or to recapitulate the wisdom of all mankind, and not only that of the Greeks, informs Eusebius's idea of a *praeparatio evangelica*. As is well known, this theological standpoint entailed a relativization of the Greek cultural tradition. What is not emphasized often enough, and clearly enough, is the fact that it could also lead to some measure of ethnological curiosity toward other cultures.

> And in the darkened solitudes of India, those who practice philosophy in nakedness (and are hence called gymnosophists), nevertheless have coverings on their genitals, although they have none on the rest of their body.[57]

This description of the barbarian philosophers of India, by Diogenes Laertius in the third century C.E., is fairly typical of what was known and repeated in the Roman world about Indian wisdom. As mentioned above, the traditional conception of India in Hellenistic and Roman literature followed the detailed and authoritative account given by Megasthenes in his *Indica*.[58] In the words of J. W. Sedlar: "All later Hellenistic writers on India (Arrian, Quintus Curtius, Strabon, Plinius, Philostrates) depended for their view of India primarily upon the Alexandrian tradition, three to five centuries old."[59]

Thanks to the important trade contacts between India and the Roman Empire, a more concrete knowledge of India became available. It remains a puzzling matter that this new knowledge is not really reflected in the image of India in late antique literature. In his fundamental work on *India and Europe,* Wilhelm Halbfass offers as a partial explanation of this fact "a certain classicism, which defined and stylized India as the country Alexander subjugated and Megasthenes lived in."[60] A case in point is the almost complete lack of reference to Buddhism, by then the chief religion of India, in the literature of the Roman period.

---

[57] Diogenes Laertius, *Lives of the Philosophers*, 1.22.

[58] See esp. A. Dihle, "The Conception of India in Hellenistic and Roman Literature," *Proceedings of the Cambridge Philological Society* 190 (n.s. 10) (1964): 15–23; reprinted in *Antike und Orient: Gesammelte Aufzätze,* eds. V. Pötschl and H. Petersmann (Supplemente zu den Sizungsberichten der Heidelberger Akademie der Wissenschaften, Phil.-hist. Klasse, 2; Heidelberg 1984).

[59] J. W. Sedlar, *India and the Greek World: A Study in the Transmission of Culture* (Totowas, N.J. 1980), 262. We must remember, moreover, that in the literature of the times *India ulterior* refers to the Ethiopian kingdom of Axum, evangelized by Frumentius in the fourth century. See for instance the figure of Theophilus the Indian. See G. Fiaccadori, *Teofilo indiano* (Biblioteca di Felix Ravenna; Ravenna 1992). See also the description of the *Expositio totius mundi et gentium*, 35: "Beyond the limits of Thebaid, [Egypt] touches the people of the Indians"; see ibid., 16N-18 (I quote according to the edition of J. Rougé (SC 124; Paris 1966). See further the discussion in Thélamon, *Paiens et chrétiens au IVe siècle*, 49–50.

[60] W. Halbfass *India and Europe: An Essay in Understanding* (Albany 1988), 15.

A long list of Patristic authors deal with the ancient wisdom of the Brahmans. Clement, Origen, Tertullian, Hippolytus, the Pseudo-Clementine *Recognitiones,* Jerome, Ambrose, Augustine, Prudentius, all at least refer to their barbarian philosophy, although many offer only a few passing remarks, and do not provide any new information.[61] Of all these authors, Clement has probably the most interesting things to say on our topic:

> The Indian philosophers are also in the number [of the barbarian philosophers] and the other barbarian philosophers. And of these there are two classes, some of them called Sarmanae, and others Brahmins. And those of the Sarmanae who are called Hylobii neither inhabit cities, nor have roofs over them, but are clothed in the bark of trees, feed on nuts, and drink water with their hands. Like those called encratites in the present day, they know not marriage nor begetting of children ... Some, too, of the Indians obey the precepts of Buddha, whom, on account of his extraordinary sanctity, they have raised to divine honors.[62]

Perhaps it is not by chance if the Christian Clement is the first author to offer an explicit reference to Buddhism. Here as elsewhere when dealing with matters of religious beliefs and cults, Clement is particularly trustworthy and knowledgeable. On the Greek mystery cults, for instance, he tells us more than anybody else. Similarly, he shows a remarkably accurate knowledge of both Egyptian cult and traditions.[63]

Clement is of course an intellectual with no direct Indian contacts, but he interprets anew the traditions which he inherits. It is particularly interesting to note the parallel he draws between Indian and Christian asceticism, i.e., philosophy. His knowledge about things Indian, however, may come from his admired master Pantaenus, who traveled to India. Pantaenus was a famous Christian teacher at the catechetical school in Alexandria.[64] Eusebius tells us of his visit to India:

> It is said that [Pantaenus] went to the Indians, and the tradition is that he found there that among some of those there who had known Christ the Gospel according to Matthew had preceded his coming.[65]

On the originality of Clement's perception of Indian wisdom, Halbfass writes, almost in passing: "In the works of some Christian writers, especially Clement,

---

[61] See J. Duncan M. Derrett, "The History of 'Palladius on the Races of India and the Brahmans,'" *Classica et Medaevalia* 21 (1960): 67, n. 22. See further B. Breber and F. Bömer, eds., *Fontes Historiae Religionum Indicarum* (Bonn 1939), 105ff.

[62] *Strom.,* 1.15; on Clement's knowledge of Indian philosophy, see esp. A. Dihle, "Indische Philosophen bei Clemens Alexandrinus," in *Mullus: Festschrift Theodor Klauser* (*JAC*, Ergänzungsband 1; Münster 1964), 60–70; reprinted in Dihle, *Antike und Orient*, 78–88.; see also Sedlar, *India and the Greek World*, 263.

[63] *Strom.,* 6.4.

[64] See for instance S. Lilla, "Pantaenus," in *EEC*, vol. 2, 639.

[65] *H. E.,* 5.10.3; I, 462–3 LCL (translation by Kirsopp Lake).

the thesis of the Oriental 'barbarian' origin takes a new and peculiar turn: it becomes a means of criticizing the Greek confidence in human reason, the uniqueness of the Hellenic tradition, and their proud proclamation of philosophy and theory."[66] Halbfass is certainly correct in referring to a new attitude towards the concept of "barbarian philosophy" which can be detected in the thought of the Church Fathers. This new attitude does not reflect the influence of Numenius, as argued by Waszink. Rather, as the example of Brahman wisdom shows, it stems directly from their own particular viewpoint and sensitivity as Christian intellectuals. It is thus Christian self-fashioning which permitted the development of a new interest in alien wisdom, an interest different from the pagan romantic infatuation with "barbarian philosophy."

As Albrecht Dihle points out, the Christians were able, more than contemporary pagans, to learn from sailors and tradesmen.[67] Dihle, however, does not tell us the reasons for this ability. It seems to me that it should be looked for in a combination of their missionary activity on the one hand, and their lack of commitment to the Hellenistic literary tradition on the other. Cosmas Indicopleustes, in the 6th century, is of course the most famous example of such Christian travelers and sailors to India. Like the fourth-century anonymous *Expositio totius mundi,* Cosmas is interested only in geography, not in ethnography. The picture of India that he develops is not different from the one known to his pagan contemporaries, and stems from early Hellenistic sources.

To sum up, we can say that when Clement speaks about the barbarian philosophy of the Brahmans, he presents an image of India slightly different from the one usually reproduced by his pagan contemporaries. This new image is directly related to both his religious universalism and his cultural relativism. Through both, he violates some literary taboos, and succeeds in keeping a certain distance from classical culture.[68]

The perception of India and of its wise holy men in the Hellenistic world and in early Christianity differs considerably from the traditional view of Arabs in ancient literature. While the Indians, as we have seen, were widely perceived as being the inheritors of a perennial tradition of wisdom, no such representation of the Arabs was available. The opposite is true. Indeed, the Arabs are consistently presented in late antique literature, including in many Christian texts, as "real" barbarians, desert tribes devoid of any respectable cultural tradition. For instance, the Ismaelites are described by Rufinus, in terms inherited from the Biblical representation of Ismael, as a *gens ferocissima,*[69] while Eusebius, referring to their raids on the Roman lines, calls them "thieves," and also *skènites,*

---

[66] Halbfass, *India and Europe,* 9.
[67] A. Dihle, "The Conception of India," 91.
[68] As noted by Dihle, "The Conception of India," 91, this enables him, for instance, to present a new picture of South India.
[69] Thélamon, *Païens et chrétiens au IVe siècle,* 149.

tent-dwellers, addicted to repulsive social and religious practices such as human sacrifice. Eusebius mentions the yearly sacrifice of a young boy to an evil demon, and his burial under the altar.[70] Perhaps under the influence of Eusebius, the same picture obtains in the writings of Jerome, who also speaks of the "barbarian" character of Semitic languages.[71] Augustine, too, holds a similar pejorative view of Arabs as barbarians.[72]

The Christianization of the nomadic tribes had begun in the second half of the fourth century with the conversion of Queen Mavia, who can be called "the founder of an Arab national church."[73] The emergence of a Saracen Christianity in the 370s, as told in Mavia's story, reflects the fact that conversion to Christianity was experienced by the barbarians as a factor of integration into the Roman Empire.[74] In some cases, the newly converted Arabs appeared to be orthodox barbarians, in an empire where heresy of various kinds was rife. This was, however, far from being the rule, and more often than not the Arabs were perceived to be heretics. The Palestinian Epiphanius, for instance (he was born in Eleutheropolis) associated the Arabs with heresy. It is from his heresiographical *summa*, the *Panarion* that we know about the Audians, a still barely known sect on the borders of heresy, whose probably Arab members we meet in fourth century Judea.[75] Hippolytus's *Philosophoumena* tell us of Monoïmus (probably Mun'im), the Arab leader of a Gnostic sect. From various sources, we also know of early Manichaean influences among the Arabs.[76]

The most important Patristic source on the Arabs is probably the testimony of Sozomen on their religion in his *Ecclesiastical History*.[77] Sozomen shows an impressive ethnological ability. Moreover, he must have come into contact with the

---

[70] Eusebius, *Praep.Ev.,* 4.16.17. See I. Shahid, *Rome and the Arabs: A Prolegomenon to the Study of Byzantium and the Arabs* (Washington, D.C. 1984), 108. I should like to emphasize my debt in this section to the pioneering work of Irfan Shahid, the best specialist of Greek and Latin sources on the Arabs. See esp. his *Byzantium and the Arabs in the Fourth Century* [=BA-FOC] (Washington, D.C. 1984), and *Byzantium and the Arabs in the Fifth Century* [=BAFIC] (Washington, D.C. 1989.

[71] References in Shahid, *BAFOC*, 293–95. This last point is argued by Shahid in *BAFIC*, 534.

[72] See V. Christides, "Arabs as *barbaroi* before the rise of Islam," *Balkan Studies* 10 (1969): 315–24, and idem, "Once again the 'Narrations' of Nilus Sinaiticus," *Byzantion* 43 (1973): 38–50. For further details on Cyril of Scythopolis's image of the Arabs as *barbaroi*, see Shahid, *BA-FIC*, 208. The Saracens are considered to be *barbaroi* particularly when they are not Christians; see ibid., 139.

[73] Shahid, *BAFOC,* 158.

[74] See Thélamon, *Païens et chrétiens*, 138.

[75] See chapter 15 of this volume.

[76] On Manichaeism among the Arabs in Palestine, see G. G. Stroumsa, "Gnostics and Manichaeans in Byzantine Palestine," in *Studia Patristica,* ed. M. Livingstone 10 (Kalamazoo 1985), 273–78; in French translation, in G. G. Stroumsa, *Savoir et salut* (Paris 1992), 291–98. See further, Shahid, *BAFOC,* 31–35, who speculates on Imru el Qais's father as a protector of Manichaeism in Hira in the period that followed the execution of Mani.

[77] On this text, see Shahid, *BAFOC,* 274–77. This text has long attracted the interest of Islamicists; see, e.g., M. Cook, *Muhammad* (Oxford 1983), 80–81.

Negev Arabs in his early years, since he was born in Bethelia, near Gaza, toward the end of the fourth century. His words, hence, should be taken seriously. Sozomen tells us that in the 370s (at about the time of Valentinian the younger, and of Ulfila's conversion to Arian Christianity) the Arab queen Mavia, who had led her troops into Phoenicia and Palestine, demanded the ordination of a Christian holy man, Moses, in exchange for peace with the Romans.[78] Reflecting the radical semantic transformation of the concept *philosophia,* Sozomen describes Moses as someone "who practiced philosophy in a neighboring desert," that is to say someone who leads a monastic way of life.[79]

Sozomen then offers an overview of the religious history of the Arabs. The tribe had its origin from Ismael, son of Abraham. Later, they called themselves Saracens, *sarakènoi,* in order to claim that they were the progeniture of Sarah, rather than of the slave Hagar. Indeed, the Arabs are usually called *sarakènoi* in late antique and early Byzantine literature.[80] The term retains clear pejorative connotations, implying nomadic life in the desert, i.e., uncultured barbarians.[81]

> Such being their origin, they practice circumcision like the Jews, refrain from the use of pork, and observe many other Jewish rites and customs.

With the lapse of time, however, the Jewish origin of many of these religious practices became blurred, until

> the inhabitants of the neighboring countries, being strongly addicted to superstition, probably soon corrupted the laws imposed upon them by their forefather Ismael.

This departure from the laws of their forefathers then became reflected in the Arabs' acceptance of various idolatrous practices common among the neighboring nations, although

> some of their tribe afterwards happening to come in contact with the Jews, gathered from them the facts of their true origin, returned to their kinsmen, and inclined to the Hebrew customs and laws.[82]

This famous text thus testifies to a strong Jewish influence upon pre-Islamic Arab society. It also refers to a Judaising trend, or sect, among contemporary Arabs. It is hard to know whether Sozomen refers more particularly to the Negev Arabs, or whether his testimony is also valid for Arabs from the Hijaz. But the details and the whole tone of Sozomen's report make it very probable

---

[78] Sozomen, *Hist. Eccl.* 6.28.

[79] On Moses, see Shahid, *BAFOC*, 152–58.

[80] The name *Sarakènoi* (a word with a puzzling etymology) is said to come from the name Sarah. See also I. Eph'al, "'Ismael' and 'Arab(s)': a Transformation of Ethnological Terms," *JNES* 35 (1976): 225–35. See also S. Krauss, "Talmudische Nachrichten über Arabien," *ZDMG* 70 (1916): 321–53

[81] On which see Shahid, *Rome and the Arabs*, appendix, ch.9, 123 sv., and *BAFOC*, 282.

[82] Sozomen, *Hist. Eccl.* 6.38.

that he was using some concrete sources, and that his report does not simply reflect a traditional image. It fits together with other sources, which mention important Jewish influences in the pre-Islamic Hijaz.[83] The main implication of Sozomen's text for our present purposes is that it shows that some Christian
authors could perceive the Arabs as more than uncultured desert tribes.
Through their kinship with the Jews, the original "barbarian philosophers," the
Arabs were thought to have some share in the *Heilsgeschichte*. Obviously, such
an approach could not have been developed by pagan writers. It is clearly a
Christian novelty in the representation of the Arabs. As Fergus Millar has recently shown, the new image of the Arabs in late antiquity stemmed from the
perception of the Ismaelites presented by Josephus, that is, of a people having
some kinship with the Israelites.[84]

The new perception of the Arabs' share in Israel's nobility permitted the development of new, less pejorative attitudes towards them. Thus we can read in
Theodoretus' *Graecarum Affectionum Curatio,* for instance:

> As to our neighbors, the nomads (I mean the Ismaelites who live in the desert and who
> have not the least conception of Greek letters), they are endowed with sagacity and in-
> telligence, and they have a judgment capable of discerning truth and refuting false-
> hood.[85]

Like the image of India, then, the image of the Arabs in late antique Christian
literature is slightly different from the one reflected in pagan texts. This specificity of the Christian texts permits the development of a more open, more
curious attitude toward the barbarians and their traditions.

4. Christians and Manichaeans

A look at some aspects of the interaction between Christianity and Manichaeism in the late antique Near East might help sharpen the analysis. The syncretistic and ecumenical nature of Manichaeism, as well as the intimate relationships between the two religions, can shed some light on the similarities and differences between the two religions in their representations of other spiritual
traditions. This comparison, in its turn, should permit a better understanding of
the nature of Christian attitudes to foreign cultures.

---

[83] See for instance M. J. Kister and M. Kister, "On the Jews of Arabia: Some Notes" (in Hebrew) *Tarbiz* 48 (1979): 231–47; cf. U. Rubin, in *JSAI* 13: 99, who quotes this passage from Sozomen; on strong Jewish influences in the Yemen, see M. Lecker,"Judaism among Kinda and the
Ridda of Kinda," *JAOS* 115 (1995): 333–56.

[84] F. Millar, "Hagar, Ishmael, Josephus and the Origins of Islam," *JJS* 44 (1993): 23–45.

[85] Theodoretus, *Graec. Affect. Curatio* 5.73; I quote according to P. Canivet's edition, *Théo-
doret de Cyr, Thérapeutique des maladies helléniques* (SC 57, Paris 1958), vol. 1, 250; this passage is discussed by Shahid, *BAFIC*, 157. Theodoretus mentions elsewhere that together with the
Phrygians, the Arabs were the first to consult augurs (1.19; I, 108 Canivet).

A double list of prophets, sent throughout history and to the different regions of the world, is typical of the Manichaean structure of prophecy. On the one hand, there is a diachronic list of prophets, from Adam to Christ to Mani, which includes prophets of the antediluvian times such as Enoch – but not the Biblical prophets properly so called. The synchronic list, on the other hand, mentions Buddha in the East, Zarathustra in the central lands, and Jesus in the West, all preceding Mani. Each was sent only to one area of the world, while Mani, the only prophet to offer a total revelation, valid for all peoples, in the entire *oikoumenè,* seals prophecy.[86]

The double chain of prophecy has been known for a long time from various Manichaean texts, but a new Coptic *Kephalaion,* recently published and analyzed by Michel Tardieu is most explicit:

> The Lord Zoroaster came in Persia to king Hystaspes. He has revealed the law still really established in Persia.
> The Lord Buddha the wise, the blessed: he came in the land of India and among the Kushans.
> He has revealed the law still really established in the whole of India and the Kushans. After him came Aurentes and Pkedellos in the East; they have revealed the law still really established in the East: the Middle of the world and Parthia; He has revealed the law of truth among all of them.
> Then Jesus Christ in the West of the Romans came to the whole land of the West.[87]

As far as my knowledge goes, the Manichaean double chain of prophecy, both through the ages and through the universe, has always been considered by scholars to be an original theme, devised by Mani himself, the first thinker to have established a consciously universal religion. If my analysis above is correct, this *communis opinio* should be qualified. The Manichaean double chain of prophecy is highly reminiscent of Tatian's and Clement's conception of two chains of *barbaros philosophia,* that of the Hebrews and those of the Eastern barbarian peoples. The similarities between these two mythological frames seem too close to be the fruit of chance. It stands to reason, therefore, that the basic structure of Manichaean revelation throughout the generations and among the different cultures was not a total novelty. Rather, it appears to be a

---

[86] See G. G. Stroumsa, "Seal of the Prophets: the Nature of a Manichaean Metaphor," *JSAI* 7 (1986): 61–74; in French translation, in *Savoir et salut*, 275–88. See also C. Colpe, *Das Siegel der Propheten* (ANTZ 3; Berlin 1990), 227–43.

[87] See M. Tardieu, "La diffusion du bouddhisme dans l'empire kouchan, l'Iran et la Chine d'après un kephalaion manichéen inédit," *Studia Iranica* 17 (1988): 153–82. As Tardieu points out, this very important text represents the oldest literary document on the expansion of Buddhism in the Kushan empire. The Kushan empire was from the late first to the third centuries C.E. an important Buddhist power, where Greco-Roman, Indian, and Iranian cultures mixed to a remarkable extent, and known for its widespread cultural, artistic, and religious syncretism. Moreover, the *Kephalaion* emphasizes the formative importance of Buddhist influence in the early stages of Manichaeism.

new development, stemming from an already existing Christian scheme. This
scheme had been accepted, in particular, by those Christian thinkers who kept a
particular interest in traditions of the East.

On the so-called "Ka'ba of Zarathustra" at Naqsh-i-Rustam, in the south east
of the Iranian plateau, is found the famous Pahlevi inscription written on order
of Kirdir, chief-mobed under Vahram I (273–76). The inscription describes the
eradication of all religions from the Sasanian Empire:

> The doctrines of Ahriman and of the demons *(dev)* have been expelled from the Em-
> pire and have been proscribed. The Jews *(yahud)*, the Buddhists *(?saman)*, the
> Brahmans *(braman)*, the Nazoreans *(nacaray)*, the Christians *(kristian)*, the *maktak*
> (?), the Manichaeans *(zandik)* have been chased, the idols broken, the hiding places of
> the demons destroyed and transformed into temples for the gods. ...[88]

When the Zoroastrian clergy, headed by Kirdir, induced king Vahram to arrest
and execute Mani, the Christians were identified with the Manichaeans in the
ensuing persecution. The same identification occurred during the new outbreak
of persecution under Vahram II (276–93). There were some obvious and deep
differences between the two religions. Unlike the Manichaeans, the Christians
never tried to integrate various Zoroastrian concepts and deities into their theology. Manichaeism, indeed, appeared to Kirdir as a threat precisely because it
was so close to the Zoroastrian orthodoxy which sought to establish its monopoly. As we can read in Denkart, a *summa* of Sasanian theology: "The most dangerous enemy of religion is the heretic who betrays the stronghold from
within."[89] In a sense, the perception of Manichaeism as a Zoroastrian heresy in
the Sasanian empire parallels its perception as a Christian heresy in the later
Roman Empire. Yet, it would seem that the Christians were persecuted in Iran
together with the Manichaeans both because of the similarities between the two
religions, and because the Manichaeans themselves claimed to be Christians:

> Seeing that the Manichaeans called themselves Christians ... he believed, because of
> his evil intentions, that the two religions were identical. He thus ordered to kill the
> Manichaeans and to destroy their churches. Then the Magians persecuted the Chris-
> tians without any distinction.[90]

Except for the fifteen years or so of the persecution under Varham, the Christians were tolerated in Iran until 337, when Constantine, having established

---

[88] The inscription is translated and discussed in M.-L. Chaumont, *La christianisation de l'empire iranien, des origines aux grandes persécutions du Ive siècle* (CSCO, subsidia 80; Louvain
1988), 111–17. See further G. Fowden, *Empire to Commonwealth: Consequenses of Monotheism in Late Antiquity* (Princeton 1993), 28–29.

[89] This text is quoted by S. N. C. Lieu, *Manichaeism in the Later Roman Empire and in Medieval China* (Manchester 1986), 79, who also offers a description of Kirdir's role in the fall and
execution of Mani.

[90] Chronicle of Seert 1.1, Nestorian text quoted by Chaumont, *La christianisation de l'empire
iranien,* 105–106.

Christianity as the official religion of the Roman Empire, sought to enroll the Christian communities of Iran as supporters of his cause. He succeeded to a certain extent, and the Christians, who had become "sympathizers" of the Romans, were perceived by the Sasanians as a sort of fifth column.[91]

The Iranian perception of the Christian communities was the exact reflection of the perception of the Manichaeans as a Persian fifth column in the Roman Empire.[92] Both Diocletian and Maximian, for instance, speak of Manichaeism as of a systematic ideological threat emanating from Persia.[93] This radical rejection of the Manichaeans in the Roman Empire stemmed from a combination of causes, which included both the geographical provenance of the Religion of Light and the nature of its teachings. The evil sect came from enemy land, and its teachings, in particular perhaps the prohibition of reproduction, sounded not only strange and perverse, but also threatening the security of the state. Manichaeism remained outlawed when the Empire became Christian. The Christian rulers added theological arguments of their own against the dualist heretics, but they also retained, lock, stock and barrel, the Roman perception of the Manichaeans as Iranians, i.e., barbarians. For instance, Titus, bishop of Bostra in the fourth century, and author of an important theological refutation of Manichaeism, could speak of the madness (*atopia*) of the Manichaeans' *barbarikos dogma*. (*Adv. Man.* 1.7).[94] To sum up, the fate of Manichaeism in both the Iranian and the Roman empires reflects the case of a community appearing to be at once from within and from without, and whose believers are perceived as trespassers of intellectual as well as political borders, or as threatening barbarians without a respectable philosophy.

The case of the Christians of Iran was indeed rather special, due to their numbers, the particularly high political and military stakes, and also their close similarities with the Manichaeans. They were not, however, the only Christian communities outside the Roman Empire. The Christian historians of the fourth and fifth centuries, Eusebius, Rufinus, and Sozomenus, tell us about these communities, many of which had been in existence since the second century. Their establishment had been the direct result of the intensive missionary efforts in the early Church. In the mid-third century, Origen is witness to the Christian

---

[91] This was shown by T. D. Barnes, "Constantine and the Christians of Persia," *JRS* 75 (1985): 126–36.

[92] On the Roman perception of the Manichaeans as a Persian fifth column, see Lieu, *Manichaeism*, 91–95.

[93] For instance: "nova et inopinata prodigia in hunc mundum de Persia adversaria nobis gente progressa," *Mos. et Rom. legum Collatio*, 15.3, quoted by F. Millar, "Byzantium Persia and Islam: the Origins of Imperialist Monotheism," *Journal of Roman Archaeology* 7 (1994): 509–11. For a detailed analysis, see Lieu, *Manichaeism*, 91–95.

[94] On polemics and perceptions, see S. Stroumsa and G. G. Stroumsa, "Anti-Manichaean Polemics in Late Antiquity and under Early Islam," *HTR* 81(1988): 37–58 [= Stroumsa, *Savoir et salut*, 354–77].

goal of converting the whole world.[95] The missionary efforts of the early Church in the East are reflected, for instance, in the cycle of Thomas in general, and in the *Acts of Thomas* in particular. The Thomas tradition of the third and fourth centuries is directly related to the mission of the Parthian and Syrian Church to North India.[96]

Converting the whole world: on this goal, Christians and Manichaeans did not differ. Both understood themselves as belonging to missionary religions. As we have seen, even the overall structure of revelation by two series of prophets, both through history and through the different religions of the world, does not seem to have been quite specific of the Manichaeans. This structure, indeed, seems to be at least implicit in some early Christian writers.

As the fate of both religions in the Sasanian empire shows, however, there were also some basic differences between Manichaeism and Christianity, in both their understanding of their missionary nature and their attitudes to other religions. In radical opposition to Christian attitude, the Manichaeans decided to break loose from Judaism. Since the first dualist and Gnostic temptations in the early second century, most Christian intellectuals had consistently refused to cut the umbilical cord which attached the new religion to the tradition of Israel. The radical theological antisemitism of the Manichaeans is here highly significant. Manichaean mythological theology permitted to all peoples and cultures of the enlarged *oikoumene* (except of course the Jews, who remained on the side of Satan) to see themselves as part of the divine plan, the *praeparatio manichaeica*, as it were. Another abyss between Christians and Manichaeans lies in their different attitudes to traditions and cultures, in other words, to "barbarian philosophies." The Christians did not only insist on maintaining links of kinship with the Jews and their Law. Despite their wide diaspora outside the Roman Empire, they also retained some clear terms of reference to the Roman Empire.

It is often repeated that the Manichaeans established the first consciously universalist religion. One should perhaps say more precisely that they created the first consciously *multi-cultural* universalist religion. This subtle but fundamental difference between Christians and Manichaeans entailed a different attitude toward other religions and cultures, and different ways of defining their own identity vis-à-vis outsiders.

For the Manichaeans, much more than for the Christians, syncretism was the preferred, legitimate way of dealing with the meeting of cultures. This apparent openness and flexibility entailed the disappearance of any ethnological *curiositas*. Paradoxically, the concept of "barbarian philosophy" became meaningless for the Manichaeans, since they did not stand firmly in one cultural tradition that

---

[95] Origen, *Contra Celsum* 3.9. On the place of mission in early Christianity, see M. Goodman, *Mission and Conversion*, ch. 5.

[96] See A. Dihle, "Neues zur Thomas-Tradition," *JAC* 6 (1963): 54–70; reprinted in Dihle, *Antike und Orient*, 61–77.

they could consider their own. For them, all cultural and religious traditions had, at least theoretically, an equal share in the universal *Heilsgeschichte*. In a sense, one can say that the radical denigration of Judaism by the Manichaeans was the ultimate step permitting a complete universalization of the religious message of Christianity.

Conclusions: ambivalence and evolution of barbaros philosophia

Concluding his reflections on the knowledge of alien wisdoms in the Hellenistic world, Arnaldo Momigliano noted that it had all the instruments of knowing other civilizations – except the knowledge of foreign languages.[97] One important factor for understanding the parameters of early Christian attitudes to barbarian wisdom does not seem to be often pointed out. Christians had distanced themselves from the Greek cultural tradition, but also from the Jewish conception of the Sacred Tongue in which the Holy Scriptures had been revealed. The religion they established was, for the first time in history, it seems, devoid of any inhibitions about translating its Holy Scriptures, and Christian liturgy was developed in the vernaculars of believers from all origins. This Christians' linguistic openness partly explains their willingness to accept the claims to truth of barbarian cultures.

In conclusion, we can say that early Christian literature reflects an ambiguous approach to ethnological representations. On the one hand, both the ecumenism of the early Christian thinkers and their cultural relativism permitted a more open attitude to foreign cultural traditions than the one reflected in pagan contemporary literature. On the other hand, however, and despite this attitude, we cannot really speak of a true anthropological openness in early Christianity. Some of the causes for this lack lie in deep-seated theological structures, while others stem from the transformation of Christianity, in the fourth century, into the official religion of the Roman Empire. The very universal character of Christianity had also some surprising consequences. The Christian interest in the salvation of the soul and in the human person, for instance, entailed a lack of serious interest in mores, in whatever could appear as contingent in the forms of human existence. Ethnic terms were deeply irrelevant for the Christians.

With time, the Christians gave up on being called barbarians, and started to identify with the traditional Roman spite and fear from the threatening barbarians. In the fifth century, the barbarians had become either those who stubbornly remained pagan within the Christian empire, or those who fought this empire. This transformation of the concept of barbarian reflected the integration of Christianity into late classical culture. Christian culture was born, becom-

---

[97] A. Momigliano, *Alien Wisdom*, 149.

ing more or less identical to European civilization. For many centuries, it would show very little interest in foreign ways of life or systems of thought.

In 1495, the young Erasmus published a pamphlet written against the Christian fundamentalists of the day, in which he argued for the cultural importance of classical learning, i. e., of pagan literature. The very title of this pamphlet, *Antibarbari,* may allude to the dramatic changes that had occurred since late antiquity, and to those still to come. Batt, Erasmus's spokesman, argues in the defense of pagan learning that the achievements of the pagans are part of a divine plan. For Erasmus, the barbarians are those Christians who refuse to read anything but the Scriptures, who object to the integration between Christianity and pagan culture. Since late antiquity, the relationships between barbarism and civilization had indeed turned around in radical fashion.

It is only with the great discoveries at the dawn of the modern times that we can discern the birth of a true ethnological interest in the Christian West. Bartolomé de Las Casas took a real interest in the newly-discovered Indians of America, and Matteo Ricci was fascinated by the alien wisdom of Chinese civilization. Montaigne would epitomize the impact of this new meeting between cultures and the rise of *curiositas*. Rather than a syncretism *à la manichéenne,* which implies that all cultures reflect different aspects of the same and unique deep (and esoteric) truth, this *curiositas* assumes that foreign cultures are different but legitimate, or at least that they do not represent a danger for the observer. In other words, a certain measure of skepticism, or at least of relativism, is necessary for the development of ethnological curiosity. At the dawn of modern times, however, this curiosity was too directly connected with imperialism and colonialism to have a chance to be convincing.

Christianity and Europe: the cultural identification born in late antiquity seems to come to an end together with the second millenium (incidentally, this happens concomitantly with the weakening of the strong links between Judaism and European civilization). Both in the Catholic Church and in various branches of Protestant Christianity, there seems to be an intense awareness, and also a certain acceptance, of this fact. (Where in Europe could the Pope draw a crowd of four millions, as he did in Manila during his Asian trip in the fall of 1994?). Today, Christianity seems indeed to be seeking new ways of integrating the different cultures to its traditional message, looking for a new identity as *barbaros philosophia.*

Part II

Living with the Other

Chapter 5

Internalization and Intolerance in Early Christianity

1.

Early Christian teachings have often been perceived as nothing less than revolutionary. Hegel, for instance, referred to the Sermon on the Mount as revolutionary in character.[1] Paul's teaching, too, has been similarly qualified. One of the main aspects of this revolutionary character of earliest Christianity is, beyond the religious intensity and new structures featured by the Christian movement, the phenomenon called internalization, which was no doubt of crucial importance during the first steps of the movement. This phenomenon is usually perceived in most positive terms, and is thought to have represented real "progress," whatever this may mean, in the history of religious attitudes.

The following pages may be considered a case study, an analysis of some relationships between psychological changes, religious transformations, and social attitudes at a major crossroads in the history of Western consciousness. I shall first seek to point out some major aspects of early Christian internalization processes. I shall then try to show that the patterns of transformation that characterize early Christianity are so complex that insistence on internalization alone may be misleading. In fact, trends that lead in another, opposite direction can also be discerned in early Christianity. To these I shall refer here, for brevity's sake, as cosmicization processes. The last part of this chapter will call attention to possible connections between the paradigmatic change revealed by early Christian internalization processes and the growth of religious intolerance in late antiquity.

Processes of internalization appeared in Greek and Hellenistic culture from the classical period, and with more intensity during the Hellenistic times.[2] The disappearance or weakening of the archaic and traditional frames of collective life, in particular of civic consciousness connected with the *polis,* encouraged new attitudes both in religion and in philosophy. A man who could not feel that

---

[1] See for instance Hegel, *Vorlesungen über der Philosophie der Geschichte,* III.3.2 (Das Christentum), in *Sämtliche Werke,* vol. 11 (Stuttgart 1928), 409–30, where Hegel insists on the new sense of *Innerlichkeit* disclosed by Jesus' teachings, and inexistent in Judaism. For Hegel, Jesus' ethics as expressed in the Sermon on the Mount destroy the world order.

[2] See esp. P. Hadot, "Exercices spirituels antiques et 'philosophie chrétienne,'" in his *Exercices spirituels et philosophie antique* (Paris 1981), 59–74. Hadot speaks there of "*Innenwendung*" [*sic*] processes active in Greek philosophy from the third century B.C.

his identity was immediately and almost solely defined by his belonging to his city-state could turn to the broader framework, the whole *oikoumenè*. The Stoic sages, for instance, identified themselves as "citizens of the world," of the *cosmopolis*. But the world is a big place, where the individual might easily find himself lost. The dimensions of the cosmos encourage the individual to find in himself the principle of his self-definition. This is the origin of the idea of autarchy, as developed, again, by the Stoics.[3]

Similar transformations may be observed in religious ideas and in patterns of behavior in the Hellenistic world. Disengagement from civic religion, or more precisely, from the official cult or cults, brought with it the development of personal religion, i.e., inward rather than outward religion, the expression of feelings, and the reflection on the truth of traditional cult and myths – or on the lack thereof. All these trends, which had begun already in the fifth and fourth centuries, became much more dominant among intellectuals from the third century B.C. onwards.[4] (Of course, we have no easy way of appreciating changes in popular religious consciousness). This evolution is well known, and has often been perceived (for instance by Father A. J. Festugière) as preparing the way, so to speak, for the appearance of Christianity.[5] E. R. Dodds, on his side, preferred to describe the phenomenon in psychological terms, and to speak of a pervasive "fear of freedom" as symptomatic of the Hellenistic age.[6]

It would however be mistaken to see these new trends in religiosity as the only *praeparatio evangelica,* as it were. No less important in the search for the roots of the internalized Christian consciousness are the deep changes in Jewish religiosity during the same period, namely the second Commonwealth. The religion of biblical Israel had undergone some radical changes, not so much in its structures – that would happen later, with the destruction of the Temple and the emergence of Rabbinic Judaism – but rather in the more delicate terms of religious sensitivity. David Flusser, among others, has called attention to this new sensitivity that emerged in Palestine toward the end of the second Commonwealth.[7] This new sensitivity, based not so much on apocalyptic trends as on sapiential literature and its offshoots, reflects the pervasive influence of the Hellenistic world on Judaism.

Seen together, both trends – in the Hellenistic world and in Judaism – provide

---

[3] On the Stoic movement as a whole, the best book is still M. Pohlenz, *Die Stoa*, 2 vols (Göttingen 1948). [new ed.]

[4] See in general M. Nilsson, *Geschichte der griechischen Religion*, 3rd. ed., vol. 2 (München, 1974), 185–309.

[5] A. J. Festugière, *Personal Religion among the Greeks* (Sather Classical Lectures; Berkeley 1954).

[6] E. R. Dodds, *The Greeks and the Irrational* (Sather Classical Lectures 25; Berkeley 1951), 236–69.

[7] D. Flusser, "A New Sensitivity in Second Temple Judaism and the Christian Message," *HTR* 61 (1968): 111–18.

the background to the radical transformation of religious structures and sensitivities in early Christianity. The early Christian attitude toward the pagan cults is
one of categorical rejection; it denies them any religious authenticity, and hence
any legitimacy.[8] In this, it reflects quite accurately the Jewish attitude. One can
state with little exaggeration, to use Ramsey MacMullen's terms, that sincerity is
almost nowhere else an issue in religious life in the ancient world.[9] The new insistence was on faith, i.e., on subjectivity, on feeling, as an essential element of
religious identity. Now, it may be observed that faith appears when at least two
conditions are fulfilled. First, when there is a conflict between two alternative
ways of understanding reality and interpreting the cosmos, or *Weltanschauun-
gen* (sociologists speak today of "cosmologies"). Second, a choice between
these alternatives has to be made by the individual.

The emergence of a new conception of the individual in early Christianity is a
very complex phenomenon, which cannot be dealt with here.[10] For our present
purpose, suffice it to mention the fact that the Christian person is to a large
measure set in opposition to Greek conceptions, particularly the Platonic dualism between body and soul. For the Christians, as for the Jews, the creation of
man by God, and the idea of resurrection – an idea quite alien to the Greek mind
– did not permit, at least from a theological point of view, a radical denigration of
the body. To this, the Christians added the incarnation, death, and resurrection
of Jesus Christ, which was set as an example and a promise to humankind. *Caro
salutis cardo,* as Tertullian said: the body is central to the Christian concept of redemption.

Another correlate Christian heritage from Jewish conceptions is the centrality of ethics in religious life. Religion is not centered only around the cultic
practices but around the practice of justice in daily life. This conception, directly
derived from biblical prophecy, is founded upon the idea of repentance (Hebrew *teshuva;* Greek *metanoia*) and the fear of sin. Early Christian texts attest to
the same sensitivities as those characteristic of second Commonwealth and
Rabbinic Judaism. They show relatively little interest in the soteriological tendencies of Hellenic intellectuals.[11] But it is not so much in opposition to Hellenic
attitudes that one usually speaks of the internalization phenomenon typical of
early Christianity. Christianity is usually seen as rejecting forms of belief and re-

---

[8] See for instance the good survey of R. P. C. Hanson, "The Christian Attitude to Pagan Religions up to the Time of Constantine the Great," *ANRW*, 23.1, 910–73.

[9] R. MacMullen, *Christianizing the Roman Empire* (New Haven and London 1984), 116.

[10] See chapter 10 of this volume.

[11] This point is emphasized by D. Flusser, "Das Schisma zwischen Judentum und Christentum," *Evangelische Theologie* 40 (1980): 214–39. The same conclusion is reached by J. Behm in
his article "*Metanoia*" in *TDNT,* 4: 975–1008), where he expresses sorrow on the "fatal relapse
into Judaism" witnessed in the Apostolic writings. Behm's attitude reflects Christian (mainly
Protestant) theological postulation of a "kerygma": of the earliest strata of Christianity essentially uncontaminated by Jewish attitudes).

ligious behavior typical of contemporary Judaism. This attitude is perceived of as typical of both Jesus and Paul.

As regards Jesus, let us refer here only to his teaching on the pure and the impure, as expressed in Mk 7: 14–23 (cf. Mt. 15: 10–20):

> There is nothing from without a man *(ouden estin exôthen tou anthrôpou),* that entering into him can defile him: but the things which come out of him *(alla ta ek tou anthrô-pou),* those are they that defile the man ... . Do ye not perceive, that whatsoever thing from without entereth into the man, it cannot defile him; because it entereth not into his heart, but into the belly.... For from within, out of the heart of men *(esôthen gar ek tès kardias tôn anthrôpôn),* proceed evil thoughts, adulteries, fornications, murders. ...

The context of this passage is clearly anti-Pharisaic polemics. It nevertheless reflects the very Jewish demand of ethical integrity, of the purity of intention which should sustain all cultic behavior, rather than a polemic against Jewish food taboos – as the ending of verse 19 ("and he declared all food pure"), which is probably a gloss, would suggest.

Paul's conception of the interior man *(ho esô anthrôpos)* is of course much more specific and reflects Greek, to be precise Platonic expressions.[12] It would seem, however, that Paul's use of the term corresponds to the Biblical *lev,* "heart."[13]

A famous passage, Rom 7: 14–25, reads:

> For we know that the law is spiritual *(ho nomos pneumatikos estin)*: but I am carnal, sold under sin. For that which I do I allow not: for what I would, that do I not; but what I hate, that do I... For the good that I would I do not: but the evil which I would not, that I do.... For I delight in the law of God after the inward man *(kata ton esô anthrôpou)*: But I see another law in my members, warring against the law of my mind, and bringing me into captivity to the law of sin which is in my members.

In these terse sentences Paul expresses the excruciating psychological paradox of a divided will. This paradox stands at the basis of Paul's rejection of the Torah, and it will be stated anew, in no less pregnant terms, by Augustine in his *Confessions.*[14] The same tradition is also reflected in Goethe's Faust: "Zwei Seelen wohnen, ach, in meiner Brust." In Paul's conception, the interior man is clearly set in opposition to "the exterior man" *(ho exô anthrôpos),* although the expression itself does not appear in Paul's Letters.[15] Paul's anthropological dual- *[2 Cor 4:⚹ 16*

---

[12] See for instance Plato, *Resp.* 9. 589a: *ho entos anthrôpos.* Cf. Plotinus, *Enn.* 5.1.10: *hoion legei Platôn ton eisô anthrôpon).*

[13] See Behm, *"esô,"* *TDNT,* 2: 698–99. Cf. R. Bultmann, *Theologie des Neues Testaments,* 9th ed. (Tübingen 1984), 204ff, who emphasizes the Hellenic origin of the conception. See already A. Bonhöffer, *Epiktet und das neue Testament* (Giessen 1911), 115–17.

[14] On the closeness of Augustine to Paul, see P. Fredricksen, "Paul and Augustine: Conversion, Narratives, Orthodox Traditions and the Retrospective Self," *JTS,* n. s., 37 (1986): 3–34.

[15] *hoi exô* in I Cor. 5:12 refers to "those who are outside," a common phrase in Greek; cf. also Mk 4:11, where they are set in opposition to Jesus' disciples; the problem of esoteric versus exo-

ism is also defined as the opposition of the real versus the false self, the spirit versus the flesh. To the interior or spiritual man corresponds the spiritual Law, while the body remains in bondage under the law of matter, or of sin.

Hence, the only way for man to reach redemption is to free himself from this bondage. Liberation: the dynamic character of the term reflects the dramatic newness of Paul's conception of the inner man. In the Platonic tradition, the inner man is a given. The philosopher's task consists in turning inwards and discovering his true self. According to Paul, on the other hand, the search for one's inner man is perceived as a fight, and the accent is put on the process itself. Moreover, the omnipresence of sin means that only through Christ is the liberation process rendered possible:

> Stand fast therefore in the liberty wherewith Christ hath made us free *(tèi eleuteriai hèmas Christos èleutherôsen),* and be not entangled again with the yoke of bondage. (Gal 5:1).

Much more than its traditional Greek homonym, the Pauline concept of freedom *(eleutheria)* describes a process of internalization. In a seminal paper, the late Shlomo Pines analyzed the Pauline stance and its context.[16] Let me summarize here his argument, which bears directly on our theme.

Pines analyzes some of the uses of the Hebrew word *herut,* freedom, in the first century B.C. and the first century C.E. He notes that there is no biblical equivalent to the Greek term *eleutheria* (or to the Latin *libertas*), and that during the Hellenistic period, the word *herut* came to be used to convey the meaning of the Greek term. Pines adds, however, that in the process the meaning of the word had undergone a deep change, which made the new meaning of *herut* "one of the most consequential events in Jewish history." The Greek term referred primarily to a state of affairs, namely the political experience of freedom in the *polis.* The Hebrew word, in contradistinction, was used in a society under foreign domination and referred to a process: that of the people of Israel freeing itself from foreign yoke. According to Pines, the Jews were thus the first people to speak of "national liberation."

The next step in the transformation of the term, adds Pines, was achieved by Paul, who effected a radical internalization of the word. For him, *eleutheria* no longer meant liberation from foreign yoke, but from the yoke of the Torah. He says:

> Because the creature itself also shall be delivered *(eleutherôthèsetai)* from the bondage of corruption into the glorious liberty of the children of God (Rom 8:21).

---

teric teaching in early Christianity is a different, albeit related, question, and will not be dealt with here.

[16] Sh. Pines, "On Transformations of the Term 'Freedom'" (in Hebrew), in *Between Reflection and Action, Festschrift for Nathan Rotenstreich,* eds. Y. Yovel and P. Mendes-Flohr (Jerusalem 1984), 247–65.

Thus the opposition to foreign government became primarily an opposition to religious authority, a transformation with obvious and ominous consequences for Western history.

The process described by Pines is that of the early Christian internalization of the Torah, and more generally, of the Jewish tradition. To the interior man corresponds the internalized Law. As we have seen, this internalized Law is also identical to the spiritual Law. The internalization process is ipso facto a spiritualization process. These transformations reflect a new kind of religiousness, not found elsewhere in Palestinian Jewish literature. The path is open which leads straight from Paul to Augustine's discovery of the intricacies of the human psyche and to the mature Christian utilization of Platonic thought for the development of a Christian spirituality and mysticism. For Augustine, the way to God becomes identical to the way to oneself. God will be reached in self-knowledge, in the discovery of oneself. The way upward will become a way inward, a process underlined by the equivalence of the metaphors in patristic spiritual and mystical literature, and strongly influenced by Platonic thought.

Plotinus had expressed, in Plato's name, the idea that God is inside man: "God is not exterior to any being, said he [Plato]. He is in all beings but they don't know it. They flee far from Him, or rather from themselves." (*Enn.* 6.9.7). The Plotinian formulas are found almost unchanged in Augustine's writings. "You were within me, and I was outside myself, and I was looking for You outside....You were with me, and I was not with you." (*Conf.* 10.27). Or again: "They incline to get out of themselves, abandoning their intimate being, while God is more interior to them than themselves." (*De Trin.* 8.7.11). The most pregnant Augustinian formula reflecting the need of internalization in order to reach God is perhaps that of the *De Vera Religione,* 39.72: "Do not go abroad. Return to yourself. In the interior man dwells truth *(Noli foras ire, in teipsum redi; in interiore homine habitat veritas)*."

Despite the similarities of the vocabulary, there are some basic differences between the position of Plotinus and that of Augustine. These differences are found not only in the conception of the person and the ontological background, but also in the quality of the impulse which brings one into oneself. The cause of the distance from oneself is obviously very different in Platonism and in Christianity. For the Christians, the distance from oneself is more a "loss of touch," to use a rather anachronistic expression, than an ontological statement about the embodied soul. The dynamic character of the Christian's simultaneous search for oneself and for God is alien to the much more static Platonic tradition. The Platonic conception of the Divine does not permit the same kind of constant progress towards God, kindled not by the knowledge of the *sungeneia* of the soul to God, but by love for the transcendent God. It is precisely this voluntaristic movement, so well analyzed by Endre von Ivanka, which gives its character to the Christian pattern of internalization and which distinguishes it from Platonic spirituality.[17] Although the above quotations are taken from Augustine, the most eloquent spokesman for the new turning into oneself, the same attitude is found among other Patristic writers.

Gregory of Nyssa, for instance, states: "To take away what is foreign is to come back to the true and authentic nature of the soul," and thus to be again what Adam was before his sin (PG 46, 372c). This attitude became the very foundation of Christian mysticism, and the mystical vision is rendered possible only at the end of the long process of internalization, which is identical to the ascetic purification of oneself. So Evagrius Ponticus, foremost representative at once of the Platonic influence in Patristic literature and of desert spirituality, writes: "The intellect will not be able to go and accomplish this beautiful emigration and arrive to the region of the incorporeal, if it has not corrected the inside. For domestic troubles usually bring it back to what it had left." (*Praktikos,* 61). In the mystical writings, internalization reaches its peak. The mystical attitude, all inwardness, is often considered to be uninterested in, and tolerant of externalized religion; behavioral patterns are considered to be, in the best case, of little relevance for the goal of the mystic. More often than not, such a perception is dispelled by historical evidence.

Gnosticism in this respect presents a rather special case, on which I would like to add a few comments. In a famous dictum, A. D. Nock has called Gnosticism a "Platonism run wild."[18] John Dillon has referred to some of the dualistic trends of late antiquity as "the Platonic Underworld."[19] To be sure, Gnostic origins, which remain in the mist, lie far apart from Platonic thought, even from a Platonism for the poor. Yet various Gnostic thinkers in the second century developed ways of thought, or at least a vocabulary, strongly influenced by Middle Platonism. The dualism inherent in Gnosticism, which is both theological and anthropological, became expressed in terms that oppose matter to the realm of the spirit. It perceived salvation as a radical departure from the material world and the body. Encratism, the strongly negative attitude to the body that such a conception entailed, is quite different in its roots and consequences from the asceticism common in religious movements and among philosophical schools in late antiquity.

What appeared as a radical rejection of the cosmos by the Gnostics (see for instance Plotinus' strong words in *Enneads* 2.9) may obviously be described, in some ways, as a movement of internalization within the still-loose boundaries of early Christianity. Christ Himself is spiritualized by the Gnostics (the term is used here in a generic sense). Docetic trends developed precisely among those for whom the bodily existence of Christ either had no meaning or was a source

---

[17] E. von Ivanka, *Plato Christianus* (Einsiedeln 1964); chapter 5 is devoted to Augustine.

[18] For a summary of Nock's views on Gnosticism, see his "Gnosticism" in A. D. Nock, *Essays on Religion and the Ancient World*, ed. Z. Stewart (Oxford 1972), 2: 940–59.

[19] J. Dillon, *The Middle Platonists* (Ithaca, N.Y. 1977), 384–96.

of religious or intellectual embarrassment. Those milieus where the idea of the Messiah or of incarnation made no sense also could not be interested in Christ's Resurrection. *Christos,* the anointed one, meaningless for them, became *Chrèstos,* the excellent, a spiritual entity having nothing to do with Jesus of Nazareth.[20]

There is also another aspect of Gnostic teachings which is directly related to internalization, this time not only in an anthropological sense, but also at the social level. I am referring to the esoteric character of Gnostic teachings, a character noted by all students of Gnosticism but more rarely analyzed in depth. Gnostic myths are not to be revealed to outsiders, but only to those who belong to the inner circle, the spiritual ones, freed from the bonds of the material body, or *pneumatikoi,* as they are called in the Valentinian tradition. Ptolemeus' *Letter to Flora* shows that the presentation of the doctrine is made on two levels, for two different kinds of public. The various Gnostic traditions preserved by the Christian heresiologists repeat in various ways warnings and prohibitions concerning the revelation of secret teachings to outsiders. To be sure, similar esoteric trends were common in late antique religion, including Judaism and early Christianity. Indeed, it is in this context that Gnostic esotericism, which claimed to go back to the Apostolic tradition, should be understood. But the latter went much further, and in a much more radical way, than either of its predecessors. The extinction, during the first Christian centuries, of Christian esotericism, can be shown to be directly related to the importance of esoteric teaching among the Gnostic sects. It is to a great extent in order to distance themselves from such claims that the Church Fathers gave up the deeper, esoteric level of Christian teaching. In a sense, it can be argued that Gnosticism represents a radicalization of trends which were present in the earliest strata of Christianity.

To Gnostic esotericism one must relate the willingness of some Gnostics (and of the Manicheans after them) to hide their true religious beliefs in order to avoid persecution. The Patristic writers report that the Gnostics were willing to sacrifice to the idols, for instance, in order to escape martyrdom. The phenomenon, which later became common among Shî'î Muslims, and is more widely known under its Arabic name, *taqiyya,* is directly linked to the consciousness of internalization. It is precisely the feeling that the only meaningful religious attitude is the interior conviction of possessing truth in a world of falseness, under the rule of the power of darkness, which permits the development of *taqiyya.*[21]

This attitude should be seen as corollary to the well-known antinomian behavior of some Gnostic sects. If truth is exclusively an interior matter, a state of

---

[20] See, for instance, the Gnostic *Treatise on Resurrection* (also called the *Epistle to Rheginus*) found in Coptic at Nag Hammadi (CG I. 4).

[21] E. Kohlberg, "Taqqiya in Shî'î Theology and Religion," in *Secrecy and Concealment: Studies in the History of Mediterranean and Near Eastern Religions,* eds. H. G. Kippenberg and G. G. Stroumsa (SHR 65; Leiden 1995), 345–80.

mind, as it were, then there is no need for commandments and for religious practice. The Pauline rejection of the Torah can be perceived to be in the background
of the much more radical antinomianism of the early Christian dualist heretics.
The difference between the two is roughly similar to the difference between
Christian asceticism and an encratism established upon dualist premises, and a
hatred for both the body and the whole cosmos.[22]

2.

It would be mistaken, however, to think of the transformations of religious consciousness accomplished by early Christianity as being only, or mainly, reflected
in the internalization processes. The very figure of Christ, the eschatology in
which it appears and which provides the setting for much of early Christianity,
the idea of the original sin, the new conception of the person, the urge, finally, to
preach the new religion to the whole *oikoumenè,* all these – and the list is representative, not inclusive – point to a process quite opposite to internalization,
namely a *cosmicization* of religious attitudes and conceptions in the world of
early Christianity.

It may be stating the obvious, but one should first refer to the early Christian
figure of Jesus Christ. It is first of all a transformation of the Jewish messiah
figure. As such, and as a new interpretation of the Son of Man figure of Apocalyptic literature, it is a very concrete figure, possessing at least some of the characters of the divine, and often described as an angelic character, sometimes of gi-
gantic, or even cosmic dimensions. The very deutero-Pauline concept of *kenôsis*
(Phil. 2:7) entails a mode of thinking about Christ that is at once spatial and cosmic: before the *kenôsis* Christ was indeed a cosmic figure.[23] These patterns of
thought are well represented in various trends of early Christian literature. The
expectation of Jesus' second coming at the end of time, the *parousia,* adds to the
very concrete perception of Christ. In various ways, therefore, the Christ figure
of early Christianity defies internalization. This phenomenon should be seen in
the background of contemporaneous religious perceptions in nascent Rabbinic
Judaism. After the destruction of the Temple, the lamentable failure of the great
revolt, and the Christian challenge, Jewish messianism seems to have been
tuned down, so to speak. In some ways, one can speak of a *neutralization* of activist Jewish messianism.[24] The belief in the coming of the messiah became inter-

---

[22] See G. G. Stroumsa, *Savoir et salut,* ch. 8, 147–62.

[23] I have argued this point in "Form(s) of God: Some Notes on Metatron and Christ," *HTR*
76 (1983): 269–88, esp. 282–83 (= Stroumsa, *Savoir et salut,* ch. 3, 65–84).

[24] G. Scholem has argued that such a "neutralization" of messianism is to be found in .Ea-
stern European Hassidism; see his "The Neutralization of the Messianic Element in Early Hassidism," in G. Scholem, *The Messianic Idea in Judaism* (New York 1971), 176–202.

nalized, while the figure itself became less concrete. In this respect, and in opposition to traditional conceptions, it would seem that the Christian attitude is rather less internalized than the Jewish one.

The figure of Christ itself should be seen within the frame of eschatology. Direct heir to Jewish eschatology of the times, as reflected mainly in apocalyptic literature, eschatology belongs to the earliest strata of Christian literature. This is witnessed not only by the Revelation of John, but also by the synoptic apocalypse. It is only progressively and at a rather late date, after the hope for the Second Coming had become blurred by the fact that history seemed to go on despite the Incarnation, that Christian thinkers succeeded in ridding themselves of a rather dysfunctional eschatology. To cite but one example, the first major Christian theologian after Paul, Irenaeus, ends his magnum opus, the *Adversus Haereses,* with a few millenarian chapters describing the war between Christ and the Antichrist in the last days, the conquest of Jerusalem by the Antichrist, and its final *reconquista* by Christ, ending with the rebuilding of the Temple. It is symptomatic of the later changes of attitudes that these chapters disappeared from most manuscripts, and were rediscovered in a single codex in the seventeenth century. Here too, it is hard to see the sole contribution of Christianity in promoting the internalization processes in religious patterns of thought.

In this context, the early Christian conception of sin is of capital importance. There are actually two kinds of sin reflected in the early Christian sources. First, of course, the concept of individual sin, essentially inherited from Judaism, which is of either a cultural or moral nature. Sin, in this sense, should be avoided, and the believer should fear it in his consciousness (*yr'at ḥet* in Hebrew). The New Testament concept of conversion, or *metanoia,* which is already the one preached by John the Baptist in the desert, is repentance *(teshuva)* for one's sins, accomplished first and foremost in the inner conscience of the believer. Later, Christian penance will be the direct heir of this Jewish repentance.

Together with this first meaning of sin, however, there developed in early Christianity another sense of sin, which soon became the hallmark of the Christian conception.[25] This is the idea of original sin, which became dominant in later, medieval Christianity mainly thanks to Augustine (if one should thank him for that), but which appears already with Paul, as is well known, particularly from Rom. 5:12:

> Wherefore as by one man sin entered into the world *(hè hamartia eis ton kosmon eisèlthen),* and death by sin; and so death passed upon all men, for that all have sinned.

Sin is described as entering not in the individual, but in the world. Sin is present in everyone because it is present in the whole cosmos, at any time since the beginnings of mankind. Paul's conception of the cosmic dimensions of sin necess-

---

[25] See in particular P. F. Beatrice, *Tradux Peccati: Alte fonti della dottrina agostiniana del peccato originale* (Milan 1978).

arily meant a lessening of the onus of possible sin on the individual. If I am a sinner from birth, the weight of my actions (or thoughts) on my possible salvation or damnation is limited. Indeed, only Christ's death can save us from the consequences of sin conceived as cosmic in its dimensions. Atonement, rather than penance, is the proper remedy for sin so conceived. The emphasis is no longer on the searching of the individual conscience. In other words, the Pauline conception of sin limits, to a certain extent, the process of internalization – that is, of the development of conscience – which had grown in Judaism during the Second Commonwealth. In a way, one may hence speak of a certain "de-ethicization" of sin in early Christianity, of a process quite opposed to internalization.

Early Christian thinkers transformed in some very significant ways the conception of the person that they had inherited from the Greek philosophers, that is, mainly, from Platonist thought. For weighty theological reasons, they integrated the human body into the definition of the person: creation ex nihilo by a transcendent God, resurrection, the incarnation, these were some of the essential differences between Christian and Greek thought which imposed the development of a new anthropology by the Church Fathers. This integration of the body ran counter to the definition of the real essence of man as his soul or his spirit, in other words as the interior man, which was the widest accepted conception in later Greek thought. Thus, in this sense, early Christianity also brought the development of some trends very different from internalization.

As it developed into a religion in its own right, Christianity soon saw as its main task the conversion of the nations of the world to the new faith. To be sure, such an active ecumenism does not in itself carry conceptions either of internalization or of externalization. But it points to the urgent need, on the part of a new religion, to concentrate its efforts on the definition of new social boundaries, and the invention and development of structures of authority. This expansionism does not square with the reflective, minor mood needed for internalization processes. It does not in itself prevent such processes, but it renders them more complex, or ambivalent in nature.

On all the points mentioned above: the figure of the messiah, eschatology, sin, the conception of the person, of the boundaries of the community, it seems that the position of the Rabbis, explicit or implicit, is strikingly different to that of the Church Fathers. These differences bear upon internalization processes. A comparative analysis between the two religions, developing simultaneously according to new patterns, would be in order, and might lead to interesting results.

Here too, Gnosticism deserves special mention. The radical spiritualization occurring in Gnosticism has been mentioned above. But spiritualization is not internalization. Besides its dualist proclivities, Gnosticism is characterized by its attempt, on a grand scale, to develop mythical ways of thought. Hans Jonas has dealt with this topic. His conclusions, which seem to have remained widely unnoticed, are important for our purposes. In "Myth and Mysticism: A Study of Objectification and Internalization in Religious Thought,"[26] Jonas states that "the objective representation of reality found in myth precedes in time the subjective realization of different stages of being," which is a prerequisite for the development of mystical thought. For Jonas, myth and mysticism are rooted in a common existential experience. Mystical ascent corresponds in mental immanence to the representational transcendence of myth. Focusing on Origen's *apokatastasis,* he claims the Gnostic reinterpretation of myth to have been a decisive step on the way from mystery to mysticism in late antiquity.

For Jonas, Gnosticism cannot represent internalization processes because the mythic structure of Gnostic thought does not permit the growth of a real concept of the person, and is not interested in subjectivity. Hence, we could say that Gnosticism does not permit the development of conscience. Conscience implies ethical judgment. We know already from Plotinus' moving protest against the Gnostics in the name of intellectual sanity that this very point, the lack of Gnostic ethics, was considered to be a shocking trait of Gnostic mythmaking in late antiquity. The Gnostics accomplished a neutralization of the body, one may even speak of pneumatization, but their lack of interest in the human person as a moral agent prevented them from internalizing religious life.

3.

From Paul to Constantine and Augustine, as we have seen, two radical changes occurred in the perception of identity.

The new parameters of personal identity emphasized the integration of soul and body into the definition of the human person as a composite. It has been noted above, however, that in the emerging conception, the person was not quite a harmonious one. Instead of the divide between soul and body typical of Platonism, the idea of original sin brought with it a new break, this time within the soul itself. This break was due to a sense of guilt, inescapable because sin was inherited and ever-present.

This state of affairs strengthened the need for a salvation far beyond that of the individual and his behavior. Repentance for one's sins, indeed, expressed this need of salvation only in part. Christian salvation entailed ridding oneself of a sin that went far beyond the individual. Such an attitude was bound to enhance a tension within the soul unknown among Greek philosophers. In this framework, faith became not only the condition sine qua non of salvation, but also al-

---

[26] Hans Jonas, "Myth and Mysticism: A Study of Objectification and Internalization in Religious Thought," *JR* 49 (1969): 315–29. We shall not deal here with all aspects of Jonas' argument, which at times suffers from a certain lack of clarity.

most equivalent to it. Faith in Jesus Christ and His redemptive sacrifice, in itself, saved.

Social identity, on its side, was also submitted to a radical reinterpretation in early Christianity. For the first time in the ancient world, identity became defined in religious terms, not in ethnic or cultural-linguistic ones (as was the case in the Hellenistic and Roman worlds). This new approach of social identity is perhaps best reflected in the new corpus of laws established from Constantine to Theodosius II, in the first decades of the fifth century, and collected in the *Codex Theodosianus*.

These laws show the importance of defining the Church and the centers of authority within it. This implied a constant effort at defining the boundaries of the Christian community. Since the traditional Jewish criteria, such as ethnicity, language, and *halakha,* were no longer available, only dogma could provide the definition of the new social identity. Dogma referred to the proper way to understand Jesus Christ, His nature and His mission. Hence, for the first time, collective identity was defined in terms directly rooted in internalization, in belief. True belief, or orthodoxy, was itself defined by its negation, and reflected the many faces of error: heterodoxy, or heresy, from within, and Judaism and paganism from without.[27]

The social definition of Church boundaries, however, not only reflected opposition to error, but also the desire, inherent to Christianity from its very beginnings, to broaden its appeal; in other words, the church boundaries reflect Christianity's very catholicity, its strong and successful urge to convert. Conversion is the other side of the essentially dogmatic definition of the new religion: it implies a choice between truth and error.

The consequences of this state of affairs for our present purpose are as follows: both individual and collective identity were redefined in early Christianity in direct relation to the internalization process. As pointed out above, both also reflect the limitations of this process. The fight between faith and sin within the individual and the fight between truth and error at the collective level seem to follow parallel patterns. Since truth comes from Jesus Christ, error comes from the Antichrist, or from Satan. A choice of belief stands at the basis of the formation of both individual and collective identity, and establishes an element of intolerance in the very definition of Christian identity. To be sure, intolerance has many faces, not all of them religious, and religious intolerance itself did not start with Christianity. But what seems to happen very clearly in early Christianity, and will remain an ominous legacy in the Western world, is the following: the two sides of intolerance related to identity formation seem to strengthen each other. A strong sense of the unavoidable presence of sin does not prevent self-

---

[27] On Christian self-definition see E. P. Sanders, ed., *Jewish and Christian Self-Definition,* vol. 1: *The Shaping of Christianity in the Second and Third Centuries* (London 1980).

righteousness (paradoxically, the contrary seems sometimes to be true), while an internalized strong sense of certainty leads directly to religious persecution. These processes, which deserve serious study, are very complex, and can be studied only in the *longue durée*. I have been able here only to allude to them.

In conclusion, I should like to come back to the revolutionary character of early Christian beliefs, with which I began. If the direction followed here is basically correct, it is less these beliefs in themselves than the overall structure and status of internalization in the new religion which is responsible for the growing religious intolerance that is one of the hallmarks of late antiquity. Like other revolutions, the Christian revolution succeeded to a remarkable extent in suppressing freedom in the name of liberation.

Chapter 6

Tertullian on Idolatry and the Limits of Tolerance

1.

"Let one man worship God, another Jove" *(Colat alius Deum, alius Iovem).*[1] With this lapidary plea Tertullian establishes himself as one of the earliest advocates of religious tolerance in the Christian tradition. In the Roman Empire of the late second century, the Christians were in great need of some religious toleration.[2] Those Christian writers whom we call the Apologists aimed precisely at convincing Roman intellectuals in the corridors of power that toleration of the Christians and of their religious beliefs would in no way harm the state, and that such a toleration was, moreover, congruent with principles of reason shared, at least in theory, by all men.[3]

One of the major historical paradoxes reflected by the development of early Christianity is its transformation, during the course of the fourth century, from a *religio illicita* seeking recognition and tolerance into an established religion refusing to grant others (and its own dissenters from within, the "heretics") what it had sought for itself until the recent past.[4] The traditional answer to our paradox, is that as long as the Christians were in need of religious toleration for themselves, they knew how to make a case for its necessity. As soon as they came to power, however, they forgot their early virtues and learned how to deprive others of what they had just acquired. Christian intolerance, in such a view of things, would be seen to be rooted in human nature, rather than in some implicit aspects of Christian theology.[5]

---

[1] *Apologeticus* 24.5 (132–33 LCL). On our problem, one can still refer with profit to T. R. Glover, *The Conflict of Religions in the Roman Empire* (London 1909 and multiple later editions). For a recent bibliography, see for instance the entry on Tertullian in *EEC* 2:818–820.

[2] On religious repression in the Roman Empire, see for instance A. Momigliano in M. Eliade, ed., *ER* 12: 469–70, with bibliography. The classic work is of course W. H. C. Frend, *Martyrdom and Persecution in the Early Church* (Oxford 1965).

[3] Such principles the Stoics called *koinai ennoiai*. On the intellectual context of the Apologist movement, see for instance R. M. Grant, *Gods and the One God* (Philadelphia 1986).

[4] For a recent overview of the relationships of Christianity with the Roman authorities, see M. Sordi, *The Christians and the Roman Empire* (London 1988; Italian ed. 1983).

[5] See for instance R. MacMullen, *Christianizing the Roman Empire, A.D. 100–400* (New Haven and London 1984), ch. 10: "Conversion by Coercion."

This explanation no doubt suffers from an oversimplification of complex phenomena. Moreover, it seems to me to be a mistake to focus only on the fourth century if we want to understand how this transformation was made possible. Indeed, an ambivalent attitude to religious toleration had been inherent to Christianity from its very beginnings. I have sought to analyze this ambivalence elsewhere, and cannot repeat my argument here.[6] In the second and third centuries, Christian intellectuals were arguing for toleration, and yet they were unwilling (or unable) to accept the basic premise of religious toleration: a certain relativism in religious matters.

In these few pages, I cannot deal with the whole historical problem of early Christian tolerance and intolerance. Rather, through the case of Tertullian (the first Christian writer to offer a lengthy discussion of Christian attitudes to paganism, in his *De Idololatria*), I propose to reflect here on some aspects of this ambivalence toward religious tolerance in early Christian thought. I hope to shed some light on the boundaries of Christian identity and the construction of Christian life in a pagan society, as well as the implications of such a life. Tertullian shows us how arguments in favor of religious toleration could be developed which did not entail a deep transformation of thought-patterns, a real internalization of the idea of tolerance. In a sense, therefore, the following pages are an attempt to understand how different, even contradictory ideas can live together in the same mind, and how they can come to bear on wider historical issues.

Tertullian was a gifted polemicist, for whom tolerance cannot be a major virtue. Rather, in the heat of the argument, he wrote numerous and fierce invectives against various enemies from all sides: besides the pagans, the Jews, and Christians who happened to establish their theology along lines different from his, such as Praxeas or Hermogenes, as well as the traditional arch-heresiarchs Marcion and Valentinus.

2.

Interpreting the new religious pluralism under the early Empire, John North has recently argued that we have here, throughout the Mediterranean, a case of what he calls, in an appropriate metaphor, "a market-place of religions." This "market-place" forms the sociological background to Tertullian's thought. Perhaps for the first time in antiquity, individuals could now choose that religious practice and identity that best suited them.[7] No more the single choice of following the *patrioi nomoi,* the religious tradition of the city. To be sure, this religious

---

[6] See ch. 1 of this volume.

[7] See J. North, "The Development of Religious Pluralism," in *The Jews among Pagans and Christians in the Roman Empire,* eds. J. Lieu, J. North, and T. Rajak (London and New York 1992), 174–93.

pluralism remained more a matter of fact than a recognized value. It was the Christians, to be sure, who gained most from that transformation of the relationships between religion and identity.

North's study develops some conclusions of A. D. Nock on conversion as a new dimension in religious history in the Hellenistic period.[8] The central fact of religion under the early Empire, according to North, can be encapsulated in his metaphor of this open competition for minds and hearts. In other words, religion was no longer a given of one's native identity, together with ethnicity. A new religious identity could be freely chosen by the individual, from different possibilities. In such a new situation of religious pluralism, the Christians had clear advantages over their competitors. More than any other group, they had the ability to formulate the need for conversion in religious discourse, and to express the higher truth value of their own religion. Such a discourse, part of their Jewish heritage, remained quite alien to their pagan adversaries, until they, too, developed a similar discourse – but this happened only under Christian influence, in the third and fourth centuries.[9] But by that time, it was too late. It is in such a broad frame that we must try to read Tertullian's plea for tolerance: a Christian intellectual in late second century Africa sought to convince pagan readers that Christianity should be allowed in the "religious market-place." On the other hand, he knew that coexistence meant competition. Therefore, he tried to delegitimize (on intellectual, ethical, and religious grounds – the only ones available to him) the party in power at the same time that he appealed to it. Hence the basic ambivalence in his discourse on religious tolerance. This ambivalence tells us much about the ways invented by early Christian intellectuals for living as a Christian in a pagan society.

3.

The sentence quoted at the opening of this paper stems from the famous chapter 24 of the *Apologeticus*, where Tertullian's argument for religious toleration reaches its peak:

> Let one man worship God, another Jove; let this man raise suppliant hands to heaven, that man to the altar of Fides; let one (if you so suppose) count the clouds as he prays, another the panels of the ceiling; let one dedicate his own soul to his god, another a goat's. Look to it, whether this also may form part of the accusation of irreligion – to do away with freedom of religion, to forbid a man choice of deity *(Videte enim ne et hoc ad inreligiositatis elogium concurrat, adimere libertatem religionis et interdicere optionem*

---

[8] A. D. Nock, *Conversion* (Oxford 1933).

[9] This seems to be the case for the great interest devoted to the *Chaldean Oracles*, and also to some aspects of Julian's thought, and argued by G. Bowersock in his *Julian the Apostate* (Cambridge, Mass. 1978).

divinitatis), so that I may not worship whom I would, but am forced to worship whom I would not. No one, not even a man, will wish to receive reluctant worship.[10]

Tertullian eschews here the reasons for the Roman perception of Christianity as a *religio illicita*. Now Christianity, in contrast with native and traditional cults, considers Roman religion not as just another, competing and legitimate tradition, but as a *false* religion. For Tertullian, Roman religion is a cult not of gods, but of demons, which does not even deserve the name of religion. In the same chapter Tertullian rejects the charge of treason against Roman religion hurled at the Christians: since the Roman "gods" are not real gods, then Roman "religion" is not really a religion, and the Christians cannot be accused of a crime against religion: "*Si enim non sunt dei pro certo, nec religio pro certo est: si religio non est, quia nec dei pro certo, nec nos pro certo rei sumus laesae religionis*".[11] He then develops an argument according to which by common consent, men understand the concept of god as similar to that of the emperor, namely entailing the idea of a single supreme power ruling above the various gods assigned to different functions, just as the Emperor is the single supreme political power.[12] Tertullian further lists various deities in the provinces of the empire. Although these provinces are Roman, their gods are not Roman. It appears, then, that religious freedom is granted to all but the Christians. Tertullian's argument about true and false deity *(de vera et falsa divinitate)* concludes with the statement that only the Christians, who honor the true God in the midst of all idolaters, are forbidden to practice religion.

4.

According to Tertullian, moreover, idolatry is not simply to be defined as "false religion." It represents the supreme offence in the eyes of God: "*Atquin summa offensa penes illum idololatria est.*"[13] So paganism, i.e., idolatry, is shown by Tertullian to be religiously illegitimate. He further argues that it is also to be condemned from an ethical point of view.[14] But what is, for him, the precise nature

---

[10] *Apol.* 24.5 (132–33 LCL). Tertullian, *Apology, De Spectaculis*, T. R. Glover, tr., (LCL; Cambridge, Mass. and London 1978).

[11] *Apol.* 24.1 (130 LCL).

[12] On the importance of this comparison, see E. Peterson's seminal essay, *Der Monotheismus als politisches Problem: ein Beitrag zur Geschichte der politischen Theologie im Imperium Romanum* (Leipzig 1935), on which see A. Schindler, ed., *Monotheismus als politisches Problem? Erik Peterson und die Kritik der politischen Theologie* (Gütersloh 1978).

[13] *De Spectaculis* 2.9 (236 LCL). Cf. *de Spect.* 4.4 on the cult of the dead among the pagans as equivalent to idolatry, since the dead are honored like gods.

[14] For many insights on monotheistic views of paganism, see a book written by two philosophers, M. Halbertal and A. Margalit, *Idolatry* (Cambridge, Mass. 1992), *passim*. For a more balanced historical overview, see, for instance, J.-C. Fredouille, "Götzendienst." *RAC* 11 (1981): 828–95.

of idolatry? Since Tertullian devotes an entire treatise to this question, we should turn our attention to his *De Idololatria*.

In this treatise, written before his Montanist period, (probably between 203 and 206),[15] Tertullian asks the two related questions on the nature of idolatry and on the conditions of Christian life in a world filled with idols and idolaters. These two questions are related to each other since the definition and scope of idolatry will dictate Christian attitudes toward it. Moreover, one should recognize at the onset that many forms of idolatry are hidden, and should first be unveiled. The first point to be emphasized is the recognition of the incompatibility between the two realms of true religion and of idolatry. The realm of idolatry is also that of Caesar, and one cannot be at once a soldier of both Caesar and Christ. One is the camp of darkness, *castris tenebrarum,* totally opposed to the camp of light, *castris lucis.*[16] Hence, a Christian cannot swear an oath to Caesar, and is therefore forbidden from becoming a soldier in the Roman army. To use another metaphor of Tertullian, Athens and Jerusalem have nothing in common: *Quid ergo Athenis et Hierosolymis? Quid academiae et ecclesiae?*[17]

There was a time, to be sure, when there existed no idols: *Idolum aliquamdice retro non erat.*[18] But that was only in the *Urzeit*, before the devil "brought into the world the makers of statues, portraits, and every kind of representation." Through human error, everything but the Creator began to be worshipped.[19] As Tertullian argues in the *Adversus Praxean*, an *idolum* (a loan word which Tertullian introduces into Latin) is everything that functions as an intermediate entity between human beings and *daimones. Idololatria,* therefore, is the worship given to demons.[20] The same concept is reflected in *Apologeticus* 23.11: "Those whom you had presumed to be gods, you learn to be demons *(daemonas esse cognoscitis).*"[21]

The most important trait of idolatry is perhaps its ubiquity. Tertullian further warns that idolatry does not even need temples and statues in order to be practiced.[22] That means that idolatry is everywhere. Indeed, all sins reflect idolatry,

---

[15] These are the dates considered most probable by the most recent editors of *De Idololatria.* Tertullian, *De Idololatria*, ed. and tr. J. H. Waszink and J. C. M. van Winden, (Suppl. to *Vigiliae Christianae* 1; Leiden 1987), 10.

[16] *De Idol.*, 19.2.

[17] On this, see J.-C. Fredouille, *Tertullien et la conversion de la culture antique* (Paris 1972), ch. 6.

[18] *De Idol.*, 3.1; cf. Rom 1.

[19] *De Idol.,* 4.

[20] *De Idol.,* 18; see J. C. M. van Winden, "Idolum and Idololatria in Tertullian," *VC* 36 (1982): 108–14; and C. A. Contreras, "Christian Views of Paganism," *ANRW* 23.1, 974–1022, esp. 993; Cf. *De Idol.* 4.2, 5.2, 15.6 for the relationships between Enoch, the fall of angels, and the origin of demons.

[21] (126–27 LCL). One may note that the same assimilation of *dii* and *daemones* is found in Minucius Felix's *Octavius*.

[22] *De Idol.,* 3.4

in hidden as well as in open form, insists Tertullian in the introduction to his treatise.[23]

From this analysis follow various consequences. Idolatry is not only a product of metaphysical error; it is also morally reprehensible. And since it is ubiquitous, Christians cannot be too careful in seeking to avoid sin and idolatry. Tertullian devotes the bulk of his treatise to the ramifications of idolatry and their implications for the daily life of Christians in the Roman world. He enumerates, first of all, the professions that should be avoided by Christians, because they deal directly with idolatry. This list includes, obviously, the makers of idols, but also astrologers, teachers, and traders. Secondly, he tackles the indirect forms of idolatry, contact with which is almost inevitable through participation in social life. He goes here also into great detail, seeking to delineate rules of conduct, and distinguishing between permissible and forbidden behavior in the surrounding pagan world. How to live – and, more prosaically, how to make a living – in a world permeated with idolatry is a very serious question: the borders should be drawn in each case, and principles constantly weighed against feasibility. This discourse, it has been pointed out, is quite new in Christian literature. The fight against the *daimones*, or the pagan gods, is a very concrete one, against live adversaries rather than against a system.[24] Tertullian presents a sharp critique of Roman values: the very greatness of the Romans is linked to war (i.e., to violence and the destruction of temples). War and religion are mutually exclusive, and the very greatness of Rome comes from irreligiosity: *de irreligiositate provenit*.[25]

5.

In the course of his argument in the *De Idololatria*, Tertullian comes to answer some concrete questions about daily life and religious practice, in a way not unknown in Rabbinic literature of the same period. Indeed, some puzzling parallels in tone and detail exist between this treatise and the Mishna *Avoda Zara*, a more-or-less contemporary text, which deals with the interactions between Jews and pagans in Palestine.[26] In order to understand the nature of the similarities

---

[23] *De Idol.*, 1 and 2. Cf. *Spect.* IV.4, on the cult of the dead as a kind of idolatry. It should be noted here that Tertullian's attitude is not typical of all early Christian authors. For instance, he is here poles apart from Origen, as pointed out by Carlo Ginzburg, "Idols and Likenesses: Origen, *Hom. Ex.* VIII. 3, and its Reception," in *Sight and Insight: Essays on Art and Culture presented to E. H. Gombrich,* ed. J. Onians (London 1994), 55–78, esp. 58.

[24] This point is emphasized by J.-M. Vermander, "La polémique de Tertullien contre les dieux du paganisme," *RSR* 53 (1979): 111–23, esp. 116.

[25] *Apol.* 25.14–17.

[26] On these parallels, see Fredouille, "Götzendienst," and esp. C. Aziza, *Tertullien et le Judaïsme* (Paris 1977), 177ff. The *communis opinio* is that the Mishna was redacted in the last

and differences between the two texts, we should first say a few words on the concept of *latreia*.

As we have seen, idolatry, or false religion, is the most common form of cult, of *latreia*. We have here a clue as to Tertullian's implicit line of argument. If there can be idolatry without idols, this is because for a Christian, the boundaries of "cult" are very broad indeed. *Latreia* is, first and foremost, an affirmation, explicit or implicit, about the nature of the divinity. This affirmation is expressed in words or deeds, since Christianity itself is a religion defined through words, through the affirmation of a few truths, the *kerygma*. The Christians – more than in any other religious community in antiquity, the Jews included – developed a concept of religion in which truth and its proclamation was a central element, more important even than traditional forms of cult.

For Jews, the domain of *latreia* is defined much more sharply than for Christians. Jewish *latreia* ('*avoda* in Hebrew) consists essentially of Temple sacrifices (or their equivalent – prayers – after the destruction of the Temple). Since for Jews their own cult is precisely delimited, the Jewish conception of idolatry will also be more specific than the Christian one. In Rabbinic texts, it refers, mainly, to pagan *cult*, to sacrifices or prayers to idols. For the Jews, unlike the Christians, idolatry is essentially the cult of idols; it has less the quality of ubiquity. The implications of this semantic difference are significant, and reflect different approaches to new patterns of interaction between competing religious communities. Since the Christian conception of *latreia,* and hence of *eidolo-latreia* are broader, there remains a smaller margin for toleration of alien patterns of thought and behavior. For a theologian like Tertullian, almost any interaction with pagans may entail contacts with idolatry, and this will involve its toleration. Such toleration, needless to say, is to be most strictly condemned.

Early Rabbinic Judaism did not really develop tolerant attitudes towards gentiles and idolaters.[27] But various structural differences between Judaism and Christianity are reflected in some differences in the attitude of both religions to idolatry. The more stringent Rabbinic definition of idolatry permitted the toleration of a broader spectrum of interaction with pagans than Tertullian was willing to admit. Such toleration is reflected in Mishna *Avoda Zara*.[28]

One major structural difference between the two religions is the fact that Judaism remained a *religio licita* throughout our period, while Christianity was still, of course, a *religio illicita*. It is certainly quite difficult, if not impossible, to

---

decades of the second century. See brief discussion and references in G. G. Stroumsa, *Hidden Wisdom: Esoteric Traditions and the Roots of Christian Mysticism* (*SHR* 70; Leiden 1996), 132–46.

[27] See D. Novak, *The Image of the Non-Jew in Judaism: An Historical and Constructive Study of the Noahide Laws* (Toronto Studies in Theology, 14; New York and Toronto 1983).

[28] See further M. Halbertal, "Coexisting with the Enemy: Jews and Pagans in the Mishnah," in *Tolerance and Intolerance in Early Judaism and Christianity,* eds. G. N. Stanton and G. G. Stroumsa (Cambridge 1998), 159–72.

expect a religious group which does not enjoy even a modicum of toleration to grant its persecutors any kind of recognition. Another factor emphasizing the different Jewish and Christian attitudes is the fact that in the late second century, the Jews had, for all practical purposes, abandoned serious attempts at proselytism, while proselytism was the Christians' very raison d'être. As has often been recognized, the violence of the clash with the pagan world was partly due to the centrality of mission in the Christian mind.[29]

A third difference between Jewish and Christian self-perception, crucial from our perspective, lies in the boundaries of collective identity. The Mishnaic tractate *Avoda Zara* was written in Palestine when Roman occupation was bitterly felt. The rabbis could not avoid acknowledging the existence of various cults and religions on the ancestral soil.[30] But it was also clear to them that the Land of Israel belonged to God, and that He had given it to His people, Israel. The Romans, thus, were unambiguously considered to be invaders. They and their cult had to be avoided, but ways could be found which prevented pollution through contact with idolatry without paralyzing necessary contact (mainly in the field of commerce). In other words, Jews learned to live side by side with pagans. Such a limited interaction between the communities was not felt to endanger Jewish identity, because it had very clear ways of expressing itself, in language, territory, dress, or food habits.

Such clear-cut patterns of self-definition were of course precluded for the Christians. It is the *Epistle to Diognetus*, perhaps, which formulated this lack of all objective criteria of Christian identity in the most meaningful way: Christians have neither a territory, nor a language, nor special dress or food habits of their own. This strange people without any of the usual identifying criteria of peoplehood, is like the heart in the body of nations.[31] It is precisely their complete territorial, linguistic, and social osmosis with the pagan majorities (in Africa as elsewhere) which forced them into stricter rules of interaction with the pagans. One could say that Christian identity is formulated, in contrast to Jewish identity, *exclusively in religious*, and not in ethnic terms.

The combination of all these factors, it seems to me, goes a long way in ex-

---

[29] On this one can still refer to A. von Harnack, *Die Mission und Ausbreitung des Christentums in den ersten drei Jahrhunderten*, 2nd. ed., (1924); English tr. *The Mission and Expansion of Christianity in the First Three Centuries* (London 1908). On some implications of Christian proselytism, see chapter 4 of this volume.

[30] For a survey of paganism in Roman Palestine, see D. Flusser, "Paganism in Palestine," in *The Jewish People in the First Century*, eds. S. Safrai and M. Stern, vol. 2 (*CRINT*, Assen and Amsterdam 1976), 1065–1100. On Rabbinic attitudes to pagan cults, see E. E. Urbach, "The Laws of Idolatry in the Light of Historical and Archeological Facts in the Third Century" (in Hebrew), *Eretz Israel, Archeological and Geographical Studies*, 5 (1958): 189–205. See further Y. Baer, "Israel, the Christian Church, and the Roman Empire," *Scripta Hierosolymitana* 7 (1961): 79–149, esp. 88–95 (on Tertullian); and M. Hadas-Lebel, *Jérusalem contre Rome* (Paris 1990), 301 ff., on Roman religion and the Imperial cult as perceived in Rabbinic literature.

[31] *Ep. Diognetus* 5–6.

plaining why Tertullian's *De Idololatria* seems to reflect in part a more radical rejection of interaction with pagans than the Mishna *Avoda Zara*. The rather close similarities between the two treatises have often been emphasized. Claude Aziza, in particular, has argued for a Jewish influence on Tertullian's discourse on, and perception of, idolatry.[32] Although direct literary influences between the two texts are unlikely (Tertullian had no Hebrew), there is a distinct possibility that Tertullian was aware of the Jewish patterns of thought and behavior toward idolatry.[33]

What is more important than the question of the sources, however, is the internal logic of the parallel discourses of the two treatises. Tertullian, who did not like the Jews, did not hesitate to say so, in strong language.[34] None the less, he has been accused by various Patristic scholars of being "too Jewish." One may quote here, for instance, Hans von Campenhausen: "[Tertullian] ist in dem allen doch mehr ein Christ des Alten als des Neuen Testaments geblieben; er ist, theologisch geurteilt, beinahe ein Jude."[35] One should go beyond the author's intention, which was obviously meant *in malam partem,* and inquire into the interesting parallels in Christian and Jewish attitudes toward idolatry. The narrow limits of religious tolerance, or rather the intolerance reflected in the writings of Tertullian help us understand better the intellectual and religious presuppositions which rendered possible, in the course of the fourth century, the progressive limitation of religious freedom and toleration.

Last, but not least, it should be pointed out that Christian intellectuals in the first centuries did not necessarily consider religious intolerance to be a vice. On the contrary, it could also be praised as a virtue, since it reflected a readiness to martyrdom, as Origen argues emphatically.[36] In this short chapter, I have sought

---

[32] See n. 26 above.

[33] Against Aziza's opinion, see M. Turcan, ed. and tr., Tertullien, *Les spectacles* (SC 392; Paris 1986), 51: "Au lieu de parler d'emprunts, ne faut-il pas plutôt penser que Tertullien et les rabbins ont, chacun de leur côté, réagi aux excès dont ils étaient les témoins?," and T. D. Barnes, *Tertullian* (Cambridge, Mass. 198), 92 "Any similarity which he displays in contemporary Judaism does not originate in direct derivation," or ibid., n. 10 "The undeniable affinities between Tertullian and Judaism may be analogical, not genealogical." For a clear link between Tertullian and Jewish post-Biblical literature, see W. Horbury, "Tertullian and the Jews in the Light of *De Spectaculis* XXX. 5–6", *JTS* 23 (1972): 455–59, reprinted in W. Horbury, *Jews and Christians in Contact and Controversy* (Edinburgh 1998), 176–79.

[34] See for instance, beyond his *Adversus Judaeos*, a typical remark as in *de Spectaculis* 30.1–7, on which see A. De Vogüé, *Histoire littéraire du mouvement monastique dans l'antiquité, vol. 1* (Paris 1991), 133.

[35] H. von Campenhausen, *Lateinische Kirchenväter* (Stuttgart 1983 [1960]), 35–36. This is the last sentence of his chapter on Tertullian.

[36] Origen, *C. Celsum* 7.64 (see H. Chadwick's translation [Cambridge 1953], 448). On the willingness to die for the faith, see A. J. Droge and J. D. Tabor, *A Noble Death: Suicide and Martyrdom among Christians and Jews in Antiquity* (San Francisco 1992). On hatred in Tertullian, see for instance M. Turcan, ed., Tertullien, *Les Spectacles* (SC 332; Paris 1986), 54–56, and esp. *Spect.*, 16.6; 5.6; 2.11.

to point out a fundamental ambivalence, a double tradition within the early Christian psyche: a demand for tolerance together with an acceptance of intolerance, its presuppositions and its consequences. This double tradition of two contradictory trends explains why a real conception of religious tolerance did not develop in late antique Christianity.

Chapter 7

Religious Contacts in Byzantine Palestine

In 382, Gregory of Nyssa went to Palestine on ecclesiastical business. What he saw in Jerusalem did little to endear its inhabitants to him. "Nowhere else on earth are people more prone to killing each other," he wrote home, and his words strike the modern observer as possessing some ominous and eerie permanence. Elsewhere, Gregory tries to dissuade his correspondent from undertaking a pilgrimage to the Holy Land. According to him, God can be found in Cappadocia as well.[1] Gregory's strikingly reticent attitude towards the Holy Places, which had been gaining high status throughout the Christian world during the fourth century, requires explanation. The ambivalence inherent to the complex and evolving religious situation in Byzantine Palestine – and in particular to Christian attitudes towards non-Christians – can shed some light on the crystallization process through which different religious communities were living in an uneasy cohabitation before the Islamic conquest.[2]

From one conversion to another, from the fourth to the seventh century, Byzantine Palestine remained in many ways a rather special place. Despite its privileged status, it never became one clearly defined entity, be it from the geographic and administrative, the ethnic, or even the religious point of view.[3] Moreover, it should be noted from the outset that the "Holy Land" did not necessarily refer to Palestine as a whole, but rather to the very vaguely defined land "belonging" to the Holy City.[4] In a sense, Palestine had less an identity its

---

[1] See Grégoire de Nysse, *Lettres,* ed., tr., P. Maraval (*SC* 363; Paris 1990). In the Jaeger edition, see G. Pasquali, ed. *Gregorii Nysseni Epistolae* (Leiden 1959), 13–27. On these texts see I. Grego, "San Gregorio Nysseno a Gerusalemme e lo scontro con i giudeo-cristiani," in his *I giudeo-cristiani nel IV secolo* (Jerusalem 1982), 133–46. For a similar ambivalence toward Jerusalem on Jerome's part, see his epistle 58, to Paulinus (written in 396):"It is not to live in Jerusalem that is worthy, but to live there well." In this letter, Jerome advises Paulinus not to come on pilgrimage to the Holy Land.

[2] For a pertinent conceptual framing of the issues related to the study of religious changes in a given society, see R. F. Gombrich, *Precept and Practice: Traditional Buddhism in the Rural Highlands of Ceylon* (Oxford 1971), 1–17.

[3] For general introduction to our period, see F. M. Abel, O.P., *Histoire de la Palestine,* vol. 2 (Etudes Bibliques; Paris 1952); L. Perrone, *La chiesa di Palestina e le controversie cristologiche* (Testi e ricerche di scienze religiose, 18; Brescia 1980), and G. Stemberger, *Juden und Christen im Heiligen Land: Palästina unter Konstantin und Theodosius* (Munich 1987).

[4] The emergence and evolution of the concept of "Holy Land' in Christianity is studied in depth in R. Wilken, *The Land Called Holy: Palestine in Christian History and Thought* (New Haven, Conn. and London 1992).

own than other Near Eastern lands such as Egypt, Armenia, or even Syria. The religious and ethnic strife that plagued Palestine during the period under consideration is particularly complex. The boundaries of the religious communities were defined to a great extent in the process of confrontation with other communities, and the new shape they took as a result would have a notable impact in the future, on the community unified under God's Caliph rather than the Christian Emperor. This shape and this process can be observed particularly well in Byzantine Palestine.[5]

To a great extent, the Christian elite in Palestine was a society of immigrants, who had come to the Holy Land to practice there the new monastic virtue of *xeniteia* i.e., learning to become a stranger on earth.[6] The monastic immigrants were confronted with a multiplicity of ethno-religious groups living in less than perfect harmony on the land. It is this confrontation, together with the religious intolerance inherent to monotheist tradition, which gave rise to a new sense of collective identity within the communities, as well as to a demonization of the outsiders. This collective identity was neither purely ethnic nor purely religious; in order to describe it we may follow the suggestion of the folklorist Alan Dundes and use the term "folk identity."[7]

For more than half a century before Gregory visited the country, since Constantine's conversion, both Palestine and Jerusalem had been submitted to an intensive transformation process, concretized by the new churches established throughout the land thanks to the devotion of Helena, Constantine's mother, and of course with the help of the imperial treasury.[8] Both the land (in the vague, limited sense referred to above) and the city had been redefined as *holy,* promoted to a new status in the Christian system of beliefs which was fast becoming the official ideology of the Roman Empire. From "the holy places," a new concept "the holy land," *hagia gè,* was soon coined; the expression appears already in sixth century monastic texts from the Judean wilderness.[9] A similar sanctifica-

---

[5] S. Greenblatt, *Renaissance Self-Fashioning* (Chicago 1980), 8–10, lists the various ways in which the definition of the self is related to the confrontation with the alien, perceived as a hostile power. Relatively little attention has been devoted to the late antique and early Byzantine heritage of early Islam. For a recent approach along these lines, see J. Herrin, *The Formation of Christendom* (Princeton 1987).

[6] On this concept, see A. Guillaumont, "Le dépaysement comme forme d'ascèse dans le monachisme ancien," *Annuaire de l'Ecole Pratique des Hautes Etudes; Sciences Religieuses* 76 (Paris 1968): 31–58; reprinted in Guillaumont, *Aux origines du monachisme chrétien: pour une phénoménologie du monachisme* (Bégrolles en Mauges 1979), 89–116.

[7] See A. Dundes, "Defining Identity through Folklore," in *Identity: Personal and Socio-Cultural, a Symposium,* ed. A. Jacobson-Widding (Uppsala 1983), 235–61. For various anthropological approaches to problems of identity, cf. J. M. Benoist, ed., *L'Identité* (Paris 1977).

[8] On Helena's buildings, see in particular the chapter devoted to her in E. D. Hunt, *Holy Land Pilgrimage in the Later Roman Empire, A.D. 312–460* (Oxford 1982).

[9] See for instance a letter written by Palestinian monks to Emperor Anastasius and quoted by Cyril of Scythopolis in his *Vita Sabae,* ch. 57, 152–57 Schwarz.

tion process may be traced concerning Jerusalem, the home of the mother-church. After having been known since 135 as Aelia Capitolina, it had regained its name of old and was fast becoming the spiritual center, or at least one of the spiritual centers, of the triumphant religion. Although Jerusalem was a relatively minor urban center, by the mid-fifth century it had become one of the five patriarchal sees, on a par with Rome, Constantinople, Antioch, and Alexandria.[10] This had by no means been the case in pre-Nicene Christian writings, where the birthplace of the new religion was first and foremost identified as the city of Christ's killers.[11] But now it was "the holy city," a place of pilgrimage from the four corners of the *oikoumenè*.

It was precisely against this new status, or rather against the new religious attitudes which it reflected, that Gregory protested. The *engouement* for pilgrimage, to be sure, usually lured only a limited number of affluent people (among them many a Roman *matrona*) into a trip to the Holy Land, or rather the Holy Lands. The grand tour, more often than not, included a visit to some of the famous holy men who had taken to making the desert bloom with the flowers of the spirit in Egypt and in Syria, to their pillars, their caves, their monasteries, or their tombs.[12] Many poorer pilgrims who could not afford a return ticket went nonetheless, and stayed as monks.[13] In any case, the attraction of the Holy Land was fast modifying the structure of Christianity, encouraging patterns of religious behavior which were quite independent of the theologians' influence.

The monastic newcomers to the Holy Land had come from both East and West, although their respective situations cannot be described in quite symmetrical terms.[14] The Latin speakers were a minority within the Christian popula-

---

[10] For the evolution of Jerusalem's status, one might refer to the introduction of A. A. Stephenson, *The Works of Saint Cyril of Jerusalem*, vol. 1 (Fathers of the Church, 61; Washington, D.C. 1965). See also Z. Rubin, "The Church of the Holy Sepulchre and the Conflict between the Sees of Caesarea and Jerusalem," in *Jerusalem Cathedra,* ed. L. I. Levine, 2 (Jerusalem and Detroit 1982), 79–105. See especially P. W. L. Walker, *Holy City, Holy Places?* (Oxford 1987).

[11] Bibliography in G. G. Stroumsa, "Which Jerusalem?" (in Hebrew), *Cathedra* 11 (1979): 119–24.

[12] For a remarkable survey of pilgrimage in early Christianity, see P. Maraval, *Lieux saints et pèlerinages d'Orient* (Paris 1985).

[13] On monasticism in the Holy Land, see J. Binns, *Ascetics and Ambassadors of Christ: The Monasteries of Palestine 314–631* (Oxford 1994), together with J. Patrick, *Sabas, Leader of Palestinian Monasticism: A Comparative Study in Eastern Monasticism, Fourth to Seventh Centuries* (Washington D.C. 1995); L. Perrone, "Monasticism in the Holy Land: From the Beginning to the Crusades," *Proche Orient Chrétien* 45 (1995): 31–63.

[14] In his Epistle 107.2, Jerome reckons that "everyday we receive in Jerusalem troops of monks coming from India, Persia, Ethiopia, ... Armenians, Huns, Goths, Scyths." Its rhetorical flourish notwithstanding, this text testifies to the cosmopolitan atmosphere in Jerusalem in the late fourth and early fifth centuries. A group not mentioned by Jerome and whose presence was felt early in Jerusalem are the Georgians. See R. Janin, "Les Géorgiens à Jérusalem," *Echos d'Orient* 16 (1913): 32–38, 211–219. Hunt notes (*Holy Land Pilgrimage,* 151) that the establishment of the Christian Jerusalem contributed enormously to the cosmopolitan nature of the city's inhabitants.

tion of Jerusalem and Bethlehem, which could perhaps be compared to the small society of White Russian émigrés in Paris between the World Wars. But they often developed rather close links with the local ecclesiastical elite, and cultivated too many contacts to be adequately described as living in a cultural ghetto of sorts. Yet it seems fair to state that they never became quite integrated to the surrounding society.

In one of his most interesting letters about the nature of the land, Jerome notes that the holy men of Palestine are all foreigners (an argument meant to speak against the Jewish belief in the sanctity inherent to the land itself).[15] Similarly, Cyril of Scythopolis notes in his hagiography of Euthymius, the Armenian founder of cenobitic monasticism in the Judean wilderness, that of all his disciples, only one was a native of Palestine. Their various cultural, ethnic, and linguistic backgrounds help to explain why and the Christian elite of the Holy Land seem to have retained for a long time their minority sensitivities.[16] More than elsewhere, perhaps, the religious conflicts in Byzantine Palestine preserved patterns of communal conflict. One could almost speak of a land of *peregrini:* Jerome, the *homo ciceronianus* from Dalmatia in his Bethlehem cell, keeping remarkably well in touch with the world at large through his extensive correspondence[17]; Euthymius, the founder of monasticism in the Judean wilderness, coming, as did many of his followers, from Armenia[18]; the Egyptians Isaiah and Barsanuphius in the surroundings of Gaza[19]; or the Monophysite leaders John of Beith-Rufina and especially Peter the Iberian, who transformed Maiuma, Gaza's port, into a stronghold of anti-Chalcedonian resistance, established upon a core of autochthonous "old believers" and which held fast until Justinian eventually broke it (although Severus of Antioch had failed to bring Palestine into Monophysite orbit).[20]

---

[15] Epistle 129, to Dardanus, written after 413. Text and French tr. in J. Lebourt, *Saint Jérome, Lettres,* vol. 7 (Paris 1961), 154–66. This letter is referred to by F. Stummer, "Die Bewertung Palästinas bei Hieronymus," *Oriens Christianus* 32, n. R. 10 (1935): 60–74, esp. 68–69; by R. Wilken, "The Restoration of Israel in Biblical Prophecy: Christian and Jewish Responses in the Early Byzantine Period," in *"To See Ourselves as Others See Us": Christians, Jews, "Others" in Late Antiquity,* eds. J. Neusner and E. S. Frerichs (Chico, Cal. 1985), 443–71.

[16] As pointed out by W. H. C. Frend, *The Rise of the Monophysite Movement* (Cambridge 1972), 152, much of the rural population of Palestine had retained strong anti-Christian feelings.

[17] In "From Dalmatia to the Holy Land: Jerome and the World of Late Antiquity," 67 (1977): 166–71, E. D. Hunt describes Jerome's carreer as being at "the intersection of magnetic fields of various cultural foci" (168).

[18] Euthymius was born in Mytilene, the capital of Lesser Armenia. On Armenian monks and pilgrims in Byzantine Palestine, see M. E. Stone, "An Armenian Pilgrim to the Holy Land in the Early Byzantine Era," in *Mélanges Bogharian, Revue des Etudes Arméniennes* 18 (1987): 173–78.

[19] See D. J. Chitty, "Abba Isaiah," *JTS,* n.s. 22 (1971): 47–72, esp. 66.

[20] See R. Raabe, *Petrus der Iberer: ein Charakterbild zur Kirchen- und Sittengeschichte des fünften Jahrhunderts* (Leipzig 1895); as well as P. Devos, "Quand Pierre l'Ibère vint-il à Jérusa-

The varied ethnic origins of the Christian elite may also account for the noticeable absence of a local theological school. Jerusalem remained too cosmopolitan in character to permit the development of a tradition of its own. Perhaps
one should refer to it as to an *ouranopolis*[21] rather than a full-fledged *metropolis*.
Its theologians usually exhibited either Antiochene, or Alexandrian and Origenist influences. As a whole, the Holy Land remained a refuge and a pole of magnetic attraction – an attraction reflected, for instance, by the coming of Pelagius
to Jerusalem in the early years of the fifth century – rather than a genuine center
endowed with a natural hinterland of its own. In any case, Jerusalem and Palestine retained remarkably good links with overseas centers.

During the course of the fourth century, the fast sliding of imperial legislation
from religious toleration, through religious privilege, to a near-monopoly of orthodox Christianity, had in the Holy Land in particular very direct repercussions
on the relationships between the communities, or more precisely on Christian
attitudes towards other communities. In other words, social relations became,
much more than under the pagan emperors, invested with religious dimensions
and implications. The various religious communities were not quite alien to each
other. Commerce, at least, brought people into some contact, although usually
on a modest scale. From the few reports in the rabbinic sources – which, to be
sure, are usually rather laconic – we can infer that the daily contacts between pagans and Jews did not amount, on the whole, to very much.[22] The same must have
been true, mutatis mutandis, of their relations with the Christians.

Both Greek and Aramaic served as linguae francae, and diglossia seems to
have been widespread in Palestine. Egeria is a witness of this situation, when she
describes in her *Travels* how the liturgy at the *Anastasis* was being translated
from Greek into Aramaic for the benefit of those who did not understand
Greek.[23] One may also refer to two Christian texts from both ends of our period.
In his *Vita Hilarionis,* Jerome reports about a meeting between the thaumaturge
and the native (non-Christian) population of Elusa (a town in the north-west
Negev that would become the capital of *Palestina Salutaris* after the partition of
358), on the occasion of a pagan festival of the morning star. The crowd sur-

lem?" *An Bol* 86 (1968): 337–50. Peter reached Jerusalem in 437–438. See now A. Kofsky, "Peter the Iberian: Pilgrimage, Monasticism, and Ecclesiastical Politics in Byzantine Palestine," *Liber Annuus* 47 (1997), 209–222.

[21] I borrow this term to C. von Schönborn, *Sophrone de Jérusalem: vie monastique et confession dogmatique* (Théologie historique 20; Paris 1972), 20.

[22] So D. Flusser, "Paganism in Palestine," in *The Jewish People in the First Century C.E.,* eds.
S. Safrai and M. Stern (Aassen and Amsterdam 1976), 1065–1110, esp. 1093. See now J. Geiger,
"Aspects of Palestinian Paganism in Late Antiquity," in *Sharing the Sacred: Religious Contacts
and Conflicts in the Holy Land,* eds. A. Kofsky and G. G. Stroumsa (Jerusalem 1998), 3–17.

[23] Latin, too, was used as a third liturgical language in Jerusalem, as can be inferred from Gerontius's *Vita Melaniae.* Cf. Hunt, *Holy Land Pilgrimage,* 152. For Egeria's *Travels*, see the new
edition and translation of P. Maraval and U. du Bierzo, *Egérie, Journal de Voyage* (S.C. 296; Paris 1982).

rounded the holy man, asking him in the semitic vernacular to bless them: *"Ba-rekh!"*[24] And John Moschus tells us in his *Pratrum Spirituale* how a monk addressed a woman in her native Semitic tongue: *"Legei autoi hebraisti"* [i.e. in Aramaic, rather than in Hebrew].[25]

These examples are enough to testify to the existence of some contact between the communities. But a smattering of knowledge was never a guarantee against prejudice, in the Near East as elsewhere. On the contrary, one may argue that the acquaintance with the alien deprived the latter of any of the exotic charm and seductive power which were often attached to Eastern peoples and their presumed traditional wisdom.

Some remarks should be devoted here to basic relations between competing and conflicting systems of thought in Late Antiquity. These remarks are not necessarily specific to Palestine, but are needed in order to understand the implications of the religious revolution in the Holy Land. The fact that inter-communal contacts remained minimal does not mean that there was no shared life, regulated by similar patterns and ruled, equally for all, by the whims of the climate. Prayers for rain, for instance, crossed religious boundaries. There was indeed a *koinos bios,* but it was never recognized as such, never translated into conscious feelings of closeness. In a small world of micro-climates and clashing minorities with no clear majority group, or at least no group perceiving itself as a natural majority and acting accordingly, identity was often reduced to show business. A person was what he or she claimed and showed himself to be. Language, or at least accent, added to traditional dress and to food customs, in a word appearance, probably defined one rather well.[26]

Besides the way of life, pagans, Jews and Christians partook in late antiquity in a sort of *religious koinè,* i.e., similar patterns of religious behavior. This *koinè* covered the huge if amorphous field of religious practices and beliefs that change least, or most slowly, with time. The most obvious example of such practices and beliefs is probably the field of magic, which one is tempted to call, to borrow Descartes' words, "la chose du monde la mieux partagée." Bowls, phylacteries, incantations of various sorts, belong to all denominations; even their language – both in Greek and in Aramaic documents – often seems to cross "official" religious boundaries.[27] One could perhaps speak in this context of *cold* (as

---

[24] *Vita Hilarionis* 16. I have used the edition of A. A. R. Bastiaenesen, *Vita di Martino, Vita di Ilarione, in memoria di Paola* (Fondazione Lorenzo Valla; A. Montadori 1975), 72–143 and notes, 291–317. The *Vita Hilarionis* was written in 386–391. Cf. I. Shahid, *Byzantium and the Arabs in the Fourth Century* (Washington, D.C. 1984), 288–93. Jerome's probable source for his *Life* is Epiphanius, himself a disciple of Hilarion in some measure.

[25] Ch. 136, PG 87.3, 3000 A-B.

[26] On identity as show-business, cf, M. Fortes, "Problems of Identity and Person," in *Identity,* ed. A. Jacobson-Widding, 389–401.

[27] The continuous flow of publications by Shaul Shaked on Aramaic magic from Late Anti-

opposed to *hot,* in Levi Straussian parlance) religious history. Besides radical differences in theological outlook, both through time and between groups, some patterns seemed to be endowed with a certain permanence: beliefs in spiritual beings, angels or demons, or magical practices, would have been obvious topics of this religious *koinè.* But it should be at once pointed out that this closeness, too, usually remained hidden and unacknowledged, since relations with other religions or deviant interpretations of the Christian message had been defined by orthodox Christianity exclusively in terms of polemics – again, quite a new phenomenon in the classical world.[28]

Needless to say, the utmost importance of polemics in the crystallization of religious identities in late antiquity did in no way entail close relations or some kind of understanding between the various religious groups. In religious polemics, as in other kinds of polemics, one does not speak to each other, but rather to oneself about the other, the demonized other. The patterns of self-definition achieved through this very special genre deserve a study of their own. Suffice it here to say that these texts often seem to border on the incantatory rather than on any rational pondering of arguments. Their goal is not to convince, but to strengthen already existing conviction. Indeed, cases of genuine religious dialogue can be safely said to have been non-existent in our period.

The insistence on common patterns of life and religious attitudes is not intended to deny the radically new sensitivities introduced into the pagan world by Christianity. Without resorting to teleological reasoning, we should recognize that the impressive victory of Christianity over hearts and minds must have been founded on some advantages of the new *Weltanschauung* over existing systems. In his remarkable study of the Spaniards' conquest of America, Tvetan Todorov shows that the Indians, who had a very sophisticated symbolic view of the cosmos and of man's place in it, lagged far behind the *Conquistadores* in inter-human communications – a weakness that proved fatal to them.[29] It is impossible to dwell on this important issue in the present context, but we should at least note the decisive advantage held by the Christian world-view over its pagan rivals (including the major philosophical systems, Platonism and Stoicism) in the idea of religious truth. This idea offered a new pole through which the empire could be unified. It entailed a radically new concept of identity, founded

---

quity is fast transforming our knowledge. See, e.g., J. Naveh and Sh. Shaked, *Magic Spells and Formulae: Aramaic Incantations of Late Antiquity* (Jerusalem 1993), with bibliography.

[28] On religious polemics in late antiquity, their forms and role, see R. Lim, *Public Disputation, Power, and Social Order in Late Antiquity* (Berkeley, Calif. 1995); D. Rokeah, *Jews, Pagans and Christians in Conflict* (Studia Post-Biblica 33; Jerusalem and Leiden 1982). On specific sides of the issue, see S. Stroumsa and G. G. Stroumsa, "Aspects of Anti-Manichaean Polemics in Late Antiquity and under Early Islam," *HTR* 81 (1988),:27–58 (= Stroumsa, *Savoir et salut,* 355–77).

[29] T. Todorov, *La conquête de l'Amérique: la question de l'autre* (Paris 1982).

exclusively on criteria of religious truth, rather than on cultural or ethnic criteria, as had been the case until then. Together, religious identity and a new approach to the state's ideology ensured that the religious nonconformist would become rather quickly an outsider, the outsider par excellence.[30]

The victory of Christianity and its Establishment meant that throughout the empire the main criterion of identity, which since Hellenistic times had been cultural, had now become religious. In the ancient world, *barbaros* designated him who did not speak Greek, and later, more broadly, an alien to Greco-Roman culture.[31] Even the imperial cult, the observance of which was required of all citizens of the empire, functioned mainly as a duty of *civil* religion, which in no way prevented other religious affiliations. Christianity was a religion of a new kind, which cut across all barriers. Class, ethnicity, language – none of these was considered a hindrance which could prevent one from joining the Church. Believers were spread even beyond the empire's borders. Hence, refusal to acknowledge Christ as Savior became, soon after Constantine's conversion, the main criterion for defining the outsider. Before the end of the fourth century, with Theodosius I, this perception was enshrined in imperial legislation. The famous edict *Cunctos Populos,* published in Thessaloniki in 380 by Theodosius, defined Christianity as the state religion. When everybody could and should belong, those who refused to do so were held fully responsible. According to this conception there was no, or almost no, neutral outsider. It is this attitude that explains the tendency to demonize the outsider, in particular the heretic and the Jew, which has been so widespread in Christian history.[32]

When we seek to unveil the roots of the specific kind of religious intolerance in the Christian empire, the significance of the new emphasis on *religious truth* among Christian thinkers can hardly be overemphasized. Together with the unity and unicity of God, any monotheistic system is bound to insist on the idea of a single truth in religious matters.[33] What was not truth was error, and could in no way remain "value-free," independent of and unconnected to the Christian message. It was not the activist monks, but the practicing pagans, chased from their *templa* and moving into *fana* inside the land in order to practice their cult, who were defined as *fanatici.*

The new centrality of *truth* in religious matters, coupled with the emphasis on

---

[30] In the pagan empire, the outsider had been defined in a very different way, as shown by R. MacMullen, *Enemies of the Roman Order: Treason, Unrest and Alienation in the Empire* (Cambridge 1966). See also B. Kötting, *Religionsfreiheit und Toleranz im Altertum* (Rheinisch-westfälische Akademie der Wissenschaften 1977).

[31] See E. Fascher, "Fremder," *RAC* 8: 306–48. Cf. chapter 4 of this volume.

[32] See J. Gager, *The Origins of Antisemitism* (Oxford 1983), and cf. my review, in *Numen* 32 (1986): 287–89.

[33] The double truth theory in medieval philosophy and the late antique idea of esotericism related to mystical conceptions only confirm the primacy of Truth. On the latter, see chapter 2 of this volume.

religion as a prime factor of identity, radically transformed the status of religious outsiders. Two lapidary Latin formulas express this attitude well. On the one hand, *anima naturaliter christiana,* coined by one of the first Latin Christian writers, Minucius Felix, implies the universalist self-perception of early Christianity, coextensive in theory with human nature despite its revelatory character. On the other hand, *extra ecclesiam nulla salus,* the famous (or should one say infamous?) phrase of Cyprian adopted and popularized by Augustine during his fight with the Donatists. These two formulas are not poles apart, as they might appear prima facie. Rather, they reinforce each other in their main implication, namely the rapid growth of religious intolerance into a central element of religious, and also political, behavior in the Christian empire.[34] Although it was still *religio illicita* at the beginning of the fourth century, Christianity had managed before the century was over to either outlaw, delegitimatize, persecute, or greatly impede in their normal life all competitors, from within (the heresies) as well as from without. To be sure, daily *praxis* did not necessarily follow patterns shaped by theologians, yet the coercive powers of the church and its close relationships with political authorities greatly contributed to the long-term shaping of patterns of thought and of behavior throughout the Christian realm. From now on, the real outsider, the "other," would be defined in religious rather than in social, ethnic or cultural terms. This new situation entailed heightened tensions between the religious groups.

One could have expected the attitudes briefly described above to have been prevalent in Byzantine Palestine. To some degree they were indeed, but the very de facto pluralism of the population qualified them to some extent. Christian attitudes towards Jews, Hellenized pagans, and Arabs in Palestine present some interesting characteristics to which we shall now turn.

Due to its special character, Palestine was kept in some ways under particularly close watch from imperial quarters. When Juvenal, bishop of Jerusalem around the middle of the fifth century, converted to orthodoxy (that is to say, accepted the emperor's line against the Monophysite view on matters of dogma), the ecclesiastical rank of the city was upgraded to a Patriarchate.[35] The move was sealed in 455, when Eudocia, in Jerusalem, was reconciled with the emperor.[36] Such a symbolic importance had not always been the case.

Before the Peace of the Church, relatively little can be inferred from our dearth of sources on the development of Christianity in Palestine. The only monographic source, Eusebius's *The Palestinian Martyrs,* sheds light mainly on

---

[34] "If there were men who recommended tolerance and peaceful coexistence of Christians and pagans, they were rapidly crowded out," writes A. Momigliano, in "Pagan and Christian historiography," in idem., *The Conflict between Paganism and Christianity in the Fourth Century* (Oxford 1963), 80.

[35] On Juvenal, see E. Honigmann, "Juvenal of Jerusalem," *DOP* 5 (1950): 211–79.

[36] Cf. the chapter on Eudocia in Hunt, *Holy Land Pilgrimage.*

the late third and early fourth centuries. Two trends about this development, however, appear quite clearly. First, the relatively small scale and belatedness of the Christianization process.[37] Related to this fact, perhaps, is the lack of evidence for serious clashes between Christians and Jews in the second and third centuries. As Saul Liebermann reminds us, despite the Jews' national humiliation, Judaism retained its status of *religio licita;* and the Palestinian Jews do not seem to have suffered martyrdom under the pagan Roman empire.[38]

In the mid-fifth century, the ecclesiastical writer Sozomen is so puzzled by the following paradox that he states it at the very beginning of his *History of the Church:* at a time when even the Barbarians are converting, only the Jews have not yet recognized Christ.[39] It may not be irrelevant that Sozomen himself was a native of Palestine; he himself tells us that his grandfather, who had been converted by Hilarion, belonged to the first Christian community in the surroundings of Gaza. It stands to reason that precisely in Palestine, Jewish stubbornness in refusing to admit the claims of *Verus Israel* would strike the Christians as particularly offensive. This specific tension inherent to the nature of the relationships between Christians and Jews was fueled by a fact that has only begun to be recognized at its true value in recent scholarship. Even as late as the fourth century, Judaism, far from having become fossilized and retrenched upon itself, was actively and successfully proselytizing.[40]

Moreover, the Christians had a particular theological argument with the Jews about Palestine. As mentioned above, anti-territorial tendencies, already perceptible in the New Testament, had carried the day in Christian writings until the fourth century. But now everything was changed. The new Christian attitude had given the Holy Land a new ideal unity and special quality which matched the Jewish conception of *Eretz Israel.*

In Palestine even more than elsewhere, the fourth century represented the real watershed. Despite Origen's school in Caesarea, which provided a major intellectual and spiritual center of gravity in the third century, Christianity seems to have made only slow progress in its native land before Constantine's conversion. As late as towards the end of the fourth century, when the state's power was thrown massively on the side of the church, it seems that popula-

---

[37] The rhythm of conversion remained rather slow for some time. It is only under Theodosius II that Christians become a majority in Palestine. See L. Perrone, "Vie religieuse et théologie durant la première phase des controverses christologiques," *Proche Orient Chrétien* 27 (1977): 212–49, esp. 213.

[38] S. Liebermann,"Palestine in the Third and Fourth Centuries," *JQR* 36–37 (1946): 329ff., reprinted in idem., *Studies and Texts* (New York 1974), 112–79.

[39] Sozomen, *Historia Ecclesiastica,* I. 1, in Sozomène, *Histoire écclésiastique I-II,* ed. J. Bidez and tr. A. J. Festugière (Sources chrétiennes 306; Paris 1983), 108–13.

[40] This is emphasized by both Gager, *Origins of Antisemitism,* and R. L. Wilken, *John Chrysostom and the Jews: Rhetoric and Reality in the Late Fourth Century* (Transformation of the Classical Heritage; Berkeley 1983).

tions both urban and rural, were sometimes rather reluctant to accept Christianity.[41]

This fact may be due to the abovementioned history of religious and ethnic pluralism in a land that had never been perceived as a single entity by its inhabitants. Only the coastal cities were thoroughly Hellenized. Caesarea, the provincial capital, had been more rapidly Christianized, but cities such as Ascalon, and particularly Gaza, remained pagan strongholds for some time. The Samaritans, who during their revolt were to offer a serious military opposition to Justinian's troops, had expanded beyond their mountainous region, and were to be found also in the cities.[42] The Arab tribes, known to the Romans and Byzantines as *sarakênoi,* lived mainly in the Judean wilderness and in the Negev, as well as in the Sinai.[43] The Jews, prohibited by Hadrian from living in Jerusalem (the decree was renewed and reinforced by Constantine),[44] had remained in the neighboring villages and throughout the Judean hills, although their main population centers were in the Galilee. Later on, in order to avoid the heavy hand of the Byzantine power as much as possible, the Jews also moved to more eccentric and isolated areas, such as the Jordan valley. Imperial design could not transform this ethnoreligious mosaic into a monolith, i.e., a society united through the new faith. What it could and did achieve was to grant the Christians religious predominance.

Jerusalem offered a case sui generis. Here both the Christian ambivalence and the effects of the transformation were at their peak. Eusebius is one of our main witnesses of the sanctification of the city where Christ had been executed, as well as being himself one of the major artisans of this process. In theory, at least, Jerusalem remained forbidden for Jews, but no Imperial edict could erase the Jewish dimension of Jerusalem, the city of David and the locus of Solomon's temple. As Amnon Linder has shown, this dimension was prominent in the Christian Hierosolymitan liturgical tradition, which emerged in the fourth century and was to have such a major impact on the overall development of Chris-

---

[41] Cf. n. 17 above. See F. R. Trombley, *Hellenic Religion and Christianization, 370–529,* 2 vols. (Leiden 1992–1994).

[42] For a contemporary description of the Samaritan revolt, see Procopius of Caesarea, *Anecdota,* 11. 26 and 27. 27.

[43] On the original meaning of *sarakênoi,* see the detailed discussion by I. Shahid, *Rome and the Arabs* (Washington, D.C. 1984). 123–41. After the partition of Palestine in 358, the Sinai became known as *Palestina tertia.* Despite monastic presence, it remained known for a long time as Saracen land. Jerome speaks about "desertum Saracenorum, quod vocatur Faran." See *Onomasticon,* ed. Klostermann, 167–73. On the progress of Christianity in the area, see R. Devreesse, "Le Christianisme dans la péninsule sinaïtique des origines à l'arrivée des musulmans," *RB* 49 (1940): 205–23.

[44] Cf. A. Linder, "Roman Power and the Jews in Constantine's Time"(in Hebrew), *Tarbiz* 44 (1975): 95–143, esp. 136–41; but see O. Irshai, "Constantine and the Jews: The Prohibition against Entering Jerusalem – History and Hagiography" (in Hebrew), *Zion* 60 (1995): 129–78. Irshai casts doubt on the traditional view.

tian liturgy.[45] By the early fourth century, various eschatological trends in early Christian thought, which had ventilated hopes for the rebuilding of the Temple, had been suppressed and rejected as heresy, but not so the *Jewish* hopes for the return to Zion and the rebuilding of the Temple.

Jewish messianic and revivalist trends, similar to those known later in the Orient as the *avelei Sion* (mourners of Zion) were no doubt greatly encouraged by Julian's short-lived attempt in 363 to rebuild the Temple; and equally deflated the following year with the abandonment of the project and the Apostate's death. Whatever may have been his complex reasons for attempting to rebuild the Temple of the Jews, they are not directly relevant to our present task.[46] It may nevertheless be noted here that the episode highlights the existence of some intellectual contact – one dare not call it religious – between pagans and Jews, at least on the tactical level, and often oriented against the Christians, the common enemy. Few other traces of such a contact are extant; one might refer to the correspondence between Libanius and the Patriarch in Tiberias, the leader of the Palestinian Jewish community.[47] In any case, the fear that had seized Christian intellectuals at the time of Julian's apostasy did not resolve itself either swiftly or easily, as Robert Wilken has convincingly argued.[48] Its scars on the Christian psyche were still visible in the last years of the century, for instance, in Chrysostom's writing, as Wilken points out. What had affected Antiochene Christianity to such an extent must by the nature of things have had an even stronger impact on Palestinian Christianity.

We know from Eusebius's *Vita Constantini* that the emperor had already begun to isolate Jews socially and to discriminate against them on religious grounds as "Christ's killers." After Constantine, Constantius (337–361) began to limit the Jews' rights and privileges, ushering in a dark period for the Palestinian Jews. They were not yet forced, however, to transgress their religious laws. Jerome's works, in particular his biblical commentaries, reflect the new mood fairly well. The potential return of the Jews to the Holy land and their claims

---

[45] A. Linder, "Jerusalem between Judaism and Christianity during the Byzantine Period" (in Hebrew), *Cathedra* 11 (1979): 109–17.

[46] On the various aspects of Julian's relations with the Jews, one can still consult J. Vogt, *Kaiser Julian und das Judentum: Studien zum Weltanschauungskampf der Spätantike* (Leipzig 1939). On Julian's possible reasons to rebuild the Temple in Jerusalem, see A. Momigliano, "The Disadvantages of Monotheism for a Universal State," in his *On Pagans, Jews and Christians* (Middletown, Conn. 1987), 142–58, esp. 155–58. On the Christian perceptions of Julian's attempt and its failure, see David B. Levenson, *Julian and the Jerusalem Temple; the Sources and the Tradition* (forthcoming).

[47] These letters are translated and analyzed by W. A. Meeks and R. L. Wilken, *Jews and Christians in Antioch in the First Four Centuries C.E.* (Missoula, Mont. 1978), 59–66. As a *restaurator templorum,* Julian gained the Jews' sympathy; for both, the Christians were the common enemy; cf. G. W. Bowersock, *Julian the Apostate* (Cambridge, Mass. 1978), 88–90.

[48] R. L. Wilken,"The Jews and Christian Apologetics after Theodosius I *Cunctos Populos"* *HTR* 73 (1980): 451–71.

upon it seem to have preoccupied him. His abovementioned letter to Dardanus is particularly telling.[49] In this small treatise, which reflects a more ambivalent attitude towards the Land than elsewhere in his writings,[50] Jerome argues against the Jewish conception of the *promised land (terra repromissionis)*. His basic argument in rejecting any particular inherent sanctity to a land that he paints in rather dark colors insists that it is only Christ who sanctified the land on which he lived. The letter shows traces of a major, although latent and implicit, theological argument between Palestinian Christians and Jews on the topic. Other ecclesiastical texts coming from fourth- or fifth-century Jerusalem (which I have analyzed elsewhere) – by Cyril or by Hesychius, for instance – strengthen this impression.[51]

About one Jewish group, the Christian attitude is particularly ambivalent. This group, a small one to be sure, was particularly meaningful precisely because it stood right across ideological and ethnic boundaries that were becoming harder and harder to cross. The continued presence of Jewish-Christians in Palestine, perhaps even in Jerusalem (they saw themselves as the direct heirs of the mother church), at least up to the fifth century and probably throughout the Byzantine period, does not seem anymore in doubt.[52] The ambivalence and the annoyance shown on the part of Christian authors towards them was not always expressed directly. Yet the traces of their presence in various texts can be identified with reasonable certainty.

If the existence of the Jewish-Christians appears to be so fraught with problems that it is hard even to follow their track, this stems from the very nature of their *community*. Origen had once said about the Ebionites that attempting to be both Jews and Christians, they ended up being neither. For both established communities – and it is irrelevant here that the Jews were fast becoming a disenfranchised community – the Jewish-Christians were both, from within and from without, and hence perceived as a doubly pernicious danger. They threatened not only the "orthodox" Jews' and Christians' claims for theological legitimacy, but also those groups' very identity.

Despite the dearth of sources, it appears that in some cases at least, the Jewish-Christians were considered as Jews by gentile Christians of Palestine. In one of his homilies, pronounced in the basilica of the *Anastasis* in 350 or 351, Cyril of Jerusalem, turning to the "Jews," wonders why, since they worship

---

[49] Cf. n. 16 above.

[50] Cf. Stummer, "Die Bewertung Palästinas bei Hieronymus," (n. 16 above). F. M. Abel, "Jérome et Jérusalem," in *Miscellanea Gerominiana* (Rome 1920): 131–55, deals more with topography than with attitudes.

[51] G. G. Stroumsa, "*Vetus Israel:* les juifs dans la littérature hiérosolymitaine d'époque byzantine," *RHR* 205 (1998): 115–31 (= Stroumsa, *Savoir et salut*, ch. 6, 111–23). Cf. J. Taylor, *Christians and the Holy Places: The Myth of Jewish-Christian Origins* (Oxford 1993).

[52] Cf. ibid., passim, for discussion and references.

Jesus Christ, they continue to use the old name (i.e., *ioudaioi*), which remains limited to a geographic province, rather than adopting the new name of *christianoi,* now known throughout the *oikoumené*.[53] This testimony is buttressed by a similar remark on the Nazoreans by Epiphanius of Salamis.[54] It is easy to conceive that for the growing community of the church *ex gentilibus,* the continued separate existence of even a small Jewish-Christian community in Jerusalem or in its neighborhood was perceived as a threat to their legitimacy. In a word, all sides rejected the Jewish-Christian pretension to be at once *verus* and *vetus Israel.*

Towards the rabbinic Jews, Christian enmity was clear. Under Byzantine rule, the Jews witnessed worsening legal and social standing, continuous insults – both intended or perceived as such – to their already wounded ethnic pride, along with religious frustrations, attempts to convert them, and sometimes even pogroms.[55] The latter were more often than not enacted by thugs donning the monastic *schema* like the vicious Bar Sauma and his band around the middle of the fifth century, roaming around the land and terrorizing the population.[56]

All these were probably frequent enough, although the sources are far too spotty to permit any precise reconstruction of the course of events during the fifth and sixth centuries. In any case, it should not come as the least surprise that the Jews joined the Sassanian Persians in 614 aiding them in their conquest of Jerusalem and in the subsequent massacre of the city's Christians, which appears to have been on a large scale.[57] The Byzantine authorities, no doubt, had sufficient time to make the Jews pay for their treachery before the Holy City was to fall, this time for good, to the Muslim Arab invaders in 642.

In Palestine, where Hellenization had been less thorough than in either Egypt or Syria, it remained largely limited to the population of the coastal cities. As a result of the religious revolution brought by the Christian victory, the meaning

---

[53] *Cat.* 10.16, P.G. 33, 681 C.

[54] *Panarion* 29.1.2, P.G. 41, 389 A.

[55] For a general overview, see M. Avi-Yonah, *The Jews under Roman and Byzantine Rule* (repr. Jerusalem 1984).

[56] The monks' exactions were common knowledge in the empire. Elsewhere, but in a situation fairly similar to the one that obtained in Palestine, Symmachus, the head of Theodosius's cavalry, exclaimed after the arson of the Callinicum synagogue in 388 :"monachi multa scelera faciunt." On Bar Sauma's raids, see Z. Rubin, "Christianity in Byzantine Palestine – Missionary Activity and Religious Coercion," in *Jerusalem Cathedra,* ed. L. I. Levine 3 (Jerusalem and Detroit 1983), 97–111, esp. 107–108. Cf. E. Patlagean,*Pauvreté économique et pauvreté sociale à Byzance, 4ème.-7ème. s.* (Civilisations et sociétés 48; Paris and the Hague 1977), 225–26.

[57] See for instance the description of the Armenian historian Sebeos, *Histoire d'Héraclius,* tr. F. Macler (Paris 1904), 68. See also "Vie de Georges Koziba" *An Bol* 7 (1888): 134. Cf. Avi-Yonah, *The Jews,* 259–65. For the impact of the Persian conquest on Christian consciousness, see further the Greek and Arabic texts edited and translated by A. Couret, "La prise de Jérusalem par les Perses, en 614," *ROC* 2 (1897): 125–64.

of *hellenismos,* stripped from most of its former cultural connotations, was rapidly changing, becoming more or less identified with the old-fashioned pagan religion, and its adepts perceived as reactionaries (to use an anachronistic term) and arch-heretics.

The coastal region, for instance, from Caesarea to Gaza, which was to provide one of the major Hellenic centers in late antiquity, could be said to belong to the Holy Land in the fourth century only in a loose sense, although strong links were developed between the Church in Jerusalem and that in Gaza throughout the period under discussion. In the early fifth century, these links are represented by the friendship between John II, patriarch of Jerusalem, and Mark the Deacon,[58] or a little later by the move of Peter the Iberian from Jerusalem to Gaza. The close relationship between the two cities seem to have been maintained throughout this period, since the eighth-century witnessed the ecclesiatical writer Cosmas of Jerusalem becoming bishop of Maiuma, Gaza's harbor, in 743. Yet, the diverging lines taken by development of the coastal cities are conditioned by their particular background.

What is most striking in the coastal cities is the remarkable strength of paganism there, in its various garbs, which had inherited a long tradition. From the Roman period, we know of the cult of Atagartis in Gaza, Ascalon, and Jaffa. In this latter city, the legend of Andromeda and Perseus was told as a local story. Yet pagan religious cults and Hellenistic culture, although present throughout Palestine, do not seem to have had a major impact inside the land. Carried mainly by merchants, they remained for the most part concentrated along the sea shore and in a few major pagan cities such as Scythopolis or Sebastia. In the mountainous inland, including Jerusalem, which did not have a very large non-Christian Hellenized population, these cults and this culture were not overwhelmingly present. Palestinian schools of rhetoric in the coastal cities were sufficiently famous in the fourth century to have attracted, as a young Christian student, Gregory Nazianzen.[59] Libanius, on his side, spoke of Gaza with respect, and had friends in Elusa.[60]

After the conversion of its Hellenized elite, these schools retained their fame. In the late fifth century and in the first half of the sixth century, barely a hundred years belore the Islamic conquest, Choricius's discourses bespeak the vitality of Hellenic culture in Gaza. So does the active Christian Platonic circle of Gaza, with an Aeneas writing dialogues in the Platonic vein on the creation of the world or the immortality of the soul.[61] In Jerusalem, too, Hellenic literary culture is present in the fifth century, thanks in particular to the presence of the Em-

---

[58] On Mark, see G. Couilleau's article in *DS* 10: 265–67.

[59] On these schools, see G. Downey, "The Christian Schools of Palestine: A Chapter in Literary History," *Harvard Library Bulletin* 12 (1958): 297–319.

[60] Libanius, Epistle 334 Förster (=337 Wolf).

[61] A good portrait of the city is drawn by G. Downey, *Gaza in the Early Sixth Century* (Nor-

press Eudocia, who surrounded herself with a literary salon of sorts, and cultivated her taste for writing poetry (of a rather mediocre quality).[62] One should
add that even some of the monks happened to be men of letters, as is clear in the
case of their most famous hagiograph, Cyril of Scythopolis.[63] *The Life of Porphyry, Bishop of Gaza,* by Mark the Deacon, is a remarkable text documenting
in particular the Christianization of Gaza in the last years of the fourth century.[64]
What is of special interest is to note that until a relatively late date (towards the
end of the fourth century), the Christian community seems to have remained a
small minority – of at most a few hundred souls – in Gaza and its surroundings.
The text also witnesses the impressive resistance of the pagan population to the
state-supported efforts of the Church in suppressing pagan cults and philosophical culture (the Julia presented in the extant version of the text as a Manichaean
missionary appears to have been originally a philosopher).[65] Eventually, the
great temple of Marnas, the pride of the Gazans, was indeed destroyed.[66] Similar
clashes between pagans and Christians happened elsewhere. In Sebastia, for instance, the main Hellenistic center of Samaria, Rufinus kept record of religious
violence around shrines.[67]

Incidentally, it may not be pure chance if the first attested suppression of a
pagan temple in which a bishop played some role happens to have taken place in
fourth-century Palestine. Eusebius quotes from a letter of Constantine to Maca-
rius, bishop of Jerusalem, and to the other bishops of Palestine, describing how a
pagan temple at Mambre, near Hebron, where Abraham had received the three
angels of God, was destroyed and replaced with a church.[68]

---

man, Okla. 1963). See also F. M. Abel, "Gaza au sixième siècle d'après le rhéteur Chorikios," *RB* 40 (1931): 5–31.

[62] See for instance A. Cameron, "The Empress and the Poet: Paganism and Politics at the Court of Theodosius II," *YCS* 27 (1982): 217–89, esp. 280. Cf. her poem recently published by J. Green and Y. Tsafrir, "Greek Inscriptions from Hammat Gader: A Poem by the Empress Eudocia and Two Building Inscriptions," *IEJ* 32 (1982): 77–96.

[63] On Cyril and the significance of his work, see B. Flusin, *Miracle et histoire dans l'oeuvre de Cyrille de Scythopolis* (Paris 1983).

[64] Marc le diacre, *Vie de Porphyre, évêque de Gaza,* eds. and trs. H. Grégoire and M. A. Kugener (Paris 1930). See now Z. Rubin, "Porphyrius of Gaza and the Conflict between Christianity and Paganism in Southern Palestine," in *Sharing the Sacred,* 31–66.

[65] See G. Fowden, "Bishops and Temples in the Eastern Empire A.D. 320–435", *JTS* 29 (1978): 53–78, esp. 72–73. On the identity of Julia, see G. G. Stroumsa, in *CR,* n.s. 37 (1987): 95–97 (following Couilleau, n. 60 above), which corrects my previous "Gnostics and Manichaeans in Byzantine Palestine," in *Studia Patristica,* ed. M. Livingstone 10 (Kalamazoo 1985), 273–78. On religious coercion in Gaza, see R. MacMullen, *Christianizing the Roman Empire, (A.D. 100–400)* (New Haven 1984), 86–89 and notes. Gaza had witnessed riots against Christians during Julian's reign; cf. Gregory Nazianzen, *Disc.* 4.93 and Sozomen, *H.E.* 5.9.

[66] The importance of Marnas for Gazans is also refered to in the *Vita Hilarionis,* 8.5.

[67] The testimony is analyzed by F. Thélamon, *Paiens et chrétiens au IVe. siècle: l'apport de l'Histoire Ecclésiastique de Rufin d'Aquilée* (Paris 1981), 290–93.

[68] *Vita Constantini* III.52–53, pp. 105–107 in F. Winkelmann, *Eusebius Werke, über das Leben des Kaisers Konstantin* (Berlin 1975). Cf. Fowden, "Bishops and Temples," 58.

The destruction of the Marneum in Gaza may remind the reader of the burning by the Christian mob of Alexandria's famous Serapeum, so well described by Rufinus in his *Ecclesiastical History*. The vignette is symbolic, in a way, of the proximity of Egypt and Gaza. It is through Gaza that Egyptian influences reach Palestine, then as in previous or later times. In particular, there is every reason to believe that it is through Gaza that the new phenomenon of monasticism reached Palestine in the late third and early fourth centuries. Famous holy men such as Abbot Isaiah or Barsanuphius had come from Egypt, where they had learned the new way of life, the new *politeia*.[69] Hilarion, the semi-legendary first monk of Palestine, himself born in Thavata, fifteen miles from Gaza, about 293, had been schooled in Alexandria, and then spent some months in "the inner desert" with Saint Anthony before returning to Palestine.

Incidentally, the posterity of Gazan spirituality – which does not seem to be related to the Christian Platonism flourishing in Gaza in the sixth century – was to be oriented after the Islamic conquest towards the Sinai peninsula, where its mystical inclinations were to fully blossom. There it offered some of the most fragrant flowers of Byzantine mysticism, well after the Islamic conquest, by personalities such as John Climacus.

Yet this monastic spirituality should not be conceived as occurring among secluded communities of ascetics. The importance of the monks' role in the transmission of Christianity to the native population cannot be overrated. Cities like Elusa were flourishing before the seventh century, and had been Christianized by charismatic holy men such as Hilarion. In his *Vita Hilarionis,* Jerome describes Hilarion's appeal to non-Christian inhabitants, semi-sedentary Arabs who would flock to him.

Replacing the Temple's Holy of Holies, Golgotha was now construed as the new *omphalos*.[70] At the same time, the Barbarian nations were undergoing a rapid process of conversion, and hence the concept of "barbarian" itself became radically transformed. The whole world would soon be Christian, or so it seemed. It is one of the major paradoxes of the new Holy Land that right next to the center of the universe one stepped into the fringes of the civilized world. Civilization, since *Christianitas* was becoming more and more closely related to the *Romanitas* of which Jerome was the High Priest in the post-Constantinian empire.[71]

---

[69] On Isaiah, see D. F. Chitty, "Abba Isaiah," *JTS* n.s. 22 (1971): 47–72, esp. 66. On Barsanuphius, see Dom L. Regnault, *Maîtres spirituels au désert de Gaza: Barsanuphe, Jean et Dorothée* (Abbaye de Solesmes 1966).

[70] The significance of this transformation has recently been studied anew by J. Z. Smith, *To Take Place* (Chicago 1987).

[71] On Western Christian attitudes towards Rome, see F. Paschoud, *Roma Aeterna: Etudes sur le patriotisme romain dans l'occident latin à l'époque des grandes invasions* (Bibl. Helv. Romana; Rome 1967).

Jerusalem was both the *oikoumenè*'s center and periphery. Right outside the City stretched the Judean wilderness, appropriately called "Jerusalem's desert" by the monks who were settling it at a fast pace in the fifth and sixth centuries.[72] The monks had not simply retreated from the city. In many ways, their monasteries had become its intellectual and spiritual pole, as witnessed by the serious arguments fought in these monasteries over the Origenian controversy in the early sixth century.[73] This pole was also perceived as eminently political, and the monks' often stormy relations with the Patriarchate of Jerusalem form an important chapter in the history of the Palestinian church. The monastic *lavra,* the typical Palestinian form of monastic community, was at the crossroad between Egyptian cenobitism which first shaped Palestinian monasticism in the fourth century, and the Syrian, more individual, forms of ascetic life which became more influential in the fifth and sixth centuries.[74] This monasticism in our period played a distinct and major role in the life of ideas. Although to some extent the *lavrai* remained isolated Greek-speaking enclaves, this role was not only intellectual, but also involved an active part in the Christianization of the desert "Barbarians." These Arab nomadic tribes, the *Sarakènoi* (as the Byzantines) called them, were feared for their ability to stage successful razzias against border settlements.[75] Their threat was less serious from a military point of view, but more persistent, than that of the Huns, who had brought destruction on a large scale in northeast Syria at the turn of the fifth century, and had sown panic in Palestine.

Our main witness to Judean wilderness monasticism at its acme is, of course, Cyril of Scythopolis. His hagiographies possess much of historical value, and through him we can partially enter the monks' *Sitz im Leben.*[76] They had neighbors in the desert – not only the tribes that they were actively seeking to convert

---

[72] Cf. G. G. Stroumsa, " From Cyril to Sophronius: Hierosolymitan Literature from the Byzantine Period" (in Hebrew), in *Sefer Yerushalaim*, eds. M. Stern, S. Safrai, and Y. Tsafrir (Jerusalem, forthcoming).

[73] Justinian's edict against Origen and Origenism was published in 543 in Jerusalem. The best discussion of this controversy is in G. Guillaumont, *Les "kephalaia Gnostica" d'Evagre le Pontique et l'histoire de l'origénisme chez les Grecs et les Syriens* (Patristica Sorbonensia 5; Paris 1962).

[74] On the lauras in the Judean wilderness, see R. Rubin, "The lauras in the Judean wilderness during the Byzantine Period" (in Hebrew), *Cathedra* 23 (1982): 25–46. See also Y. Hirschfeld, *The Judean Desert Monasteries in the Byzantine Period* (New Haven, Conn. and London 1992).

[75] On the relationships between them and the monks, see Abel, *Histoire de la Palestine*, vol. 2, 344–54. Jerome witnesses to this fear of raids; see for instance *Quaest. in Gen.,* on Gen. 16:12, or Epistle 126.2, about a raid in Tekoa. See also Cyril of Scythopolis, *Vita Sabae,* 13–14, and *Vita Johan. Hesych.,* 13. John Moschus reports, in the name of one Gerontius of Madaba, how the Saracens had slaughtered three monks on the shores of the Dead Sea during the terrible invasion of 509; *Pratrum Spirituale* 21, 124.

[76] For a proper use of hagiographies by the historian, see E. Patlagean, "Ancienne hagiographie byzantine et histoire sociale," *Annales E.S.C.,* 1 (1968): 106–26; reprinted in her *Structure sociale, famille, chrétienté à Byzance, 4ème-11ème siècles* (London 1981).

thanks to their thaumaturgic powers – but also competitors vying for the nomads' spiritual allegiance, motley groups of cranks or heretics, mostly located
around the shores of the Dead Sea: Jewish-Christians, Gnostics, baptists of
various affiliations, and Manichaeans. Cyril sometimes refers to them, but we
also know of their continued existence thanks to John of Damascus, a denizen of
the great monastery of Mar Saba, located midway between Bethlehem and the
Dead Sea, in the first half of the eighth century.[77] "Arabia haeresium ferax": the
dictum seems to reflect well the secret life of the desert. It should not come as a
surprise when we hear of Manichaean converts among the Arab tribes, or when
we note some striking examples of Judaizing among them – or at least practices
perceived as such by the ecclesiastical writers.[78]

It is through the Christianization of the nomads that the monks contributed
to the expansion of Christianity. They were wise enough soon to realize that the
success of the enterprise demanded the integration of the newly-converted into
the clergy. Euthymius, for instance, managed to appoint as bishop a tribal chief,
Aspabetus, whose son Therebon he had cured and converted. Aspabetus became known as Peter of the *Parembolai*.[79] Some of these Arab converts
 reached influential positions in the Church. The monophysite writer John
Rufus, for instance, was an Arab of Ascalon.[80] The most famous case, however,
is that of Mavia, queen of the Saracens.[81] After having organized for some time
attacks against the Palestinian *limes* and the *limes arabicus* southeast of Bostra,
she converted to Christianity and around 370 had Moyses, an Orthodox monk,
consecrated as a bishop to the Arabs (despite the Arianism of the emperor
Valens). Through her story we discover another noticeable aspect of the tribes'
conversion – its military dimension. Converting them was indeed – or so it was
perceived – the best way of securing the integration of tribes that had already
for some time played a buffer role between the Byzantines and the Sassanians.
Following the new parameters of identity in the Christian empire, political in-
dependence was possible only as a sequel to religious autonomy. This fact at
least partly explains the tendency to religious splitting that resulted in the

---

[77] Cf. Stroumsa, "Gnostics and Manichaeans," passim.

[78] See for instance Ps. Nilus, *Narratio* III, P.G. 79, 612–13, on Judaizing practices among the
Arabs. Cf. Eusebius, *In Psalmos* 59.10, P.G. 23, 567–70, esp. 568 B (on Jewish-Christian converts
among the Moabites and the Ammonites. Cf. further Sozomen, *H.E.* 38, P.G. 67, 1408–1413 (on
Judaizing practices of Mavia).

[79] For another story of cure and conversion of Saracens by Euthymius, see Cyril, *Vita Euthy-
mii,* 51 (130–31 Schwarz).

[80] See F. Nau, ed., *Jean Rufus, evêque de Maiouma, Plérophories,* PO 8 (1911): 6. John (who
 died in 488) had known Isaiah and Peter the Iberian at the Maiuma *lavra*.

[81] On Mavia, see G. Bowersock, "Mavia, Queen of the Saracens," in *Studien zur antiken So-
zialgeschichte; Festschrift Friedrich Vittinghoff* (Kölner historische Abhandlungen 28; Cologne
1980), 477–95, *non vidi*. Cf. Shahid, *Byzantium and the Arabs in the Fourth Century,* 199ff. See
also Thélamon, *Chrétiens et paiens,* 123ff. Cf. Z. Rubin, "On Mavia, Queen of the Saracens" (in
Hebrew), *Cathedra* 47 (1988): 25–49, see p. 76 above.

emergence and development of the Monophysite and Nestorian churches in the East (though not, of course, the birth of Monophysite or Nestorian conceptions).

Unfortunately, the few details that we are able to collect about religious change do not help much in understanding the ways in which groups – as distinct from individuals – converted in late antiquity (one should keep in mind what was noted above, namely that religious change is not necessarily identical with conversion). There was no more an Augustine among the Arabs of the Negev or of Judea, than there was one among any of the other "barbarian" peoples of the Near East converting to Christianity, and we know pitifully little about their thoughts or feelings. In any case, events of earth-shaking power reshuffled the cards before long. In 634, it was not a band of thugs that prevented Sophronius, the patriarch of Jerusalem, from going to Bethlehem at Christmas. This time, the *troubles fête* were Saracens newly-converted to another faith, that of their false prophet from Arabia. They were occupying the city of Christ's birth in the all too real war they were waging on the Byzantine forces, and that they were soon to win in Palestine.[82]

The Islamic conquest brought upon Palestine as a whole, and upon Palestinian Christians in particular, some radical changes, first and foremost of a linguistic nature. Although Greek letters survived for some time, in particular within the monasteries, and continued throughout the eighth century to show signs of creativity, the new idiom, Arabic, was making fast headway.[83] Sidney Griffith was able to show recently that, partly due to their isolation from Constantinopol, Palestinian Christians were the first of their faith to use Arabic as a respectable intellectual tool for the expression of theological ideas.[84] Since the Jews also began to use Arabic, a new *koinè* was emerging, which was to render possible a quite new phenomenon throughout the Islamic realm: a theological exchange, real if limited, between monotheists.[85]

---

[82] The Christmas sermon of Sophronius, printed in an incomplete Latin version in PG 87.3, 3201ff., was edited by H. Usener, *Rheinisches Museum*, n.F. 41 (1886): 500–16. A few days later, in his Epiphany sermon, Sophronius complains about massacres, the destruction of monasteries, the plundering and burning of towns and villages by the Saracens "who claim to conquer the whole world". Cf. F. M. Abel, "La prise de Jérusalem par les Arabes (638)," in *Conférences Saint Etienne,* 1910–1911 (Paris 1911), 107–44. For the broader historical context of these events, see also Herrin, *The Formation of Christendom,* 194–98.

[83] On the last stages of Greek culture in Palestine, see R. P. Blake, "La littérature grecque en Palestine au VIIIe. siècle," *Le Muséon* 78 (1965): 367–80.

[84] Griffith has been publishing recently a series of important articles on connected topics; see for instance "Stephen of Ramla and the Christian Kerygma in Arabic in Ninth-Century Palestine," *JEH* 36 (1985): 23–45.

[85] For a good introduction to Jewish medieval literature in Arabic, see A. Halkin, "Judaeo-Arabic Literature," in *The Jews: their Religion and Culture,* ed. L. Finkelstein (New York 1971), 121–54. On the theological exchange of ideas, see J. Wansbrough, *The Sectarian Milieu* (Oxford 1970). Cf. S. Stroumsa, "Jewish Polemics against Islam and Christianity in the Light of the Ju-

Ramsay MacMullen has suggested that the Islamization process in the Near East followed patterns rather similar to the Christianization process, often putting economic, legal, and social pressure on potential neophytes rather than using more direct coercion. Hence the Christians (and the Jews) would become second-class citizens in the Islamic commonwealth.[86] This important observation should be tested in various specific contexts. I believe that it offers a fruitful insight about fundamental historical processes, although MacMullen plays down the radical difference between monotheist attitudes towards other monotheists and towards pagans. A more precise understanding of the nature of the religious changes in Palestine towards the end of the Byzantine rule and during the first stages of the Islamic caliphate might be of crucial importance for our comprehension of the very nature of early Islam.[87]

In any case, the new ruling religion reversed a trend that we saw growing under Byzantium. Limits were put to religious intolerance. This was achieved through the combined pressure of two conditions, which we can observe intertwined in Palestine. The first, mentioned above, is the rapid predominance of a new intellectual *lingua franca,* which permitted a modicum of communication between the elites of the different faiths. The second was the fact that the Islamic conquest did not suppress the ethno-religious mosaic that we saw established in late antiquity. Rather, the fact that they had fought against monotheists strengthened the tendency to grant some religious legitimacy, although limited and precarious, to the various communities in the land. Indeed, Both Christianity and Islam recognized each other in an awkward way from the very beginnings of their encounter: as heresies, i.e., as distortions of the monotheist message, not as pagans. Hence, although the Muslims developed much faster than the Christians and had a real sense of majority, thanks to their sweeping conquests, religious intolerance remained checked by the respect for the boundaries of the religious minorities. To sum up, the status of the Christians under Islam was meaningfully different from the status of pagans in the Christian realm.

A legend, preserved by Ibn Batriq, alias Eutychius, Monophysite patriarch of Alexandria in the tenth century, has it that when the Caliph Omar al-Khattab conquered Jerusalem, the old patriarch Sophronius, after handing him the keys of the city, invited him to pray in the church of the *Anastasis.* To the gallant offer Omar replied even more gallantly. He declined the invitation, saying that he did not want the Muslims to reclaim the church after his death as a Muslim holy place.[88] He would rather remove the *omphalos* back to its original locus, the

---

daeo-Arabic Texts," in *Judeo-Arabic Studies: Proceedings of the Founding Conference of the Society for Judeo-Arabic,* ed. N. Golb (Amsterdam 1997), 241–50.

[86] See R. MacMullen, *Christianizing the Roman Empire,* 58.

[87] One of the most challenging approaches is that opened by P. Crone and M. Cook, *Hagarism* (Cambridge 1977).

[88] Ibn Batriq, *Annales,* II.17. Cf. S. D. Goitein, "Al-Kuds, histoire," *EI,* 5: 321–40, esp. 322–23.

Temple mount.[89] Religious power and religious pluralism had been secured as established in an uncomfortable, limited coexistence, but at least not quite exclusive of one another, in Palestine.

---

[89] On the building of Muslim Jerusalem, see O. Grabar, "Al-Kuds, monuments," *EI*, 5: 340–45, esp. 340–42. On the holiness of Jerusalem in Islam, see esp. S. D. Goitein, "The Sanctity of Jerusalem and Palestine in Early Islam," in his *Studies in Islamic History and Institutions* (Leiden 1968), 135–48. See esp. 146 on the influence of Christian monks.

Chapter 8

From Anti-Judaism to Antisemitism in Early Christianity?

Modern racial antisemitism is essentially a secular phenomenon. Nonetheless, its Christian roots, a *praeparatio antisemitica* of sorts, are not called into question.[1] The difficulty lies in identifying these roots precisely. Not unexpectedly, scholars in different fields point to their own area of specialty as the most crucial for discovering the roots of modern antisemitism. Thus, Reformation scholar Heiko Oberman detects these roots in the thought of the reformers during that period.[2] Similarly, medieval historians like Gavin Langmuir, Gerhard Ladner, and Jeremy Cohen insist on the deep transformation of attitudes toward Jews in the twelfth and thirteenth centuries.[3] According to Cohen, it was the friars who, from the twelfth century on, were primarily responsible for transforming traditional anti-Judaism into a new, radical demand that Jews be completely excluded and expelled from Christendom. And Gerhard Ladner points out that the theme of the collective guilt of contemporary Jews for the sins of their fathers does not seem to appear clearly in the literature before Abelard.[4]

I shall seek here to identify the roots of this later development in the first Christian centuries, and to trace the origins of the medieval demonic image of the Jew back to the construction of the Jew in Patristic literature. I shall further analyze the transformation of early Christian attitudes toward Jews and Judaism that followed the religious revolution of the fourth century. In other words, I shall ask whether, side by side with the anti-Judaism characteristic of Patristic polemical literature, some traits may be detected, which should be viewed as antisemitic.[5]

---

[1] On the taxonomy of anti-Semitism, see for instance Y. H. Yerushalmi, *Assimilation and Racial Anti-Semitism: the Iberian and the German Models* (The Leo Baeck Memorial Lecture No. 26; New York 1982), 5.

[2] H. A. Oberman, *The Roots of Anti-Semitism in the Age of Renaissance and Reformation* (Philadelphia 1984). The work was originally published in Berlin in 1981, under the title *Wurzeln des Antisemitismus*.

[3] G. L. Langmuir, *History, Religion, and Antisemitism* and *Toward a Definition of Antisemitism* (Berkeley, Los Angeles, and Oxford 1990); G. Ladner, "Aspects of Patristic Anti-Judaism," *Viator* 2 (1971): 355–63; J. Cohen, *The Friars and the Jews: The Evolution of Medieval Anti-Judaism* (Ithaca 1982).

[4] Ladner, "Aspects," 362.

[5] Anti-Judaism and antisemitism are not interchangeable terms, and both need to be used. While Samuel Sandmel and John Gager speak of "antisemitism" in the titles of their books, both acknowledge that in some ways it would have been more precise to speak of "anti-Judaism." (Sandmel, *Antisemitism in the New Testament?* [Philadelphia 1978], xxi; cf. J. Gager,

The purpose of what follows, therefore, is not to offer a new synthetic study or overview of Jewish-Christian relations in the first centuries, but rather to clarify the relationships among early Christian anti-Judaism, the formation of Christian identity, and Christian antisemitism.

The various possibilities call for different questions. For example, if the postulated roots of antisemitism are found in all strata of early Christian literature, from the text of the New Testament on, do all texts display the same level of prejudice and aggressiveness toward Jews, or can some sort of evolution be detected that would lead from theological polemics (reflecting "anti-Judaism") to ethnic prejudice ("antisemitism" proper) toward the end of our period? Or perhaps, should we give up the attempt to see a linear evolution, and recognize two different trends in the writings of the Church Fathers on Judaism and the Jews, one more courteous or civil, the other more aggressive? If we decide on the latter, there is a subsidiary question: whether we should attribute these two trends mainly to the different situations in which the authors lived and wrote, to their different theologies, or even to different psychological attitudes or frames of mind. These options must all be weighed.

A caveat is in order here. When using such words as "antisemitism" or "religious intolerance," we run the risk of anachronism, and should therefore proceed with utmost caution. Peter Brown reminds us that religious toleration was at best a fragile notion in the ancient world[6]; and indeed, the concept of "toleration" does not appear before the seventeenth century.[7] Yet, the fact remains that in ancient societies, acceptance was more or less easy for those outside the leading or ruling tradition, according to circumstances.[8] We must therefore assume that there must be either progress or regression in the acceptance of foreign

---

The Origins of Antisemitism: Attitudes Toward Judaism in Pagan and Christian Antiquity [Oxford 1983]). Langmuir has sought to define these terms anew. According to him, anti-Judaism is "the total or partial opposition to Judaism – and to Jews as adherents of it – by people who accept a competing system of beliefs and practices and consider certain genuine Judaic beliefs and practices as inferior" See "Anti-Judaism as the Necessary Preparation for Antisemitism," in his *Toward a Definition*, 57). He defines antisemitism as: "chimerical beliefs or phantasies about 'Jews,' as irrational beliefs that attribute to all those symbolized as 'Jews' menacing characteristics or conduct that no Jews have been observed to possess or engage in"; see "From anti-Judaism to Antisemitism," in his *Toward a Definition*, 297. The difference between religion and religiosity, upon which Langmuir insists, bears some similarity with that between theology and popular religion. This opposition between religion and religiosity is not a new one. It played a major role in the thought of the young Buber, a fact apparently ignored by Langmuir. On this last point, see my, "Martin Buber as an Historian of Religion: Presence, not Gnosis." *Archives des Sciences Sociales des Religions* 101 (1998), 87–105.

[6] See P. Brown, *Authority and the Sacred: Aspects of the Christianisation of the Roman World* (Cambridge 1995).

[7] Apparently, the concept appears for the first time in Locke's *On Tolerance*, first published as *Epistola de Tolerantia* in 1689.

[8] See P. Garnsey, "Religious Toleration in Classical Antiquity," in *Persecution and Toleration in Classical Antiquity,* ed. W. J. Sheils (Oxford 1984), 1–27.

traditions and their followers. And it appears that there was less room for religious freedom and religious difference in the Christianized Roman Empire than there had been under the pagan emperors. Since Gibbon, the traditional explanation for this situation identifies Christianity with the religious zeal, *sive* fanaticism, typical of monotheistic religions. However, since this explanation does not take religious evolution into account, it fails to provide an adequate interpretation of historical reality. I shall therefore propose here to insist on the transformation not only of doctrines, but also – more importantly –of perceptions and attitudes during the first Christian centuries, on what might be termed the dynamic character of early Christian identity.[9]

After a short presentation of the current state of research on early Christian anti-Judaism, and of the *Adversus Judaeos* literature, I shall present the two main competing scholarly approaches to early Christian anti-Judaism. The first, which has been fashionable in the last generation, insists on the social dimension of the conflict between Jews and Christians in the towns of the empire, while the second considers anti-Judaism as mainly belonging to the Christian discourse of self-definition. I shall then try to show how the static character of both approaches is misleading, and that early Christian anti-Judaism must be understood in light of the dynamic character of religious identity in the Roman world. I shall endeavor to underline the implications of the fourth-century revolution in religiosity for understanding the transformation of anti-Judaism.

1. Early Christian anti-Judaism

Anti-Judaism and antisemitism in antiquity

Between the ambivalent attitudes towards Jews and Judaism in antiquity and the modern hatred of Jews, both essentially non-religious and non-theological in nature, or at in intention, early Christian perceptions of Jews and Judaism appear to be sui generis.

The existence of a strong dislike, or even hatred of Jews in the ancient world is well-known, but it does not appear to have been based on racial prejudice. Side by side with it, moreover, flourished a rather remarkable "philosemitism."[10]

---

[9] See chapter 1 of this volume. For speaking about "attitude" rather than "doctrine," see P. Brown, "St. Augustine's Attitude to Religious Coercion," *JRS* 54 (1964): 107–16, reprinted in his *Religion and Society in the Age of Saint Augustine* (London 1972), esp. 260–61.

[10] See Gager, *Origins of Anti-Semitism*. For a good summary of the *status quaestionis,* see L. H. Feldman, "Anti-Semitism in the Ancient World," in *History and Hate: the Dimensions of Anti-Semitism,* ed. D. Berger (Philadelphia, New York and Jerusalem 1986), 15–42, and the response by Sh. Cohen, "'Anti-Semitism' in Antiquity: the Problem of Definition," ibid., 43–47. See now P. Schäfer, *Judeophobia: Attitudes toward the Jews in the Ancient World* (Cambridge, Mass. 1997).

Even Tacitus, an author notorious for his derogatory descriptions of Jews in his *History,* can also at times express himself in positive terms about them.[11] As A. N. Sherwin-White has shown, it is misleading to refer to *racial* prejudice against Jews in the ancient world, particularly in Imperial Rome.[12] The antagonism against Jews there seems rather to have been based on what was perceived as Jewish religious "separatism" and rejection of patterns of Hellenistic culture. Louis Feldman detects the following traits attributed to Jews by their pagan enemies: hatred of mankind, credulity, double loyalty, aggressiveness in proselytism; moreover, the Jews were also perceived by their detractors as beggars. To be sure, our information about such trends in antiquity is very limited. We hear something about the beliefs of intellectuals, as well as about the attitude of governments, but we can learn very little about the feelings of the masses.

It is the great merit of John Gager's *Origins of Anti-Semitism* that it analyzes – within the same context – both the pagan and the early Christian attitudes. This enables Gager to emphasize the deep ambivalence of both traditions to Judaism and the Jews, a phenomenon too often forgotten or undervalued. In the ancient world, indeed, negative perceptions of Jews and Judaism should be understood only together with strong philosemitic trends among pagan and Christian intellectuals (i.e., the Fathers), as well as within less-educated social groups. Such an approach underlines the fundamental differences between pagan and Christian attitudes.

Understandably, many scholars have often sought to avoid speaking of Christian antisemitism while dealing with early Christian literature, namely the Patristic texts and, a fortiori, the New Testament. It obviously makes little sense to speak of Christian antisemitism in the earliest stages of the new religion, since the belief in Jesus Christ was at first held within a Jewish sectarian movement. But although Christianity appears on the scene of history as a Jewish sect, it soon grew into the direct competitor of Judaism, claiming to be its inheritor. No wonder that the opposition to the mother religion and the polemic against it are embedded in early Christian literature. Anti-Judaism is hence perceived as inherent to Christianity, while antisemitism would represent an attitude of a rather different nature, appearing later, or elsewhere. It is also true, however, that the radical character of the anti-Jewish polemic soon gave it undeniably violent undertones. Indeed, texts of the New Testament written before the end of the first century already reflect such a transformation: "the Jews," and "the Pharisees," typified as the opponents of the young movement, are blackened and even presented as responsible for the death of Jesus. One cannot overemphasize the consequences of this accusation, which soon led to the description of the

---

[11] See L. H. Feldman, "Pro-Jewish Intimations in Tacitus' Account of Jewish Origins," *REJ* 150 (1991): 331–60.

[12] A. N. Sherwin-White, *Racial Prejudice in Ancient Rome* (Cambridge 1967), esp. 99–100.

Jews' sin as *deicide*. This transformation of theological language can already be observed in the writings of Melito in second-century Sardis. To be sure, it does not necessarily reflect a simultaneous change for the worst in social relations between Jews and Christians. The question of anti-Judaism in the New Testament has been raised recently from several quarters, and this is not the place to dwell on it.[13] I do, however, at least wish to recall that these texts were written in rather diverse milieus, and that it is therefore quite meaningless to speak about a single New Testament attitude.[14] What counts for us here is the fact that, as early as the second century, the texts embedded in the New Testament were considered by Christians to represent one single authoritative view.

Finally, it should be pointed out that anti-Jewish attitudes can be felt on three different levels, correctly distinguished by Langmuir.[15] Side by side with the theological writings, popular expressions of anti-Jewish sentiment should be taken into account, although they are not always easy to detect or document precisely. Some time after the establishment of Christianity as the preferred, then the only legal, religion, Roman legislation on Jews in late antiquity began to reflect the constant shrinking of the Jews' privileges and rights. The theological, the popular, and the legal levels are not quite autonomous and independent of each other, and we should be able to detect dialectical relationships between them. Theological doctrines, which are in part informed by biblical texts or expressions, help shape popular attitudes as well as legal developments. These last two, on their side, do have an impact on theological reflections about Jews and Judaism.

At the popular level, it is extremely difficult to draw a clear line between anti-Judaism and antisemitism. Rather, Christian anti-Judaism is rooted in theological polemics in contradistinction to pagan antisemitism, it is essentially an intellectual phenomenon, launched and developed by literati, and stemming from an insurmountable theological confrontation. To be sure, there were intellectuals among the pagan enemies of the Jews, and of course it is mainly the intellectuals who have left us written records about their opinions; but their negative attitude toward the Jews does not seem to have been dictated by the nature of their intel-

---

[13] For some recent studies, see for instance S. Freyne, "Vilifying the Other and Defining the Self: Matthew's and John's Anti-Jewish Polemic in Focus," in *To See Ourselves as Others See Us,* eds. J. Neusner and E. S. Frerichs (Chico, Calif. 1985), 117–43; J. D. Levenson, "Is there a Counterpart in the Hebrew Bible to the New Testament Antisemitism?," *JES* 22 (1985): 242–60; A. Reinhartz, "The New Testament and Anti-Judaism: a Literary-Critical Approach," *JES* 25 (1988): 524–37; L. T. Johnson, "The New Testament's Anti-Jewish Slander and the Conventions of Ancient Polemic," *JBL* 108 (1989): 419–41.

[14] See D. R. A. Hare, "The Rejection of the Jews in the Synoptic Gospels and Acts," in *Antisemitism and the Foundations of Christianity,* ed. A. Davies (New York, Sydney and Toronto 1979), 27–47. Hare distinguishes between three consecutive sources of anti-Jewish imagery in the New Testament: Prophetic anti-Judaism, using Old Testament language; Jewish-Christian anti-Judaism (mainly in Luke and Acts); and Gentilizing anti-Judaism (mainly in Matthew).

[15] Langmuir, "Anti-Judaism as the Necessary Preparation for Antisemitism," in *Toward a Definition,* 58.

lectual life. That a popular odium can, and indeed did, grow out of such a phenomenon is obvious. But we should recognize that popular traditions and behavior against Jews and Judaism are rooted in more elemental prejudices. As to the legal aspects of anti-Judaism, they also appear to be derivative from theological conceptions and (mis)perceptions. Indeed, the legal system in Christian late antiquity, as reflected for instance in the Theodosian Code, remained essentially Roman law, and hence retained for some time, and to some degree, some protection of the Jews as citizens, and of Judaism as *religio licita*. It was only with Justinian that the last legal protection of the Jews disappeared.[16]

According to Langmuir, "three main nonrational reactions stand out" in the formation of anti-Judaism: the belief in the deficiency of Jewish understanding, the accusation of deicide, and the belief that historical events demonstrated that God was punishing the Jews for their deicide. These three reactions he sees as "the core of Christian anti-Judaism."[17] They do not, however, seem to have appeared simultaneously, but rather in successive order. Originally, the conflict between the early followers of Jesus and most other Jews revolved around hermeneutical issues: how to interpret the Holy Writ. The accusation of deicide was not formulated clearly until a later stage (the second century), while the perception of the tragic events of Jewish history as divine punishment developed only after the failure of the Bar Kochba revolt in 130.

The Adversus Judaeos *literature and the teaching of contempt*

The early Christian texts dealing specifically with the Jews and Judaism are well known, and various studies in the last fifty years have focused upon the development of Christian anti-Judaism in the first Christian centuries. The literary documents, to which we refer usually as the *Adversus Judaeos* literature, have been well charted, and their social and religious background has been duly analyzed. It consists of some ten extant texts, to which should be added at least eight lost treatises "against the Jews" from the Patristic period.[18] The extent to which these texts reflect actual hatred toward the Jews or only a virulent polemic

---

[16] The standard collection of Roman laws on the Jews and Judaism is now A. Linder, *The Jews in Roman Imperial Legislation* (Detroit 1987). For references to recent works on the legal status of the Jews in the Roman Empire, particularly in late antiquity, see A. Demandt, *Die Spätantike* (Munich 1988), 431–37, and K. L. Noethlichs, "Judentum und römisches Staat," in *Judentum, Antisemitismus und europäische Kultur,* ed. H. O. Horch (Tübingen 1988), 35–49. For the fourth century, see for instance G. Stemberger, *Juden und Christen im heiligen Land* (Munich 1987), 237–46.

[17] Langmuir, "From anti-Judaism to antisemitism," 285.

[18] For a broad general survey, see K. Hruby, *Juden und Judentum bei den Kirchenvätern* (Zurich 1971). See also L. M. McDonald, "Anti-Judaism in the Early Church Fathers," in *Anti-Semitism and Early Christianity: Issues of Polemics and Faith,* eds. C. A. Evans and D. A. Hagner (Minneapolis 1993), 215–52.

against their religion remains a moot point among scholars, whose views usually depend upon their own religious preferences.

Such traditions and perceptions were repeated and amplified throughout the centuries, not only in church, but also on the market place. Their major impact on the crystallization of the new, radical rejection of the Jews, both within and then without the tradition of the churches, is beyond dispute. In a series of seminal studies published in the fifties and sixties, the French historian Jules Isaac sought to show the ways through which the various polemical texts against the Jews permitted, encouraged, and carried what he called "l'enseignement du mépris" toward the Jews.[19] For him, this research was meant as an effort to unearth the roots of modern, racial antisemitism and its culmination in the mass murder of the Jews on European soil.

Slander and opprobrium do not make their first appearance in post-Constantinian Christianity. In the Gospel of John, "the Jews" (*hoi ioudaioi*) are described in no uncertain terms as belonging to the devil.[20] In the early second century, Basilides, whom we should probably learn to see as the first Christian philosopher,[21] could also use libelous terms in order to describe the Jews and their God as being in radical opposition to Christianity and to the norms of decency. The same century is not only that of Justin Martyr's *Dialogue with Trypho*, but also of Melito of Sardis's sermon *On the Pascha*, with its graphic description of the murder of the Lamb in Jerusalem. Melito, indeed, has been called "the first poet of Deicide."[22]

If we exclude the writings of the New Testament which reflect, to varying degrees, some sort of anti-Judaism, the *Adversus Iudaeos* literature can be said to begin with the anonymous *Epistle of Barnabas*, probably written in early second-century Alexandria, and Justin Martyr's *Dialogue with Trypho*, written around 150. From the *Dialogue*, which has been called "the last piece to be at least partially based on reminiscence of real contests,"[23] stems a long list of polemical texts, written in Greek, Latin, Syriac, and then in other Oriental as well as European languages, throughout the Patristic period, the Middle Ages, in By-

---

[19] On Jules Isaac and his work, see Gager, *Origins of Antisemitism*, 15–16 and notes.

[20] See esp. John 8: 44.

[21] See B. Layton, "The Significance of Basilides.in Ancient Christian Thought," *Representations* 28 (1989): 135–51.

[22] On Melito and his work, see S. G. Hall, ed., *Melito of Sardis, On Pascha and Fragments* (Oxford 1979). On Melito's attitude to the Jews, see S. G. Wilson, "Melito and Israel," in *Anti-Judaism in Early Christianity*, ed. S. G. Wilson, vol. 2 (Studies in Christianity and Judaism, 2; Waterloo, Ont. 1986), 81–102.

[23] A. Funkenstein, "Basic Types of Christian anti-Jewish Polemics in the Later Middle Ages," *Viator* 2 (1971): 373–82. See esp. M. Mach, "Justin Martyr's *Dialogus cum Tryphone Iudaeo* and the Development of Christian Anti-Judaism," in *Contra Iudaeos: Ancient and Medieval Polemics Between Christians and Jews*, eds. O. Limor and G. G. Stroumsa (Tübingen 1996). 27–47, and H. Remus, "Justin Martyr's Argument with Judaism," in *Anti-Judaism in Early Christianity*, ed. S. G. Wilson, 59–80.

zantium and in Western Europe, and, with renewed passion, since the Reformation. This traditional literature, which is rather repetitive in its argumentation, is now well mapped, thanks to the pioneering study of Lukyn Williams, published in the thirties,[24] and more recently, in the two hefty volumes of Heinz Schreckenberg. Both scan the literature in systematic fashion and will remain the basis for any serious investigation in the future.[25] One may divide the period that interests us here between the pre-Nicene times and the "golden centuries" of Patristic literature. From the former, Tertullian's *Adversus Judaeos* and *Adversus Marcionem* (two closely-related works) are the only Latin evidence.[26] More texts are extant from the later period. We may refer here at least to Eusebius of Caesarea's *Evangelical Demonstration*, the relevant chapters of Epiphanius of Salamis's *Panarion*, John Chrysostom's *Homilies against the Jews*, some of Aphrahat's *Homilies,* and Augustine's *Adversus Judaeos.*[27]

Charles Munier points out that a certain evolution in the argumentation and the themes can be detected from the second to the late fourth or early fifth centuries: "while the defensive genre prevails up to the third century, the authors of the third and fourth centuries can write more to demonstrate the Christian faith; finally come works containing invectives against the irreductible obduracy of the Jews".[28] Munier adds that "the writers of the Great Church express ever more strongly its members' awareness of being the true Israel, which has received the inheritance of the old Judaism, now rejected because of the infidelity of its members and because of the death of the Just one." This dynamism, reflected in the progressive radicalization of attitudes towards the Jews, is perhaps the most interesting characteristic of the *Adversus Iudaeos* literature. Yet, it has until now elicited very little attention.

In order to understand this radicalization, however, we should focus not so much on the polemical texts themselves as on their bearing on the question at hand, namely the transformation of Christian attitudes towards the Jews. As significant as it may be, the *Adversus Iudaeos* literature cannot alone adequately reflect the evolution of Christian attitudes toward Jews and Judaism. It is in the nature of these treatises to express anti-Jewish sentiments. But the conflict be-

---

[24] A. L. Williams, A*dversus Judaeos; a Bird's-Eye View of Christian Apologiae until the Renaissance* (Cambridge 1935).

[25] The first volume is of direct interest to us here: *Die christlichen Adversus-Iudaeos-Texte und ihr literarisches und historisches Umfeld (1.-11.Jh.)*, (Frankfurt and Bern 1982).

[26] The *Dialogue between Jason and Papiscus about Christ*, by Aristo of Pella, as well as the treatises *Against the Jews* by Miltiades and Apollinaris of Hierapolis are lost.

[27] There are also some rather fragmentary or spurious texts, while at least four treatises – by Eusebius of Emesa, Diodore of Tarsus, Theodoret of Cyrrhus, and Nestorius – seem to be lost. For the later anti-Jewish polemics in the East, see G. Dagron and V. Déroche, "Juifs et chrétiens dans l'Orient du 7e. siècle," *Travaux et Mémoires* 11 (1991): 1–273, and ibid., V. Déroche, "La polémique anti-judaïque au 6e. et au 7e. siècle; un mémento inédit, les *Kephalaia,*" 275–311, which includes a "catalogue raisonné" of the polemical texts.

[28] C. Munier, "Jews and Christians," in *EEC*, vol. 1:436 a-b.

tween Christians and Jews cannot be seen in isolation from the continuing polemic, throughout our period, between Christians and pagans. As David Rokeah has recently argued, what we have here is a triangle, in which the polemics among all sides are interdependent.[29] To refer to only two cases, within the context of his polemic against the pagan philosopher Celsus, Origen is able to show a clear recognition of the fundamental kinship between the faith of Israel and that of the Church[30]; and Eusebius wrote his *Evangelical Preparation* and *Demonstration* as twin works dealing with both anti-pagan polemics and Christian self-definition versus Judaism.[31]

The radicalization of attitudes toward the Jews reflects the growing estrangement of Christians from Jews in the Roman Empire. We often work under the assumption that the closer the ties, the harsher the conflict. This traditional postulate of historical research, however, seems to fail us here, for the fast-developing chasm between the two communities was not accompanied by any weakening of the polemic. Later Christian discourse hence reflects a different kind of conflict situation than the close, family-like argument of the first and the second centuries. Estrangement may entail lack of adequate knowledge about the opponent, but ignorance seems to be reflected not in a milder, but in a different, kind of intolerance.[32]

From the second to the fourth centuries, we can follow the birth, out of the traditional faith of Israel, not of one, but at least of two religions. Rabbinic Judaism, which emerged at Yavneh before the end of the first century, grew into a full-fledged religion with the development of Talmudic culture during the same centuries in which Christianity developed into a new religion with a structure and identity that were quite different from those of its genitor. Of necessity, the conflict between these two intimately related but quite different religions would differ from the internal conflict of the first two centuries. It is to the dynamics of this conflict that we now turn.

2. Religious conflict and Christian discourse

The Formation of Anti-Judaism

The social milieus in which the ecclesiastical writers lived and confronted the Jews or polemicized against Judaism have been carefully investigated in recent

---

[29] See D. Rokeach, *Jews, Pagans and Christians in Conflict* (Studia post-Biblica; Jerusalem and Leiden 1982).

[30] See G. G. Stroumsa, "The Hidden Closeness: on the Church Fathers and Judaism" (in Hebrew), *Mehkarei Yerushalaim be-Mahshevet Israel* 2 (1982): 170–75.

[31] A. Kofsky, "Eusebius of Caesaria and the Christian-Jewish Polemic," in *Contra Iudaeos: Ancient and Medieval Polemics between Christians and Jews,* 59–83.

[32] *Pace* Funkenstein, in his article quoted n. 23 above.

research. Not surprisingly, early second-century Alexandria has been found to be different in this regard from Sardis in approximately the same period, or from third-century Carthage, or from late fourth-century Antioch. In each case, the situation, and hence the tensions between Jews and Christians, are neither similar, nor even comparable. Contemporary interest in social history, fostered by the healthy disengagement of some Patristic scholars from traditional theological stances, has encouraged a perception of things which may be called the "conflict theory."[33] According to this theory, which is consciously at the antipodes of the traditional Christian attitude, anti-Judaism would reflect competition between the new religion and a Judaism that had not lost any of its dynamism and combativeness.

Brought about by new trends in historical research, the social background of religious ideas and attitudes has become prominent in the last generation. The many blessings brought by the new scholarly sensitivity are obvious: the study of religious ideas and of their development has become a full-fledged part of historical inquiry. It is in this context that much emphasis has recently been put on the social background of the anti-Jewish polemical texts. Much of the contemporary research has been based on the pioneering studies of James Parkes[34] and Marcel Simon.[35] While Parkes sought to follow the path of Christian attitudes towards Jews up to the early medieval period, Simon focused upon the early stages of the conflict between Jews and Christians in the Roman Empire, up to Constantine. Both started their research in the 1930s, under the growing shadow of racial antisemitism, and both intended their scholarship to deal courageously with the question of the early Christian roots of modern antisemitism.

Simon strove to show early Christian antisemitism unfolded only in the fourth century, arguing that the compelling reason for antisemitism was the continued religious vitality of Judaism. He was arguing against a long tradition that postulated that Judaism, having been disinherited by Christianity, had lost all dynamism or spiritual power of attraction by the second century, and had become a closed system with no interest in proselytism or religious competition.[36] Simon was rightly impressed by the theological background of such a view of things and by its historical inadequacy. For him, the social relationships between Jews and Christians in the Roman Empire were the context in which we should under-

---

[33] I borrow the phrase from Miriam S. Taylor, *Anti-Judaism and Early Christian Identity: A Critique of the Scholarly Consensus* (Studia Post-Biblica, 46; Leiden, New York and Köln 1994).

[34] See esp. J. Parkes, *The Conflict of the Church and the Synagogue: a Study in the Rise of Antisemitism* (London 1934).

[35] M. Simon, *Verus Israel: Relations entre juifs et chrétiens dans l'empire romain (135–425)* (Paris 1948).

[36] See the most recent study of Edouard Will and Claude Orieux, *"Prosélytisme juif"? Histoire d'une erreur* (Paris 1992). Will and Orieux argue convincingly that the commonly stated Jewish proselytism is in many ways a historiographical myth.

stand the development of Christian attitudes toward Jews and Judaism. Simon's discovery of the surprising dynamism of Judaism in the first centuries led him to conclude that this was the basis of contemporary Christian anti-Jewish attitudes. His explanation should be seen as reflecting the competition between the two religions. [37] To emphasize the social background of polemical expressions stood to reason, and Simon's work has had a far-reaching influence. In the last generation, scholars have sought to identify the difference between the various contexts of Jewish Christian relations in the Roman Empire. To each context, its own kind of anti-Judaism. The more dynamic Judaism was, the more it would have been a competitor of Christianity, and hence the more virulent Christian anti-Judaism would have been. The debate was thus moved from the theological to the historical level. Implicit in Simon's thesis was the assumption that anti-Judaism was not inherent to Christian doctrine or to its earliest sources.

Robert Wilken has devoted a full-fledged sensitive study of John Chrysostom's famous eight sermons *kata tôn ioudaiôn* read in church in Antioch in 386, and of their background.[38] Wilken agrees with Simon's basic approach, which insists that anti-Jewish views reflect the social and religious vitality of Judaism in late antiquity. Scholarship showed long ago that the sermons are directed mainly against *judaizantes*, i.e., Christians Judaizers, attracted by Jewish cultic practices, rather than against Jews. Yet as Wilken readily admits, the text shows a repetition and amplification of anti-Jewish arguments known from earlier Patristic literature. The sermons reflect, then, the conflict between Jews and Christians in the Eastern Mediterranean towards the end of the fourth century, and it is the background of this conflict that Wilken primarily seeks to reconstruct. As he rightly points out at the beginning of his study, however, it would be a serious methodological mistake to seek to describe Jews and Christians as if they were simply confronting each other. The scene, rather, should be represented in its full complexity: even toward the end of the fourth century, it included the "pagans" and Hellenism as a "real presence" that colored relationships between Jews and Christians. Indeed, for Christians, the threatening shadow cast by Julian and his attempts to de-establish Christianity and re-build the Temple were still present. Wilken's vivid reconstruction of the Antiochene scene is quite remarkable. We end up understanding Chrysostom's background and the patterns of the rhetoric of late antiquity so well that we almost forget the violence of his wording and the direct and indirect threat that it presented for Jews, hit first by

---

[37] The faith of Israel had undergone a major transformation after the destruction of the Temple, and hence one may legitimately alter the traditional filial metaphor and speak about two "sister religions"

[38] R. L. Wilken, *John Chrysostom and the Jews: Rhetoric and Reality in the Late Fourth Century* (The Transformation of the Classical Heritage; Berkeley, Los Angeles, and London 1983). See also W. A. Meeks and R. L. Wilken, *Jews and Christians in Antioch in the First Four Centuries of the Common Era* (Sources of Biblical Study, 13; Missoula, Mont. 1978).

theological discourse, soon afterwards by disenfranchizing laws and, from time to time, subject to blatantly violent attacks on their persons or property.

In a recent publication, Robert MacLennan has presented a detailed study of four of the most important pre-Nicene anti-Jewish writings.[39] According to him, anti-Judaism only arose in the third and fourth centuries, from misreadings of these early writings.[40] For MacLennan, they primarily reflect attempts at Christian self-definition, using conceptions about Jews and Judaism which in all probability did not reflect a concrete knowledge of Jews or of social and intellectual interaction with them.[41] Altogether, MacLennan's research is more informative than convincing. It does strike one as an attempt, rather apologetic in spirit, at exonerating the early Christian polemicists from "embarrassing" attitudes towards Jews and Judaism.

Anti-Judaism as Part of Christian Discourse

Proponents of the second trend of research, which grew out of a certain dissatisfaction with the previous approach, stress that, in most cases, early Christian anti-Judaism seems to cater more for an internal Christian need of identity or definition than to reflect active confrontation between two communities. For this school of thought, Patristic anti-Judaism must above all be understood as an inner Christian discourse, having little to do with social external challenges.

In a recent study, Luke Johnson has argued that anti-Jewish slander in the New Testament should be understood in the context of ancient polemics and its conventional nature, which "means that its chief rhetorical import is connotative rather than denotative."[42] In other words, what is said about opponents (here, "the Jews") should be understood as expressing their perceived identity as opponents rather than reflecting "reality." What is true of the New Testament texts is also, of course, true of later literature. Thus Michael Mach can write, in his study of Justin's *Dialogue:* "It does not really matter whether Justin's accusations are "historically" given facts – they are prescribed by his system, which

---

[39] R. MacLennan, *Early Christian Texts on Jews and Judaism* (Brown Judaic Studies, 194; Atlanta 1990). MacLennan studies *Barnabas,* which he calls "a moderate approach," Justin ("an apologetic essay"), Melito ("a poetic defense"), and Tertullian ("a legal defense"). He states, rightly, that these and similar texts cannot be understood out of the context within which they were written. A major aspect of this context is the cities of the Mediterranean themselves, where Jews and Christians lived. Thanks to important new archeological discoveries, this context can now be studied more closely. Seeking therefore to understand the conflictual social background of the *Adversus Iudaeos* literature, MacLennan concludes each of his studies with a "verdict of acquittal": in each case, he finds the author not guilty of having propounded anti-Jewish ideas or of "degrading Jews."

[40] Ibid., 153. MacLennan does not seem to distinguish between anti-Judaism and antisemitism.

[41] Ibid., 152

[42] See n. 13 above.

keeps the Old Testament safe for the Church and the Church safe from Marcion's non-Jewish Christianity."[43] In Rosemary Ruether's words, the Jewish pro-
tagonist in most of the *Adversus Iudaeos* texts is only a "straw figure."

Ruether's *Faith and Fratricide* became very influential soon after its publication in 1974, particularly among North American Roman Catholic scholars.[44] In
this work, Ruether argued with great verve that Patristic anti-Judaism reflected
an intrinsic need of Christian self-affirmation. She pointed out the relative lack
of appeal to Jews in the *Adversus Iudaeos* literature. Her fundamental argument
seems to be rooted in the fact of the Christian supercession of Judaism. As both
communities, and very soon both religions, vied for the same heritage, and for
the same sacred texts, conflict was inevitable, particularly on the part of the new-
comer. Gerhard Ladner has expressed similar ideas. According to him, it is essentially the fight over the proper understanding of the Hebrew Bible that triggered, perforce, Christian anti-Judaism. Following in Ruether's footsteps from
Protestant quarters, Lloyd Gaston perceives Christian anti-Judaism as arising
out of an inner-Christian theological debate, rather than out of rivalry with a living Judaism.[45] For him, Patristic anti-Judaism is a by-product of a Christian self-
definition in which the Church was led to deny to Judaism certain central characteristics of its own self-understanding.

In an interesting study, David Efroymson has insisted on the fact that Patristic
anti-Judaism is the other side of the Fathers' opposition to Marcion and to Gnostic dualism.[46] Efroymson calls attention to a very important aspect of the debate
that had been oddly ignored: the role played by the fight of the Church Fathers
against Gnostic dualism in the broader framework of their constant attempts at
a better, sharper, and also more limited definition of legitimate Christian identity. For this emerging identity, the rejection of Judaism and of Gnosticism are
perceived to be parallel steps: for the heresiologists, both Jews and Gnostics, indeed, sin essentially by their inability to properly understand the Bible by reading it in spiritual fashion. Judaism, in the eyes of the Christian heresiologists, had
become a proto-heresy of sorts, the model of all later willful distortions of the
Christian message. In Efroymson's words, it is by means of the "anti-Judaic
myth" that the Fathers "retrieve" Jesus from Marcion for "orthodox" Chris-

---

[43] Cf. n. 23 above.

[44] R. Ruether, *Faith and Fratricide: the Theological Roots of Anti-Semitism* (New York Press,
1974). See also idem., "The *Adversus Judaeos* Tradition in the Church Fathers: the Exegesis of
Christian Anti-Judaism," in *Aspects of Jewish Culture in the Middle Ages,* ed. P. E. Szarmach
(Albany 1979), 27–50, reprinted in *Essential Papers on Judaism and Christianity in Conflict,* ed.
J. Cohen (New York 1991), 174–89. For the impact of *Faith and Fratricide,* see the debate in *Au-
schwitz: Beginning of a New Era?* ed. E. Fleischner (New York 1974), 73–108, and A. Davies,
ed., *Antisemitism and the Foundations of Christianity* (cf. n. 14 above).

[45] G. Ladner, "Retrospect," in *Anti-Judaism in Early Christianity,* ed. S. G. Wilson, 164–74.

[46] D. Efroymson,"The Patristic Connection," in *Antisemitism and the Foundations of Christianity,* ed. A. Davies, 98–117.

tianity. Like Gaston, then, Efroymson views anti-Judaism as a by-product of a Christian self-definition that did not take Jewish self-understanding into account.[47] The same path has been followed by John Gager, who insists on the role of "anti-Judaism in the theological response to Marcion and the Christian Gnostics."

Most recently, the focus on social context in the study of early Christian anti-Judaism has been challenged on methodological grounds by Miriam Taylor. In an original piece of work, Taylor offers a thorough analysis of what she calls "conflict theory," and finds it lacking on various counts.[48] Taylor argues that "conflict theory," of which Marcel Simon is the main proponent, "underestimates the traditional character of anti-Jewish writings, because of its focus on the social foundation of anti-Judaism."[49] At the root of her criticism lies the claim that this approach exonerates Christianity too easily from the accusation of a deep, inherent anti-Judaism, because of its "reluctance to view the theological as a genuine order of motivation."[50] Thus, in sharp contrast to the "conflict theory," Taylor argues forcefully that anti-Jewish polemics lie at the very core of Christian discourse. Her thesis "aims at establishing that the Jews in the writings of the Church Fathers are neither 'men of straw' nor 'formidable rivals,' but symbolic figures who play an essential role in the communication and development of the Church's conception of God's plans for the chosen people, and in the formation of the Church's own cultural identity."[51] If this is the case, she claims, the Judaism negated by the Fathers arises not from contemporary pressures on the part of Jews, but rather from an internal dynamic that negates a symbolic rather than a living Judaism.

In this approach, therefore, the roots of anti-Judaism are said to lie in Christian discourse itself. Being at the antipodes of the "conflict theory," it seems to suffer from opposite weaknesses. While the first approach looked only at the social context, ignoring the autonomous power of theological beliefs and their ability to shape perceptions of the other, the "intrinsic anti-Judaism thesis" seems to approach "Christian discourse" as if it were a well-defined and fixed entity, unchanged by historical circumstance. In each case, the model suffers from a static character that seriously weakens its ability to persuade. I shall seek here to offer an alternative analysis of early Christian anti-Judaism between the second to the fourth centuries.

Gerhard Ladner has argued that the puzzle of anti-Judaism is inherent to the conflict about the Old Testament and its meaning. For Ladner, it is the dispute about the proper interpretation of the Old Testament that has been at the very

---

[47] Ibid., 100.
[48] M. Taylor, *Anti-Judaism and Early Christian Identity.*
[49] Ibid., 173.
[50] Ibid., 253.
[51] Ibid., 7.

heart of the Christian polemic against Judaism throughout history. "The real Jewish-Christian problem then for Chrysostom as for all the Fathers of the Church was the relation between the Old and the New Testament. We can see this perhaps most clearly in Saint Augustine's treatise against the Jews."[52] In other words, one could say that the conflict is one of inter-textuality. The conflictual basis of Christian anti-Judaism, then, should be identified primarily as an intellectual rather than a social conflict, or, more precisely, as a conflict involving identity. The truth of Christianity is perceived as demanding the demise of Judaism, and hence the opprobrium upon the *perfides iudaei*.

3. The dynamic character of religious identity

Religious pluralism in the Roman Empire

I have presented above the two main trends of contemporary research. As we have seen, both offer important contributions and insights. Both approaches, however, leave us with some unanswered questions. The "conflict theory" and the "Christian discourse" approaches seem to be based upon false or at least incomplete assumptions. Both are established upon rather simplistic postulates, which do not adequately reflect changing historical reality. The "conflict theory" approach tends to ignore the deep transformation of the Jews' situation and hence of Jewish-Christian relationships from the second to the fourth century.[53] Change in this period was multiform, and did not follow a single vector. The virulence of a Basilides' theological or metaphysical antisemitism (his radical hatred of the God and the religion of Israel), for instance, cannot really be explained solely on the basis of references to social frictions between Jews and Christians in early second-century Alexandria, as Bentley Layton has recently attempted to do.[54] Something else is at work here, a deep ambivalence that transcends social conditions and the tense relations between two urban groups. Similarly, the lack of deep animosity toward, and of vicious expressions about the Jews on the part of Augustine, in the late fourth and early fifth centuries reflects more than the lack of tensions between Jews and Christians in Africa at the time. In both cases, it is the overall theological attitude that informs their approach to "the Jewish question."

Ruether's argument that anti-Judaism is inherent to Christian discourse assumes that there is one essential discourse, and does not take into account the

---

[52] "Aspects of Patristic Anti-Judaism," 360.

[53] This radical transformation has been emphasized anew by Judith Lieu in her "History and Theology in Christian Views of Judaism," in *The Jews among Pagans and Christians in the Roman Empire,* eds. J. Lieu, J. North, and T. Rajak (London and New York 1992), esp. p. 94.

[54] See. n. 21 above.

deep transformations of Christian discourse itself during our period. The context and meaning of the rejection of the Jews in the Gospel of John, for instance, are vastly different from Chrysostom's anti-Jewish invective. We cannot speak of a single early Christian or Patristic attitude towards Jews and Judaism, or imply its existence. Both the relationship of Christianity to Judaism and the Christians' perceptions of Jews are totally different at the end of the fourth century than they had been three hundred years previously.

What has changed, essentially, is the self-perception of Christians – the parameters of Christian identity. With the conversion of the emperor, Christians no longer perceived themselves primarily in relationship to *vetus Israel*. Their newly-acquired self-confidence was reflected in their clear identity as a religion sui generis, expressing truth and God's revelation, now resounding throughout the *oikoumenè*. In front of such miraculous and providential behavior, the obstinate, unexpected, and inexplicable rejection of truth by the Jews deeply transformed the Christian perception of *vetus Israel*, of the Jews, and of their land. The relationship then becomes almost reversed, with the Christians moving to the top, the Jews to the bottom, and the perceived spiritual reality becoming a major element in the future deterioration of the legal and social situation of the Jews in late antiquity.[55]

Therefore, it is not sufficient to study *both* history and discourse. It is the history of Christian discourse, its transformations throughout the first centuries, which must stand at the core of our research, if we are to understand the paradoxical radicalization of anti-Judaism in theological discourse over time. This radicalization, which reflects the growing intellectual and religious, although not necessarily social, distance between Christians and Jews in the Roman Empire.

John North has recently offered a fresh overview of the development of religious pluralism during the first Christian centuries.[56] Following the insights supplied by A. D. Nock in his classic study of conversion, North points out that in the Hellenistic world, and then in the Roman Empire, religion is no longer a direct function of the city-state, but was perceived as implying a choice of the individual between competing systems, between "differentiated groups offering different qualities of religious doctrine, different experiences, insights, or just different myths and stories to make sense of the absurdity of human experience."[57] The process of what North describes with the metaphor of the "supermarket of religions" had already started at Rome under the Republic. North himself has analyzed with remarkable acumen (although his terms may sometimes smack of anachronism) the "secularization" which occurred in the late Republic together

---

[55] See. G. G. Stroumsa, *Savoir et Salut* (Paris 1992), 111–23.
[56] J. North, "The Development of Religious Pluralism," in *The Jews among Pagans and Christians*, 174–93.
[57] Ibid., 178.

with the retreat of the sacred from areas it had occupied until then, and the emergence of new religious institutions specializing in the "sacred," and hence concentrating its manifestations within defined, limited areas.[58] According to North, it is this "secularization" that permitted the development of religious pluralism on a scale previously unknown. As North points out, however, together with pluralism we can follow the sharpening of religious conflicts, and "the emergence of persecution as a new possibility." As the new religious associations began striving to gain followers, competing on the market, as it were, the competitors sought to prevent their opponents from "stealing their clientele." Among the new competing groups, the Christians held pride of place, since, in contradistinction to "oriental cults" or Judaism, the whole religion was established upon the idea of conversion, i.e., choice, and since the structure of the new religion quite explicitly rejected any cultural or ethnic tradition for its self-identity (except, of course, in the metaphorical sense of *verus Israel*).

This is the general background of the development of religious polemics under the Roman Empire. Polemics, then, is the literary reflection of the conflictual relationship between competing religious groups. But it serves multiple purposes. It does not intend only, or even mainly, to convince and convert, but also to strengthen the faith, or the self-confidence, of those who are already converted. Polemics, indeed, serves as a major tool in group-identity building and affirmation.

In the fourth century, however, the "market situation" described by North changed in some drastic ways, with the transformation of non-religious "institutions" – first among them the person of the Emperor – which gained a new religious identification and the aura that comes with it. In the Christianized empire of late antiquity, we can discern a clear advance of the sacred, a new invasion of religious themes, motifs, beliefs, and practices which pervaded different levels and corners of society from which they had until then been absent. This process, which has been recently analyzed anew with much insight by Robert Markus,[59] entailed the profound transformation of the "free religious market" known in the first few centuries. In other words, the conversion of the emperor brought with it the disappearance of religious pluralism, i.e., of the legitimation rather than of the actual existence of religious plurality. When Christianity was still a *religio illicita,* and the early Christian intellectuals were striving for intellectual respectability, they had been the first in the ancient world to develop a coherent argument about the need for religious tolerance, and hence pluralism. Oddly enough, it is their fourth- and fifth-century heirs who carried out the de-legitimation of religious pluralism.

---

[58] See J. North, "Religious Toleration in Republican Rome," *Proceedings of the Cambridge Philosophical Society* 205, N.S. 25 (1979): 85–103, esp. 96.

[59] R. Markus, *The End of Ancient Christianity* (Cambridge 1991).

In the Hellenistic world, the rise of faith as a central component of religion had displayed the *mos maiorum* as the core of religious identity and behavior. The victory of Christian *pistis* that ushered in late antiquity closed the circle, in a sense, as it transformed the parameters of identity and brought to the drastic curtailing of religious pluralism. It is in the context of this revolution in religiosity that we must understand the radicalization of anti-Jewish attitudes.

The revolution in religiosity and the demonization of the Jews

Justinian dropped the important law in the Theodosian codex that explicitly declared Judaism a *religio licita*. But such a radical step did not go unheralded, nor did this momentous demise of the Jews come as a surprise. Judaism had been deprived of religious value and respect long before the Jews were disenfranchised legally. Indeed, Justinian's measure appears as the last step in a series of limitations of Jewish self-expression and respectability. After the Christians' political victory in the empire, the new triumphalism did not intend so much to annihilate as to humiliate the vanquished. As Peter Brown has expressed it recently, the Jews' newly lowered position was supposed to remind all of Christ's victory.[60] After the fourth century, orthodox Christians treated their vanquished competitors – pagans, Jews, and particularly heretics – in a manner similar to how Islam treated monotheistic non-believers, labeling them *ahl al-kitab*.

But, in sharp contradistinction to the situation under Islam, that of late antiquity was anything but stable. What counts most here is the vector, the direction of trends and patterns. And there is no doubt that what followed was a constant degradation of the legal status and social standing of the Jews and of popular attitudes towards them. While non-toleration of the Jews was limited during this period, it seems to have increased over time. To be sure, this degradation was not a linear process, and could be observed only in the *longue durée*.

In the Hellenistic and Roman worlds, religious pluralism was predicated upon identity being formulated in ethnic or cultural rather than religious terms. The religious revolution of the fourth century meant, among other things, that religion became a major component of identity. In many ways, this revolution reflected a passage from cultural to religious identity. Indeed, the entire world seemed to recognize the new truth, to follow the new faith. The optimistic conviction that the conversion of all and sundry throughout the *oikoumenè* reflected the perception of the manifest destiny of Christianity was strongly expressed toward the end of the fourth century in the verses of Prudentius: there was one God, one law, one king.[61] Theodoret, more or less, a contemporary of Prudentius, opened his *Ecclesiastical History* with an exposition of wonder at

---

[60] P. Brown, "Christianization and Religious Conflict" (n. 6 above).
[61] Prudentius, *Peristephanon*, II, 429.

the sight of the conversion of the most exotic peoples. From the Armenians and the Georgians to the Abyssinians and the Indians, foreign and barbarian peoples all converted to the newly-revealed truth. But he completed this statement with a sharp expression of disappointment at the sight of the "irredentist" Jews – the very people of Judea to whom Christ had been sent – who were still refusing to recognize the Messiah announced by their own prophets.

As I have already noted, animosity usually seems to be greater between closely-related groups than between more distant enemies. Thus, Christian heretics were treated with particular animosity, and suffered much more than either pagans or Jews at Christian hands. Yet Christian anti-Judaism appears to have grown with time, even though social relations between Jews and Christians do not seem to have been particularly rocky during most of that period. The key to understanding this historical paradox lies in the continuing frustration of Christian intellectuals and leaders. The continued refusal of Jews to accept Christianity set them apart more and more clearly from the growing Christian majority. The mass conversions of pagans, and the almost complete demise of paganism and of the dualist heresies in the fourth century, removed them as perceived threats to orthodox Christianity. In the Christianized empire, Judaism came to be perceived as the only remaining major negation of the universally proclaimed truth. What had been a family argument came now to be perceived as a permanent and public insult to God and His true faith. Julian, who tried to think and to behave as a pagan, but felt as a Christian, knew intuitively that the deepest symbolic violence he could inflict upon the Galileans was to let the Jews rebuild their Temple. Indeed, Christian sensitivities remained hurt for a generation after the failed attempt. This may partly explain the verbal violence of Chrysostom, as Robert Wilken has shown. If our evidence is to be trusted, the radicalization of anti-Judaism shows that the continuing existence of the Jews seems to have become with time less and less tolerable for the Christian mind, or at least for the minds of Christian theologians.[62]

Theological anti-Judaism is identical neither with legal discrimination nor with popular defamation, but it is hard to avoid the conclusion that it set the stage for both. In this instance, intellectual perceptions fueled the transformation of social attitudes. Still, there is little evidence to show that the beliefs and practices of Judaism in the fourth century were considered threatening, or, on the other hand, had been rendered powerless by the appearance of Christianity.[63] Thus, it seems that the Church Fathers were more than the carriers of anti-Jewish sentiment. Rather they seem to have been its "aggravators," whose aggressive rhetoric helped transform anti-Jewish theological argument into what can be called antisemitic prejudice.

---

[62] See J. Lieu, "History and Theology in Christian Views of Judaism."
[63] Gager, *Origins of Antisemitism*, 133.

In a sense, to the extent that there was a qualified religious toleration of the Jews in the social reality of late antiquity, it can be said to have come about despite theology. It is thanks to the legal tradition of Rome, which the theologians could not quite erase or transform overnight, and to the limited measure of Christian conviction or enthusiasm on the part of the populace (a trait true in any society), that the Jews retained for several centuries some kind of economic integration, social status, and legal standing within "Christian" society.

Fourth-century Christian thinkers were the inheritors of an ever-growing tradition of literary polemics with Jews and Judaism. This tradition, as we have argued, was not stable. Rather, the texts show a growing propensity to identify contemporary Jews with the killers of Christ, and to perceive them in sharp contradistinction to both the ancient Hebrews, sons of the promise, and their spiritual heirs, the Christians, *verus Israel*. Such expressions and vocabulary, however, became radically transformed in the aftermath of the Constantinian revolution. To use Weberian parlance, one can speak here of *Politisierung*. Weber referred to *Entpolitisierung* as the process through which intellectuals in different societies of the ancient world, when ejected from the corridors of power, developed new religious conceptions usually having salvation at their center.[64] If the earliest strata of Christianity can legitimately be described as stemming from such *entpolitisiert* milieus, fourth-century Christian writers reflect the inverse trend: they learned to express anew ideas originally developed without any direct contact with political reality and power. Throughout the fourth century, from Eusebius to Ambrose, Christian writers taste the new proximity of political power, and most of them found it sweet.[65]*Neutralization* is a process common in the history of religions, whereby concepts once understood literally become less pregnant with immediate meaning under new conditions. *Politisierung*, on its side, is rendered possible by the activization that occurs in the new framework. Activization, then, is the opposite of neutralization. As such, it helps explain the new semantics of traditional attitudes carried by the theological literature.

The transformation of the context in which the Christian religion had been expressing itself led to deep changes within religiosity itself. Acting upon one's beliefs no longer meant the willingness to suffer for their public affirmation. It now meant insisting that these beliefs be proclaimed and respected up to the highest levels of the state. This resulted in a lack of tolerance toward those who publicly denied God's Word and Truth, on the part of the heirs of the second-century Apologists, who had been the first to articulate a conception of religious tolerance. Pagan cult, heresies, and the Jewish presence were all felt to sully the

---

[64] See H. Kippenberg, *Die vorasiatischen Erlösungsreligionen in ihrem Zusammenhang mit der antiken Stadtherrschaft: Heidelberger Max-Weber-Vorlesungen 1988* (Frankfurt 1991).

[65] See G. W. Bowersock, "Architects of Competing Transcendental Visions in Late Antiquity," in *The Origins and Diversity of Axial Age Civilizations,* ed. S. N. Eisenstadt (Albany 1986), 280–87.

newly-shining splendor of Christianity in varying degrees. In seeking proper
ways to react to this new challenge to their feelings, subtly crossing the boundaries between private sentiment and public decency, Christian intellectuals
came to rely on their literary baggage. But in applying the texts and themes of
the past to the new political reality, they seriously distorted the meaning of texts
written under radically different conditions. In this way, the semantics of themes
of anti-Jewish polemics first developed in the second century soon became deeply transformed.

In December 388, Ambrose, bishop of Milan, wrote a letter to Theodosius
from Aquilea, upon hearing that the Emperor had ordered the bishop of Callinicum to pay for rebuilding the local synagogue that a Christian mob had
burned in a pogrom. In his letter, Ambrose argued that it should not be said
that Christians, in the Christian empire, submitted to the humiliation of helping
the cult of the Jews, who do not recognize Christ.[66] The letter expresses in the
strongest possible terms Ambrose's inability to accept the legally binding order
of the emperor. Indeed, he forced Theodosius to recant by cancelling his previous order. A few years after the turn of the century, in 414, Cyril, bishop of
Alexandria, instigated the expulsion of the Jews from the city.[67] And as early as
the mid-fourth century, Ephrem had vituperated violently against the Jews in
his hymns.[68]

One should note, of course, that the attitude and the abusive language of Ambrose, Chrysostom, Ephrem, or Cyril was not universal among the Church
Fathers. Suffice it to mention two examples. From the East, Aphrahats' tone
against the Jews in his *Demonstrationes*[69] is strikingly different, and eminently
more civilized, than that of Ephrem; while Augustine in the West was able, like
Aphrahat, to polemicize against the Jews while retaining a modicum of decency
in his language.[70] As we now know from his recently-discovered letters, in radi-

---

[66] Ambrose, letter 40. See *Ambrose, Letters*, tr. M. M. Beyenka (The Fathers of the Church;
Washington, D. C. 1954), 6–19. Cf his letter to his sister Marcellina, also written in December
388 (Letter 41), pp. 385–97. Ambrose reveals, incidentally, that the assembly place of the Valen-
tinians which was destroyed on the same occasion was not ordered by the emperor to be rebuilt.
Cf. n. 95 to Gibbon, *Decline and Fall*, ch. 27, which refers to a law from September 393 (*Codex
Theodosianus* XVI. 8. 9). On another occasion, when Ambrose was absent, Theodosius forba-
de the destruction of synagogues. On Ambrose's attitude toward Jews, see also his Letter 77.3.
On his general attitude toward violence, see L. J. Swift, "St. Ambrose on Violence and War,"
Transactions and Proceedings of the American Philological Association 101 (1970): 533–43.

[67] See M. Simon, *Verus Israel*, 156.

[68] See A. P. Hayman, "The Image of the Jew in the Syriac Anti-Jewish Polemical Literature,"
in *To See Ourselves as Others See Us*, eds. J. Neusner and E. S. Frerichs, 423–41.

[69] Aphrahat refers to the Jews mainly in *Demonstr.* 16 and 19. For a recent work, see J. Neusner, *Judaism and Christianity in the Age of Constantine* (Chicago 1987), 191–202.

[70] See esp. B. Blumenkranz, *Die Judenpredigt Augustins* (Basler Beiträge zur Geschichtswis-
senschaft, 25; Basel 1946), and his "Augustin et les juifs; Augustin et le judaïsme," *Recherches
Augustiniennes* 1 (1958): 225–41.

cal contradistinction to his former spiritual guide Ambrose, Augustine insisted that the law should protect Jews as well as Christians.

Nonetheless, it seems that the more radical attitude carried the day, and had more influence upon the formation of the medieval Christian construction of the Jew. As anti-Jewish arguments became increasingly radicalized, they were subtly transformed into arguments against the Jewish people. Christian literati felt the painfully public and attractive presence of the Jewish cult as a slur. In constructing the new Christian identity, they felt an almost instinctive need to redefine the legal status and perceived identity of all outsiders to the faith as a most urgent desideratum. The Jews, together with the pagans and the heretics, had to be publicly vanquished and humiliated.

The detectable growth in the verbal violence of anti-Jewish expression on the part of the Church Fathers can at least in part be explained by precisely this dissonance between the *Adversus Iudaeos* tradition and the new, *politisiert,* reality. This increase in verbal violence presaged the emergence of the multiform legal and physical violence toward the Jews throughout medieval and modern European history. It can be considered puzzling, since, as we have seen, it appeared at a time when the Jewish and Christian communities were growing apart in their social life and culture. But, while daily frictions may have been less frequent than previously, the Jew remained ever present in the Christian mind. It may even be argued that an abstract Jew was constructed precisely when Jewish presence was felt to be becoming less concrete.

It should noted that the transformation of the perception of the Jew occurred simultaneously with the weakening of the pagans' position. To be sure, the pagans remained an unavoidable presence in the world of late antiquity. But their threat had been drastically reduced.

After Julian's short but momentous reign, the fear of a possible return of paganism remained for some time,[71] but the Christians knew, in an essential way, that they were the victors and that the gods of Antiquity had been defeated forever. These gods, of course, they called demons. The *daimones* had died. Or had they? The character of the demons essentially vanished, but although they might disappear, but they did so in subtle ways, soon to reappear in another guise. As people living in late antiquity, Christians believed that demons were all around them in the air. Both demons and angels continued to be felt by all. To paraphrase Descartes, in late antiquity the *daimones* were "la chose du monde la mieux partagée".[72] So if the official believers in demons, the propagators of their

---

[71] See R. Wilken, "The Jews and Christian Apologetics after Theodosius' *Cunctos Populos,*" *HTR* 73 (1980): 451–71.

[72] See *s.v.* "Geister (Dämonen)", *RAC* 9: 688–797. On the different status of demons among pagans and Christians, see R. Lane Fox, *Pagans and Christians* (Harmonsworth 1986), 327–30. On the Christian perception of pagan demons, see Lampe, *A Patristic Greek Lexicon, s.v. "daimon"* (328–31).

cult, had been crushed, somebody else had to become their representative – the *paraklètos tou satanas*, the *advocatus diaboli* – to keep in touch with the demons. The Jews were invested with this power which the pagans had lost. In the Christian mind, the Jews became the inheritors of some of the pagans' qualities and religious (or anti-religious) identity.[73]

> Although such beasts are unfit for work, they are fit for killing. ... They live for their bellies, they gape for the things of this world, their condition is no better than that of pigs or goats because of their wanton ways and excessive gluttony. ... Do you see that demons live in their souls?

Thus Saint Chrysostom, one of the "five pillars" of the Orthodox Church, referred to the Jews of Antioch in 386.[74] In the same sermon *kata tôn ioudaiôn*, against the Jews – or more precisely, against the Judaizers – Chrysostom likened the Jewish synagogue to places of cult:

> For the synagogue is not only a brothel and a theater; it is also a den of robbers and a lodging for wild beasts... the synagogue is a dwelling for demons. God is not worshipped there. [In brief, the Jews are] doing battle with God.[75]

Few texts underline so strikingly the poignant paradox posed by Christian anti-Judaism, *sive* antisemitism: how to explain the growth of such hatred in believers in the religion of love, in particular in its spiritual and intellectual leaders? Chrysostom's discourses *kata tôn ioudaiôn* reveal a new trend in the attitude toward the Jews of some Christian intellectuals in the late fourth century: their perception as the inheritors of the pagans and of the latter's false claims and lies; their relationship with the false gods, or demons, previously associated only with the

---

[73] The "demonic" qualities attributed by the Christians to the Jews, particularly in the middle ages, have indeed been investigated, but the strange mechanism by which their "demonization" was made possible is still in need of clarification. Neither J. F. Russell, *Satan: the Early Christian Tradition* (Ithaca and London 1981), nor N. Forsyth *The Old Enemy: Satan and the Combat Myth* (Princeton 1987)], seem to mention the dubious relationships between Satan and the Jews in early Christian consciousness. For the medieval conception, see the pioneering work of Joshua Trachtenberg, *The Devil and the Jews* (Philadelphia 1983 [first published 1943]), cf. esp. 20–21. See further G. Dahan, *Les intellectuels chrétiens et les juifs au moyen âge* (Paris 1990), 520–23, as well as M. Lazar, "The Lamb and the Scapegoat: the Dehumanization of the Jews in Mediaeval Propaganda Imagery," in *Antisemitism in Times of Crisis,* eds. S. Gilman and S. Katz (New York 1991), 38–80.

For a late medieval confirmation that the Jew was typically perceived as different from other human beings, indeed not quite human, see the testimony of Salomon ibn Verga, in his *Shevet Yehuda*: "The Christian...believes that the Jew is merely an animal in the guise of a human being and that his soul will end up in the lowest chamber of hell. ...", quoted by F. Niewöhner, "Are the Founders of Religions Impostors?," in *Maimonides and Philosophy,* eds. Sh. Pines and Y. Yovel (The Hague 1986), 242.

[74] *Adv. Iud.*, I. 2.6. I quote from the translation of P. W. Harkins, *Saint John Chrysostom, Discourses against Judaizing Christians* (Fathers of the Church, 68; Washington 1979).

[75] Ibid., I. 2. 7; I. 3. 1. As Simon already noted, the first homily is both the most characteristic of the eight as well as the most virulent one against the Jews.

pagans. The synagogues of the Jews were likened to pagan temples, because they were "places of the demons," and they were called "theaters." There was, how-ever, one major difference between the situation of pagans and Jews: while the pagans were outsiders par excellence, the Jews were to some extent insiders. Their ambiguous situation may be described as that of "the enemy within," the Christian's *Doppelgänger*.

This helps to explain why the perceived threat from the Jews not failed to dis-appear, but seems to grow stronger over time, alongside the demise of paganism. While the heretics were total insiders, the Jews' situation was ambiguous, sui generis. The clear boundaries between the Jewish and the Christian com-munities might be clear, and the fences strong, but the threat was perceived from within the Christian mind.

The demonization of the Jews was rendered possible not only by the weaken-ing of the pagan threat, which left the Jews as the most serious competitors of the Christians, but also by the tradition that associated Jews with Satan, a tradition inherited by Christianity from the Gospel of John. Indeed, such expressions are not surprising in a tradition that could quote Jesus, even before the end of the first century, as telling the Jews:

> You are from your father the devil, and you choose to do your father's desire. He was a murderer from the beginning and does not stand in the truth, because there is no truth in him. When he lies, he speaks according to his own nature, for he is a liar and the father of lies (John 8: 44).[76]

But this trend is not universal. Other tones could still heard in Christian dis-course. First, the legal system was not immediately influenced by the new trend. It was only later that the delegitimation of Judaism by the Christian intellectuals would leave its clear mark on the laws, a process that culminated in Justinian's cancellation of the legitimacy of synagogal cult.[77] Like legal developments, popular attitudes came second. They were fueled by the conceptions of intellec-tuals, whose reactions reflected their frustration. For them, the continued un-hampered existence of the Jews puts an intolerable blemish on the ecumenical success of Christianity, otherwise shining in all nations and peoples, within and without the empire. Indeed, John Gager insists on the fact that popular Chris-tianity was not nearly as convinced as its leaders that the beliefs and practices of Judaism had been rendered powerless by the appearance of Christianity.[78] We must therefore conclude by positing the concomitant existence of two trends, two attitudes, in the *Adversus Iudaeos* literature of late antiquity.

---

[76] The demonization of the Jews should be seen as part of a broader trend which included the growth of the role of Satan, as well as the demonization of sex; cf. H. Chadwick, "*Enkrateia,*" *RAC*, 5: 349ff.

[77] See. Langmuir, "Transformation of anti-Judaism," 86: "Toleration had continued in Italy after Ambrose because of the countervailing imperial tradition of Roman Law." Cf. ibid., 99.

[78] Gager, *Origins of Antisemitism*, 133.

Through the pervasive influence it exerted, Patristic language of opprobrium against the Jews, especially their demonization after the pagan threat had more or less disappeared, became one of the main roots of European racial antisemitism. In the middle of the third century, Origen, answering the philosopher Celsus, was able to see the two biblical religions as standing, on some crucial issues, on the same side of the barricade in the war against paganism. But this was not possible for Chrysostom. By his time, it was mainly Judaism that Christianity viewed as the radical enemy – and the stakes were high: "Don't you realize," he says, "if the Jewish rites are holy and venerable, our way of life must be false."[79] It is this perception of the continued existence of Judaism as a perpetual threat to the very survival and truth of the Christian religion that was to prove so ominous of the future.

---

[79] *Adv. Iud.* I. 6. 5.

Part III

Shaping the Person

Chapter 9

From Repentance to Penance:
Tertullian's *De Paenitentia* in Context

The ritualization of repentance, the public expression of a deeply intimate trans-formation of the self, is a matter of central significance in any religion. In Christianity, the development in the first centuries of *paenitentia secunda*, an activity public by nature, and its progressive transformation, in the high Middle Ages, into private confessional practices, remains one of the most complex problems of Church history.[1] Much of what has been written, however, should be read within the context of the polemic between Catholics and Protestants. For Luther, it was inconceivable that the teaching of Jesus Christ and the Apostles would have been at the root of the corrupt penitential practices of the Catholics. For him, the reform of these practices remains, precisely, *"optima paenitentia nova vita."* Thanks to Melanchton, who showed him how the etymology of *meta-noiete,* ("Repent!") entailed change rather than penance, Luther was able to in-sist on the ethical dimensions of the conversion demanded by both John the Baptist and Paul.[2]

Around the end of the second century, the demand for individual repentance underwent a mutation, and was transformed into the ritualized public penance.[3] I propose here to offer some remarks on this transformation. The problem is crucial in the complex relationships between the anthropology developed by early Christian thinkers and the new social frameworks within which the early

---

[1] The *confessio secreta* is mentioned as early as the sixth century by Leo I (*Epistle* 168.2). For a recent study of post-Tridentine Catholic confession, see J. Delumeau, *L'aveu et le pardon: les difficultés de la confession, XIIIe-XVIIe siècle* (Paris 1990). For an anthropological approach, see T. Assad, *Genealogies of Religion* (Baltimore and London 1993), 97–105.

[2] See W. Robertson Smith, *The Old Testament in the Jewish Church,* 45, quoted by A. H. Dirksen, *The New Testament Concept of* Metanoia (Washington, D.C. 1932), 3. "Metanoiete, id est, poenitentiam agite," writes Luther, as he translates *metanoein* as "sich bessern" in his first translation of the New Testament. Only later will he use the expression "Buss tun."

[3] The question has been much studied; for a general introduction, see for instance C. Vogel, *Le pécheur et la pénitence dans l'Eglise ancienne* (Paris 1965), as well as the anthology of early Christian texts edited by H. Karpp, *La Pénitence* (Neuchâtel 1970; German version, Zurich 1970). See also K. Zinniel, "Busse," *HrwG* 2: 188–90; H. Emonds and B. Porschmann, "Busse," *RAC* 2: 802–12; D. Aune, "Repentance," *ER* 12: 337–42; P. Adnès, "Pénitence (repentir et sacrement)," *DS* 12: 943–1004; in *TRE,* no less than five articles are devoted to *Busse.* One can still consult E. Amann, "Pénitence-repentir" and "Pénitence-sacrement," *DTC* 12: 742–48 and 748–845.

Christians developed their identity. I shall then offer a reading of Tertullian's D*e paenitentia*, one of the first texts devoted to the topic of *paenitentia secunda*.

1. Metanoia

In a seminal work published long ago, Rafaele Pettazzoni analyzed the confession of sins in various religions throughout the world, focusing upon the religious systems of the ancient Near East. The chapter on Israel, in particular, analyses various kinds of confession of sins: individual, collective, and periodical (i.e., the rituals of Yom Kippur, based upon Lev. 16, their Canaanite origins, and their parallels in the Babylonian *akitu*).[4] The great importance of Pettazzoni's work was to show that the confession of sins was a central element of any religious system. How should a community react to an individual who has deviated from the norms of behavior through which the community defines itself? Fritz Stolz has recently redefined the problem, by speaking of "normal abnormality."[5] "Normal," since such a deviation from mores or laws developed or accepted by the religious community is of course a universal phenomenon, to be observed in the most different societies. By such a deviation, the individual not only sins, i.e., counters the expectation or will of the divinity, or behaves against the rules of heaven, but also crosses the symbolic boundaries through which the community defines itself. For the sinner to be reintegrated into this community, a ritual process will have to be developed, which is in some ways similar to the rites demanded in order to join the community. One can speak, then, of *rites de passage* parallel to those of conversion.

We shall see how the traditional ways of expressing repentance in ancient Israel and in Second Temple Judaism were broken or dismantled in the new religious system emerging with Christianity. The Jewish rituals of repentance and of purification needed after the pollution of the person through sin were mainly of two kinds. Those that centered around Yom Kippur were mainly of a public character; while baptism, a private act of purification through immersion in water, could be performed at any time. Now Yom Kippur had totally disappeared from early Christianity – perhaps because the whole ethos of the new religion centered upon repentance from sins, thus allowing no special, limited place for one single day, hallowed as it may be, devoted to the repentance from sins. As to baptism, it did not disappear, to be sure, from the new religion. On the contrary, its central importance was fostered as it became exclusively identified with a ritual of conversion. Baptism, however, now became a one-time ritual,

---

[4] R. Pettazzoni, *La confessione dei peccati* (vol 1, Bologna 1929; vol. 2, Bologna 1935). I have not been able to see the announced third volume. See further J. P. Assmussen, "Beichte," *TRE* 5: 411ff., and Chr. Auffahrt, "Beichte," *HrwG* 2: 116–19.

[5] F. Stolz, *Christentum* (Göttingen 1985), 80–89.

and could no longer be used repeatedly, as in Judaism, as a rite of repentance, permitting purification and offering religious and ethical rehabilitation, and re-integration into the community. During the first two centuries, the Christians developed new ways permitting and symbolizing the sinner's reintegration into the community. In a sense, these ways offer a parallel to the ritual patterns developed for conversion, and they reflect the search for a new equilibrium. As they found their way from a Jewish sect to a new, independent religious system and community, the early Christians had to invent a new ritualization of repentance. In this sense, the passage from repentance to penance reflects the passage from a *communio sanctorum* to the catholic *ecclesia*, a much broader community of believers, in which even sinners have their place.

The clear relationship between the individual and society regarding the character of repentance is stated in the earliest stages of Christian literature, which reflect a sectarian movement not yet quite distinct from Judaism. In Matthew 18: 15–18 (alluding to Deuteronomy 19: 15) it is stated that at least two witnesses are needed in order to prove guilt. Hence the possibility, or even the necessity of a public aspect of repentance. As is well known, religious as well as political groups and sects feel a need, which sometimes grows to an obsession, to establish rules regulating attitudes towards deviants or heretics. The smaller the sect, the harsher the rules. An obvious instance is provided by the Qumran texts dealing with discipline within the sect. When Christianity became a religion with universalist ambitions, did it retain some attitudes inherited from its sectarian beginnings?

The importance attributed by Christianity to repentance finds its obvious origin in the predication of John the Baptist: "Repent ye *(metanoiete),* for the kingdom of heaven is at hand. ... I indeed baptize you with water unto repentance *(eis metanoian)* ... ."[6] One is thus dealing here with a Jewish context, a fact known by all scholars who, in the footsteps of Paul de Lagarde, understand *metanoia* as alluding to the Hebrew root *shuv,* and to the many examples of its composites in the Hebrew Bible – *pace* Wellhausen, who could state in lapidary fashion: "*Metanoia* ist unjüdisch."[7] Pettazzoni had been able to show that repentance was linked to the confession of sins in the religion of Israel. This link was retained in Second Temple Judaism. Indeed, Jesus' name itself directly refers to the remission of sins: "Thou shalt call his name Jesus: for he shall save his people from their sins." (Mt 1: 21). Elsewhere, Jesus shows explicit consciousness of the centrality of the remission of sins: "For this is my blood of the new testament, which is shed for many for the remission of sins."[8]

---

[6] Mt 3: 2, 11; cf. Mk 1: 1–8; Lk 3: 1–8. For a discussion, see for instance, H.-G. Schönfeld, "Metanoia: ein Beitrag zum Corpus Hellenisticum Novi Testamenti" (Ph.D. diss., Heidelberg 1970).
[7] Quoted by Schönfeld, *Metanoia,* 10.
[8] Mt 26:28; cf. Acts 2:38. Cf. J. Murphy O'Connor, "Péché et communauté dans le Nouveau Testament," *RB* 74 (1967): 161–93, esp. 162–63.

It should be pointed out here that while the idea of a confession of sins is found in vastly different religious contexts, the problem is not phrased everywhere in the same terms. In Greek religion, for instance, the concept of *metanoia* does not play a role. Impurity does not have there the ethical dimensions of sin as in Second Temple Judaism.[9] There is no denying the presence of *metanoia* in pre-Christian Greek literature, but the fact remains that the status of sin and culpability in the Greek world is significantly different from their status in the biblical tradition.

The nature, and possible Jewish origin of *metanoia* have in the past fed some heated arguments among classical philologists. About the call to repentance in the last chapters of the *Poimandres* (esp. chapter 28), Eduard Norden had noted that the importance of *metanoia* in this text probably reflected a Jewish or "oriental" influence – a statement strongly opposed by Werner Jaeger.[10] As is well-known, *hamartia* in classical Greek means error rather than sin. This fact much weakens Jaeger's opinion. Any argument passing directly from the word to the concept, and calling attention to linguistic parallels while ignoring their contexts, sounds suspect, even suspicious. It almost seems to reflect an attempt to ignore the direct Jewish Palestinian background of nascent Christianity. The ethical dimension is central to the repentance preached by John the Baptist. The same ethical character of a practice of cultic purity is found also in Essene baptism.[11] In the new religious sensitivity developed in Second Temple Judaism, ethics stands at the very heart of religious life.[12] There is no need to insist on the fact that such an ethical demand is absent from Hellenic systems of thought, even if one can speak about a *metanoia* in mystery cults.[13]

Yet, despite the obvious roots of the concept of *metanoia* in the New Testament, the origin of the word itself remains a problem. The word, for instance, is not used in LXX in order to translate *shuv* and its composites. Those are usually translated by *epistrephein*, while *metanoiein* represents *niham* and its cognates. One finds *metanoia*, however, in Hellenistic Jewish literature. In *Joseph and*

---

[9] See R. Parker, *Miasma: Pollution and Purification in Early Greek Religion* (Oxford 1983).

[10] Norden had made this statement in his *Agnostos Theos.: Untersuchungen zur Formgeschichte religiöser Rede* (Leipzig 1913). Jaeger established his attack against this judgment upon a Greek "pagan" reference to *metanoia,* as "the feeling of he who is mistaken." According to him, this is very close to the New Testament meaning of the term as "repentance." See C. Praechter, ed., *Kèbètos Pinax, Cebetis Tabula* (Leipzig 1893) 10, 139. On Norden's approach, see B. Kytzler, K. Rudolph, and J. Rüpke, eds., *Eduard Norden (1868–1941): ein deutscher Gelehrter jüdischer Herkunft* (Palingenesia 49; Stuttgart 1994).

[11] D. Flusser, "John's Baptism and the Dead Sea Sect," in his *Jewish Sources in Early Christianity* (in Hebrew) (Tel Aviv 1979), 81–112, esp. 84ff.

[12] See D. Flusser, "A New Sensitivity in Judaism and the Christian Message," in his *Judaism and the Origins of Christianity* (Jerusalem 1988), 469–89.

[13] This was suggested by R. Joly, in his edition of the *Pastor of Hermas,* a text crucial for the evolution of repentance in early Christianity; see R. Joly, ed., tr., *Le Pasteur d'Hermas* (SC 53 bis; Paris 1968).

Aseneth, for instance, a hypostatic *Metanoia*, a figure similar to Dame Wisdom, Sophia, appears as "the daughter of the Most High."[14]

In the Mediterranean and Near Eastern world during the Hellenistic period, and then under the Roman Empire, one can observe some radical transformations of the categories of religious thought. In a classical study, Arthur Darby Nock long ago analyzed these transformations, describing in particular the birth and development of the idea of conversion in the Hellenistic and Roman world.[15] One could now choose religious identity, and leave the ethnic and religious group to which one belonged from birth, in order to join another one. For the Roman period, John North has recently followed in Nock's footsteps, by insisting on what he calls a "supermarket of religions" in the Empire.[16] *Epistrophè*, *conversio*, are ambiguous terms. They describe the passage from one religion to another, but also the passage to philosophical or even mystical patterns of thought or way of life.

To be sure, conversion existed in first-century Judaism – although it might not have been as widespread as sometimes thought.[17] Conversion to Judaism demands baptism; yet, baptism, i.e., purification through immersion, remains essentially identified with repentance of sins.

In the earliest strata of Christianity, baptism became endowed with a new meaning: it would now almost exclusively delineate the passage to the new religious identity. In a sense, one could perhaps say that from being essentially concerned with *paenitentia*, it became the ritual of *conversio* par excellence. This does not mean, of course, that the repentance from sins disappeared from Christian baptism. Quite the contrary: repentance from sins is so essential in Christian baptism that it became integrated into the profession of faith: Jesus saves. The nature of baptism thus underwent a radical transformation, as exemplified, in particular, in Paul's writings. Baptism is certainly central to Paul's thought (see, for instance, Romans 6: 1–11). But Paul insists much more upon salvation, i.e., the victory over death brought by baptism, than upon repentance. In Paul's theology, indeed, *metanoia* is included within *pistis*. A caveat is in order here: in the New Testament, *metanoia* and *epistrophè* are often synonymous terms, as in Paul's speech in front of king Agrippa (Acts 26: 20): one must "repent and turn to God, and do works meet for repentance" *(metanoiein kai epistrophein epi ton theon axia tès metanoias erga prassontas)*.

---

[14] See A. Standhartinger, *Das Frauenbild im Judentum der hellenistischen Zeit* (AGAJU 26; Leiden 1995).

[15] A. D. Nock, *Conversion: The Old and the New in Religion from Alexander the Great to Augustine of Hippo* (Oxford 1933). See also A. Momigliano, "Religion in Athens, Rome, and Jerusalem in the First Century B.C.," in his *On Pagans, Jews, and Christians* (Middletown, Conn. 1987), 74–91.

[16] J. North, "The Development of Religious Pluralism," in *The Jews among Pagans and Christians,* eds. T. Rajak, J. Lieu, and J. North (London 1992), 174–93.

[17] For a recent re-evaluation of the question, see Sh. J. D. Cohen in *JQR* 86 (1996): 429–34.

Despite the importance of repentance, Christian baptism, since it is above all a confession of faith, must remain a one-time event. There is only one baptism possible for the Christian, since it defines the conversion to the new religious identity. This highlights an essential difference between the Jewish and the Christian attitudes towards repentance and conversion. Despite its obvious character, this observation does not seem to be widely recognized.[18] While Jewish baptism deals especially with the internal regulation of religion, the reintegration into a state of purity; Christian baptism focuses upon the passage from within to without, i.e., the acceptance within the community.[19] Early Christian identity was defined in terms profoundly different from those defining Jewish identity after the first century. Christianity was a *religio illicita,* and the communities were often constituted of religious *virtuosi,* to use Max Weber's expression. In such intense communities, the reintegration of fallen members is notoriously difficult. Outlawed communities, moreover, cannot exert any real kind of pressure or sanction. Thus Augustine could explain, toward the end of the fourth century, why the clandestine Manichaeans were unable to force even their *electi* to repentance and penance.[20] In the case of ancient Christianity, one should add the intensity of eschatological expectations, the belief in the imminent end of the world and second coming of the Savior: " The time is fulfilled, and the kingdom of God is at hand: repent ye, and believe the gospel." (Mark 1: 15).

Since baptism functioned for them as the ritual of conversion, and since Yom Kippur had disappeared from their ritual, the early Christians had to develop a new system permitting the solemn reintegration of serious sinners into the community. Baptism was identified as an act of *metanoia*. The act of re-integration into the community, therefore, would be a second *metanoia*, a *paenitentia secunda*. This new development is particularly well-exemplified in Tertullian's *De paenitentia*, where we can follow some key elements of a new ritualization of repentance.

This new system had to recognize the duplication of repentance. Since the new ritual was a duplication of baptism, it had to respect the latter's unique character. Just as there was only one baptism, there would also be a single *paenitentia secunda*. In the early church, indeed, one can detect a clear parallel between neophytes and penitents. Just as the catechumens existed as a separate class, there existed in the first centuries an *ordo paenitentibus*. This system worked for a rather long time. Ambrosius's *De paenitentia* shows that public penance was

---

[18] See for instance K. Berger, *Historische Psychologie des Neuen Testaments* (Stuttgart 1991), which does not devote special discussion to repentance.

[19] On repentance in Rabbinic thought, see for instance E. E. Urbach, *The Sages* (Jerusalem 1975), ch. 15 and bibliography. Among older studies, see esp. A. Büchler, *Studies in Sin and Atonement in First-Century Judaism* (London 1958).

[20] Augustine, *De mor. eccl. cathol. et de mor. manich.,* 2.19.68.

known in Milan towards the end of the fourth century; Augustine himself knew a semi-public penance.[21] Yet this compromise remained unstable; its application proved too difficult, and it was far from satisfying the needs of the faithful. It did not succeed in imposing itself, and eventually became obsolete. The invention of *paenitentia secunda,* actually, ran against the grain of Christian logic, a fact reflected, for instance, by the Letter to the Hebrews (6: 4–8) and the *Pastor of Hermas,* for which there is no possibility of forgiveness for sins committed after baptism.[22] Clement of Alexandria, too, only barely agrees to tolerate the *paenitentia secunda,* since he who has received in baptism forgiveness for his sins should not sin anymore.[23]

2. Tertullian's De paenitentia *in Context*

Tertullian wrote the *De paenitentia* in 203, before his Montanist period. This text is crucial for the history of ecclesiastical penance.[24] Years later, Tertullian published the *De pudicitia,* a violent polemic against the penitential discipline of the Catholic Church in Africa, and in particular against the edict of Pope Callistus, who forgave sins of adultery and fornication to penitents. The *De pudicitia* is the first source to mention explicitly the three capital sins, idolatry, fornication, and murder.[25] It offers a distinction between *peccata remissibilia* and *irremissibilia,* a distinction absent from the *De paenitentia.* One should underline the fact that the three capital sins (see Acts 15: 20–28 and I Cor 10: 7) are also found in Rabbinic literature: one should willingly accept death rather than offering sacrifice

---

[21] See R. Gryson, ed., tr., *Ambroise de Milan, La pénitence* (SC 179; Paris 1971); Gryson's introduction provides a broad discussion of the question in the Early Church, focusing upon the Novatians, Ambrosius's opponents. On the public character of the remission of even *peccata minora,* see P. Galtier, "La rémission des péchés moindres dans l'Eglise du troisième au cinquième siècle," *RSR* 13 (1921): 97–129. The ritual, public dimension is still to be found in some Eastern churches; see J. Isaac, *Taksa d-hussaya: le rite du Pardon dans l'Eglise syriaque orientale* (Orientalia Christiana Analecta 233; Rome 1989).

[22] See I. Goldhahn-Müller, *Die Grenze der Gemeinde: Studien zum Problem der zweiten Busse im Neuen Testament, unter Berücksichtigung der Entwicklung im 2Jh. bis Tertullian* (Göttingen 1989).

[23] See J. Reiling, *Hermas and Christian Prophecy: A Study of the Eleventh Mandate* (Leiden 1973). On Clement, see especially *Strom.* II.13; and *Quis dives salvetur* 40 (352–353 LCL).

[24] I am using the text of E. Preuschen, ed., Tertullian, *De paenitentia. De pudicitia* (Freiburg 1891). One can still read with great profit the fundamental analysis of H. Windisch, *Taufe und Sünde im ältesten Christentum bis auf Origenes* (Tübingen 1908), 412–33. Oddly enough, Windisch refers to Tertullian's approach as "Jewish" on the problem at hand. See also K. Rahner, "Zur Theologie der Busse bei Tertullian," in *Abhandlungen über Theologie und Kirche: Festschrift für Karl Adam,* ed. M. Reding (Düsseldorf 1952), 139–67. On Tertullian and Montanism, see P. de Labriolle, *La crise montaniste* (Paris 1913), ch. 3.

[25] *De pudicitia* 5. One should note that Augustine condemned Tertullian's limitation to these three sins; cf. P. F. Beatrice, "Sin," *EEC,* 2: 781a.

to the idols, or committing incest or murder. For Tertullian, just as for the Rabbis, adultery is a close relative of idolatry, and it is impossible to separate the field of religion from that of ethics (5.4; cf. *De pudicitia*). The great contrast between Tertullian's two works has occasioned many studies. The following analysis will focus upon the *De paenitentia*.

Tertullian begins with a psychological analysis of *paenitentia*. The term itself, which is not Christian, denotes an emotion *(passionem animi quandam)* stemming from a radical change of opinion on past actions. In other words, the vocable does not originally possess a moral value, and can also be used, at least theoretically, *in malam partem,* in alluding to a return to evil actions. Without the fear of God, *paenitentia* is vain, since it does not bring one to correct one's conduct.[26] Tertullian proposes to limit the meaning of *paenitentia,* by applying the term only to the rejection of *evil* actions. Doing so, he accomplishes an ethicization of the concept, based upon the idea of God's justice *(iudex deus iustitiae,* 2.12). Side by side with this ethicization of the concept, Tertullian insists also on its epistemological character: *paenitentia* reflects the passage from ignorance to knowledge. The correlate of this position is the definition of *paenitentia,* returning to sin, as a revolt, *contumacia.*

The idea of repentance is established also upon anthropology, not only upon theology. As is well-known, for Tertullian man is a composite, and the body as well as the soul forms an integral part of human nature.[27] Sins, then, can be corporal as well as spiritual. They are sins of the will (3.3, 4.1). Hence, penance must purify man of these two categories of sin, and repentance must find a double expression, corporal and spiritual.[28] *Paenitentia* should not express itself only in an interior change, i.e., a change of *conscientia (ut non sola conscienta praeferatur),* but must be exteriorized, visibly *(in actu;* 9.1). For Tertullian, *conscientia* hides sin, and is therefore, as a rule, guilty. Despite the strong Stoic influence upon Tertullian's anthropology, his approach here is sensibly different from that of Stoic tradition up to Seneca, for which what is exterior always belongs to the *adiaphora,* while good and evil things remain interior.[29] Thus, according to Tertullian, Christianity permits the exteriorization of consciousness.

Originally, repentance *(paenitentia)* is identical to baptism, through which one enters into the Church. As such, it is required by God. Now we have seen that for Tertullian, the concept of *paenitentia* entails a vector, a direction. The movement of the soul must therefore be a continuous progress, and a Christian,

---

[26] "Sed ubi metus nullus, emendation proinde nulla; ubi emendatio nulla, paenitentia necessario vana." (2.2).

[27] See chapter 10 of this volume.

[28] "Ut corporale sit, quod in facto est, quia factum, ut corpus, et videri et contingi habet; spiritale vero, quod in animo est, quia spiritus neque videtur neque tenetur." (3.8–9).

[29] See H. Cancik-Lindemaier, "Gewissen," *HrwG* 3, 17–31. On the process of internalization in Early Christianity, see chapter 5 of this volume.

in theory, should not sin anymore (6.17). In principle, therefore, repentance is not possible after baptism, and the idea of a *paenitentia secunda,* as noted above, is a concession of God's grace to human weakness (5.1).

A sinning Christian has lost the fear of God, and revolts against Him. Doing so, he returns to the service of God's enemy, Satan.[30] In other words, says Tertullian, the Christian sinner "repents from repentance" (5.9). Tertullian then polemicizes against Anomians, for whom faith alone saves, while the expression of sorrow for past sins is not needed. In a word, he says, according to them one may commit adultery or parricide and remain pure (5.10)!

In order to refer to *paenitentia secunda,* Tertullian uses the Greek term *exhomologèsis.* This is an act through which one confesses one's sins to God.[31] In opposition to *dissimulatio,* indeed, *confessio,* or exteriorized acknowledgment, lightens sins.[32] As has often been noted, we have here the first mention of *exhomologèsis* in ancient Christian literature. What is for Tertullian of capital importance is the public character of this confession. Three arguments are advanced to justify this character. Firstly, it is an act of (renewed) adhesion to a community. Secondly, human nature entails the exteriorization of behavior. Thirdly, public humiliation is the best warrant of the Christian reversal of values.

This reversal of values is explicitly presented as the passage from an ethic of shame to an ethic of guilt.[33] "Some care more about shame than about salvation," says Tertullian.[34] He himself does not care at all about shame.[35] Now one must choose. Is it better to be secretly damned than to be saved, at the price of a public humiliation?[36] Since sin hides deep at the bottom of conscience, inward repentance must be accompanied by exteriorization. While it humiliates the sinner in a public way, *exhomologèsis* purifies him inwardly:

> cum igitur provolit hominem, magis relevat,
> cum squalidum facit, magis emundatum reddit,
> cum accusat, excusat,
> cum condemnat, absolvit. (9.6).

---

[30] "Cum aemulo eius diabolo paenitentia renuntiasset et hoc nomine illum domino subiecisset, rursus eundem regressu suo erigit et exultationem eius seipsum facit ... ." (5.7).

[31] "Huius igitur paenitentiae secundae et unius... ut non sola conscientia praeferatur, sed aliquo etiam actu administretur. Is actus, qui magis graeco vocabulo exprimitur et frequentatur, *exhomologèsis* est, qua delictum domino nostrum confitemur ... ." (9.1–2).

[32] "Tantum elevat confessio delictorum, quantum dissimulatio exaggerat. Confessio enim satisfactionis consilium est, dissimulatio contumaciae." (8.9).

[33] 9.6. As is well known, the opposition between shame and guilt, first proposed by the anthropologist Ruth Benedict, has been used by R. E. Dodds in order to describe some major transformations in Greek society, from the archaic to the classical period, in *The Greeks and the Irrational* (Berkeley 1951).

[34] "Pudoris magis memores, quam salutis" (10.1).

[35] "Ego rubori locum non facio" (10.3).

[36] "An melius est damnatur latere quam palam absolvi?" (10.8).

The ritual and public character of *paenitentia secunda* is almost theatrical; it reflects indeed the demands of a cathartic process. Like the catechumen at baptism, the repentant crosses from the camp of the devil to that of the devil's enemy, God (6.7). Just like baptism, *exhomologèsis* offers protection against Gehenna (12.5). The Church, indeed, is a community, and one cannot be saved alone: "In uno et altero ecclesia est, ecclesia vero Christus" (10.5).

In contradistinction to baptism, which had been a second birth, penitence is conceived as an act of mourning. As he laments his sins, the penitent covers himself, in Biblical fashion, with a sack of ashes; in order to be forgiven, he fasts. This attitude of the repentant, expressing mourning and sadness (at the remembrance of sins past) is called *penthos*. It will later become typical of the monk in the eastern tradition.[37] These various characteristics of repentance show that *paenitentia* is a new regulating system, already developed at the end of the second century. This system permits the individual's reintegration into society, through acts as well as through a change of heart.

Various scholars, in particular among German Protestants, have characterized Tertullian's insistence on the social dimensions of repentance as reflecting a "Judaizing" tendency in the Church during the second century.[38] One has even spoken of a "fatal return" to Judaism [*sic!*].[39] This "fatal return," of course, refers to the idea of divine law and to the ethical kernel of religious life, to the integration of body and soul, and of the individual and the community, which are perceived as endangering Luther's idea of salvation *sola fide*.

---

[37] See I. Hausherr, *Penthos: la doctrine orientale de la componction* (Rome 1954).

[38] See for instance H. von Campenhausen, *Die lateinischen Kirchenväter,* in the chapter on Tertullian, *in finem,* and Windisch's view, quoted n.24 above.

[39] See J. Behm, "Metanoia," in *TWNT,* ed. G. Kittel, 4: 972–1004. One may note that this volume appeared in 1942. I quote: "Der verhängnisvolle Rückfall des nachapostolischen und altkatholischen Christentums in jüdisches Gesetztum kommt in der Wandlung des metanoia-Verständnisses zu bezeischnendem Ausdruck. Der urchristliche religiöse Begriff ist ins Moralistiche zurückgebogen." (1003). About Tertullian, *De paenitentia* 9, he speaks of a "Bussdisziplin analog der synagogalen," and concludes: "An der Schwelle der Geschichte des nt.liche metanoia-Gedankens in der alten Kirche steht alsbald das jüdische Missverständnis." (1004).

Chapter 10

Caro salutis cardo:
Shaping the Person in Early Christian Thought

1.

The body is fashionable. As with other domains of inquiry, late antique studies have greatly profited from the new focus. In particular, the accent has been put, more clearly than ever before, on the radical changes in attitudes toward the human body by those who lived in the area of the Mediterranean from the second to the fifth century C.E. In his major opus, Peter Brown studied at great length the Christian attitudes to the body, partly inherited from Judaism, and quite new to the pagan world, and their implications for the perception of the person.[1] While facets of this transformation and its varied backgrounds have been analyzed in detail and approached from various perspectives, its intellectual and theological background is still worthy of investigation. Special attention should be called to the new conception(s) of the human person which rendered this transformation possible and permitted the emergence of a newly reflective self, i.e., a subject turned back upon itself in ways unknown before. Moreover, the relationships between theological reflection on God's nature – even quite anthropomorphic conceptions of God's physical shape – and perceptions of the human person have been noticed, but by no means given the whole measure of their fundamental importance.[2]

---

[1] See P. Brown, *The Body and Society: Men, Women and Sexual Renunciation in Early Christianity* (New York 1988), e.g., 31–32 or 432–42. See also his chapter in the volume *Histoire de la vie privée,* vol. 1, ed. P. Veyne (English ed., *A History of Private Life,* tr. A. Goldhammer [Cambridge, Mass. and London 1987], 237–317, with a detailed bibliography, 650–52); One item, at least, should be mentioned: A. Rousselle, *Porneia: de la maîtrise du corps à la privation sensorielle* (Paris 1982). Brown's questions, and hence his approach and emphasis, are rather different from my own. He insists on the multiple fracturing of the ancient notion of the human person while I am here more interested in its new structure. While he treats the subject first and foremost as a social historian, I tend to ask questions of intellectual history; see G. G. Stroumsa, review of P. Brown, *The Body and Society,* in *HR* 30 (1990): 100–102.

[2] For recent approaches, see for instance J. D. Zizioulas, "Personhood and Being," in his *Being and Communion* (Crestwood, N.Y. 1985), 27–65, esp. 25–49; Zizioulas points out a radical change in cosmology as a necessary condition for the emergence of the person. Cf. J. Daniélou, "La notion de personne chez les Pères grecs," in *Problèmes de la personne,* ed. I. Meyerson (Paris and La Haye 1973), 113–21, and particularly Joseph Moingt, "Polymorphisme du corps du Christ," in *Corps des Dieux, Le temps de la réflexion,* (Paris 1986), 11: 47–62. See also G. G.

Although not quite identical, terms such as "reflective self," person, or "singular subject" belong to the same nexus and may all be used legitimately to describe the new sensitivity to the individual that appeared in late antiquity.[3] The important task of sorting out the precise differences between these terms, and best applying them to the various contexts cannot, however, be dealt with here.

Major historical developments are always overdetermined, a truth recently noted anew by Charles Kahn.[4] This fact usually spells the doom of those fruits of hubris that attempt to offer exhaustive evidence, or models that are too often sealed argumentative packages. There will be no claim in the following pages to develop a full-fledged theory or present a comprehensive interpretation; rather, the attempt will focus only on some aspects of the radical transformation of the person in late antiquity.

From our point of view, the maturing corpus of Christian thought, from the second to the fourth century, culminated with the notion of a radical reflexivity of the self, a notion introduced in its clearest form by Augustine, and, as Charles Taylor reminds us, bequeathed by him to the Western tradition of thought.[5] It

---

Stroumsa, "Form(s) of God: some Notes on Metatron and Christ," *HTR* 76 (1983): 269–88; and idem., "Origen on God's Incorporeality: Context and Implications," *Religion* 13 (1983): 345–58 (= Stroumsa, *Savoir et salut* [Paris 1992], ch. 3, 65–84, and ch. 10, 183–97).

[3] The only history of the word "person" of which I am aware is H. Rheinfelder, *Das Wort Persona: Geschichte seiner Bedeutungen mit besondere Berücksichtgung des französischen und italienischen Mittelalters* (Beihefte zur Zeitschrift für romanische Philologie, 77; Halle 1928). For a good collection of the evidence in antiquity, see R. Hirzel, *Die Person; Begriff und Name derselben im Altertum* (Munich 1914). See also the important studies of Maria Daraki, "La naissance du sujet singulier dans les Confessions de Saint Augustin," *Esprit* (1981): 95–115, and John Rist, *Human Value: a Study in Ancient Philosophical Ethics* (Philosophia Antiqua 40; Leiden 1982), esp. "Individuals and Persons," 145–63. Cf. two recent articles attempting to sort out some religious implications of this shift in the perception of the human person: R. Kirschner, "The Vocation of Holiness in Late Antiquity," *VC* 38 (1984): 105–24; and R. F. Newbold, "Personality Structure and Response to Adversity in Early Christian Hagiography," *Numen* 31 (1984): 199–215. Newbolt points out the shift of emphasis undergone by pagan values by the end of the third century, from outer to inner purity, from deed to intention – thus preparing the ground for the new Christian values. On this shift see Y. Shohat, "The Change in Roman Religion at the Time of the Emperor Trajan," *Latomus* 44 (1985): 316–36. See also M. Augé, *Génie du Christianisme* (Paris 1982), 48ff.

[4] C. Kahn, "Discovering the Will: From Aristotle to Augustine," in *The Question of 'Eclecticism': Studies in Later Greek Philosophy*, eds. A. A. Long and J. M. Dillon (Berkeley, Los Angeles, and London 1988), 234–60.

[5] This fact in emphasized by C. Taylor, *The Roots of the Self* (Cambridge, Mass. 1989). I wish to thank Professor Taylor for putting at my disposal the typescript of an important chapter of this book. See also his "The Person," in *The Category of the Person: Anthropology, Philosophy, History*, eds. M. Carrithers, S. Collins, and S. Lukes (Cambridge 1985), 257–81. For another philosophical inquiry on the concept of self and what the author calls its "myth," see A. Kenny, *The Self* (Aquinas Lecture, 1988; Milwaukee 1988). For an Islamic perspective, see H. H. Schaeder, "Das Individuum im Islam," in *Der Mensch im Orient und Okzident* (Munich 1960), 239–306. For an enlightening anthropological study, see W. A. Christian, Jr., *Person and God in a Spanish Valley* (New York and London 1972), passim. Cf. D. Sperber, *Rethinking Symbolism* (Cambridge and Paris 1975), x.

should be argued forcefully that this new notion was not only a product of the times, but was developed in Christianity. The lack of a similar reflexivity of the self in the classical world is evident in the teachings of the different philosophical schools, which, in various ways, all show a basic lack of interest or respect for the self, the individual, and the particular.[6] The absence of the subject, as we understand it, in the mental and psychological experience of the ancients, is also evident in the literature, where the self appears, more often than not, pale and stilted. To quote Paul Veyne, "No ancient, not even the poets, is capable of talking about oneself. Nothing is more misleading than the use of 'I' in Graeco-Roman poetry."[7]

It should be emphasized at the outset that, more than a new anthropology, it is first and foremost a fresh *attitude* towards the self that the Christians would discover, an attitude grounded in a few fundamental points of their theology, and which could not have taken shape without this theology.

The new sensitivity to the subject shown by the Church Fathers, and hence the emergence of the reflective self, should indeed be seen as the acme of a trend in the new epoch. This trend was prepared by the emphasis on the "care of the self" studied by Michel Foucault in the (pagan) philosophical and scientific circles of the first two centuries of the Empire.[8] Prima facie this emphasis would seem to offer something close to what the Christians would propose. Yet one should beware: Marcus Aurelius still reflected the old attitude, and offered recommendations rather than indulging in introspection. For a Stoic thinker,[9] indeed, the true man is passionless, and while the idea of conversion to wisdom plays a role, not so the process of conversion itself. Once converted to wisdom, a man should

---

[6] See for instance Rist, *Human Value,* or most recently the demonstration of this fact by Rémi Brague, *Aristote et la question du monde* (Paris 1988), esp. 141–48. In a series of learned articles, the late historian of Greek philosophy C. J. de Vogel argued against this view of things. I have not been convinced by her arguments, which seem to grant more importance to the wording of concepts than to their semantic shifts. See, e.g., her "The Concept of Personality in Greek and Christian Thought," in *Studies in the History of Philosophy,* ed. J. K. Ryan (Washington, D.C. 1963), 20–60; and idem., "Plotinus' Image of Man," in *Images of Man in Ancient and Mediaeval Thought, Studia G. Verbeke...dictata* (Leuven 1976), 147–68. See also, for a synthetic view, F. M. Schaeder, "The Self in Ancient Religious Experience," in *Classical Mediterranean Spirituality,* ed. A. H. Armstrong (New York 1986), 337–59.

[7] Brown, *History of Private Life,* 231.

[8] I refer here to the third and last published volume of M. Foucault, *Histoire de la sexualité, Le souci de soi* (Paris 1984). Foucault died before he could complete the fourth volume of his history of sexuality, which was to be devoted to early Christianity; however, see his "Le combat de la chasteté," *Communications* 35 (1982): 15–25 (on John Cassian); and "L'écriture de soi," *Corps Ecrit* 5 (1983): 3–23 (on Evagrius and the *Vita Antonii*). See also P. Hadot, "Exercices spirituels antiques et 'philosophie chrétienne,'" in his *Exercices spirituels et philosophie antique* (Paris 1981), 59–74.

[9] On Marcus's Stoicism see J. Rist ,"Are you a Stoic? The Case of Marcus Aurelius," in *Jewish and Christian Self-Definition,* eds. B. F. Meyer and E. P. Sanders , vol. 3 (Philadelphia 1984), 23–45, 190–92.

shade away, forget and ignore his previous patterns of thought and behavior. Where Plotinus sought to reach the state of contemplation *(theoreisthai)*, it is the path of sustained effort leading to it *(quaerere)* on which Augustine will most insist.

Foucault distinguishes radically between the "care of the self," the *epimeleia heautou* recommended or practiced by the pagan thinkers, and the vastly different attitude developed by the Christian intellectuals, which involved renouncing and deciphering the self.[10] The Nietzschean overtones of such an approach are obvious. Nietzsche – as well as Schelling before him[11] – loathed Socrates' attempt at retrieving the hidden self, his recoil from the archaic Greek attitude of acting out, publicly, in an altogether unreflective manner, as the healthy way of expressing the self. For Nietzsche, this attempt was not a great moment in the history of Western thought, but rather the beginning of a decline ultimately completed with the victory of Christianity. Foucault is undoubtedly correct in pointing out a major difference in attitude toward the self among pagan and Christian thinkers under the Empire, although it should constantly be kept in mind that we are dealing more with Weberian *Idealtypen* than with neatly delineated and differentiated social realities. Once again, it should be emphasized that pagans and Christians lived in the same mental world, and it often appears that they were carried away from each other by the implications, or the logical consequences of their ideas, appearing to do so, at times, more reluctantly than willingly.[12] Foucault's assessment, however, that the Christian thinkers tried to renounce the self, is profoundly mistaken. Incidentally, this radical misinterpretation is rather similar to that of the anthropologist Louis Dumont, for whom early Christianity, like Buddhism, represents, in Weberian terms, a clear case of "otherworldly asceticism."[13] On the contrary, the Christian thinkers were striving, to a great extent successfully, to establish a new conception of the human person – a person to be first retrieved, but then developed and cherished. In this respect, one of the most striking differences between the pagan and Christian

---

[10] C. Taylor, "Foucault on Freedom and Truth," in his *Philosophical Papers II: Philosophy and the Human Sciences* (Cambridge 1985), esp. 182–83.

[11] I owe this observation to Brague, *Aristote et la question du monde,* 142, n.27.

[12] For a remarkably broad picture of the social, intellectual, and religious world in which both pagans and Christians moved, see Robin Lane Fox, *Pagans and Christians* (London 1987). Cf. P. Brown, "Brave Old World," *New York Review of Books* (12 March 1987): 24ff., where Brown takes exception to Lane Fox's interpretation of Christian mentalities.

[13] L. Dumont, "A Modified View of Our Origins: The Christian Beginnings of Modern Individualism," *Religion* 12 (1982): 1–27, reprinted in *The Category of the Person,* 93–122. This article (an earlier French version of which was published in *Le Débat* 15 (1981): 124–46), launched a scholarly debate. See, e.g., three responses in *Religion* 12 (1982): 83–91, and S. N. Eisenstadt, "Transcendental Visions – Other-Worldliness and its Transformations," *Religion* 13 (1983): 1–17. Cf. G. G. Stroumsa, "Old Wine and New Bottles: On Patristic Soteriology and Rabbinic Judaism," in *The Origins and Diversity of Axial Age Civilizations,* ed. S. N. Eisenstadt (Albany 1986), 252–60, 525–27 (= Stroumsa, *Savoir et salut,* ch. 5, 99–109).

ethos seems to be in the latter's dynamic approach to the person – a dynamism grounded in the idea, inherited from Judaism and utterly unfamiliar in the Greco-Roman world, that ethics is the kernel of religious life. In the Roman Empire, the idea of moral progress, or of personal reform, so well-studied by Gehrart Ladner, is first and foremost a Christian one.[14]

It is the highly ambiguous status of the reflectivity developed by Christian thinkers that mislead Foucault into offering such a radical misinterpretation. For these thinkers, turning upon oneself and reforming oneself was perceived as part of an ongoing and indivisible process of conversion *(metanoia)*, that is, making constant efforts to turn away from former habits of thought, feeling, and behavior. This conversion was of a different nature than the one propounded by philosophers, since it was based on a very different perception of the relationships between faith and reason, and on a promise of salvation for all and sundry unknown to the elitist philosophers.[15]

Moreover, the emergence of the new subject was dependent upon two essential theological conceptions unknown to the classical world. First, the Biblical idea that man – and woman – had been created in God's image *(homo imago dei)* permitted, as we shall see, the integration of the person, body and soul together, in a way and to an extent unknown among both Stoics and Platonists, who were the Fathers' main intellectual contenders in the first centuries.[16] This conception's Jewish roots were radically concretized, recast in a totally new form in the Christian context, through the intermediary of Jesus Christ, both truly God and truly man.

Now – and here lies the core of what I have called the ambiguous status of the Christian reflective self – just as it was being enlarged and unified through the integration of the body, the subject was at once broken again, in a new fashion. This time, the great divide was no longer between soul and body as representing lofty spirit and base matter, but cut right through the subject itself. The conception of original sin, and hence of the radical asceticism appearing on a grand scale in the fourth century, was again rooted in Jewish soil, more precisely in those marginal splinter groups of Encratites familiar to us from the Dead Sea Scrolls, and who seem to have left a deep imprint on early Jewish Christianity.[17]

---

[14] G. Ladner, *The Idea of Reform: its Impact on Christian Thought and Action in the Age of the Fathers* (Cambridge, Mass. 1959).

[15] On religious and philosophical conversion in the ancient world, see the classic work of A. D. Nock, *Conversion: The Old and the New in Religion from Alexander the Great to Augustine of Hippo* (Oxford 1933), and P. Aubin, *Le problème de la conversion* (Paris 1963).

[16] The best overviews of the interrelations between these two schools and early Christian thought are M. Spanneut, *Le stoïcisme des Pères de l'Eglise* (Patristica Sorbonensia; Paris 1957), and E. von Ivanka, *Plato Christianus: Übernahme und Umgestaltung des Platonismus durch die Väter* (Einsiedeln 1964).

[17] See the important work of P. F. Beatrice, "Continenza e matrimonio nel cristianesimo primitivo (secc. I-II)," in *Etica sessuale e matrimonio nel cristianesimo delle origini,* ed. R. Cantala-

It is precisely this rift within the human person that rendered the new reflectivity possible.

Yet it is only with Augustine – to whom we shall return at greater length – that this new rift within the person became final, precisely at the same time that the new perception of the self was fully blossoming. In his thought, the tension is felt most strongly within the human will. The fundamental weakness of the will, coupled with the concept of *libera voluntas* required by the idea of responsibility, is Ariadne's thread through which we should retrace the intricacies of Augustine's new attention to the sinner's paradigmatic psychology.[18]

Incidentally, it is in this context that we should understand the paramount importance of sexuality for Augustine, who devotes to it a much more sustained reflection than any other Christian thinker before, and also probably after him.[19] If Augustine can offer such new psychological insights, the reason should be sought, first and foremost, in his new reflective attitude to his own self, whose ontological status he recognizes to be as problematic as its existence is obvious.

In other words -and this fact can hardly be overemphasized – the process which reaches its peak with the radical novelty of the *Confessions,* rests upon the two synchronic movements of the broadening of the self and its new interior breakdown.[20] With all its deep-seated ambiguities, the history of the reflective self from Paul to Augustine forms a major chapter in the history of Western consciousness.[21] This chapter is that of the transformation of a structure of thought, characterized by objectification, into another one, focusing upon the recognition of the individual's irreducibility. It is through this process, which was to be continued, at least throughout the Middle Ages, and in this recognition, that all

messa (Milan 1976), 3–68, and his *Tradux peccati: alte fonti della dottrina agostiniana del peccato originale* (Milan 1978).

[18] The bibliography on the topic is immense. A good orientation may be found in A. Schindler, "Augustinus," *TRE* 4: 646–98. On Augustine's anthropology, one can still consult E. Dinkler, *Die Anthropologie Augustins* (Stuttgart 1934); cf. G. Maertens, "Augustine's Image of Man," in *Images of Man in Ancient and Medieval Thought,* 175–198. On the vast array of problems connected to his conception of free-will, see particularly J. Rist, "Augustine on Free Will and Predestination," *JTS,* n.s. 20 (1969): 420–47, reprinted in his *Platonism and its Christian Heritage* (London 1985); Kahn, n. 4, above; A. Dihle, *The Theory of Will in Classical Antiquity* (Berkeley, Los Angeles, and London 1982), chapter 6; M. Clark, *Augustinian Personalism* (Villanova, Pa. 1970).

[19] See for instance Brown's remarks in *A History of Private Life,* 307ff.

[20] One should remember that although the *Confessions* have been widely read since their publication, many centuries will be needed for its worth to be truly recognized. In some ways, Petrarca appears to be the first author to truly relate to it. See P. Courcelle, *Les Confessions de Saint Augustin dans la tradition littéraire* (Paris 1963) See also E. R. Dodds, "Augustine's Confessions: a Study in Spiritual Maladjustment," *Hibbert Journal* 26 (1927–28): 459–73, and C. Kahn, n. 4 above.

[21] On the similarities between Paul's and Augustine's conception of the "retrospective self," see P. Fredricksen, "Paul and Augustine: Conversion, Narratives, Orthodox Traditions, and the Retrospective Self," *JTS,* n.s. 37 (1986): 3–34.

Western conceptions of personalism are ultimately grounded.[22] We shall look at some aspects of the new religious sensitivity that rendered this recognition possible.

2.

In some obvious sense, Greek philosophy does indeed provide the starting point for the development of the Western discovery of the self (in a subjective way) and of the person (in an objective way).[23] Yet, the status of the individual had to remain unclear in Greece, as long as marks of individuality were primarily perceived as signs of imperfection – a well-known fact analyzed anew by John Rist.[24]

In Plato's *Alcibiades* – a text which through Porphyry influenced Augustine – the brash, ambitious and self-satisfied young man is progressively led to acceptance of the Delphic maxim, "Know thyself," and to the recognition that introspection should seek to discover the soul, which is the essence of man.[25] In the same dialogue, Plato underlines the indissoluble links that bind the individual's search for virtue, justice, and moral wisdom to the life of the city. It may be no mere chance that for the Greeks, who put so much weight on the public locus of political life, the discovery of the interior self entailed the recognition of a fundamental chasm between body and soul, the latter alone being the real self.[26] This somato-psychological dichotomy, or dualism, might well be "the most questionable... of all [Greece's] gifts to human culture," to quote E. R. Dodds.[27]

---

[22] On the medieval follow-up of the internalization process, see M.-D. Chenu, *L'éveil de la conscience dans la civilisation médiévale* (Montréal and Paris 1969), for whom it is in the twelfth century that "man discovers himself to be a subject" (p. 15), Abélard being "the first modern man." See also C. Morris, *The Discovery of the Individual, 1050–1200* (London 1972). Cf., for the same process perceived through "la longue durée," J. Le Goff, *L'imaginaire médiéval* (Paris 1986), vii. On Christian personalism, see J. Pépin, "La notion d'idéal moral: héroisme grec et sainteté chrétienne," in his *Les deux approches du christianisme* (Paris 1961), 101–15, esp. 112. For a fresh approach which succeeds in integrating attitudes previously thought to be exclusive of one another, see C. W. Bynum, "Did the Twelfth Century Discover the Individual?," in her *Jesus as Mother: Studies in the Spirituality of the High Middle Ages* (Berkeley, Los Angeles, and London 1982), 82–109. Bynum shows that corporate awareness and the self could be emphasized at once in twelfth-century religion.

[23] For a recent study, see, e.g., S. Scolnicov, "Socrates on the Unity of the Person," *Scripta Classica Israelica* 7 (1985–86): 14–25. See also C. L. Griswold, Jr. "Self-Knowledge and the Idea of the Soul in Plato's *Phaedrus*," *RMM* 26 (1981): 189–200.

[24] J. Rist, "Individuals and Persons," n. 3 above, esp., 152.

[25] On the origins and early history of the Delphic maxim, see P. Courcelle, *Connais-toi toi-même, de Socrate à Saint Bernard* vol. 1 (Paris 1974); on *I Alcibiades,* in particular, see 14ff. On the posterity of *I Alcibiades* see J. Pépin, *Idées grecques sur l'homme et sur Dieu* (Paris 1971), part I.

[26] See J.-P. Vernant, "Aspects de la personne dans la religion grecque" in his *Mythe et pensée chez les Grecs* (Paris 1974), 79–94, esp. 93. See also E. des Places, "En marge du *TWNT*: conscience et personne dans l'antiquité grecque," *Biblica* 30 (1949): 501–508. Cf. H. Chadwick "Gewissen," *RAC*, 10: 1025–1107.

[27] Dodds, *Christian and Pagan in an Age of Anxiety* (New York 1965; reprint 1970), 29.

For Plato, therefore, and for his school of thought, to know oneself – the re-flective attitude par excellence – meant to attend to one's soul, at the exclusion of the body. The case of Aristotle is rather more complicated, since he succeeded in developing an anthropology that could not be subjected to the same kind of criticism as could Plato's. Aristotle, however, did not succeed any more than most other Greek thinkers in conceiving of a private, introspective meditation upon oneself.[28] In any case, Aristotle's influence remained largely limited to small philosophical groups in the first Christian centuries, and had little impact on the formation of Patristic theology.[29]

As hinted above, the major mutation of late antique thought deeply trans-formed the attitudes to the person and had momentous implications for the sub-sequent stages of Western culture. The discovery of the whole person as a com-posite of body and soul not subject to reincarnation should not, however, be seen in isolation from other simultaneous radical changes in attitudes, toward the world or toward society, for instance. The turn upon oneself as a legitimate, nay essential step in the search for God, occurred together with the develop-ment of a new ambivalence toward society at large, the state, and its structures. Thus, one can discern a correlation, however blurred it may be at times, between anthropological and political attitudes.[30] The cosmos, moreover, now considered to have been created ex nihilo and having hence achieved a new unity, had also by the same token lost the lofty character with which it was invested in Greek thought, when still divine.[31]

The new interest in the self had a price, which should not be ignored. Diving into oneself meant the end of the soul's immersion within the universe that had always been the core of astral mysticism in the ancient world. It is here, perhaps,

---

[28] See esp. fine analyses of Brague, *Aristote et la question du monde,* (n. 6 above), 111–70.

[29] On this limited impact, see A.-J. Festugière, *L'idéal religieux des Grecs et l'Evangile* (Paris 1932), Excursus C, "Aristote dans la littérature grecque chrétienne," 221–63. Thomas Aquinas wore Augustinian glasses when he interpreted Aristotle's anthropology. See A. C. Pegis, *At the Origins of the Thomistic Notion of Man* (Saint Augustine and the Augustinian Tradition; New York and London 1963).

[30] See the recent studies of Elaine Pagels, "The Politics of Paradise: Augustine's Exegesis of Genesis 1–3 versus that of John Chrysostom," *HTR* 78 (1985): 67–99, and "Christian Apologists and the 'Fall of the Angels': an Attack on Roman Imperial Power?," ibid., 301–25. These stu-dies are integrated as chapters of her book, *Adam, Eve and the Serpent* (New York 1988). In the case of the classical world, this correlation has been studied by S. C. Humphreys, *Anthropolgy and the Greeks* (London 1978). On the correlation between theological and political attitudes, see for instance A. Momigliano, "The Disadvantages of Monotheism for a Universal State," in his *On Pagans, Jews and Christians* (Middletown, Conn. 1987), 142–58.

[31] On the new cosmology implicit in Christian monotheism, see G. G. Stroumsa, " Gnosis und die christliche 'Entzauberung der Welt'," in *Max Webers Sicht des antiken Christentums: Interpretation und Kritik,* ed. W. Schluchter (Frankfurt 1985), 486–508 (= Stroumsa, *Savoir et salut,* ch. 9, 163–91).

that the distance between Plotinus and Augustine is greatest. For Plotinus, indeed, the self is fully recovered only when recognizing its kinship *(suggeneia)* with the heavenly or divine world.[32] To be sure, the new trend did not quite eradicate traditional attitudes. To wit, the case of Origen's *Peri archôn* and its remarkable posterity, both East and West. Although the one God may have created a united universe, he too often seemed to have left it to Satan's rule. Hence the need for the individual to recoil upon himself in his search for God. Ambiguity, indeed, might be the key word in describing Christian attitudes to the self, society, and the cosmos.

Just like biological mutations, this one was prepared by a long and subtle process of evolutionary changes. When Tertullian wrote, in his lapidary style *caro salutis cardo* – "the flesh is the axis of salvation"[33] – he already stood within a process begun before him, and which still deserves our attention. Despite the large body of scholarly work on Patristic literature, relatively little seems to have been devoted specifically to our topic.

In a seminal yet schematic paper devoted to the roots of the modern notion of the person, Marcel Mauss underlined long ago its passage from the juridical to the theological realm. Mauss pointed out that while the Stoics had begun to develop a new attitude towards introspection, Christianity was left to provide the new sensitivity with a solid metaphysical basis.[34]

A methodological presupposition of the present inquiry is that pivotal concepts around which religions or civilizations are organized tend to appear at early stages in their development.[35] In the case of Christianity, theological conceptions crucial for the shaping of a radically new conception of man are found already in the New Testament. It is, however, from the second to the fourth century that the new anthropology crystallized, as a direct consequence of the challenge to the emerging *Weltanschauung* on the part of alternative soteriological and epistemological attitudes or visions: Judaism, philosophy, and Gnosticism.

Hence, the major role played by the body in Christian soteriology is most clearly apparent in Patristic polemical literature. This role cannot be understood without recognizing the paramount importance devoted to the body of the Savior. As Joseph Moingt has reminded us recently, it is through its conception of a divine body that early Christianity could have contributed so significantly to en-

---

[32] See for instance G. J. P. O'Daly, *Plotinus' Philosophy of the Self* (Shannon 1973), passim, and P. Hadot, *Plotin ou la simplicité du regard* (Paris 1973), esp. 28 and 36.

[33] *De resurrectione mortuorum* 8.2.

[34] M. Mauss, "Une catégorie de l'esprit humain: la notion de personne, celle de 'moi'," in his *Sociologie et anthropologie* (1950, reprint Paris 1968), 331–62, esp. 357ff. An English version of this essay opens, *The Category of the Person,* note 5 above. See also C. N. Cochrane, *Christianity and Classical Culture* (1940, reprint Oxford 1980), ch.11:"*Nostra Philosophia:* the Discovery of Personality."

[35] Cf. the pertinent remarks of F. Rosenthal, *Knowledge Triumphant: The Concept of Knowledge in Medieval Islam* (Leiden 1970), 1.

nobling the human body.[36] This is the case in some of the most fundamental works composed against various Docetic attitudes, first and foremost in Irenaeus' *Adversus Haereses*. The Savior's body, moreover, was not conceived only literally, but also metaphorically. The Pauline conception of the Church as the mystical "Body of Christ" of which the believers are the members, entails a direct link between views of man and views of the "collective person," the Church.[37] It is in this light that the shift of emphasis given by the Church Fathers to the Delphic maxim (to which we shall return) should be understood, according to which the command "Know thyself" no longer refers exclusively to an epistemic attitude of the mind, but to the drawing of the Church's social boundaries.

To what extent was this shift in basic attitudes a conscious phenomenon, perceived as such by those who performed it? There can be no clear-cut answer to this question, but some elements do suggest such a consciousness. Since Christianity was born and first developed as a religion of a new kind against which arose very diverse spiritual forces, it remained for a long time *religio illicita* from the intellectual as well as from the legal point of view. Their very marginality or illegitimacy forced upon Christian intellectuals a clear recognition of their own identity. Christian polemical and apologetic literature reflects the utter consciousness of this radical stand. This is particularly clear in Africa, where, from Tertullian to Augustine, the new conception of the person and the discovery of the reflective self took shape decisively. This discovery has been hailed as "Christianity's greatest contribution to philosophy."[38]

3.

In the Roman world, a Christian was defined, above all, by his staunch belief in a few narrative statements presented as historical and centered around the life, teachings, death, and resurrection of a man[39] – who also happened to be divine.

---

[36] Moingt, "Polymorphisme du Christ," n. 2 above.

[37] The bibliography of research on Paul's *soma christou* is immense. See, e.g., the well-documented study of C. Colpe, "Zur Leib-Christi-Vorstellung im Epheserbrief," in *Judentum, Urchristentum und Kirche, Festschrift für J. Jeremias* (BZNW 26; Berlin 1964), 172–87.

[38] G. Florowsky, "Eschatology in the Patristic Age: an Introduction," in *Studia Patristica, I*, vol.2 (*TUGAL* 64; Berlin 1957), 235–50, esp. 249. See also V. Lossky, "The Theological Notion of the Human Person," in his *In the Image and the Likeness of God* (Crestwood, N.Y. 1974), 11–123, who points out that despite a Christian anthropology, there is no elaborated doctrine of the human person in Patristic writings. Cf. J. Daniélou, "La personne chez les Pères Grecs," n. 2 above; Daniélou points out that we witness in fourth-century writings the emergence and development of the concept of person, linked to the divine hypostasis, but not yet of a specifically *human* person. See also P. Hadot, "De Tertullien à Boèce. Le développement de la notion de personne dans les controverses théologiques," ibid., 123–34.

[39] "You have forsaken God and put your trust in a man – what salvation can await you?" asks the rabbi in Justin Martyr's *Dialogue with Trypho*, 8.4.

Faith in this supreme "Exemplar," as Peter Brown has called Him,[40] offered a
new sense of identity, both personal and collective, which cut through all established criteria. Paul is both the first and the most eloquent exponent of this new
conception: "There is neither Jew nor Greek, there is neither bond nor free,
there is neither male nor female: for ye are all one in Christ Jesus" (Gal. 3: 28).
The believers become members of Christ's body, of His flesh and of His bones
(Eph. 5: 30). A new social unity is thus achieved: "So we, being many, are one
body in Christ, and every one members one of another" (I Cor. 12: 5).

From its inception, the powerful Pauline metaphor of Christ's mystical body
exerted a major influence on the shaping of Christian thought. Its influence on
the emerging anthropology and new sensitivity was compounded, however, by a
few basic theological conceptions, which should at least be referred to here.

From Judaism, Christianity inherited both the belief in man's being made in
the image of God – a belief expressly stated in the first chapter of Genesis – and
belief in the bodily resurrection of the dead – a doctrine slower to emerge fully
in Jewish thought, but already well-established in the first Christian century.[41]
This doctrine was rejected as a striking and insane novelty in the pagan world.
To these two beliefs Christianity added a third, the idea of Christ's incarnation.
Seen as a whole, these doctrines offered a formidable stumbling block for pagan
philosophical thought.[42]

The philosophers first objected to the idea that man had been made in the
image of a transcendent God: this ran against the Platonic conception of a *suggeneia,* a genetic affinity, between the human soul and the divine.[43] In the Platonic tradition – which for various reasons turned out to be (much more than
the Stoa), the main rival of the new faith in late antiquity[44] – the philosopher was
an intellectual embarrassed by or even ashamed of his body, to quote Porphyry's description of Plotinus,[45] and looking forward to the moment when,
freed from the bonds of flesh, he would be able to return, for eternity, to a spiritual afterlife of pure contemplation. Hence the philosophers' profound repulsion for the Jewish and Christian belief in the resurrection of the dead. "Furthermore, are not these notions of yours absurd? For on the one hand you long

---

[40] P. Brown, "The Saint as Exemplar in Late Antiquity," *Representations* 1 (1983): 1–25,
esp. 10, where he refers to the "Exemplar of all Exemplars."

[41] See A. Marmorstein, "The Doctrine of the Resurrection of the Dead in Rabbinic Theology," in his *Studies in Jewish Theology* (Oxford 1950), 145–61. For the earliest Christian belief,
see O. Cullmann, *Immortalité de l'âme ou résurrection des morts? Le témoignage du Nouveau
Testament* (Neuchâtel and Paris 1956).

[42] On philosophical anti-Christian polemic see R. T. Wallis, *Neoplatonism* (London 1972),
100–105. Cf A. H. Armstrong and R. A. Markus, *Christian Faith and Greek Philosophy* (London 1960), 46–57.

[43] A. Louth, *The Origins of the Christian Mystical Tradition* (Oxford 1981), esp. 1–17.

[44] One might note in this context that from Clement of Alexandria on, the Platonic influence
on Christian thinkers becomes predominant and bypasses by far that of the Stoics.

[45] So does Porphyry begin the description of his hero in *The Life of Plotinus.*

for the body and hope that it will rise again. ...." writes Celsus, around the mid-second century, adding that "persons who believe this ... are absolutely bound to the body."[46]

In so categorically rejecting the idea of resurrection from the dead, which Christian thinkers fused only later with the idea of the soul's immortality,[47] late antique philosophers were the direct heirs of the classical Greek dichotomy between body and soul. The divine had nothing in common with matter, and should by all means seek to avoid it. For matter was directly related to evil, according to Platonic conceptions, and hence was deeply repulsive. Thus Origen had to answer Celsus: "For what is properly abominable is of the nature of evil. But the nature of the body is not abominable, for in itself bodily nature is not involved in evil which is the originating cause of what is abominable."[48] It is in order to counter Celsus that Origen adopts the Stoic view according to which the body was morally neutral.[49] But there is more here than a Stoic conception confronted to a Platonic idea. For the Christian, the body could be no *adiaphoron,* but rather was possessed in itself of major value. Pagan philosophers also rejected the idea of incarnation. For them, this was a grotesque contradiction in terms: how could God ever seek to incarnate Himself, to enter of His own will a human, corruptible body?

Most pregnant on this point are the famous words of Augustine in his *Confessions,* telling of the many deep-seated similarities which he found between Platonic and Christian teachings, as well as of the major difference he discovered between them: "There also did I read that God the word *(verbum, deus)* was not born of flesh nor of blood, nor of the will of man, nor of the will of the flesh, but of God. But that the word was made flesh and dwelt amongst us, did I not read there (i.e., in the books of the Platonists)."[50] More precisely, what shocked pagan intellectuals in the idea of incarnation was not only the desire of the invisible God to appear in the world – after all this was a well-known problem of pagan theology, emphasized by the all-too present statues of the gods – but the idea of flesh and its corruptibility, and the fact that, according to Christian doctrine, incarnation had happened once, and only once, in history.[51] This

---

[46] These are the words of Celsus, a second-century philosopher, as quoted by Origen, *Contra Celsum* 8.49. I cite the translation of H. Chadwick, (Cambridge 1953), 488. Cf. ibid., 5.14, where Celsus refers to Jesus and Christians who reject the idea of resurrection.

[47] See, for instance, F. Refoulé, "Immortalité de l'âme et résurrection de la chair," *RHR* 163 (1963): 11–52; H. A. Wolfson, "Immortality and Resurrection in the Philosophy of the Church Fathers," in his *Religious Philosophy* (New York 1965), 69–103; A. H. Armstrong, *Expectations of Immortality in Late Antiquity* (Milwaukee 1987). Cf. J.-Y. Lacoste, "Les anges musiciens," *RSPT* 68 (1984): 549–75.

[48] Origen, *Contra Celsum* 3.42.

[49] This was shown by H. Chadwick, "Origen, Celsus, and the Resurrection of the Body," *HTR* 41 (1948): 83–102.

[50] Augustine, *Confessions* 7.9.

[51] For one instance among many, see the fifth treatise of the *Corpus Hermeticum,* in A. D.

disturbed the pagan thinkers most. Here again, the uniqueness of the divine paradigm, the unity of the person of Jesus Christ, formed the core of the pagan argument against Christianity.

For the Christians, of course, theological and anthropological conceptions were intimately linked. If God had made man in His image, it was through Jesus Christ that he had created him. If Christ had incarnated Himself, He had done so in order to save man: through His own death and resurrection, He had offered victory over death and the gift of resurrection to everyone.

The unity of Christ, possessor of two natures but remaining nonetheless one single *persona,* is of course, in a nutshell, the main achievement of centuries of Christological and Trinitarian pugnacious investigations. From our present perspective, one can only recall how this unity became the most powerful of models for Christian thought and behavior. At the personal level, the *imitatio Christi* was soon interpreted – beyond the martyrs' readiness to experience on their flesh what Jesus had suffered on His own – as the duty of unification of the human person through the integration of will and thought. On that issue, the Syriac tradition is particularly enlightening, which interprets Matt. 18: 20 "For where two or three are gathered in my name, there am I in the midst of them" as "Those who, being two or three, have unified their own self, with them I am."[52] On that basis, the monk (*monachos;* Syriac *iḥidaya*), by virtue of his name, must succeed in unifying his whole person, becoming one on all counts, and remaining alone with himself and Christ, who resides in him. This exegesis is propounded not only by Philoxenus of Mabbug, but also by no less a representative of mainstream Greek tradition than Gregory Nazianzen.[53]

At this point, one may cast doubt upon the truth of the rather commonly held conception according to which Christian asceticism, i.e., since the fourth century, monasticism in its various forms, together with Gnostic dualist trends and in opposition to the more sober asceticism of the philosophers, manifested in the extreme, in the words of E. R. Dodds, "a contempt for the human condition and a hatred of the body" that was an endemic disease of the period.[54]

There is no denying that Christian ascetic attitudes sometimes took aberrant forms. But norms, even when those of rather marginal groups or situations, should be dealt with here, rather than aberrations. We shall see how much of

---

Nock, ed. and A.-J. Festugière, tr., *Hermès Trismégiste,* vol. 1 (1946, Paris 1972), 58ff.. Cf. the excellent presentation of the problem in social and historical context in Lane Fox, *Pagans and Christians* (n. 12 above), 102–67.

[52] This exegetical tradition is studied by A. Guillaumont,, "Monachisme et éthique judéo-chrétienne," in *Judéo-Christianisme, Recherches en hommage au Cardinal Daniélou, RSR* 60 (1972): 199–218, reprinted in his *Aux origines du monachisme chrétien* (Abbaye de Bellefontaine 1979), 47–66, esp. 55–58.

[53] Gregory Nazianzen, *Epigr.* 20, *PG* 38, 93 A, quoted by Guillaumont, *"Aux origines,"* 56, n.28.

[54] E. R. Dodds, *Pagans and Christians in an Age of Anxiety* (Cambridge 1965), 35.

Christian anthropology crystallized around the vehement rejection of Gnostic dualist attitudes. Suffice it here to note that Christians, more often than not, conceived of asceticism as an effort to strengthen and not to weaken the body. So does Athanasius, in his *Life of Saint Anthony,* one of the most influential books in the history of Christianity, describe how the father of all monks underwent fasts and vigils in order to fortify his body for the fight against the demon, not to mortify it.[55] It might be useful here to refer to phenomenological analysis, a method with which positivist historians feel uncomfortable but without which I fail to see how the historian of intellectual or religious trends can even begin to interpret the facts which he studies in their broader context.[56] Such a phemomenological analysis, I believe, reveals the ethos of Gnostic encratism to stand in radical contrast to Christian asceticism, despite some obvious blurring of the boundaries between them. This contrast is evident from the points of view of theological grounds, of practice, and of implications.[57] If the Christian holy man, whose imposing figure we have learned to recognize as rising over the horizon of late antiquity like a stylite saint on his column, could have become a total incarnation of values, it is precisely because he appeared in popular consciousness – in stark contrast with the pagan holy man, the philosopher – as an entity of body and soul, a "Christ-bearing exemplar."[58]

4.

For the collective as well as for the individual, the sense of identity is directly related to the perception of the outsider, the "Other," to use a term borrowed from the French. Polemics, therefore, play a most important role in the development of self-awareness, of reflective consciousness.[59] For the early Christian theologians, heresies appeared as the closest, hence the most immediate and dangerous threat to their emerging collective identity. They also realized very soon that Christian doctrine was progressively defining and refining itself through he-

---

[55] Athanasius, *Vita Antonii* 5, *PG,* 848 B.

[56] This was a methodological assumption of my *Another Seed: Studies in Gnostic Mythology* (Nag Hammadi Studies, 24; Leiden 1984). For a strongly dissenting view, see B. Layton's review, in *RB* 94 (1987): 608–13.

[57] See G. G. Stroumsa, *Savoir et Salut,* ch. 8, 145–62.

[58] See especially P. Brown's seminal study, "The Rise and Function of the Holy Man in Late Antiquity," *JRS* 61 (1971): 80–101, reprinted in his *Society and the Holy in Late Antiquity* (Berkeley and Los Angeles 1982), 102–52. P. Brown coins the "Christ-bearing exemplar" in "The Saint as Exemplar," n. 40 above. On the figure of the philosopher, see G. Fowden, "The pagan Holy Man in Late Antique Society," *JHS* 102 (1982): 33–59.

[59] Studying a very different literary corpus and cultural area, S. Greenblatt reaches important conclusions on self-fashioning and its relation to the "threatening Other," which are also valid in our context. See his *Renaissance Self-Fashioning* (Chicago 1980), 9. I owe this reference to the kindness of Peter Brown.

resiological discourse. *Opportet haereses esse,* they liked to quote the Apostle (I Cor. 11:9). In this discourse, too, the place of the body, of flesh, both of Christ and of man, very soon became cardinal.

Few problems would seem to epitomize the main drive of Gnostic thought better than that of personal identity, of the anguished quest for the real self – "Who were we? What did we become? Where have we been thrown?..." These were the crucial questions asked in the school of Theodotos, one of the leading Valentinian teachers.[60] But the self sought by the Gnostic, and whose redemption he sought, was only his spirit, his *pneuma,* in sharp contradistinction to his corruptible body, and sometimes also his soul. In order to find his own self, the Gnostic thus sought to free himself from his body: "Everyone should practice in many ways to gain release from this element," reads the *Treatise on Resurrection* found at Nag Hammadi.[61]

Indeed, Harnack's famous dictum, according to which Gnosticism was the "acute Hellenization of Christianity," seems nowhere as true as in the field of anthropology. Of course, such a basic attitude had direct implications on the nature of Christ's body and of the resurrection. For the Valentinians, for instance, the body of the Savior was either psychic or spiritual, "pneumatic" (but never of a material or "hylic" nature), while resurrection was spiritual and immediate, that is, understood metaphorically rather than as an eschatological, actual resurrection of the body.[62] In their own way, the Marcionites expressed similar ideas, but our interest here lies in the Fathers' reaction to the Gnostic challenge, rather than in a taxonomy of Gnostic conceptions.

A mere perusal of some of the early Patristic treatises reveals the urgency with which anthropological questions were asked and answered.[63] This urgency reflects the existential intensity with which the new sensitivity was emerging, and its importance is felt best in the context of the Gnostic challenge. Irenaeus insists so much on the humanity of Christ because he sees it as a warrant of the "salvation of our flesh, since were not the flesh to be saved, God would not have become flesh."[64]

---

[60] *Excerpta ex Theodoto,* 78.2. F. Sagnard, ed. and tr. (Sources Chrétiennes, 23; 1948, reprint Paris 1970), 202. The analysis of this anguished quest, unfortunately expressed in rather anachronistic Heideggerian parlance, formed the core of H. Jonas' classical study, *Gnosis und spätantiker Geist, I* (Göttingen 1934).

[61] *C.G.* II; 49, 26ff., B. Layton, ed. and tr. (Harvard Dissertations in Religion, 12; Missoula, Mont. 1979), 30–31.

[62] Irenaeus, *Adversus Haereses* 1.21.4, A Rousseau, L. Doutreleau, eds. and trs. (Sources Chrétiennes, 264; Paris 1979), 302–304. On Gnostic anthropology in general, see K. Rudolph, *Die Gnosis: Wesen und Geschichte einer spätantiken Religion* (Göttingen 1980), 98–131.

[63] On Patristic anthropology, see H. Karpp, *Probleme altchristlicher Anthropologie* (Beiträge z. Forderung christl. Theol., 43.3; Gütersloh 1950), and E. Osborn, *The Beginning of Christian Philosophy* (Cambridge 1981), 79–110.

[64] Irenaeus, *Adv. Haer.* 5.14.1, A. Rousseau, L. Doutreleau and C. Mercier, eds. and trs. (Sources Chrétiennes, 153; Paris 1969), 181–187. The importance of this text is underlined by J. Daniélou, *Message évangélique et culture hellénistique* (Paris 1961), 365–74.

Hence a radical break with the Platonic conception of man and the elaboration of a new anthropology, which saw the essence of man not in his soul, but in the composite of soul and body: "It is man, and not a part of man, who becomes to the image and the resemblance of God."[65] The perfect man is thus the mixing and the union *(sugkrasis kai henosis)* of soul and flesh.[66] "Soul and body together constitute the animal" is one of the main motifs in Aristotle's *De Anima.* It is rather puzzling at first to notice the Aristotelian antecedents of this new anthropological sensitivity. Although the presence of Aristotelian elements in Augustine's anthropology has been noticed, they do not appear to have been the direct source of Patristic teachings.[67]

Similar anthropological principles appear in Pseudo-Athenagoras' *De Resurrectione,* the first Christian work to have been devoted to the problem. The author affirms: "There is one living being composed of two parts, undergoing all the experiences of soul and body." He goes on, getting more specific: "It is man, not simply soul, who received understanding and reason. Man, then, who consists of both soul and body must survive forever; but he cannot survive unless he is raised."[68]

One can hardly accuse Tertullian of being an *esprit de système.* Yet, if there is one theme to which he keeps coming back, approaching it from various angles, each time with all the force of his conviction, it is that of the body, or rather the flesh (both terms, *corpus* and *caro* are more or less equivalent, although *caro* is less ambiguous)[69] and its status. In his case, as in that of Irenaeus, the polemical context is obvious: it is against Gnostics (Valentinians, Marcionites, even Cainites) that he fights in his treatises *On Baptism, On the Resurrection of the Dead, On the Flesh of Christ,* or *Against Marcion* (all written between 200 and 211). "But remember that man is properly called flesh – a term which first expressed the name 'man'" (Gen. 2: 7–8). There is no need to refer to Aristotle, indeed,

---

[65] See the synthesis of A. G. Hamman, *L'homme, image de Dieu: anthropologie patristique* (Paris 1986).

[66] Irenaeus, *Adv. Haer.* 5. 6.1.

[67] On the limited exposure to Aristotle of early Christian authors, see A. J. Festugière, *L'idéal religieux,* note 29 above. On the Aristotelian grounding of Augustine's anthropology, see P. Henry, *St. Augustine on Personality* (New York 1960), esp. 8–11. Cf. A. C. Lloyd, "On Augustine's Concept of the Person," in *Augustine: a Collection of Critical Essays,* ed. R. A. Markus (Garden City, N.Y. 1972), 191–205; and W. R. O'Connor, "The Concept of the Person in Saint Augustine's *De Trinitate,*" *Augustinian Studies* 13 (1982): 133–43. Cf. A. C. Pegis, *At the origins of the Thomistic Notion of Man,* n. 29 above, who claims that the Augustinian reinterpretation of Aristotle holds the key to the Thomistic doctrine of man.

[68] Athenagoras, *De Resurrectione,* W. R. Schoedel, ed. and tr.(Oxford 1972), respectively *De Resurrectione,* 15.2 and 15.6, pp. 122–23 and 124–25. According to the editor, the text was probably written as an anti-Origenian tract.

[69] On the semantic fields of *corpus* and *caro* in Tertullian's vocabulary, see R. Braun, *Deus Christianorum: Recherches sur le vocabulaire doctrinal de Tertullien* (Paris 1962), 298–317, esp. 304. *Corpus* is more broadly defined than *caro,* and is ambiguous. Thus Tertullian uses *caro christi* much more frequently than *corpus christi.*

when the Biblical roots are so obvious. Tertullian goes on: "I would readily insist on this.... everything planned for man and given not to the soul alone, but also to the flesh."[70]

Elsewhere, he argues from the very weakness of the flesh against assigning to it sole responsibility for sin: "What absurdity, however, it is to attribute sin and crime to that substance to which you do not assign any good actions or character of its own."[71] Flesh, then, is ancillary to the soul in the commission of sin. On the other hand, it is usually through flesh, or at least with its help, that sin is committed. Thus, any full-fledged conception of the Final Judgment requires the presence of the entire man (i.e., flesh and soul) at the end of days.[72] In other words, divine justice itself demands the integral resurrection of man.[73] Through sin, the whole man was lost. Through Christ, therefore, it is the whole man who will be saved.[74]

The treatise *On the Resurrection of the Dead* is in many ways a powerful apology of the flesh – both the flesh of man and that of Christ. In order to be able to fight Gnostic Docetism effectively, Tertullian must show that in the wake of Irenaeus, the Gnostic interpretation of Paul's harsh words against the flesh is mistaken: the Apostle only seems to condemn flesh. Actually, he refers to the sins of flesh. The vocable "flesh" in Paul's Epistles is a generic term for carnal practices.[75] Christ was thus really born in the flesh. Mary gave birth literally, not figuratively. The status of Christ's flesh is utterly respectable, since it was the model according to which God created man. Respecting the flesh of Christ is the prerequisite for respecting the human body: the soul that hates the body is also that which despises its creator, or which denies or alters it in the very person of Christ.[76]

Through his insistence on the resurrection of the whole human composite, Tertullian is brought to some quite interesting reflections on the preservation of human identity: the notion of change must be clearly distinguished from that of destruction. "To be transformed is to be in a different way. Thus, when one is dif-

---

[70] *De resur. mort.* 5.8–9. Text in E. Kroymann, ed., *Tertulliani Opera* III (CSEL 47; Vienna and Leipzig 1906), vol. 3. See J.-P. Mahé's detailed analysis of the work in his introduction to Tertullian, *La résurrection des morts* (Paris 1980). Cf. R. Sider, "Structure and Design in the *de resurrectione morturum*," *Vigiliae Christianae* 23 (1969): 177–96.

[71] *De anima* 40.

[72] *De resur. mort.* 14.10.

[73] Ibid., 56; 57.6.

[74] Ibid., 34.1–2. On the belief in resurrection of the dead and for good presentation of the evidence and a useful bibliography, see R. Staaks, "Auferstehung," *TRE* 4: 441 ff. Cf. in particular R. M. Grant, "The Resurrection of the Body," *JR* 28 (1948): 120–30; 188–208 (who is unable to answer the main question, namely *why* the Fathers insisted on a physical conception of resurrection).

[75] *De resur. mort* 46 and 49.7.

[76] Ibid., 20. 3; 6. 44; 63. 6.

ferently, one can still be oneself."[77] In *The Flesh of Christ,* Tertullian insists on Christ's love for man, the whole man, and in particular for his flesh, weak and humble. It is this man, in the flesh, that Christ loved and saved.[78]

The implications of these texts, chosen almost at random among many others, seem to me momentous. No pagan philosopher could have wished or dared express such love for the human body, a love that God was the first to show. *Caro salutis cardo:* the discovery of the person as a unified composite of soul and body in late antiquity was indeed a Christian discovery.[79]

This love which God so generously offered to man opened the way to repentance, forgiveness of sins, and salvation. While sins soil the soul (which Tertullian, in good Stoic fashion, conceives as corporeal), baptism cleanses it: although the water runs on the body, its benefits to us are spiritual. "The rite of baptism is a corporeal action, but its effect is spiritual since it delivers us from sin."[80] Baptism is thus a purification of the whole person; this rite is also the condition sine qua non of salvation. Since the passion and resurrection of the Lord, faith is naked without baptism, and needs it as a garb of sorts.[81]

In other words, baptism accomplishes and symbolizes both the purification and integration of the individual as a whole, and entry into the Church, that is, the mystical Body of Christ. The same rite which is the condition of salvation for the person also acts as the identification principle for the Church – thus excluding from possible salvation not only pagans and Jews, but also heretics, since they do not partake in the same baptism.[82] The unity of the individual person, as well as the unity of the person of Christ, entails the unity of the Church, Christ's Body.

Similar anthropological conceptions were very widely adopted in both the East and the West, and were securely established by the fourth century, as shown for instance by Nemesius of Emesa's *De Natura Hominis,* a work more remarkable in its synthetical character (including the full integration of philosophical and scientific accepted wisdom of the day) than in its originality.[83] Yet, it

---

[77] Ibid., 55.1; 55.6.

[78] Tertullian, *De carne Christi* 4.3–4, in Mahé, ed. and tr.; Tertullien, *La Chair du Christ* (SC 216–217; Paris 1975), 1: 222–25.

[79] The central importance of the body since the earliest strata of Christian thought was the strongest insight of Nygren's classic *Eros and Agape*; cf. J. Rist, "Some Interpretations of Agape and Eros," in his *Platonism and its Christian Heritage,* vol. 1, n. 18 above.

[80] Tertullian, *De baptismo* 7.2.in *Tertulliani Opera I*, A. Reifferscheid and G. Wissowa, eds. (CSEL 20; Vienna, Prague and Leipzig 1890), 207.

[81] Ibid., 12.1; 13.2.

[82] Ibid. 15.2. On the whole array of problems related to the symbolical meaning of early Christian ritual and theology pertaining to the body, see J. G. Gager, "Body-Symbols and Social Reality: Resurrection, Incarnation and Asceticism in Early Christianity," *Religion* 12 (1982): 345–463.

[83] For a detailed presentation of Nemesius' thought, see the introduction to G. Verbeke and J. R. Moncho, *Némésius d'Emèse, De Natura Hominis* (Corpus Latinorum Commentatorium in Aristotelem Graecorum, suppl. 1; Leiden 1975).

was in the West that the most radical breakthrough occurred. A direct line of influence joins Tertullian to his great African successors. Cyprian would state that there is no salvation outside the Church, while Augustine would make liberal use of a rather far-fetched biblical exegesis in order to fight the Donatists. *Deus dilectatio est* (I John 4: 8, 16): according to Augustine, the Donatists do not love God's Body, since they do not love its members, i.e., the whole Christian community. "One cannot love the head without the members."[84] The Donatists cannot be accused of professing Docetic doctrines, since they recognize that Jesus Christ came in the flesh, but they behave as if they were Docetists. Indeed, to break the unity of the Church is to divide the Body of Christ, showing a total lack of respect for it. Only with the end of the schism will Christ be one, loving Himself; for when the members love each other, the body loves itself.[85]

For Augustine, both the Incarnation and the resurrection of the body played a major role in his reevaluation of the human body, after he had succeeded in partly disentangling himself from the Neo-platonic web of his early days as a Christian.[86] For him, moreover, the parallelism between personal and collective identity is particularly striking. After Origen, Basil the Great, Gregory of Nyssa, and Ambrose, he comments on Canticle 1:8 "Nisi cognoueris temetipsam, opulchra inter mulieres ..."[87] Ambrose had pointed out that the verse shows Solomon – as well as Moses – to have predated the Delphic maxim, stolen from them by Apollo. Ambrose had insisted that knowing oneself meant recognizing that we are mortals and sinners in our body, but also capable of a conversion of all our being through reason. Augustine, on his part, notes that this commandment is not addressed only to the soul, but also to the Church: she must know herself, recognize herself as catholic. In other words, the verse offers a weapon threatening the Donatists, who boast of being an African Church.[88]

Augustine, who deals with this verse in several places, usually tries to prevent

---

[84] *Commentary on I John,* 10.3, in P. Agaesse, ed. and tr. (Sources Chrétiennes, 75; Paris 1961), 414.

[85] Ibid., 6. 10. Et erit unus Christus amans seipsum. Cum enim se invicem amant membra, corpus se amat.

[86] See in particular H.-I. Marrou, *The Resurrection and St. Augustine's Theology of Human Values* (Villanova, Pa. 1966). The French original was first published in *REA* 12 (1966): 111–36, and reprinted in Marrou, *Patristique et Humanisme: Mélanges* (Patristica Sorbonnesia 9; Paris 1976), 429–55. This article made use mainly of later texts. M. R. Miles has shown more precisely the evolution of Augustine's thought on this topic, in her *Augustine on the Body* (American Academy of Religion, Dissertation Series 31; Missoula, Mont. 1979). On the different sensitivities in the East and in the West about the resurrection of the flesh, see for instance Y. M. Duval, "La discussion entre l'apocrisiaire Grégoire et le patriarche Eutychius au sujet de la résurrection de la chair: l'arrière plan doctrinal oriental et occidental," in *Grégoire le Grand* (Colloques internationaux du C.N.R.S.; Paris 1986), 346–65.

[87] Augustine, *In Psalmos* 66. 4. 22, quoted by Courcelle, *Connais-toi toi même,* n. 25 above, 1: 145, n. 148; cf. 147. The Latin retains a mistake already made by the LXX.

[88] Ibid. 118. 2. 13–14, quoted by Courcelle, ibid., 117; 118, n.16; 147, n.160.

an exegesis of the *Nosce te ipsum* that would place man at the end of the intro-spective process. Already in the *De vera religione,* the famous phrase "Noli foras ire, in teipsum redi; in interiore homine habitat veritas" implies that man be passed over at the end of introspection, which should culminate with a *conversio* to God.[89] On all grounds, then, for Augustine, *nosce te ipsum* means something quite different than what it had meant for pagan philosophers: it is not only his soul that man must seek to attend to; collective identity is as important as per-sonal identity; self-knowledge does indeed lead to the knowledge of God, al-though it does not end up in Him directly (since there is no *sungeneia* between the soul and the divine).[90] Moreover, introspection also leads to one's neighbor, whom one cannot love without self-knowledge. Above all, Augustine recog-nizes the fundamentally ambiguous character of introspection, a descent into the self that reveals both the misery and the greatness of human nature.

The new sensitivity to the human person was nowhere better expressed than in the *Confessions:* "As long as I accomplish my pilgrimage far from Thee, I am more present to myself than to Thee." Augustine departs here from both Neo-platonists and Stoics: there is neither a continuum between the soul and God, nor an immanence of the divine. The continuum, for Augustine, is the temporal dimension, within which the recognition of the self takes place – a dimension ig-nored by the Greek philosophers and which links the subject to the cosmos in a new, historical, way. According to his own testimony, the *Confessions* were writ-ten so that we know "out of what depths one must cry unto Thee".[91] The chasm between God the creator and the soul of the individual, which is that of a sinner, can be bridged, but only through love, not directly through knowledge. Self-knowledge is necessary, but as a catalyst of love – first self-love and then love of other souls and love of God. It is in the *De Trinitate,* from Book 9 on and particu-larly in Book 14, that Augustine developed his well-known view of the threefold process through which the soul remembers itself, understands itself, and loves it-self, as an image of the Divine Trinity.

The *Confessions* are a book *sui generis,* which bears little resemblance to other autobiographies in antiquity. In the *Confessions,* the contrite conscience brings a man to throw himself at God's mercy. Georg Misch has noted that

---

[89] Augustine, *De vera religione* 39. 72. Cf. Courcelle, ibid., 148–49.

[90] To be sure, Augustine's early writings, particularly those of the Cassiciacum period, were written under the spell of the *Libri Platonicorum*. R. J. O'Connell has argued in a sustained way that Augustine's early anthropology was shaped in a fundamental way by Plotinus. While the argument carries conviction to a large extent for the young Augustine, he later learned to di-stance himself from these early views. See in particular O'Connell, *St. Augustine's Early Theory of Man, A.D. 386–391* (Cambridge, Mass. 1968).

[91] Augustine, *Confessions* 10.5: "et ideo, quamdiu peregrinor abs te, mihi sum praesentior quam tibi."; *Confessions* 2. 3:"ut videlicet ego et quisquis haec legi cogitemus, de quam profun-do clamandum sit at te".

"Here began one of the most profound changes in European self-disclosure."[92] If one is to look for spiritual – although not literary – antecedents of the *Confessions,* Paul comes to mind first.[93] Already, in the story of his conversion, individual existence was given a transcendental structure – even though, or precisely because, it was that of a sinner. The total involvement in the imperfect person qua person, which Augustine revealed in his autobiography, has remained one of the major acquisitions of both European literary history and spiritual consciousness.[94] The *Confessions* represent nothing less than the majestic peak of a revolution within the ancient spirit, the first expression of the modern and paradoxical conception of the person, that is to say a subjectivity at once entire and broken, and therefore established in an immediate way through its reflectivity. In other words, it is the urgent need to close the gap within itself that permits the emergence of a new, reflective attitude to the self.

5.

I have tried here to refer briefly to some of the main articulations, in early Christian thought, which led to the mature expression of the new sensitivity to the subject exemplified in the *Confessions*. I have also argued that these articulations stemmed from both a few pivotal theological conceptions and the urgent need to refute deviant interpretations of the Christian message. Hence the direct correlation between conceptions of the individual and the reflectivity of the collective person, the Church.

It is a fact only partially accounted for that this new existential sensitivity remained the acquisition of the Western Church, where it was activated, while it was kept dormant in the East, where the Greek theologians developed a rather essentialist thought.[95] Although one is on very slippery ground indeed when trying to radicalize the differences between East and West in the largely unified urban culture of the Roman empire, as Peter Brown has reminded us, the process of self-awareness on both sides was rather dissimilar.[96] Brown himself has

---

[92] See G. Misch's seminal *A History of Autobiography in Antiquity* (London 1950), 2: 625–67; The quotation is from p. 531. One might add that Augustine's literary originality began already with the *Soliloquia,* which were the first example of that genre.

[93] Fredericksen, n. 21 above.

[94] See P. Courcelle, *Les Confessions de Saint Augustin,* n. 20 above.

[95] It may be no mere chance if *persona* was the only technical term to designate the aspects of trinity in Christian Latin, while the Greek theologians long preferred *hupostasis* to *prosopon.* See Braun, *Deus Christianorum,* n. 69 above, 240–42; and G. L. Prestige, *God in Patristic Thought,* ch.8 (I used the French translation, *Dieu dans la pensée patristique* [Paris 1955], 142–57).

[96] P. Brown, "Eastern and Western Christendom in Late Antiquity: a Parting of the Ways," in *Society and the Holy in Late antiquity,* n. 58 above, 166–95.

pointed out that in the West Christians retained a "twice-born" attitude much longer and kept their distance from the *saeculum,* remaining to a large extent outsiders. He has also referred to what he calls Augustine's rejection of the Eastern monastic paradigm, a rejection closely related to his own direct interest in sexuality.[97] One might add that the more fully developed cult of the martyrs in the West permitted a greater emphasis on the individual – first as a model (the martyr or the saint), then also as a follower of that model. Apologies written in Latin are much less intellectual or "philosophical" in character than those written in Greek. Rather than attempting to show that Christianity, the "barbarian philosophy," was a philosophy none the less,[98] Latin apologists more simply argued for religious tolerance; thus, for instance, Tertullian's *Apologeticum* or his *Ad Scapulam.* In the intellectual and spiritual synthesis of the Cappadocian Fathers, which was to remain the hieratic heritage of Byzantium, the emphasis of the religious experience is on the ideal of the soul meeting God in the *homoiôsis theôi.* Following Jesus' behavior and precepts in daily life, the *imitatio Christi,* remained a more specifically Western ideal that was to shape medieval spirituality up to the Reformation.[99] Indeed, the radical reflectivity bequeathed by Augustine to the Western tradition was, even more than a new anthropology, a new attitude – grounded in the recognition of the inescapable paradox of the human subject. When it gave birth to the reflective self, it also delivered its twin brother: the person in search of his like, that is, intersubjectivity. Both attitudes, rendered possible simultaneously through the presence of God's love, were to become the two sides of the Western humanist tradition.

It would be the task of another, major study in historical and philosophical anthropology to analyze the complex relationships between these twin brothers. Such a study of the "intersubjective circle," as we may call it, would seek to describe the ways in which the wounded and contrite self develops at once humility towards itself and compassion towards others. This compassion becomes the new basis of ethics. The recognition of one's duties towards others as the only possible way to retrieving the *imago dei* and achieving a total reunification of the self. If this new ethics supposes religious foundations, it also has political implications: from Paul to Augustine, the communal and political dimensions of the *Corpus Christi* were progressively discovered until their integration in the *Civitas Dei.* It is throughout the creation that the traces of God are to be found (to use a concept developed by Augustine and surviving to this day in the philos-

---

[97] Ibid. 174–75, see also his chapter in *A History of Private Life.*

[98] On this topic which would need further research, see for instance J. H. Waszink, "Some Observations on the Appreciation of the 'Philosophy of the Barbarians' in Early Christian Literature," in *Mélanges Christine Mohrmann* (Utrecht 1963), 41–56.

[99] For the difference of emphasis in Eastern and Western Christian attitudes to the human person as the Image of God, see B. McGinn, J. Meyendorff, J. Leclercq, eds., *Christian Spirituality: Origins to the 12th Century* (New York 1986), ch. 2.

ophy of Emmanuel Lévinas). In its very brokenness and incompleteness the created cosmos reflects, just like the human person, the hidden presence of its Creator. Christian ethics and politics are hence possessed of a double and ambiguous character: together with their orientation towards the salvation of mankind, between mythical past and eschatological future, they are, fundamentally,
the ethics and politics of imperfection. Just as the *polis,* as noted above, was the
context of the Greek conceptions of the person, so the Christian attitude is directly linked to a new perception of society. Only through compassion for one's
neighbor can one hope to reach oneself. Some basic traits of early Christian
thought may hence be shown to have transformed in depth the relationships between the person and society, as well as the very concept of the person.

Chapter 11

Dreams and Magic among Pagans and Christians

"Dream-producing charm using three reeds. The picking of the three reeds is to be before sunrise. After sunset raise the first, look to the east and say three times: Maskelli Maskellô ... I am picking you up in order that you might give me a dream ..."[1]

"Slander spell to Selene, which works for everything and every rite. For it attracts in the same hour, it sends dreams, it causes sickness, produces dream-visions *(oneirothauptei),* removes enemies when you reverse the spell, however you wish. But above all be protected by a protective charm and do not approach the procedure carelessly or else the goddess is angry ..."[2]

These two texts, picked out almost at random among the Greek magical texts on papyrus, underline the close connection between dreams and magic in Hellenistic and Roman Egypt. The place of both dreams and magic was rather different in early Christian discourse from what it had been in the pagan world. The purpose of the following pages is to assess the change in the relationships between dreams and magic in the passage from paganism to Christianity in the Roman Empire. By focusing on two phenomena at once universal and marginal to official religion, I hope to shed some light on the transformation of religious experience in late antiquity.

1. Dreams and magic in the ancient world

Samson Eitrem has offered the only study, to this day, specifically devoted to the relationships between magic and dreams in the ancient world.[3] Eitrem's analysis is based principally on the Greek Magical Papyri, where he found abundant material regarding magical dream visions. Eitrem first describes and analyzes various examples of dream request, which involve various divinities, such as

---

[1] PGM IV, 2172–3208; English according to H. D. Betz, ed., *The Greek Magical Papyri in Translation* (Chicago and London 1986), 99ff.

[2] PGM IV, 2622ff (86 Betz). See K. Preisendanz, ed., *Papyri Graecae Magicae* (2nd. ed. by A. Henrichs, Stuttgart 1973), I.176.

[3] Although this text was written a long time ago (Eitrem died aged ninety three in 1966), it was published only recently. See "Dreams and Divination in Magical Ritual," in *Magika Hiera: Ancient Greek Magic and Religion,* eds. Ch. A. Faraone, D. Obink, (New York and Oxford 1991), 175–87.

Hermes, the Greek dream sender, Apollo, or Helios. He then studied the topic of dream transmission, i.e, the magical methods in order to send a dream to someone else, insisting on the important figure of the attendant (*paredros*), who is instrumental in sending a dream revelation to someone through a magical procedure that includes the pronunciation of a formula. Eitrem ends his study with a few brief remarks on the horrified reactions of the early Christians regarding the transmission of dreams and the related magic of sorcerers.

The magical papyri that concern dreams fall into two categories, as Eitrem pointed out. There are requests for a dream for oneself, and requests for sending a dream to another person. There are also procedures for requesting dream-revelations. These often require ritual purification. The vision is preceded by ascetic practices. In one case, at least, the revelatory dream stands beside the dreamer in the form of a friend.[4] A recent study of dreams in late antiquity rightly connects this to the Homeric figuration of dreams as autonomous presences speaking to the dreamer.[5] In short: "The therapeutic value of magical dreams lies in such revealing confrontation. Just as Asclepian dreaming healed the body, so magical dreaming provided a therapy for the mind."[6] Hence, when we speak of the relationships between dreams and magic, we refer both to magical dreams, which themselves are possessed of magical powers, and to dreams as part of the preparation of magical rites. Moreover, incubation – the practice of sleeping in the god's temple in order to receive a revelation through dream – may be considered close to the world of magic.

The most important recent contribution to our topic is Peter Kingsley's *Ancient Philosophy, Alchemy and Magic.*[7] In this highly original and important piece of work dealing with the relationships between Greek religion and philosophy, Kingsley notes that "in the ancient world a fixed centre for the interpretation of dreams invariably implied the existence of a dream oracle." In southern Italy and in Sicily, craters and openings were viewed as points of access to the underworld. "This was true in particular of oracle centres specializing in the interpretation of dreams."[8] Indeed, the dream prophets of the Etna region, for instance, were renowned throughout Italy.[9] Kingsley notes further that there are striking similarities between the Pythagorean food taboos and the requirements of abstinence in Greek ritual and magic, especially for people using dream

---

[4] PGM VII, 798–99. See G. Fowden, *The Egyptian Hermes: a Historical Approach to the Late Pagan Mind* (Princeton 1986), 82: "PGM IV, [the Paris Papyrus] reveals "the injection of more or less spiritual elements into magic."

[5] P. Cox Miller, *Dreams in Late Antiquity* (Princeton 1994), 119–20. Cf. my review in *JR* 76 (1996): 626–28.

[6] Ibid., 123.

[7] P. Kingsley, *Ancient Philosophy, Alchemy and Magic: Empedocles and Pythagorean Tradition* (Oxford 1995). Cf. my review in *Numen* 44 (1997): 211–13.

[8] Ibid., 282.

[9] Ibid., 281.

oracles.[10] For Kingsley, the importance of dreams in the magical papyri shows that the idea of divination through dreams, which had been present among the early Pythagorean communities, continued not only to be understood, but also to be put into practice.[11] Kingsley summarizes: "In this shared concern with dreams and dream oracles there is an obvious affinity between Pythagoreism and the magical papyri."[12] The importance of Kingsley's study from our perspective stems from his insistence on the thread which leads from early movements like Empedocles or the Pythagoreans to the highly syncretistic world of the Hellenistic magical papyri. Magic was not a phenomenon limited to "popular religion," and dreams retained a central place within the magic practices of intellectuals.[13]

As with dreams, magic appears to be a universal phenomenon, most often practiced during the night, far from the light of official, public practices. It is to this nocturnal nature that both dreams and magic owe their secret, esoteric, hidden character.[14] Like dreaming, magic appears in a multiplicity of forms, heavily conditioned by the cultural and religious milieu. Last and not least, magic, like dreaming, offers a direct and close contact between our world and the realm of the divine (or of the demonic). Both dreams and magic permit the passage from our usual self to another self, and this crossing of boundaries between realms usually distinct can give the dreamer or the magician a special ecstatic power, similar to that of the shaman.[15] Although dreaming is by definition a private activity, and magic almost always a social, though not an official one, both often played rather similar roles in the ancient world in the lives of individuals. In the words of Plutarch, for instance:

> People with chronic diseases, when they have despaired of ordinary remedies and customary regimens, turn to expiations and amulets and dreams.[16]

In the Roman Empire, magic appears to have grown in popularity from the second to the fifth century C.E. (probably at the expense of astrology), together with the growth in popularity of Christianity itself.[17] The fact that magic was con-

---

[10] Ibid., 283.

[11] Ibid., 286.

[12] Ibid., 287. This link had been already pointed out by L. Deubner, *De Incubatione* (Leipzig 1900), 30; cf. Kingsley, 288.

[13] See Kingsley, 246, n. 43, on PGM LXX.4–19, rejecting Henrichs and Betz's suggestion of a reference to the mysteries of the Idean Dactyls. See further G. Stroumsa, *Hidden Wisdom: Esoteric Traditions and the Roots of Christian* Mysticism (SHR 70; Leiden 1996), 169–83, where I accept this identification uncritically.

[14] F. Graf, *La magie dans le monde gréco-romain* (Paris 1995), 33, insists on the nocturnal character of magical rites.

[15] The shaman often experiences initiatory dreams; see M. Eliade, *Le chamanisme et les techniques de l'extase* (Paris 1951), 45–75.

[16] Plutarch, *De facie lunae*, 920 B, cited by Aune, see n. 17.

[17] D. Aune, "Magic in Early Christianity," in *ANRW*, II. 23.2 (New York and Berlin 1980), 1507–1557, esp. 1519.

sistently prohibited by Roman law reflects the power with which it was endowed. Had the emperors not been afraid of magic, they probably would not have sought so consistently to neutralize it. At the same time, we can detect a clear transformation of attitudes to dreams, their nature, their source, their value, and their interpretation. As I try to show in the next chapter, the victory of Christianity led to a transformation of the discourse on dreams in late antiquity.[18] In brief, the spectrum of significant and legitimate dreams in the Christian mind-set shrunk a great deal from what it had been in the classical world, as most dreams were suspect and thought to have been sent by Satan.

Since Frazer, the relationship between magic and religion have been the topic of many studies.[19] I want here to ask a different, less general question. Did the religious revolution of late antiquity also provoke a similarly deep change in the perception and representations of magic? In other words, can we detect a transformation of magic concomitant to the transformation of religion in late antiquity and the establishment of Christianity as the state religion in the Empire?

In their seminal study of magic, written more than ninety years ago, Marcel Mauss and Henri Hubert pointed out the private, irregular, ecstatic, and abnormal character of magical rite.[20] Magic remained secret, mysterious, and the magician often provoked his own states of *ekstasis*. According to them, this character differentiates magic from religion, or rather from organized cult, in a striking way. But it also reveals close affinities between dreams and magic: dreams are also held in an abnormal state – albeit a very common one – and hence are conducive to affective states which can generate a great power unknown in diurnal states. In other words, both magic and dreams are part of the uncanny, and answer to rules different from the ones of daily, official life and cult. Both dreams and magic, therefore, encourage contacts with demonic forces.

Religions have a tendency to define as magic the rites of another religion with which they are in conflict. That does not necessarily mean that these rites are vain, but rather that they are to be avoided, that they make use of wrong, dangerous, or prohibited knowledge. While the pagans often accused the early Christians of magical practices, the latter soon came to perceive the pagans as believing in magic and offering a cult to demons.

In the ancient world, the magician is the specialist of the passage, which is relatively easy and common, between the realm of the gods and the world of men. This passage, in particular, is effected in dreams, since the body rests while

---

[18] See chapter 12 of this volume.

[19] For a classical statement of the problem, see for instance L. Deubner, *Magie und Religion* (Freiburg 1922).

[20] M. Mauss and H. Hubert, "Esquisse d'une théorie générale de la magie," in *Sociologie et anthropologie* by M. Mauss (Paris 1950). The "Esquisse" was first published in 1902–1903 in the *Annales de Sociologie*.

the soul wanders, including in the netherworld. Among our various sources on magic in the Greek world, none is as important as the corpus of the Greek Magical Papyri. These texts, which offer recipes and technical injunctions for the magician, often refer to various rites of incubation. Sleep is often recommended in the PGM.[21]

In a highly perceptive synthesis on the nature and function of magic in the ancient world, Fritz Graf does not discuss dreams in their relationship to magic.[22] Neither does he deal with the question of the transformation of the nature, role, and image of magic that occurred with the triumph of Christianity. Graf only refers in passing to magic in Christian texts, noting that the Christian saints would come to be considered the best and most efficacious *paredroi*.[23] Moreover, he points out the difference between the system of mental representations, which rejects the use of magic, and daily reality, which entails perforce such a recourse to magic (what we usually call "cognitive dissonance").[24] An interesting point in Graf's book is his insistence on the fact that in the Greco-Roman world, any peculiar religious belief or behavior is likely to raise a suspicion of magic. Magic is close to excessive religious fervor of any kind (for instance the Gnostics and Marcion are accused of magical practices by the heresiologists).

We have learned to reject the traditional categories for which magic was a phenomenon of "popular religion." Indeed, we now know, as noted by A. A. Barb, that "the majority of popular incantations are the product of highly educated people."[25] Intellectuals were not only interested in magical practices and believed in its implicit presuppositions; some also showed an active interest in magic, and wrote many of the magical documents that we possess, incantations on bowls, gold tablets, or papyri.

In this context, a special case is that of Greek philosophers and magic. We can detect a pagan influence on Christian dream-oracles, the commonest form of divination, and the only one, as Franz Cumont noted long ago, which was not prohibited by the early Church.[26] A philosopher like Plotinus condemned the magicians' concentration on technical knowledge and their lack of interest for personal virtue, hence his judgment of the magical texts as unspiritual.[27] Jamblichus, on his side, discusses "divine dreams" which give one some revelation about the

---

[21] Deubner, *De Incubatione*, 15, 29, 32: *oneiraitèson, oneirou aitèsis.*

[22] Graf, *La magie dans le monde gréco-romain.*

[23] Ibid., 137, with a reference to P. Brown, *The Cult of the Saints* (Chicago 1981), ch. 3.

[24] Ibid., 214.

[25] A. A. Barb, "The Survival of the Magic Arts," in *The Conflict between Paganism and Christianity in the Fourth Century,* ed. A. Momigliano (Oxford 1963), 100–25, esp. 124, with a reference to M. Eliade, *Traité d'histoire des religions,* 258.

[26] See P. Athanasiadi, "Dreams, Theurgy and Freelance Divination: The Testimony of Iamblichus," *JRS* 83 (1993): 115–30, who also deals with magically-produced dreams.

[27] See G. Fowden, *The Egyptian Hermes,* 79.

future.[28] Mantic dealt with these sacred dreams, which often precede divine epi-
phanies. We can thus reach the future "not in an excited *ekstasis* (since the body
remains at rest), but with no more consciousness of facts that in wakefulness."
These are dreams quite different from all human dreams, since they occur while
one is in a limbo of sorts between sleep and wakefulness. In them, one hears
voices that reveal the future (*mantikè*). Jamblichus adds that such dreams partially precede divine epiphany.[29] Thus, in the sanctuaries of Asclepios illnesses
are stopped by divine or "sacred" dreams.

2. *Dreams and magic in Christianity*

The Christians soon learned to return the accusation of being irreligious hurled
against them by the pagans, and accused the latter of magic since their cult was
addressed to demons, not to the one and only God. But it is difficult to avoid perceiving some magical aspects in Christianity. Should anyone be reminded that it
was only a few years ago that the Catholic Church suppressed the official position of exorcist?

For Christians, magic obviously has a bad name. "Magical" are the practices
and beliefs of others, not of Christians. Magic, in a sense, is the false religion of
the pagans. The early Christian attitude to magic directly reflects Mauss's perception, according to which the essence of magic lay in its illegality, as a phenomenon of social deviance.[30] The practices of Christians that strike us as closely
similar to those called magical by the Church Fathers, are described in quite a
different fashion in early Christian literature.

On the other side, the Christian approach to dreams is quite different from
traditional attitudes. It ignores or distrusts most as stemming either from Satan
or from the body, and refers to other dreams, considered to be religiously significant, as either dreams or visions, without marking the differences clearly. Hence
what our texts call "visions" *(oraseis)* often refer to visions of God, Christ,
angels, or another heavenly figure obtained in a dream.

Long ago, Erik Peterson argued that many of the revelatory visions mentioned in the *Shepherd of Hermas* are described using terms and concepts taken
from ancient magic and magical techniques, particularly those relating to divination. Peterson noted that although there were no striking parallels to the *Shepherd* in Jewish and Christian Apocalyptic literature, strikingly similar themes
could be found in Hermetic, Gnostic, and magical literature. He was referring,

---

[28] *De Mysteriis*, III.2–3, ed. and tr. E. Des Places (Paris 1966), 97–103.
[29] Ibid., 99, n. 32.
[30] See also J. Z. Smith, cited in Aune, *Magic,* 1514.

for instance, to the famous case of Thessalos the doctor.[31] He also pointed out the throne *(kathedra, thronos)* of the divinity, comparing it to Apollo's *thronos* in PGM I.2.[32] Oddly enough, Peterson – who was aware of the Jewish background of early Christian literature – makes no connection to similar patterns in some late antique Hebrew texts.[33]

In early Christianity, we can clearly perceive an ambiguous attitude to magic, as well as to dreams: on the one side, magic is vain, because demons have no real existence. If magic is prohibited, it is not because it is useless, but rather due to the dangers inherent in its practice. Origen, for instance, takes magic very seriously indeed.[34] For him, the theory of language and the ontological value of letters and words, which lie at the basis of sympathetic magic, are to be taken with the utmost seriousness.[35] According to Origen, Christian exorcisms are profoundly different from magical actions, although their morphology may seem superficially similar. Christian exorcisms operate ethical transformations in souls, while the magician operates under the assumption "ex opere operato."[36]

For Tertullian, there is a clear and direct connection between dreams and magic:

> To proceed, if magicians produce phantoms *(si et magi phantasmato edunt)* and give a bad name to the souls of the dead; if they kill children to make an oracle speak; if by mountebank tricks they play off no end of miracles; if they send dreams to people *(si et somnia immitunt)*. ...[37]

Following Justin Martyr, his disciple Tatian a few decades previously, before Tertullian, had perceived the demons as being able to send dreams to people:

> The demons do not heal, but by craft they make men prisoner. The most admirable Justin was right in pronouncing that demons are like bandits, for just as bandits are in the habit of taking men prisoner and then releasing them to their families on payment, so too those supposed gods visit men's bodies, and then in dreams create an impression of their presence and order their victims to come forward in sight of all.[38]

---

[31] See A. J. Festugière, "L'expérience religieuse du médecin Thesssalos," *RB* 48 (1939): 45–77.

[32] E. Peterson, "Beiträge zur Interpretation der Visionen im *Pastor Hermae,*" in his *Frühchristentum, Judentum, Gnosis* (Rome, Freiburg, and Vienna 1959), 254–70, esp. 255.

[33] Ibid., 255–68. Cf. Aune, 1556, cf. J. Reiling, *Hermas and Christian Prophecy* (Suppl. to *Novum Testamentum* 37; Leiden 1973), and D. Hellholm, *Das Visionenbuch des Hermas als Apokalypse* (Lund 1980).

[34] See especially G. Bardy, "Origène et la magie," *RSR* 18 (1928): 126–42.

[35] *Contra Celsum*, 1.24, 25.

[36] Among early Christian authors, Julius Africanus's view of magic strikes one as rather original, since for him magic belongs to science, not to religion. See F. C. R. Thee, *Julius Africanus and the Early Christian View of Magic* (Hermeneutische Untersuchungen zur Theologie 13; Tübingen 1984), 56.

[37] Tertullian, *Apologeticus*, 23.1 (LCL 122–23).

[38] Tatian, *Oratio ad Graecos*, 18; ed. Whittaker (Oxford 1982), 36–37.

Justin and Tatian had expressed what later became the traditional perception of dreams in early Christianity. What Tertullian adds is the demonization of magicians: they act in the same perverse ways as the demons do, by sending us dreams, i.e., phantasms on which we have no influence whatsoever, since we are asleep.

A similar view is reflected by Minucius Felix:

> These unclean spirits, or demons, as revealed to Magi and philosophers *(Isti igitur impuri spiritus, daemones, ut ostensum magis ac philosophis)*. ... These spirits keep busy perturbing men's lives, and especially disquieting their slumbers *(somnos inquietant)*. For the same perception of demons being present everywhere, and in particular in these, since spirits are without substance and not to be grasped, insinuate themselves into the bodies of men; and secretly working in their inward parts, they corrupt the health, hasten diseases, terrify their souls with dreams, harass their minds with frenzies, that by these evils they may compel men to have recourse to their aid.[39]

In the fourth century, this perception of demons would reach its logical conclusion, when Lactantius will say in so many words that the pagan gods are actually demons.[40] The great enemy, besides the Devil, is divination, which is one aspect of Satan's fight against God. This forms the core of Augustine's argument in his *Liber de divinatione daemonum,* written in 406–411.[41]

3. Dreams and magic among pagans and Christians

If the Christian Fathers were "horrified" by the transmission of dreams and the related magic of sorcerers, to use Eitrem's wording, it was mainly because "there were Christians who believed in mantic dreams without reservation."[42] As is well known since the seminal studies of Ludwig Deubner and the Bollandist Hippolyte Delehaye at the beginning of this century, the pagan practice of temple incubation was transformed into the early Christian practice of sleeping at the shrine of a saint.[43] Ludwig Deubner was able long ago to show how the early Christian saints and martyrs had become, like new heroes of sorts, semigods who had their own cult. Sleeping at night the shrine of these saints could bring one a vision of the saint or martyr. This vision could be sought for curative purposes. Deubner's monograph is rich in examples of such visions and cures at the shrines of the saints.[44]

---

[39] Minucius Felix, *Octavius*, ch. 27 (LCL 396–401).

[40] Lactantius, *Inst. Div.* II.15.17; cf. Tatian, *Adv. Graecos,* 18.

[41] See H. Leclercq, "Divination," *DACL* 4, 1198–1212.

[42] Eitrem, "Dreams and Divination," 181–82.

[43] L. Deubner, *De incubatione* (Leipzig 1900), H. Delehaye, *Les origines du culte des martyrs* (Bruxelles 1912). See further P. Brown, *The Cult of the Saints* (Chicago 1981).

[44] See n. 43 above.

Incubation is no doubt the most important magical procedure involving dreams common to both pagans and Christians in antiquity. H. Leclercq reluctantly admits the fact in the following way: "le rite de l'incubation tient une place plus ou moins envahissante dans la religion paienne et le culte chrétien, le fait est au dessus de toute contestation."[45] In its essence, incubation is connected to divination through dreams, but it is also directly connected to magic and to the cult of chtonian gods. In his *Psyche,* Erwin Rohde argued that the Greek heroes, who did not die, lived for eternity in the Underworld. They had become chtonic gods, who could be contacted through dreams.

For a Catholic scholar such as H. Leclercq, the Church did not encourage incubation, but reluctantly accepted what it could not fight: "L'Eglise a plutôt subi qu'approuvé ce qu'elle nétait pas en mesure de combattre."[46] Among the Christians, incubation is done at the shrine of holy men or martyrs. Among many examples: a Jew suffering from sciatica dreamed in the basilica of Saint Dometius in Syria; the saint appeared to him and healed him.

We know that in various ways, the perception of magic was greatly changed by the triumph of Christianity.[47] In other words, the change of religion in the ancient world also entailed a transformation of magic. Morton Smith points out that one cannot speak of a single attitude toward magic in such a highly complex reality as early Christianity. In the early fifth century, under Honorius and Theodosius II, pagan gods would be identified with demons in Roman law. The reversal was then complete; Roman religion was now identified as magic. To practice magic, moreover, was to enter the service of Satan, the great enemy of the good God.[48]

Possession, and, more generally, the middle world of demons (with the devil at their head) and their action through dreams, retains a central importance in the early Christian discourse on dreams.[49] Under the Empire, however, most aspects of demonology were shared by pagans and Christians. Topical examples are Plutarch's *De superstitione*, and Apuleius's *De deo socratis*, a work that contains the essential doctrines of demonology at the time. Arnobius is the only Christian author to turn the warnings received through dreams by the pagans into ridicule. The oniric action of demons is for him equivalent to possession.

Possession calls for exorcism. Magical evocations of demons and the theme of *praestigiae daemonis* had great success in fourth-century monastic literature.[50] *Praestigiator* in Prudentius is one of the devil's titles. Such vocables show that

---

[45] H. Leclercq, "Incubation," *DACL* 7, 511–17.

[46] Ibid., 512.

[47] See M. Smith, "How magic was changed by the triumph of Christianity?," in *Graeco-Arabica*, eds. V. Christides and M. Papathomopoulos (Athens 1982–1983), 51–58.

[48] Smith, 58.

[49] See J. Amat's beautiful book, *Songes et visions dans la littérature latine* (Paris 1985), 159–96

[50] Ibid., 176.

the devil has replaced the magician for all practical purposes in Christian consciousness. There are no recognized magical practices, and the devil, the supreme magician, acts particularly at night, in one's dreams. Dreams became the
locus par excellence of magical action. The devil, rather than the sorcerer, is the
"rival" of the saint, as Peter Brown has phrased it: "In all Christian literature,
the ambivalent and somewhat faceless *daemones* of pagan belief are invested
with precise, unambiguous negative attributes and motives ... .": in other words,
Christian dreams reflect a different world.[51] According to Brown, this growth of
magic is directly related to a precise malaise in the structure of the governing
classes of the Roman Empire.[52] Brown points out that ordeals had demanded an
easy passage in pagan texts between the sacred and the profane. This was becoming less easy in late antiquity, as the Christian belief in the creation of the
world *ex nihilo* emphasized the radical separation between God and men. In a
sense, the appearance of the ordeal in the early Middle Ages reflects a turning
back to the traditional attributes of antiquity.

Probably the most interesting early Christian text dealing with the relationships between dreams, visions, and magic is found in the Pseudo-Clementine
Homilies.[53] As is well known, this pseudepigraphical text redacted in the fourth
century preserves much older materials, stemming in particular from Jewish-
Christian milieus.[54]

In Book 17 of the *Homilies*, we find a long argument between the Apostle
Peter and his opponent Simon Magus, about the nature and the legitimacy of
dreams and visions. Simon begins by pointing out that apparition or vision "not
merely presents an object to view, but inspires him who sees it with confidence,
for it comes from God." In other words, Simon defends the view that religious
certainty is achieved through direct revelations sent to the individual in visions,
that is to say either through dreams or in moments of ecstasy. The experience of
vision constitutes its own proof, and testifies to its divine origin.

Peter answers by stating that those who claim to be the recipients of dreams
and visions cannot claim in any way that they are the inheritors of the Biblical
prophets.

> The prophet, because he is a prophet ... is believed in confidence. ... But he who trusts
> to apparition or vision or dream is insecure. For he does not know to whom he is trust-
> ing. For it is possible either that he may be an evil demon or a deceptive spirit, pretend-
> ing in his speeches to be what he is not ... for any one that sees by means of dreams can-

---

[51] P. Brown, "Sorcery, Demons and the Rise of Christianity: from Late Antiquity into the
Middle Ages," in his *Religion and Society in the Age of Saint Augustine* (London 1972), 119–46,
esp. 137. Cf. his *Society and the Holy in Late Antiquity* (Berkeley and Los Angeles 1982), 307.

[52] Brown, "Sorcery," 122.

[53] Parallel to the Greek *Homilies*, we possess a Latin romance, the Pseudo-Clementine *Recognitiones*.

[54] See especially H.-J. Schoeps, *Die Theologie des Juden-Christentums* (Göttingen 1949).

not inquire about whatever he may wish. For reflection is not in the special power of one who is asleep. Hence we, desiring to have information in regard to something in our waking hours, inquire about something else in our dreams ...

To this Simon answers:

If you maintain that apparitions do not always reveal the truth, yet for all that, visions and dreams, being God-sent, do not speak falsely in regard to those matters which they wish to tell.

In his turn, Peter says:

You were right in saying that, being God-sent, they do not speak falsely. But it is uncertain if he who sees has seen a God-sent dream.

Simon replies:

If he who has had the vision is just, he has seen a true vision .... Grant me this, that the just man alone can see a true vision ... for I have come to the conclusion that an impious man does not see a true dream.[55]

What is preserved here is a very significant discussion about the criteria of religious experience. For Peter, as for the Rabbis, the gates of prophecy are now closed, and religious life must be established upon different criteria, namely the authority of the Holy Scriptures and tradition, rather than upon charisma stemming from the direct vision of God and a personal contact with the divinity. In order to fight the legitimacy of charismatic religion, Peter argues that there exists no possibility of a vision of God:

For I maintain that the eyes of mortals cannot see the incorporeal form of the Father or Son, because it is illumined by exceeding great light. ... For the power to see the Father, without undergoing any change, belongs to the Son alone.

We have here the true context of the discussion about the conditions of the vision of God in early Christianity. In a sense, we are here at the origins of Christian mysticism. Peter represents the skeptical attitude about the possibility of such a vision. He knows, indeed, of visions granted to the unjust, and therefore denies their legitimacy: "But it is manifest that the impious see true visions and dreams, and I can prove it from Scripture." Then come examples about Abimelech and Nebuchadnezzar. Hence, "I have learned that revelation is knowledge without instruction, and without apparition and dreams." The argument seems here to be directed against the claims of various charismatic and Gnostic teachings. Peter now quotes Num. 12: 6–7: "If a prophet arise from amongst you, I shall make myself known to him through visions and dreams, but not so as to my servant Moses; because I shall speak to him in an outward appearance, and not through dreams, just as one will speak to his own friend." He then adds:

---

[55] I quote the translation in the Ante-Nicene Fathers series, vol. VIII.

You see how the statements of wrath are made through visions and dreams, but the statements to a friend are made face to face, in outward appearance, and not through riddles and visions and dreams, as to an enemy. If then, our Jesus appeared to you in a vision, made Himself known to you, it was as one who is enraged with an adversary; and this is the reason why it was through visions and dreams, or through revelations that were from without, that He spoke to you. But can one be rendered fit for instruction through apparitions?

Beneath the argument between Peter and Simon, we can distinguish the watermark of the fight against Gnostic claims to revelations, dreams and visions, to a continued prophecy. Peter's argument is indeed an old one. It echoes, as it were, the pronouncements of Jeremiah against the false prophets, who claim to receive revelations through dreams: "The prophet that hath a dream, let him tell a dream; and he that hath my word, let him speak my word faithfully." (Jeremiah 23:25–28).

Do these revelatory dreams and visions of Simon, however, have anything to do with magic? Let us remember that Simon is called Magus, the magician par excellence, he who knows ways of manifesting the Power of God though magical methods, who can evoke the divinity and arrange for hierophanies.[56] This is, precisely, the very core of magical action, and the argument between Peter and Simon shows us clearly the central place of dreams in this serious argument about the nature of true religion.

Conclusion

Early Christian intellectuals accomplished nothing less than a revolution in their perception of the world, and in particular in their perception of the relationships between men, or the world at large, and the divine realm, headed by a single, transcendent creator. Years ago, I suggested the application of the Weberian phrase about the *"Entzauberung der Welt"* – with which Weber described the cosmology of the Puritans in the New World – to the Church Fathers. In particular, I argued, this "de-magicization" of the world gave the heresiologists both the power and the tools to argue against dualists and Gnostics and fight for their own understanding of the nature of Christianity.[57] There is little doubt that the early Christian *Entzauberung* also permitted a clear separation between the created world and the realm of the divine. For the Christians, crossing the boundary between these two realms had become much more difficult than for pagans. Hence, a demonization of most spirits, but also a clear distinction between the two opposite forces, that of God versus that of Satan. God and His

---

[56] See A. Destro and M. Pesce, "Essorcismo, magia e attivita pubblica dei predicatori," in their *Antropologia delle origini cristiane* (Rome and Bari 1995), 85–109, esp. 169–73.

[57] See G. G. Stroumsa, *Savoir et salut* (Paris 1992), 163–81.

Son had clear and known ways of reaching men: essentially, the Revealed Scriptures. Hence, most other ways of crossing, in particular in dreams, were to be understood as acts of magic, i.e., attacks by demonic forces. By being singled out, confronted on a dual basis to the Law and ways of God and of his servants, magic acquired a new position and power previously unknown in the ancient world.

In magic, knowledge is power. For the Christians, magic is also dangerous because it stems from another power, confronted with the single legitimate power, that of God and of His bishop. In a telling pun, *mantikè* is identified with *manikè*, a dangerous and crazy hubris. In the early Christian world, the magician disappeared from the public eye. Magic remains, while the magicians have left the scene. It is the evil spirits, led by Satan, who play tricks upon men and women, in particular in their dreams. Hubert's and Mauss's definition of magic, which emphasizes its illegal character, seems to be nowhere as true as in Christianity. In direct opposition to the evil magical power of Satan, however, the Saint, the Holy Man, who acts through the power of God's or Jesus' name, concentrates in his hands the positive aspects of magical power.

Cumont had noted that Christianity had prohibited all methods of divination except for oniromancy. Quite, but the Church did prohibit the practice of the *specialists* of oniromancy. As Synesius of Cyrene points out in the fourth century, anyone still unable by the age of twenty-four to interpret by himself his own dreams is not worth much.

Hence, there were no magicians left in Christian Late Antiquity, only invisible demons, who appear and act most easily during our sleep. In a sense, therefore, we can conclude with the paradox that the relationship between dreams and magic was actually strengthened by the victory of Christianity, a movement which sought to fight against both magic and dreams in its successful bid to redefine and limit the borders of the self, and restructure religious experience.

Chapter 12

Dreams and Visions in Early Christian Discourse

> "Who is such a stranger to human
> experience as not sometimes to have
> perceived some truth in dreams?"
>
> Tertullian, *De anima* 46.

In the absence of a Christian Artemidorus, we possess no early Christian "key to dreams." Gershom Scholem once remarked that no Buddhist monk ever dreamt of the Blessed Virgin Mary. Could we imagine a Christian monk in fifth-century Egypt, for instance, dreaming of Dionysos? The answer is most probably negative. A more serious question is whether the Christians saw their God in dreams and visions in the same way as the pagans saw theirs. What kind of impact did Christianity have upon the perception of dreams and visions? Through the specific case of the dramatic mutation of Western culture with the advent of Christianity, it is the problem of the cultural and religious determination of dreams and visions that will be raised here.

In early Christian discourse, there is no way of distinguishing clearly between dreams and visions. "I had the following vision... *(uideo in horomate hoc)*" writes Perpetua, for example, making it clear only later ("I awoke"), that it was a dream.[1] In all probability, most dreams of the early Christians were of a rather mundane nature, and did not involve visions of divine or of demonic figures. Such dreams, however, did not seem to count, and hence were not reported. On the other hand, waking visions, obtained in a state of ecstasy, were reported in the same terms as visions obtained during sleep, i.e., in dreams. Hence any study which focuses on dreams while ignoring visions is bound to remain deeply flawed.[2]

---

[1] This appears in the third dream; cf. the second and the fifth dreams. I quote according to H. Musurillo, ed. and tr., *Acts of the Christian Martyrs* (Oxford Early Christian Texts; Oxford 1972). The dreams of Perpetua have been the subject of much research. See, for instance J. Amat *Songes et visions: L'au-delà dans la littérature latine tardive* (Paris 1985), 66–86, and the feminist approach of P. Cox Miller, *Dreams in Late Antiquity: Studies in the Imagination of a Culture* (Princeton 1994), 148–83. Both studies refer to previous literature. On the broader context of martyr's dreams, see C. Mertens, "Les premiers martyrs et leurs rêves," *Revue d'Histoire Ecclésiastique* 81 (1986): 5–46.

[2] For studies treating together late antique dreams and visions, see for instance D. Del Corno, "I sogni e la loro interpretazione nell'età dell'impero," *ANRW*, II.16.2 (1978): 1605–18; J. S. Hanson, "Dreams and Visions in the Graeco-Roman World and Early Christianity," *ANRW*,

The early Christian writers, who perceived dreams and visions as referring to basically the same phenomenon, were adopting an attitude already found in the Hebrew Bible. A good example is Joel 2: 28, which was paraphrased in Acts 2: 17, and thus became a *locus classicus* for describing and justifying dreams and visions among Christians:

> And it shall come to pass afterward, that I will pour out my spirit upon all flesh; and your sons and your daughters shall prophesy *(we-nib'u),* your old men shall dream dreams *(halomot yahalomun;* LXX *enupniois enupniasthèsontai*), your young men shall see visions *(hezionot yr'u;* LXX *horaseis opsontai*).[3]

In her recent *Dreams in Late Antiquity: Studies in the Imagination of a Culture,* Patricia Cox Miller treats the subject as if both pagan and Christian dreams equally reflected late antique culture, in which both pagans and Christians would have partaken to the same extent.[4] My approach here will be precisely the opposite: In my view, religious beliefs and allegiances do make a difference, sometimes a radical one, in the perception of dreams as in other aspects of anthropology. From the second to the fifth century, Christian thinkers developed an approach to dreams which reflected a new interaction between Greek and Hebrew traditions. They also expressed serious reservations about most dreams and visions.

The striking difference between pagan and Christian dreams is a fact which has been recognized, but remains to be explained.[5] In the following pages, I shall examine to what extent the religious beliefs of Christians in the Roman Empire informed their understanding of dreams and visions. I shall also attempt to show that we can identify an early Christian discourse on dreams and visions, distinct from other similar discourses in late antiquity, and that this discourse reflects the new anthropology, the new perception of the person, developed by Christian thinkers.[6]

II.23.2 (1980): 1395–1427; F. E. Consolino, "Sogni e visioni nell' agiografia tardoantica: modelli e variazioni sul tema," *Augustinianum* 29 (1989): 237–56.

[3] Prophetic literature also reflects violent arguments about dreams, since dreams can be perceived as the instrument of false prophecy, as in Jeremiah 23: 25–28: "I have heard what the prophets said, that prophecy lies in my name saying, 'I have dreamed, I have dreamed.'" In the Hebrew Bible, dreams can come "stealthily" (Job 4: 12), but they can also be a major means of divine revelation (Gen. 28, 37: 41, I Kings 3); In Num. 12: 6–8: it is through dreams that Yahwe makes Himself known to the prophets. See further Ottoson, "Chalôm," in *TDOT,* eds. G. J. Botterweck and H. Ringgren, 4: 421–32. On the question of dreams and visions in the New Testament, see Oepke, "onar," *TDNT,* ed. G. Kittel, 5: 220–38. Oepke notes that the New Testament is relatively poor in dreams. See further K. Berger, *Historische Psychologie des Neuen Testaments* (Stuttgarter Bibelstudien 146/147; Stuttgart 1991), 125–29.

[4] See my review of her book in *JR* 76 (1996): 469–70.

[5] R. Lane Fox, *Pagans and Christians* (Hammondsworth 1987), 410, notes that approved dreams in Christianity had an obedient tone, unlike anything in Artemidorus's book.

[6] On early Christian discourse, see A. Cameron, *Christianity and the Rhetoric of Empire: The Development of Christian Discourse* (Berkeley, Los Angeles, and London 1991).

It should be noted that we do not have a record of the dreams of most Christians from the first centuries, but only the highly reflective testimonies of a few adult men, most of them intellectuals, and of a single young woman, the African martyr Perpetua. These few precious documents reflect the way or ways some Christians perceived their dreams and spoke about them – what they decided to emphasize and where they chose to keep silent. It is from these documents alone that we can attempt to retrieve early Christian "discourse" about dreams. In the words of Gilbert Dagron: "Seront donc significatifs d'une époque ou d'une culture non ses rêves, mais ce qu'on en dit et ce qu'on en fait."[7]

We cannot retrieve the dreams of the early Christians themselves. As a rule, we can assume that most of their dreams were quite similar to those of contemporary pagans and Jews, and that the Christian attitude toward these dreams was *usually* not different from that of non-Christians to their own dreams. We can, moreover, isolate the discourse on those dreams and visions that are described as being specific to the Christians and are the exception to the rule, and identify their nature.

This discourse in its turn informed the Christian perception of the world, the relationships in the Christian mind between reality and illusion, body and spirit, sleep and awakening – what the French call the "imaginaire."[8] The representation and the role of dreams reflect anthropological attitudes, as well as perceptions of the divine. The mapping of dreams and their role is directly related to cultural or theological presuppositions. In a sense, then, dreams and visions should be studied in the larger context of historical anthropology.[9]

Christianity began as an enclave culture, or even as a radical counter-culture which defined itself through the rejection of most prevalent attitudes in the Greco-Roman world. In the fourth century, however, due to the conversion of the Empire, we can witness a major mutation of the supernatural world, which involves a radical simplification or impoverishment of the pantheon. The gods have disappeared, or have become transformed into minor demons. The victory of monotheism entailed the ordering of the demonic world under the single power of Satan, forever rebelling against the good creator God, the God of Is-

---

[7] G. Dagron, "Rêver de Dieu et parler de soi: le rêve et son interprétation d'après les sources byzantines," in *I sogni nel medioevo,* ed. T. Gregory (Lessico intellettuale europeo 35; Roma 1985), 37. See also E. R. Dodds's chapter on dream patterns and culture patterns in his *The Greeks and the Irrational* (Berkeley, Los Angeles, and London 1951). His main concern is not so much the dream experience of the Greeks as the Greek attitude to the dream experience.

[8] There is no real English equivalent to "imaginaire." "Cosmology" as used by sociologists has a narrower frame of reference than "imaginaire." On the "imaginaire," see Patlagean, "L'histoire de l'imaginaire," *Encyclopedia Universalis* (1985) 9: 249–69; P. Kaufman, "Imaginaire et imagination," ibid., 9: 776–83.

[9] See n. 3 above. For a study of dreams from the perspective of social history, see the pioneering study of P. Burke, 'L'histoire sociale des rêves," *Annales ESC* 28 (1973): 329–42.

rael.[10] Christianity thus played a crucial role in the formation of the medieval "imaginaire," both in Byzantium and in the West. The analysis of the shape of dreams and visions in early Christian discourse can thus help us to better understand this dramatic process.

In a sense, however, the place of dreams in the medieval "imaginaire" seems paradoxically closer to the their place in pagan antiquity than to the place they occupied in the Christian psyche. This stems from the fact that in the Middle Ages, Christian culture was well-established and defined with clear boundaries, whereas in late antiquity we cannot yet really speak of a Christian culture.[11]

1. Hellenic divination and the second religiosity

Like everyone else, the early Christians were well aware that dreams were a universal phenomenon. In Tertullian's *De anima*, written before the end of the second century, we have the first sustained discussion of dreams by a Christian writer. Tertullian states that the majority of mankind learn to know God through dreams: "et maior paene uis hominum ex visionibus deum discunt."[12] In this statement, he recognizes clearly the universality of dreams, and yet he does not refer to the divine in general, or to the gods, but to God, *deum*, i.e., the one and true God of the Christians. But most men and women around him were, of course, pagans.

Christian intellectuals, as newcomers to a long tradition of reflection on dreams, were unable to offer a systematic alternative to the cultural premises they were rejecting. It is probably no mere chance that the classification of dreams by a pagan, Macrobius, informs all the medieval perception of dreams.[13] As Jacques Le Goff pointed out, it is only with Isidore of Seville, in the seventh century, that we can detect the birth of a specifically Christian oneirology.[14]

Chesterton's apothegm – "Dreams are like life, only more so" – would not have been easily understood in the Hellenistic world, where sleep was perceived as being dangerously close to death. Tertullian calls sleep "the very mirror" of

---

[10] J. Le Goff, "Le christianisme et les rêves, (IIe-VIIe siècle)" in his *L'imaginaire médiéval* (Paris 1985), 293. Le Goff rightly emphasizes the significance of the passage from the demons to Satan.

[11] On the western medieval reflection on dreams, see S. F. Kruger, *Dreaming in the Middle Ages* (Cambridge Studies in Medieval Literature 14; Cambridge 1992).

[12] *De anima* 47.2 (65 Waszink). We are lucky to possess an admirable edition of and commentary upon this text: J. H. Waszink, *Tertullian, De anima* (Amsterdam 1947). I quote the translation in the *Ante Nicene and Nicene Fathers*, vol. 3. The treatise on dreams extends from ch. 45 to 49.

[13] On this text, see for instance W. H. Stahl, introduction and tr., *Macrobius, Commentary on the Dream of Scipio* (New York 1952).

[14] Le Goff, "Le christianisme et les rêves," 290.

death, or its "mirror and image."[15] In sleep, as in death, the soul was separated from the body, a conception reflected, for instance, in late antiquity, by the Gnostics or by Iamblichus.[16] For Tertullian, who basically accepts Stoic ideas, sleep represents "a temporary suspension of the activity of the senses, procuring rest for the body only, not for the soul."[17] If sleep is close to death, for a Christian, awakening resembles resurrection of the dead.[18] Dreams were thus believed at once to permit communication of the soul with the dead, and to be a most fitting vehicle for divine revelations. The ambiguous status of dreams permitted a vision, blurred as it might be, of the netherworld, and offered a link to a dominion not otherwise accessible to humans. Dreams also offered, together with knowledge of the supra-human world, solutions to various daily problems. The status of dreams was also related to their power. Plutarch's attitude here is typical of traditionally minded intellectuals in the second century C.E.:

> The dreams, children of Night and messengers of the Moon... This oracle has no fixed location. It moves in all places among men, in dreams and in visions. It is from there that dreams, mixing error and confusion with simplicity and truth, are being dispersed in the whole universe.[19]

For Plutarch, then, dreams and visions can be compared to oracular phenomena. Since one observed a disconnection of soul and body in sleep, dreaming can be perceived as a shamanistic trance of sorts. The shamanistic character of vision and dreaming is reflected in various religious traditions of antiquity, from the Pythagoreans and Orphics to Sasanian Zoroastrianism.[20]

It was easy to see the gods in the ancient world. One could see everywhere the statues of the gods, in the temples and in the streets of the cities. Seeing the god was desirable, and very common.[21] The vision could happen in different conditions; it could happen while awake, in a state of ecstasy, as in the *Poimandres;* it

---

[15] *De anima* 42, end, 50, beginning.

[16] See Iamblichus, *Mysteries of Egypt*, III.7. On Gnostic perceptions, see G. W. MacRae, S.J., "Sleep and Awakening in Gnostic Texts," in *Le origine dello gnosticismo* (Supplements to Numen 12; Leiden 1976), 496–507.

[17] *De anima,* 53.. See further De *anima.* 45: in sleep, the body rests, and is disconnected from the soul. Cf. Cyprian, *Ep.* IX (*PL* 4, 253).

[18] *De anima.* 53, *in finem*

[19] Plutarch, *De sera numinis vindicta* 22.

[20] For Sasanian Zoroastrianism, see Sh. Shaked, *Dualism in Transformation (London* 1995), 49. For the Greek tradition, see P. Kingsley, *Ancient Philosophy, Mystery and Magic: Empedocles and Pythagorean Tradition* (Oxford 1995).

[21] See for instance the enlightening remarks of H. S. Versnel, "What Did Ancient Man See When He Saw a God?: Some Reflections on Greco-Roman Epiphany," in *Effigies Dei: Essays on the History of Religion,* ed. D. van der Plas, (Studies in the History of Religion; Leiden 1987) 42–55. See further A. J. Festugière, *La révélation d'Hermès Trismégiste,* (Paris 1944) 1: 310, and idem., *Personal Religion among the Greeks* (Berkeley and Los Angeles 1960), 95–98. He analyses the heavenly visions of Asclepius in Aelius Aristides' Sacred Tales. Hermann Usener had insisted long ago on the importance of seeing the gods through their images in the ancient world.

could also consist of a conversation with the god, in waking and without ecstasy, as is the case with Thessalos the doctor. It could happen during sleep; it could also be induced, through a process known as incubation, usually at the temple of the god.[22] Aelius Aristides is of course the most famous instance of such a cultivation of incubation, but he is certainly not an isolated case. Aelius Aristides was a hypochondriac intellectual living under the Antonines, a contemporary of Artemidorus, who spent years in the temple of Asclepius in Pergamon, taking careful notes of his dreams.[23] It should, however, be pointed out that the Greek interest in dreams was not shared by the Romans, who had little interest in this kind of symbolism.

The common presence of visions of the gods in the Hellenistic world reflects at least two traits of ancient thought. The first is the important role images played in it. Here the Christians, like the Jews, are the exception. The second is the relative lack of interest the ancients had for the continuity of affective life. One has even been able to consider this lack of interest as responsible for the perception of dreams as mainly divinatory, and of their visions as essentially similar to waking vision.[24]

In the early Roman Empire, religiosity underwent deep changes. A new accent was put on subjectivity and on personal choice in religious matters. In this context, one can even speak of a "second religiosity."[25] Plutarch's dramatic description of the death of Pan[26] underlines the perceived failure of oracles in the early Empire. This failure was ipso facto perceived as that of the professional seers who had been travelling through the places of heaven and Hades, telling what they had seen to simple mortals. Under such circumstances, the dream-vision report assumed a new status and dreams became the locus par excellence of religious revelation.

Early Christian attitudes reflected an ethos vastly different from the traditional ethos of the Hellenistic world. Up to the fourth century, Christianity remained essentially an aniconic religion, which did not favor visions of the Deity.[27] The success of Christianity, moreover, both reflected and encouraged

---

[22] On Christian incubation, see for instance H. Leclerq, "Incubation," *DACL* 7: 51–57. The most careful study of the passage from pagan to Christian incubation is still L. Deubner, *De incubatione* (Leipzig 1900).

[23] On him, see C. A. Behr, *Aelius Aristides and the Sacred Tales* (Amsterdam 1968), in particular ch. 8: "The Interpretation of Dreams in Antiquity." See further G. Michenaud and T. Dierkens, *Les rêves dans les discours sacrés d'Aélius Aristide* (Bruxelles 1972,[*non vidi*], and A. J. Festugière's translation of the *Sacred Tales*, with a preface by J. Le Goff and notes by H. D. Saffrey: Aélius Aristide, *Discours sacrés* (Paris 1986). In his history of autobiography in antiquity, G. Misch refers to the *Sacred Tales* as an "oniric autobiography." On Artemidorus, see A. J. Festugière's tr., Artemidorus, *La clef des songes: Onirocriticon* (Paris 1975).

[24] See F. Refoulé, "Rêves et vie spirituelle d'après Evagre le Pontique," *La Vie Spirituelle,* Supplément 14 (1961): 470–516, esp. 498.

[25] See for instance M. Dulaey, *Les rêves dans la vie et la pensée de saint Augustin* (Paris 1973).

[26] Plutarch, De *defectu oraculorum* 419 c.

the transformations of pagan religiosity. In a sense, it epitomized them. The failure of the pagan oracles was paralleled, among Jews and Christians, by the final closing of prophecy, with the contemporary closure of the canons, of both New Testament and Mishna.[28] But the widespread refusal to recognize the validity of guilds of professional seers, together with the presence of dream books, also reflects the "demotization" of both dream interpretation and of religious visions. Anyone dreamed and could cultivate visions, provided he or she reached a certain state of mind attainable through ascetic practices, in particular fasting and prayer. Methods known throughout antiquity to encourage the appearance of visions and dreams were now popularized by the Christians; on the one hand, anyone could become an ascetic (what Max Weber called a "religious virtuoso"); on the other hand, dream interpreters had been officially forbidden.

2. Divination and incubation

Dreams belong to the general field of mantics, of divination of the future. As such, they were to be encouraged and induced by various ascetic practices, such as fasting.[29] Dreams were also connected to conversion among pagans, as shown by the dream of Isis in Apuleius's *Metamorphoses*.[30]

The Christians attributed the methods of divination in use in the first centuries C.E to evil genii and polemicized in very harsh terms against them.[31] They remained, however, unable to develop theoretical arguments against divination itself.

Among the various methods of divination known in the Greco-Roman world, oneiromancy was not only widespread, it was also a science which could be learned, in principle, by everybody – although dream interpretation usually remained the privilege of specialists.[32] It was also the only method that the Christians did not reject in categorical terms, a fact noted by Franz Cumont.[33] Already

---

[27] Although some esoteric traditions, inherited from Judaism, seem to have sought the vision of God. On these traditions, see G. G. Stroumsa *Hidden Wisdom,* passim.

[28] On canonization processes in early Christianity, see ibid., chapter 5, 79–91.

[29] See for instance Philostratus, *Life of Apollonius of Tyana*, 2.37; cf. Cicero, De *divinatione*, 2.58.119; these and other texts are quoted and discussed in V. MacDermot, *The Cult of the Seer in the Ancient Middle East* (London 1971), 1: 41–45. On the practice of fasting in order to elicit dreams, see Lane Fox, *Pagans and Christians,* 396.

[30] This is in contradistinction to the thought of the Rabbis, for whom the dream of a gentile does not count as a legitimate motive for conversion.

[31] See A. Bouché-Leclercq, *Histoire de la divination dans l'antiquité* (Paris 1879–80; reprint New York 1980), 1: 93–94.

[32] On dream interpretation in the ancient world, see Th. Hopfner, "Traumdeutung," *PW*, VII.A.2, 2233–2245.

[33] F. Cumont, *Lux perpetua* (Paris 1949), 92: "L'oniromancie est le seul mode païen de divination que l'Eglise n'ait pas répudié." On oniromancy, see for instance Ps. Chrysostom, *PG* 64, 740–

the Hebrew Bible, while rejecting divination, had recognized its existence and power. Even about oneiromancy, moreover, the Christians expressed serious doubts. Tertullian not only suggests that Christians must interpret dreams in a new way; he also rejects dream interpreters.[34] Indeed, dream interpreters, the specialist intermediaries, were banned from baptism in the early Church. Any adult was considered capable of interpreting his (or her) own dreams. In the words of Synesius of Cyrene, a Neoplatonist turned Christian in the fourth century, "At 24 years of age, it is inexcusable for a man still to need an interpreter for his own dreams."[35]

Oneiromancy in its most commonly established form, incubation, lived on in late antique Christianity, where the martyr's tomb replaced the god's temple. Christian incubations in churches, where the titular saints appear, and at the tombs of martyrs, continued for a long time after the fall of paganism. In our sources, the invention of the *reliquiae* of martyrs often happens following dreams. Dreams thus played a crucial role in the invention of martyrs' relics,[36] as well as in hagiographies, a fact emphasized by Gilbert Dagron.[37] It should be pointed out in this context that Augustine, among others, fought the proliferation of such practices and that thanks to his influence, the council of Carthage put an end to a real contagion of dreams and revelations. Canon 83 of that Council objects to *martyria* where incubation is sought for the apparition of the martyr or saint.[38]

3. Prophecy

The Hebrew Bible refers, of course, to many dreams and visions, from the dreams of Joseph to those of Daniel and the visions of the prophets (or the dreams of the false prophets). The early Christian writers, who knew the rele-

---

744, = Suda, s.v. *prophèteia*. This text is quoted by Dagron, "Rêver de Dieu," 40, n. 15, as a very influential text arguing that predictive dreams also exist for Christians, but that among the pagans, such dreams come from a pernicious art, while among the Christians, they come from virtue.

[34] See Lane Fox, *Pagans and Christians,* 392. On the Christian condemnation of divinatory dreams, see D. Devoti, "Sogni e conversione nei Padri: Considerazioni preliminari," *Augustinianum* 27 (1987): 119 and n. 46.

[35] Synesius of Cyrene, D*e somniis*. This work had been translated into Latin by Marcilio Ficino.

[36] See L. Deubner, *De incubatione,* 56ff., and H. Delehaye, *Les origines du culte des martyrs* (Bruxelles 1912).

[37] See for instance B. Flusin's comment on visions in the hagiography of Saint Anastasius the Persian, from sixth-century Palestine: *La vie d'Anastase le Perse,* (Paris 1992), 2: 142: "La vision de Jean [John of the Heptastomos] est à la fois trop transparente et trop générale pour prêter à un long commentaire... Il n'est pas un thaumaturge, capable par sa prière d'infléchir le cours des événements et de protéger la ville. Il devient un simple visionnaire, en un sens le successeur des prophètes, capable, parce qu'il est dioratique, de voir et de faire connaître aux autres le vrai sens de l'Histoire. ..."

[38] See Dagron, "Rêver de Dieu," 40, n. 7.

vant Biblical passages by heart, built their hermeneutical rules on them. For Origen, the phenomena of prophecy and of dreaming are closely related to one another.

> All who accept the doctrine of providence are obviously agreed in believing that in dreams many people form images in their minds, some of divine things, others being announcements of future events in life, whether clear or mysterious. Why then is it strange to suppose that the force which forms an impression on the mind in a dream can also do so in the day time for the benefit of the man on whom the impression is made, or for those who will hear about it from him? Just as we receive an impression in a dream that we hear and that our sense of hearing has been physically affected, and that we see with our eyes... so also there is nothing extraordinary in such things having happened to the prophets when, as the Bible says, they saw certain marvelous visions, or heard utterances of the Lord, or saw the heavens opened.[39]

This important text reflects Origen's attempt at interpreting the phenomenon of prophecy, and especially prophetic vision, by comparing it with dreaming. It is also worth noting that he does not object to the predictive dimension of dreams.

Beyond the Bible, the early Christians also had at their disposal the large and varied corpus of Apocalyptic and pseudepigraphic literature, with its emphasis on visions of the divinity or of its angels. This whole literature, Bible and Pseudepigrapha of the Old Testament, constituted the foundation of the Christian attitude to dreams and visions.[40] Biblical dreams and visions were not only legitimate; they were also canonical. But it is precisely their canonical status that also highlighted the difference between them and other, more mundane and common dreams. Such common dreams could not usually boast of a similar direct divine origin. Most often, then, it was to be feared that they came from the devil. Augustine summarized the *opinio communis* of Christian thinkers when he said that any revelation that does not have its origin in God comes from the demons.[41]

For the Jews as well as for the Christians, prophecy had ended with the closure of the canon. This does not mean that there are no significant differences between Jewish and Christian approaches to dreaming and vision in late antiquity. Jews, like Christians, believed that some dreams could point to future realities, as did prophecy. But unlike the Christians, they could not make use of Hellenic literary traditions, which they ignored. Hence, perceptions of dreaming in Rabbinic texts, and in particular in Midrash, are strikingly different, in their approach as well as in their tone, from those in Patristic literature.[42] Midrash is a lit-

---

[39] Origen, *Contra Celsum*, 1.48.

[40] The New Testament apocrypha, in particular the *Apocryphal Acts of the Apostles*, are relatively rich in dreams and visions, but the status of this literature soon became problematic in mainstream Christianity, due to its popularity among various Gnostic groups and the Manichaeans.

[41] *De divinatione daemonorum*.

[42] See for instance B. Stemberger, "Der Traum in der rabbinischen Literatur," *Kairos* 18

erary genre that is much more popular than most writings of the Church Fathers. And the constant preoccupation of the Christians with Satan has no parallel in Jewish texts, where there is no obsessive fear of demons comparable to that found in many early Christian texts. Finally, in some of the Patristic texts we can identify the blossoming of a new depth of psychological insight that has no parallel in Rabbinic literature. Altogether, the perception of a radical fight between the two opposite powers carried out within the individual is much less present in Jewish than in Christian contexts.

Early Christian discourse on dreams and visions was shaped by two closely-connected phenomena: on the one hand, the encouragement given to larger numbers of people to seek visions; and, on the other hand, the attempt to discourage, repress, and limit the world of dreams. These are the two sides of a consistent effort to domesticate dreams and visions, to transform them into the instrument of a direct link with God after the closure of the Biblical canon: revelations after the age of Revelation, as it were.

In a theology that proclaimed the era of revelation to be closed, that God had already said in both Testaments whatever he wanted and needed to tell mankind, the revelatory nature of dreams was problematic. The gates of revelation cannot be hermetically closed, even in a monotheistic religion with canonical writings. In early Christianity, as well as in Rabbinic Judaism and later in Islam, dreams and visions were endowed with a new status, liminal and ambiguous, which kept open the possibility of a continued revelation of God.[43] The opening, however, remained narrow. For a Christian dream to be religiously significant, it must come from God. But since God usually reveals himself in the canon of Scripture, now closed, a true Christian dream must remain something of an exception.

Christian suspicions about dreams were enhanced by the very nature of Christianity as a monotheistic religion. As Erik Peterson showed long ago, monotheism entails a single legitimate religious authority.[44] The idea of a single God as well as that of a single bishop imply a single legitimate source of truth and thus militate against the plurality of valid dreams. The drastic limitation of valid dreams also resulted from the notion of divine transcendence (and of the world as God's creation), a notion which impedes easy passage between the world of men and the divine realm.

(1976), 1–42; and M. Niehoff, "A Dream which is not Interpreted is like a Letter which is not Read," *JJS* 43 (1992): 58–84.

[43] See R. Brague, "L'impuissance du Verbe qui a *tout* dit," *Diogène* 170 (1995): 49–74, esp. 72, where Brague points out that in medieval Islamic thought some dreams are identified to the Koranic *mubashshirât*, the continuation of prophecy after its official end, as it were.

[44] E. Peterson, *Monotheismus als politisches Problem*, in his *Theologische Traktate* (Munich 1951); cf. A. Schindler, ed., *Monotheismus als politisches Problem? Erik Peterson und die Kritik der politischen Theologie* (Gütersloh 1978).

4. Classifications of dreams

For the early Christians, Homer remained to a large extent *terra incognita*.[45] Ignorance of Homer meant the absence of the *loci classici* of dreams and their interpretation in Hellenic culture throughout the ages.[46] Instead of the Homeric writings, which were the closest that Greek culture had to a Holy Writ, the Christians had the Bible. Although the New Testament includes some highly interesting visions, which became topical in Christian literature, it is not particularly rich in dreams.[47] The Septuagint, on the other hand, provided the Christians with a large body of dreams, such as those of Joseph or Daniel. For the Christians, the only true dreams were those that had been sent by God through angels, and which possessed a symbolism grounded in Scripture. But although the Christians were unable to make a simple and direct use of the long and rich Hellenic tradition of dream interpretation, they could not invent a fresh approach to dreams. They accepted Greek ideas, seeking to adapt them to their specific needs. In particular, they made good use of the various taxonomies of dreams that they found in widely circulating dream books. The best instance of this procedure, perhaps, is found in Tertullian's reference to "the entire literature of dreams," where he singles out Hermippus of Berytus from among a long list of authors.[48]

Different methods of dream interpretation competed for attention in Hellenistic times, and there was no single authoritative theory.[49] Aristotle's tractate on dreams, for instance, had little influence. Similarly, Artemidorus' useful distinction between a mere dream *(enupion)*, and a significant, prophetic dream *(oneiros)*, which is of Homeric origin, did not leave a clear mark, and this distinction is not generally observed in Hellenistic literature.[50]

In the late fourth century, the pagan Macrobius proposed in his *Commentary to the Dream of Scipio* a taxonomy of dreams that was to become the most important single source for the perception of dreams in the Latin middle ages.[51] According to him, dreams, of which there are five main types, often tell the fu-

---

[45] Lane Fox, *Pagans and Christians,* 377.

[46] The bibliography is immense. See for instance S. Byl, "Quelques idées grecques sur le rêve, d'Homère à Artémidore," *Les Etudes Classiques* 47 (1979): 107–29.

[47] Cf. n. 3 above.

[48] *De anima* 46; see the important remarks of Waszink in his commentary, *ad loc.*

[49] On these, see for instance A. H. M. Kessels, "Ancient Systems of Dream Classification," *Mnemosyne* 22 (1969): 389–424.

[50] In *Odyssey* 14.495, for instance, *enupion* is put in opposition to *oneiros.* Elsewhere in Greek literature, *enupion* is usually the equivalent of *oneiros*, or *opsis enupiou*, the vision of a dream. See for instance Herodotus, *Hist.* 8.54. Cf. the distinction betwen *rêve* and *songe* in French. Philo, among others, does not distinguish betwen *enupion* and *oneiros.*

[51] Le Goff, "Le christianisme et les rêves," 279, reminds us that this text would be fundamental in the twelfth-century renewal of reflection on dreams.

ture. Most dreams are true, and all are interesting. This approach clearly remains in line with the Greek classifications of dreams.

Stoic approaches have a particular importance in our context. According to the Stoics, dreams could come from the gods, from the demons, or from the soul. This tripartition of dreams lies at the basis of the first Christian tractate on dreams, in chapters 45 through 49 of Tertullian's *De anima*. For Tertullian, dreams come from one of three sources: from God, from the devil, or from the soul *(a deo, a daemonio, ab anima)*:

> But the Stoics are very fond of saying that God, in his most watchful providence over every institution, gave us dreams amongst other preservatives of the arts and sciences of divination, as the especial support of the natural oracle. So much for the dreams to which credit has to be ascribed even by ourselves, although we must interpret them in another sense. As for all other oracles, at which no one ever dreams, what else must we declare concerning them, than that they are the diabolical contrivance of those spirits who even at that time dwelt in the eminent persons themselves ... .[52]

> The third class of dreams will consist of those which the soul itself apparently creates for itself from an intense application to special circumstances ...

> Those [dreams], moreover, which evidently proceed neither from God, nor from diabolical inspiration, nor from the soul ... will have to be ascribed in a separate category to what is purely and simply the ecstatic state and its peculiar conditions.[53]

Although this text is at times difficult to understand, the last passage makes clear that there are three kinds of dreams, classified according to their source, the ecstatic state *(proprie ecstasi)* excluded. The most important point, perhaps, is that Christians can rely, *grosso modo,* on Greek classifications, but that they should interpret dreams differently from pagans. Let us comment briefly on Tertullian's classification.

5. God

The *Vision of Perpetua,* in the *Acts of the Martyrs,* mentions a conversation of the future martyr with God. Perpetua is said to be "talking to God," *fabulari cum domino*. Voice and vision are mentioned together: "profecta est mihi vox, a voice was addressed to me" and also "ostensum est mihi hoc, this was shown to me." Note the passive voice: the dreamer is the recipient of a vision, rather than its active proponent. This significant fact refutes the suggestion that Christians sang and listened to texts but did not gaze on idealized forms of their God, and that their dreams emphasize singing angels rather than visions of the Divinity.[54]

---

[52] *De anima* 46.
[53] *De anima* 47.
[54] Lane Fox, *Pagans and Christians,* 394.

Indeed, many Christian texts describe dream-visions of the deity, or of angels, which often do not differ significantly from various pagan visions. The difference between pagan and Christian discourse on dream and vision must be sought elsewhere.[55]

A striking example of such a dream-vision is the so-called *Vision of Dorotheos,* an anonymous text found on a single papyrus, which has not elicited the attention its deserves.[56] The vision takes place at midday, in the king's palace, and during sleep. The vision is that of God in his own palace, similar to that of the *basileos*. I am quoting here the beginning of this text:

> Surely, it is not for me, this sinner, that from heaven the pure God has sent Christ, his own image, to the world as a bright light, while putting in my heart a desire for a graceful song. When I was sitting alone in the palace in the midst of the day, sweet sleep fell upon my eyelids. You do not know and cannot believe all the splendor that appeared to me then. I sit well awake and singing in the daytime all that has appeared, but it baffles me to describe in words all the splendid supremacy of the Immaculate that appeared to me.
>
> I deemed to be standing in the porch and to behold the Lord in His palace, who is immortal and unborn, and grown from himself. This no man on earth has ever set eyes upon, nor the moon, nor the sun, nor the stars. Neither night nor cloud comes near to where the All-seeing lives, the eternal Lord who looks to every side. This is how my heart pictures it. ...

The great interest of the text lies in its imagery of the divine palace, which is reminiscent of the late antique Hebrew texts describing the "Divine palaces," the so-called *Hekhalot* literature.[57]

One of the most famous dreams in Christian literature is that of Jerome. In a letter to his female disciple, Eustochium, Jerome tells of the dream he had "many years ago," while he was "on [his] way to Jerusalem, to wage [his] warfare."[58] Jerome's dream, or rather nightmare, was sent by God, while Satan assaulted Jerome with other methods. The theme of the dream is well-known: Jerome, "caught up by the Spirit," is brought before the shining "judgment seat of the Judge."[59] Asked about his identity, he says: "I am a Christian," but the Judge answers: "Thou liest, thou art a follower of Cicero, not of Christ (*Mentiris, ait, Ciceronianus es, non christianus: 'ubi thesaurus tuus, ibi et cor tuum'* [Mat 6:

---

[55] See Hanson, "Dreams and Visions," n. 2 above.

[56] See A. H. M. Kessels and P. W. Van der Horst, "The Vision of Dorotheus (Pap. Bodmer 29), ed. with Introduction and notes, *Vigiliae Christianae* 41 (1987): 313–59.

[57] On this literature, see P. Schäfer, *The Hidden and the Manifest God* (Albany 1992).

[58] Letter 22.30, written in 383–84; text in J. Labourt, ed. and tr., *Lettres de Saint Jérôme*, vol. 1 (Paris 1949), 144–46. On this text, see Dom P. Antin, "Autour du rêve de Saint Jérôme", *REL* 41 (1985): 350–77.

[59] "cum subito raptus in spiritu ad tribunal iudicis pertrahor, ubi tantum erat ex circumstantium claritate fulgoris ut proiectus in terram sursum aspicere non auderem." It is significant that at the end of the vision, when Jerome returns to earth, the text has:"reuertor ad superos," which makes it clear that the throne of the judge is situated in the underworld, and not in the heavens.

21])." Upon this, the dumbfounded Jerome receives the lashes of the whip, and suffers even more from "the fire of [his] conscience." Most interesting in our context, however, is the ending of Jerome's report. The proof that his dream is true, that it is of divine origin, that "this was no sleep or idle dream," lies in the fact that "long after [he] woke up from [his] sleep," he could see and feel on his shoulders the painful traces of the lashes he had received in the dream. In other words, the true dream becomes reality, ceasing ipso facto to be a dream.

Jerome's attitude to dreams is typical of the strong suspicion about dreams among Patristic writers, and in particular in monastic literature.[60] An example of this literature can be seen in Diadochus of Photike, a Greek spiritual writer, close to the Messalian movement, who had a deep influence on the Byzantine tradition. Diadochus discusses the possibility of seeing God in dreams and visions. Can the religious virtuoso (the "athlete") see the Glory of God in a vision of the physical senses, or in a dream?[61] Diadochus denies the possibility of a vision of God in this world. Such visions, of a figure of light, for instance, should be rejected as coming from the enemy (i.e., Satan). As to dreams, he recognizes the possibility of good dreams, side by side with evil ones. Since by far most dreams, however, are evil, misleading images, and diabolical mystifications, it is a sign of virtue never to trust a dream. If it so happens that God sends us a vision that we reject, Jesus Christ, in his goodness, will forgive us, since he knows well that this attitude is dictated to us by the ruse of the demons.[62] Diadochus stays here in line with Tatian, who in the second century had compared the demons responsible for sending us dreams with bandits who kidnap for a ransom.[63]

6. The Devil

Tertullian had already pointed out that while some dreams might come from God, most must be attributed to the devil. Indeed, the devil is the predominant presence in most Christian dreams.[64] He usually sends dreams to men, but can

---

[60] See A. Guillaumont, "Les visions mystiques dans le monachisme oriental chrétien," in his *Aux origines du monachisme chrétien* (Spiritualité orientale 30; Bégrolles en Mauge 1979), 136–49. E. Benz, *Dreams, Hallucinations, Visions* (New York 1961), 22 notes that the Christian distrust toward dreams came earlier than that toward visions. See further Benz's fundamental study, Benz's fundamental study, *Die Vision: Erfahrungsformen und Bilderwelt* (Stuttgart 1962).

[61] Diadoque de Photicé, *Oeuvres spirituelles*, E. des Places, S.J., ed., (Sources Chrétiennes 5ter; Paris 1966), ch. 36–40, pp. 105–108.

[62] Ibid., ch. 38, p. 107: *kalôn te kai phaulôn oneirôn.*

[63] Tatian, *Oratio ad Graecos* 18.3 ; M. Whittaker, ed. and tr. (Oxford Patristic Texts: Oxford 1982), 36–37. For other second-century warnings from dreams sent by demons, see for instance Irenaeus, *Adversus Haereses*, 1.16.3, Justin Martyr, *Apology*, 18.3, and Tertullian, *Apology*, 23.1

[64] On the devil in the early Christian tradition, see N. Forsyth, *The Old Enemy: Satan and the Combat Myth* (Princeton 1987). Forsyth, however, does not study dreams.

also appear in dreams sent by God. This is the case, for instance, in the third dream of Perpetua, who describes how she sees the devil as an Egyptian of horrible appearance *(foedus specie)*.

Perhaps the most sustained and incisive discussion of the demonic or diabolical origin of most dreams is that of Evagrius Ponticus, whom one of his best students has called "a philosopher in the desert." Indeed, Evagrius, toward the end of the fourth century, offers a theory of monastic praxis. In his *Praktikos,* written as a basic regulation for the life led by the monks of Egypt, Evagrius mentions eight categories of demonic dreams, which he parallels to the eight *logismoi,* or evil thoughts (cf. Cassian).[65] "The demons wage a veritable war against our concupiscible appetite," he tells us, employing phantasms for this combat.[66] The attacks of the devil upon man do not end with spiritual progress. On the contrary, Satan makes special efforts to wound purified souls: "The greater the progress the soul makes, the more fearful the adversaries that take over the war against it."[67] The constant war which the monks must wage against Satan and his temptations is a well-known theme in monastic and hagiographic sources, and has left a deep imprint on literature, as anyone familiar with Flaubert's *La tentation de Saint Antoine* knows.

It should not come to us as a surprise if dreams retain a central place in those trends in early Christianity that sought to revive mythological patterns of thought. Dreams and visions played a significant role in the thought of Gnostics, Montanists, and other heretics and schismatics of the first centuries. Indeed, dreams can play a double role; they can serve to establish a truth as well as to upset an authority. Hence the important role of dreams and visions in the foundation of sects.[68]

From Valentinus and Montanus in the second century to the sixteenth-century miller described by Carlo Ginzburg in *the Cheese and the Worms,* the "imaginaire" (or "cosmology") of marginal and radical groups thrives on dreams and visions, on personal, highly subjective perceptions of religious truth, which do not pass through the channels of institutionalized and hierarchical religion.[69]

---

[65] I quote according the the translation of J. E. Bamberger, OCSO, Evagrius Ponticus, *The Praktikos: Chapters on Prayer* (Cistercian Studies Series 4; Kalamazoo, Mich. 1978).

[66] *Praktikos* 54.

[67] *Praktikos* 59.

[68] On the function of dreams in sect foundation, see Benz, *Die Vision,* 253–66; Lane Fox, *Pagans and Christians,* 399. Le Goff, "Le christianisme et les rêves," 284, refers to the importance of dreams among Ebionites, Valentinians, Carpocratians and Montanists; see further Dulaey, *Le rêve dans la vie et la pensée de Saint Augustin,* 37–41.

[69] On Gnostic literature, see in particular the rich study of G. Filoramo, "Diventare Dio: la palingenesi gnostica," in his *Il risveglio della gnosi ovverro diventare* (Bari 1990). See esp. 51, where Filoramo rightly insists on the implications of a radical dualist anthropology for the perception of dreams. For some of the most important sources, see Eusebius, *Historia Ecclesiastica* 4.7.9, Irenaeus, *Adversus Haereses* 1.25.3, (about the Carpocratians honoring demons which send them dreams, *"oniropomps"*), Hippolytus, *Philosophoumena* 6.26, and the *Cologne Mani*

The Montanists, for instance, linked dream, ecstasy and prophecy. The origin of the Montanist view of prophecy must be found in their propensity for ecstatic phenomena.[70]

The *Pseudo-Clementine Homilies* is an apocryphal popular novel of the fourth century that contains much material going back to early Jewish-Christian literature. In the form of a dialogue between Simon Magus and Peter, the seventeenth *Homily,* ch. 14–18, preserves the most interesting and detailed discussion of dream, vision, and prophecy in early Christian literature.[71] The confrontation between the two radically different conceptions starts with Peter pointing out that while the prophet can be inherently trustworthy, "he who trusts to apparition or vision and dream is insecure." The main reason for this insecurity lies, of course, in the possibly demonic origin of the dream or vision: the sleeper is unable to check the dream and to ascertain its source. Simon, on the other hand, claims that the dreams and visions of just men can be trusted: "If he who has had the vision is just, he has seen a true vision." For him, "it seems impossible that impious men should receive dreams from God in any way whatever." Peter answers that from the authority of the Bible, even the impious, such as Abimelech and the pagan Nebuchadnezzar ("who worshipped images"), can see true dreams and visions. This important text has not received the attention it deserves. The argument concerning the legitimacy of dreams and visions is linked in the *Homilies* to Jewish-Christian traditions about the mystical vision of God. It seems to have stood at the very heart of the struggle of nascent Christianity to define itself as a religion rather than as a radical sect.

At this juncture it should be recalled that Simon is called Magus. The early Christian tradition associates the arch-heretic directly with magical powers. The magician has the power to evoke dreams, and he receives his power from dreams. This association of magic and dreams is already well-established in Greek literature.[72] Its reflection in early Christianity, where Satan has inherited

---

Codex 4 and 23. See also E. Pagels, "Visions, Appearances and Apostolic Authority: Gnostic and Orthodox Traditions," in *Gnosis: Festschrift für Hans Jonas,* ed. B. Aland ((Göttingen 1978), 426ff. J. Doresse, *Les gnostiques d'Egypte* (Paris 1958), 170, had already pointed out that in the vocabulary of the Gnostics, "I fell asleep" was a *terminus technicus* alluding to ecstasy. On one of the most interesting examples of vision among the Gnostics, see G. Casadio, "La visione in Marco il Mago," *Augustinianum* (1989): 123–46.

[70] This is one of the main points of P. Labriolle in his *La crise montaniste* (Paris 1913). On visions among the Montanists, see Lane Fox, *Pagans and Christians,* 404–10.

[71] Text in B. Rehm, ed., *Die Pseudo-Klementinen* (CGS 42; Berlin, 1953). Cf. Pseudo-Clementine *Recognitiones*, 2.62. I quote the translation in the *Ante Nicene and Nicene Fathers*. A. Le Boulluec is preparing a new annotated translation of this important text for the Sources Chrétiennes series.

[72] See S. Eitrem, "Dreams and Divination in Magical Ritual," in *Magika Hiera: Ancient Greek Magic and Religion,* eds. C. A. Faraone and D. Obbink (New York and Oxford 1991), 175–87. See chapter 11 of this volume.

most magical powers, is an interesting and complex problem, which deserves a separate treatment.

7. The Soul

Following his Stoic sources, Tertullian refers to sleep as a natural function:

> Since, then, sleep is indispensable to our life, and health, and succour, there can be nothing pertaining to it which is not reasonable, and which is not natural.[73]

In sleep, he goes on, we observe a temporary separation of the body from the senses: "Our only resource, indeed, is to agree with the Stoics, by determining the soul to be a temporary suspension of the activity of the senses, procuring rest for the body only, not for the soul also." Consequently, the Christians must take dreams seriously, as "incidents of sleep, and as no slight or trifling excitements of the soul."[74] According to this conception, the soul continues to be active during sleep, while the body rests, dreams being the fruit of this activity. Tertullian states specifically that dreams that do not originate in God or the devil come from the soul.[75]

The psychosomatic understanding of dreams is further developed in the fourth century by Gregory of Nyssa, in his *Treatise on the Creation of Man*, one of the most interesting examples of fourth-century Patristic anthropology.[76] For Gregory, the dream reflects a sickness of the soul. The only legitimate activity of the spirit, according to him, is that of intelligence, of rational thought, while the representations formed by imagination during sleep are only appearances. This is so because only the senses permit the union of soul and body. Since, during sleep, most faculties of the soul are resting, we cannot speak of sensorial or intellectual activity. In sleep, only the nutritive part of soul remains active, retaining images of waking vision and echoes of sensory activities, imprinted in memory. All this is shaped into a new form by chance. In other words, human imagination is at work in dreams, and the mind gets lost in muddled and inordinate confusions. The mind during sleep can be compared to smoke: at once active and powerless. Through this detailed theory, Gregory can explain the ambiguity of dreams. They do sometimes offer a certain predictive vision of things to come, but this vision must remain blurred. This is called *ainigma* by dream interpreters.

Gregory, who seeks to offer a scientific explanation of dreams, relates them to the past activities of the subject. In this context, his acceptance of the possibility of predictive dreams is slightly intriguing. But this reflects the status of Biblical

---

[73] *De anima* 43.

[74] *De anima* 45, beginning.

[75] *De anima* 47, end.

[76] *De opificio homini was* written in 379. The discussion of dreams is in ch. 13.

dreams. Such are, for instance the dreams of Joseph in Pharaoh's prison (Gen. 40: 1), and those of Daniel. But Gregory immediately limits the relevance of such examples. The prophets were granted future knowledge by divine power, and thus have nothing to do with our topic. The predictive character of dreams in the Bible, including those of the Egyptian and Assyrian kings,[77] reflects God's desire to reveal the hitherto hidden wisdom of the saints. Such needs, says Gregory, do not exist at the present.

Except for prophetic dreams, therefore, human dreams may vary in their expression, but are all influenced by the physical disposition of the subject. As a proof of the psychosomatic nexus revealed in sleep, Gregory mentions the case of an acquaintance of his whom he himself had treated, and whose serious case of indigestion had caused him delirium. Gregory notes that the very same symptoms (sweat, for instance) could have been caused by a dream. In both cases, illness and sleep, the intelligent part of the soul had been de-activated. Indeed, says Gregory, many doctors agree that illnesses are linked to what the sick see in their dreams. Moreover, he adds that the moral state of the person is also significant in the formation of dreams. He sums up his discussion of dreams saying:

> It is not reason, but the irrational part of the soul which informs these products of imagination; it is from things which kept one busy during the day that dreams fashion images.

Gregory's discussion of dreams strikes one as strongly positivistic. There may have been a religious significance of dreams in the Bible, but as a natural phenomenon, dreaming must be treated with the analytical tools of medical doctors, who should seek to identify the relationships between psychic and somatic phenomena. One should note that not only God, but also Satan is strikingly absent from this sharp analysis. This absence emphasizes the differences between Gregory and discussions of dreams and dreaming in monastic literature.

As mentioned above, Evagrius insists on Satan as the origin of human dreams. But it is in the strong psychological tone of his approach that Evagrius' real originality lies. The phantasms used by the demons in order to attack the soul are a spiritual cancer, as it were. Dreams are one of the direct consequences of such unhealthy growth of the soul:

> Natural processes which occur in sleep without accompanying images of a stimulating nature are, to a certain measure, indications of a healthy soul. But images that are distinctly formed are a clear indication of sickness. You may be certain that the faces one sees in dreams are, when they occur as ill-defined images, symbols of former affective experiences. Those which are seen clearly, on the other hand, indicate wounds that are still fresh.[78]

---

[77] Gen. 39: 20–41:57 and Dan. 2.

[78] *Praktikos* 55.

More than any Christian or pagan writer before him, it would seem, Evagrius seeks to define psychic health, and to analyze the content and tonus of dreams in order to measure this health. Health is peace, quiet, lack of movement, what Evagrius calls, after Clement of Alexandria and in the wake of the Stoic thinkers, *apatheia*.[79] Active or violent dreams, on the other hand, reflect the fight of the demons against the soul.[80] Such a fight entails what one can perhaps call a neurosis, diagnosed by the growth of passions and the terror the dreams imprint on the soul.[81] It is not possible to completely avoid the display of images during sleep, but it is possible, at least for the ascetic, to avoid being disturbed or moved by these images. Hence,

> The proof of *apatheia* is had when the spirit begins to see its own light, when it remains in a state of tranquility in the presence of the images it has during sleep and when it maintains its calm as it beholds the affairs of life.[82]

Evagrius's radical psychologization of dreams, his insistence that they reflect the state of health of the soul, sets a new tone in Western discourse on dreams. What counts most for him is not so much the fight of the devil against the individual as the concrete reaction of the soul to his attack, and the ways in which it can attain peace by identifying the source of its dreams, thus mastering them. There is no need, I think, to emphasize the modernity of this tone.

Evagrius's understanding of dreams is based on a mythological element, namely, the power of Satan and his fight against God, a fight waged on the battlefield of man, soul and body. But the strong psychological interest in dreams developed by Evagrius neutralizes this mythological element. In a sense, we may thus speak of the real *Entmythologisierung* of dreams accomplished by Evagrius.

Having recognized the psychosomatic character of dreams and the fact that they reflect a neurotic state of the soul, the monastic authors propose, as a treatment, to discuss all dreams with a therapist, i.e., a wise man, an elderly monk, or *gerôn,* who functions also as a spiritual leader and counselor. This counselor is asked to interpret the dream, (or to interpret it away), and to counsel on sexual dreams.[83]

Evagrius' deep interest in the psychological side of dreams is paralleled in the West by Augustine. Augustine's remarkable psychological sensitivity left a deep

---

[79] Ibid. 56.

[80] Ibid. 59.

[81] Ibid. 54.

[82] Ibid. 64.

[83] See Dagron, "Rêver de Dieu et parler de soi," 43, on Evagrius, Barsanuphius, and John of Gaza's *Questions and Answers*, where the devil is the source of even visions of Jesus Christ. Dagron (46–47) points out that the monastic authors question such revelations. For Barnasuphius and John, no vision whatsoever is legitimate and true. Cf. the concept of "directeur spirituel" in post-Tridentine French Catholicism.

mark on his multifaceted reflection on dreams. His writings on dreams, both autobiographical and theoretical, have been analyzed carefully in the beautiful study of Martine Dulaey, and it is unnecessary to repeat her findings.[84] I shall therefore only refer to a few passages of Augustine's capital discussion of dream and *ekstasis* in his *De Genesi ad litteram*.

Augustine notes the paradoxical status of the soul during dreams, when it is at once vigilant and the prey of corporal images which it imagines to be real bodies.[85] When asleep, he points out, one may be aware that the images which appear in the dream are not real, while at the same time retaining the illusion that they reflect reality. Altogether, Augustine's main contribution to the discourse on dreams is his emphasis on their being essentially a psychological phenomenon, and not a privileged access to truth.[86] Here, as elsewhere, Augustine stands on the dividing line between antiquity and the modern mind. He is thus able, more clearly than anyone before him, to see prophecy and dream as two phenomena opposed to one another.[87]

8. Ekstasis

Augustine's discussion of *ekstasis,* and of the difference between prophecy and dream, focuses upon the case of Paul's ascension to the third heaven (II Cor. 12: 1–4).[88] To what kind of vision did the Scripture refer? To a physical vision of the senses, or to a spiritual one? And was the Apostle asleep or awake when taken to the third heaven? In other words, should we speak of a dream or of a case of ecstatic vision?[89] In order to sort out these possibilities, Augustine is brought to distinguish between different kinds of visions. There are, he says, three types.[90] The first is in the proper sense, through the eyes, by which we read the letters. The second is vision of the human mind *(spiritus hominis),* thanks to which we can develop mental representations, while the third is the intuition of the intellectual soul *(mens),* thanks to which we contemplate through intelligence *(dilec-*

---

[84] Dulaey, *Le rêve dans la vie et la pensée de Saint Augustin*; see also Amat, *Songes et visions,* and G. Crevatin, "Agostino e il linguaggio dei sogni," *Versus: Quaderni di studi semiotici* 50–51 (1988): 199–215. In the *Confessions,* Augustine refers to various dreams of his mother Monica; see *Confessions.* 3.11; 5.9; 6.1; 6.3; 6.13.

[85] *De gen ad lit* 12.2.3. I quote according to the edition in the *Bibliothèque Augustinienne,* 332ff.

[86] Cf. Le Goff, "Le christianisme et les rêves," 300.

[87] See esp. *De gen ad lit.* 12.30.

[88] *De gen ad lit.* 12.3.6-8.19.

[89] Ibid., 12.5.14.

[90] Ibid., 12.6.15. On visions in Christian literature, see P. Adnès, "Visions," *DS* 16: 949–1002; see also "Epiphanie," *RAC* 5: 832–905.

tio) itself. This third type is intellectual *(intellectuale)* vision, and it permits what is often described as mystical vision.

In Christian vocabulary, *ekstasis* refers, first of all, to Adam falling asleep in Genesis 2: 21, where the Hebrew *tardema* is translated as *ekstasis* in the Septuagint. Tertullian had already offered a definition of ecstasy: "This power we call ecstasy, in which the sensuous soul stands out of itself, in a way which even resembles madness *(excessus sensus et amentiae instar)*."[91] For him, as we have seen, "the ecstatic state and its peculiar conditions" was to be considered a separate kind of dream, side by side with divine, satanic, or psychic dreams.[92] In such a taxonomy, therefore, ecstasy is not clearly differentiated from dreams; rather, it is a special kind of dream. In this sense, Jacques Le Goff has been able to speak about "cette forme suprême du rêve qu'est pour les chrétiens l'exstase," pointing out that only in the Middle Ages would a clear distinction between dream and vision be worked out.[93] *Ekstasis,* which involved having visions while remaining awake, was well known to the early Christians, as the above reference to Paul already suggests. Again, one should note that the vocabulary does often not distinguish between *ekstasis* and dream. Hence, in *The Pastor of Hermas* 1. 3: "I fell asleep" may either refer to *ekstasis* or to a trance.[94] The same difficulty in differentiating clearly between dreams and visions arises in monastic literature. Among anchorites*,* various phenomena such as visions, dreams, hallucinations, and ecstasy cannot easily be distinguished.[95]

The psychosomatic understanding of dreams in Patristic sources raises the question whether one can influence the content of dreams, or evoke a vision. In principle, says Tertullian, dreams remain under control of a man's will. Tertullian however points out that just as different diets will produce different sleeping conditions, so will they have a direct influence on dreams, and on ecstatic visions, which belong to the broader category of dreams. Hence Tertullian's suggestion that fasting might contribute to visions. The catch here is that ascetic practices are not the privilege of Christians alone, but are also well known to pagans: "For even demons require such discipline from their dreamers as a gratification to their divinity … ." Therefore, Tertullian points out that Daniel's fast was not meant to bring ecstasy, but rather to please God through humiliation of the body.[96] Ecstasy, indeed, should remain, as Philo said, a *sobria ebrietas*. The dreams of Perpetua, similarly, are preceded and prepared by fasting. This care-

---

[91] *De anima* 45.

[92] Ibid., 47, end.

[93] Cf. Cyprian, *Ep.* 9, PL 4, 253.

[94] Lane Fox, *Christians and Pagans,* 383.

[95] Refoulé, "Rêves et vie spirituelle d'après Evagre le Pontique," 480; Dulaey, *Le rêve,* ch. 3.1. See V MacDermot, *The Cult of the Seer* (London 1971). See further Benz, *Die Vision,* and *Dreams, Hallucinations, Visions,* passim.

[96] *De anima* 48 *in finem.*

ful and even diffident attitude of Tertullian toward fasting is characteristic of the general tone of Christian authors, and stands at the root of the use of fast and prayer in monastic literature. Their aim is not to induce dream and ecstasy, but, on the contrary, to prevent dreaming.

Conclusion

In a sense, we may perhaps speak of a demotization of dreams in late antiquity, due mainly to the Christian suppression of dream interpreters. This trend, however, does not mean that everyone had religiously important, or significant, or legitimate dreams to the same extent. With the emergence of a new perception of dreams in the early Christian centuries, the number of valid, significant dreams sent by God becomes drastically limited. But, since most dreams are sent by the demons, and in particular by their leader, Satan, significant and legitimate dreams and visions usually remain those of religious virtuosi, i.e., monks, nuns, and saints, who know best how to avoid the devil's traps.

The ambiguous developments delineated above suggest the later transformation of dreams in two directions:

1. Dreams into utopias: when the collective side of dreams is emphasized, we witness what can be called a *continuatio apocalyptica*. Dreams and visions are recruited to the cosmic war against Satan and his hosts. In the ancient world, dreams often had a political significance, particularly the king's dreams. This political significance of dreams had disappeared in early Christian discourse. This disappearance was linked to the early Christian process of *Entpolitisierung*.[97] But as we have seen, even within an "enclave culture," dreams could reflect, in various schisms or heresies, a power struggle, the claim for an alternative source of revelation and religious authority, and a direct contact with the divine, which would not be mediated through the Church hierarchy.

A new, collective approach to dreams developed. Accordingly, these dreams no longer predicted the future, but were transformed into utopias describing the ideal society. Christian utopias represent the immersion of the individual dream-vision within the apocalyptic messianic tradition.[98]

As a consequence of this apocalyptic way of thought, dreams and visions are often related to conscience, guilt, and penance. In a sense, dreams and visions will represent for Christian conscience the window into a different, new, redeemed reality. Such a dualist pattern between present reality and messianic ex-

---

[97] For an analysis of this concept in the Weberian line, see H. G. Kippenberg, *Die vorderasiatischen Erlösungsreligionen in ihrem Zusammenhang mit der antiken Stadtherrschaft* (Frankfurt 1991).

[98] For mediaval utopias, see E. Gardiner, *Medieval Visions of Heaven and Hell: A Source Book* (New York and London 1993).

pectations reflected in utopian dreams would become a major factor in the discourse on dreams, and even in the implicit perception of dreams, in Western thought throughout the centuries. In that sense, one may also argue that it lies at the root of Freudian psychoanalysis.

2. Dreams and visions as they had been known in early Christianity provided one of the major building blocks for Christian mysticism. Visions soon became reinterpreted as mystical experiences, or tours of heaven, such as in Dante's *Divine Comedy*. The birth of Christian mysticism also reflects the transformation of the psychology of dreams and visions. Christian psychology reflects a turning inward, and the equivalence of the inward/upward metaphors. Hence the visions of the upper world are also an enlightenment of the soul, and dreams come to be understood as a reflection of the state of the dreamer's soul.

If the Christian bearers of true visions are profoundly different from shamans and other specialists of religious ecstasy in ancient or archaic religions, this is at least partly due to the fact that the fundamental structure of Christianity prevents the easy dissociation between soul and body. Indeed, Christianity emphasizes, both explicitly and implicitly, the essential unity of the human composite, made in the image of God, and to be reunified after death at the time of resurrection.

As we have seen, in the new discourse, dreams reflect the state of the soul rather than predict the future. Simon Price has noted that while Artemidorus was interested in dreams as a key to the future, the Freudian revolution transformed them into mirrors of the self, as keys to the unconscious. In other words, Artemidorus' position is predictive, while Freud's is introspective.[99] As I have tried to show in the preceding pages, the basic attitude of many early Christian thinkers to dreams and their significance reflects a major departure from that of an Artemidorus.[100] One may argue, therefore, that early Christian discourse on dreams and visions represents the passage from ancient to modern attitudes. This passage is a direct consequence of the radical transformation of the supernatural world operated by fourth-century Christianity.[101] In a sense, the Freudian revolution began with the early Christian *Entzauberung der Welt*.[102] If von Grunebaum's suggestion that we no longer need *Wahrtraum* is true, we owe this, in great part, to the anthropological revolution achieved by the early Christian thinkers.[103]

---

[99] S. Price, "The Future of Dreams: From Freud to Artemidorus," *Past and Present* 113 (1986):, 3–37.

[100] Hanson, "Dreams and Visions," 1421, argues to the contrary that early Christian dream visions are not significantly different from those in the Hellenistic and Roman world.

[101] Le Goff, "Le christianisme et les rêves," 293.

[102] See G. G. Stroumsa, "Gnosis und die christliche Entzauberung der Welt," in *Max Webers Sicht des antiken Christentums: Interpretation und Kritik,* ed. W. Schluchter (Franfurt 1985), 486–508 (= G. G. Stroumsa, *Savoir et salut* [Paris 1992], ch. 9, 163–81).

[103] See G. E. von Grunebaum, "The Cultural Function of the Dream as Illustrated by Classi-

At the beginning of his *Menschliches, Allzumenschliches,* Nietzsche devotes a few pages to dreams. According to him, dreams entail the belief, common to ancient, simpler civilizations, in another world, parallel to this one. Dreaming is thus the source of all metaphysics. Nietzsche sees a direct link between this dichotomy of worlds and the dichotomy between body and soul. Hence, for him, the belief in spirits, and eventually in gods, is also a consequence of the seriousness granted to dreams. Dreaming, according to this perception, would be, to use the Marxist metaphor, an opium which lures men into abstaining from action and from revolt. It is at least an implicit conclusion of the preceding pages that the early Christian discourse on dreams and visions does not fit Nietzsche's approach. In its impoverishment and its strictures, it announces the birth of the modern, *entzaubert,* person.

---

cal Islam," in *The Dream and Human Societies,* eds. E. von Grunebaum and R. Caillois (Berkeley 1966), 20.

Chapter 13

Madness and Divinization: Symeon the Holy Fool

1.

The most radical forms of self-transformation involve leaving human nature al-together. This can be done either from the bottom or from the top: one can become either a beast or an angel. Pascal, who knew something about the *coin-cidentia oppositorum*, warned us long ago that "Qui veut faire l'ange fait la bête." In the following pages, I shall argue that in religious history, these two forms of self-transformation have not always been diametrically opposed to one another. Some examples might even suggest that one should appear to be a beast in order to become an angel.

My argument will focus on the so-called "fools for Christ's sake," the *saloi* saints of late antiquity, and in particular on the most famous among them, Sy-meon, the Holy Fool from sixth-century Emesa.[1] These odd figures, both male and female, whose behavior was meant to shock, all came from the monastic mi-lieus in Egypt and Palestine. Extravagant behavior within ecstatic or charismatic movements is, of course, well-known in the ancient world. The frenzy of the Bac-chic maenads comes immediately to mind. Ecstasy, or trance, on the part of re-ligious virtuosi is also a well-known phenomenon.[2] Israelite prophecy is here a classic example, with its connections with madness: "for every man that is mad, and maketh himself a prophet. ..." *(le-khol ish meshuga', u-mitnabe)* says, Jere-miah (29: 26), while Hosea (9: 7) refers to "the prophet [who] is a fool, the spiri-tual man [who] is mad ..." *(evil ha-navi, meshuga' ish ha-ruah)*. Beyond such phenomena as prophecy and madness, so highly different in their motivation and yet sometimes quite similar in their expression, other specialists of the spiri-tual world, such as magicians or shamans, could appear to the outsider as set in radical contradistinction to "normal" behavior. Plato, for instance, sets So-crates' wisdom in opposition to human wisdom.[3]

---

[1] For a general overview of the Fools for Christ's sake, see for instance "Fous pour le Christ," *DS* 5: 752–70, and L. Rydén, "The Holy Fool," in *The Byzantine Saint,* ed. S. Hackel (London 1982), 106–13. For a more recent study of the *salos*'s spirituality, see V. Déroche, *Etudes sur Lé-ontius de Néapolis* (Acta Universitatis Upsaliensis, Studia Byzantina Upsaliensia 3; Uppsala 1995), 154–224.

[2] For pagan and Christian examples, see F. Pfister, "Ekstase," in *RAC*, 4: 944–87.

[3] See Plato, *Apology*, 20 D-E. Cf. Plutarch, *Isis and Osiris,* § 1. On magicians and shamans in ancient Greece, see P. Kinglsey, *Ancient Philosophy, Mystery, and Magic: Empedocles and the Pythagorean Tradition* (Oxford 1995).

The radical behavior of the religious virtuoso permits him a closer contact with the divinity, and ultimately, makes possible his divinization. As is well-known, the intellectual roots of the idea of the human transformation into the divine are to be found in the Platonic tradition.[4] They had been transplanted into the biblical monotheist climate by Philo, who can be said to be the true father of Christian mysticism. For him, the ecstatic experience of the prophet represents the entering of the Divine Spirit into the soul, and the latter's seizure by a kind of *sobria ebrietas*. In his words:

> But when it comes to its setting, naturally ecstasy and divine possession and madness fall upon us. For when the light of God shines, the human light sets; when the divine light sets, the human dawns and rises ... Mortal and immortal may not share the same home. And therefore the setting of reason and the darkness which surrounds it produce ecstasy and inspired frenzy *(ekstasin kai theophorèton manian)*.[5]

To some extent, the paradoxical experience of the *salos* saint should be seen within this complex tradition of religious eccentricity and charismatic leadership in ancient societies. The phenomenon of the *salos* has indeed been compared to other forms of liminal behavior in antiquity. Recently, in particular, Derek Krueger has argued for what one could call Cynic proclivities in the behavior of the *salos*.[6] The differences between Cynics and *saloi,* however, are obvious, and as we shall see, the Christian background is essential for a better understanding of the puzzling phenomenon of the Fools for Christ's sake. The case of the *salos* should highlight, precisely, the Christian transformation of self-transformation in late antiquity.

2.

The Christian holy man who plays the fool and has a shocking social behavior, does so not only *pour épater les bourgeois,* but also as a paradoxical device for getting closer to God. This pattern is mainly found in the Eastern tradition. While the first instances come from fourth-century Egyptian monasticism, the *Fortleben* of the phenomenon spans from early Byzantium to modern Russia.[7]

---

[4] See A. Louth, *The Origins of the Christian Mystical Tradition* (Oxford 1981).

[5] Philo, *Who is the Heir*, 264–65 (*LCL* 4: 418–19). Cf. *Special Laws*, 49 (*LCL* 8: 36–38). On Philo's mysticism, see, e.g., D. Winston, "Philo's Mysticism," *Studia Philonica Annual* 8 (1996): 74–82.

[6] D. Krueger, *Symeon the Holy Fool: Leontius's* Life *and the Late Antique City* (Berkeley 1996), ch. 6. For a general overview of the phenomenon, see S. A. Ivanov, *Vizantijskoe Jurodsvo* (Moscow 1994), which I know only through F. Tinnefeld's review, in *Jahrbuch für Österreiche Byzantinistik* 47 (1997): 293–95.

[7] See, e.g., W. Nigg, *Der christliche Narr* (Zürich and Stuttgart 1956), and G. P. Fedotov, *The Russian Religious Mind* (Cambridge, Mass. 1966), 2: 316–43.

In Byzantine literature, however, the original models are the most powerful ones. Symeon is the last vagrant, and later hagiographies, such as that of the ninth-century Andrew *salos,* reflect a taming, as it were, of the original model.[8] A similar decline may be observed on the Russian scene, too, where the *yurodivi* movement, which had its heyday in the late fifteenth and sixteenth centuries, was in decline in the seventeenth century.

As is well known, there are relatively few Western examples of "Fools for Christ's sake," who appear there as *joculatores domini,* showing off a *laetitia spiritualis*. The most famous example among them is probably Saint Francis of Assisi, a case sui generis, and also one of the clearest Christ-like figures in medieval history. Mention should also be made of a special case, the seventeenth-century Jesuit and mystic Joseph-Marie Surin, who however, after having confronted an epidemic of frenzy in a nuns' convent, seems to have gone really mad, rather than simply *playing* the madman.[9]

Although religious frenzy was far from being unknown in the ancient world, in the Christian context it would come to exhibit rather distinctive features. Such features stem, first of all, from some New Testament texts. The radical rejection of the ways of the world, the almost antinomian setting of worldly wisdom in opposition to divine wisdom would never be expressed in terms stronger than those of Paul:

> For it is written, I will destroy the wisdom of the wise, and will bring to nothing the understanding of the prudent. Where is the wise? Where is the scribe? Where is the disputer of this world? Hath not God made foolish the wisdom of this world? ... Because the foolishness of God is wiser than men; and the weakness of God is stronger than men ..." (I Cor. 1: 19–26).

In Paul's new scale of values, what was wisdom in the eyes of man has become folly, while what is God's wisdom *(sophia tou theou)* appears as folly *(môria)* to men. "We are fools for Christ's sake *(hemeis môroi dia Christou),* but yet we are wise in Christ; we are weak, but yet we are strong; ye are honorable, but we are despised." (I Cor. 4: 10).[10] One should perhaps note here that *ek-stasis* can simply mean madness in Patristic as well as in classical Greek.[11]

From late antiquity on, Christian ascetics knew Paul's powerful words by heart. Metaphorically, they would first strengthen the demand of humility: no one should claim his own wisdom. In Augustine's words, "If when calling your-

---

[8] This is noted by J. Grosdidier de Matons, "Les thèmes d'édification dans la vie d'André Salos," *Travaux et Mémoires* 4 (1970): 277–328. The *Lives* of Symeon, Andrew, and Basil the Younger are sometimes copied together, for instance in a Paris manuscript; see V. Déroche, *Etudes sur Léontius de Néapolis*.

[9] See "Fous pour le Christ," *DS* 5: 769.

[10] See Bertram, *môros, ktl...* in *TDNT,* ed. G. Kittel, 4: 832–47.

[11] See "Extase chez les Pères," *DS* 5: 2104.

self wise, you become a fool, call yourself a fool, and you will become wise."[12] More precisely, Paul's words could justify a more radical opposition to the ways of the world, as in Basil of Caesarea's *Great Rule:* "How can one become a fool to this world?"[13] Moreover, these words could also be perceived as an injunction for such a behavior. Paul's passage about divine wisdom appearing like foolishness (or folly) to the outsiders, however, are not in themselves enough to explain the shocking behavior of the *salos*. For such an explanation, we must turn to an analysis of the Fool's behavior, starting from its first occurrences.

The term *salos* itself is late, and quite rare, appearing almost only in monastic literature. For some time, it was believed to stem from the Syriac *sakla,* stupid, but this rather far-fetched etymology should be abandoned, as both Antoine Guillaumont and Sebastian Brock have convincingly argued.[14] The term's probable origin is popular. It usually means imbecile, half-witted, and is attested only once in reference to mad animals rather than men.[15]

The early cases of "fools for Christ's sake," which stem from fourth-century Egyptian monasticism, are rather well-known, and a brief review of the main exemples will suffice here. The *Apophtegmata Patrum* tell us that Abba Ammonas had spent fourteen years at Scete, seeking through constant prayers to master anger, and to succeed in getting rid of his own will and thoughts, "for the sake of God." When some people asked him to arbitrate between them, he played the fool. One woman said to her neighbor: "This monk (or "old man" [*geron*]) is mad." To which he answered: "How much did I suffer in the desert in order to acquire this madness, and because of you, I should lose it today!"[16] This instance shows the monk playing the fool in order not to be bothered by any kind of social responsibility. This he does so as to concentrate on his attempt to reach the mastery of passions, *apatheia*. This ideal of the Stoic sage, indeed, was present in the early monastic movement, following its adoption by Clement of Alexandria.[17]

The other fourth-century case is that of an anonymous nun from Tabennesis, as told by Palladius in his *Historia Lausiaca*.[18] Far from being really mad, this

---

[12] "Si dicendo te esse sapientem stultus factus es, dic te stultum, et sapiens eris," *Sermo* 67, PL 38, 436d-437a.

[13] *pôs ginetai tis tôi aiôni toutôi môros;* PL 31, 1272c.

[14] A. Guillaumont, "La folie simulée, une forme d'anachorèse," in his *Etudes sur la spiritualité de l'Orient chrétien* (Spiritualité Orientale 66; Abbaye de Bellefontaine 1996), 125–30; and S. P. Brock, "Early Syrian Asceticism," *Numen* 20 (1973): 1–19. See also Krueger, *Symeon the Holy Fool,* 63 n. 14.

[15] See Lampe, *A Patristic Greek Lexicon*, s.v.*salos*. Cf. *Apophtegmata Patrum*, PG 65, 240c.

[16] *Posous kopous epoièsa en tais erèmois, hina ktèsômai tèn salotèta tautèn...Apophtegmata Patrum*, Ammonas 9; PG 65, 121c; J. C. Guy, *Paroles des Anciens* (Paris 1976), 36.

[17] Clement and Stoicism, *Strom*. 3, cf. Chadwick, Lilla.

[18] A. Lucot, ed. and tr., Palladius, *Histoire Lausiaque* (Paris 1912), ch. 34, pp. 228–33. See an analysis of the case in M. de Certeau, *La fable mystique, 1: XVIe-XVIIe siècle* (Paris 1982), 49–58.

nun "was feigning madness and the demon."[19] Unaware of her real state of mental health, the nuns called her *salè*, the term referring to the mentally ill.[20] As no
one among the monastery's four hundred nuns agreed to eat with her, she was
never seen eating throughout her life, and was assigned all sorts of menial tasks,
in particular in the kitchen, being, as it were, "the monastery's sponge."[21] Palladius adds that she was thus accomplishing the Apostle's saying: "If someone
wants to be wise among us, let him become fool *(môros)* into this world, in order
to become wise *(sophos)*." Piterum, an anchorite from Porphyrite, having heard
from an angel about the holy woman, came to look for her. She was eventually
brought to him from the kitchen, in her rags. As he asked her to bless him, the
nuns exclaimed that she was a *salè*. "It is you who are mad, answers the holy
man. She is our *amma* (i.e., spiritual mother), mine as well as yours!" The nuns
eventually ask the saintly woman to forgive them all their insults and misbeha-
vior in the past, but after a few days, she disappears forever, unable to bear their
esteem and honor.

The *salè*'s story adds some new traits to the portrait of the Fool in Christ. First,
it can be a woman as well as a man.[22] Although this is the only case of a *salè* in
Antiquity, there are various instances of female Fools for Christ's sake in the
Russian context. Secondly, the very existence of the *salos* emphasizes the fact
that the real fools are those who despise him (or her). Thirdly, this behavior can
happen within a monastic community. Fourthly, it can reflect the attitude of a
lifetime. The revelation of his secret identity literally kills the saint, who cannot
survive the public recognition of his or her holiness. In a sense, then (but only in
a sense), the *salos* is the exact opposite of the stylite saint of late antique Syria,
whose very life on the top of his pillar is a constant proclamation, as loud as a
drumroll, of his sanctity and his powers as a charismatic virtuoso.[23]

The ideal of the *salos,* for which our earliest evidence comes from Egypt, soon
reached Palestine, together with the Egyptian influence upon Palestinian monasticism. Toward the end of the fourth century or at the beginning of the fifth
century, a certain Sylvanos, who had spent years in Egypt and on Mount Sinai,
established a monastery in a village near Eleutheropolis (Beit Guvrin), a rather
significant place in Palestinian Christianity, approximately half-way between

---

[19] *hupokrinomenè môrian kai daimona.*

[20] *houtô gar kalousai tas paskhousas.*

[21] *spongos tès monès.*

[22] On the special problem of female sanctity and the need to mascarade, see E. Patlagean,
"L'histoire de la femme déguisée en moine et l'évolution de la sainteté féminine à Byzance," in
her *Structure sociale, famille, chrétienté à Byzance, 4e.-11e. siècles* (London 1981). On cases of
female madness in early Christianity, see E. A. Clark, "Sane Insanity: Women and Asceticism
in Late Ancient Christianity," *Medieval Encounters* 3 (1997): 211–30. Oddly enough, Clark does not deal with the phenomenon of the Fools for Christ's sake.

[23] See the seminal study of P. Brown, "The Rise and Function of the Holy Man in Late Antiquity," in his *Society and the Holy in Late Antiquity* (Berkeley 1982), 103–52.

Jerusalem and Gaza.[24] One of the brethren in the monastery, playing the fool,[25] would spend his days counting the stones by the river near the village (the text probably means the *wadi*, or usually dry river bed), and putting them in two bags, one for his good and one for his evil thoughts.[26] Once the *salos* ideal reached the Holy Land, it would thrive among the monks of the Judean wilderness.

The excellent ecclesiastical historian Evagrius Scholasticus, whose *floruit* is in the last decades of the sixth century, has left us a precious description of the life in the Palestinian lavras established around Jerusalem by Empress Eudocia.[27] Two main kinds of monastic life can be found there, says Evagrius. Some of the monks live as if in herds, having no earthly links whatsoever; even their clothes do not belong to them, and they circulate among the monks.[28] They eat together, but just enough in order to survive, and fast for long periods, so that they look like walking skeletons. Other monks "follow the opposite way," adds Evagrius, by living alone in their small caves.

Besides these two kinds of monks, says Evagrius, a third kind of monk, both men and women, "have invented a kind of life *(politeia)* which goes beyond anything else in terms of courage and endurance." They wander in the desert almost naked, hiding only their genitals, in winter as well as during the summer. These have become companions to the beasts, and are called *boskoi,* i.e., grass-eaters. Like beasts, they eat only whatever they can find in the desert, so that eventually they really become animals. They lose both human form and human feelings, fleeing away whenever one tries to approach them.

To the smallest but most impressive group of monks, adds Evagrius, belong those who, having reached impassiveness *(apatheia),* return to the world, pretending to be mad *(paraphorous)*. These behave without shame; they eat anything they find, even walk into the women's baths and stay there naked with them, having so well mastered their passion that they do so without experiencing any sexual arousal. Evagrius adds that they are men with men and women with women, since they wish to participate to the nature of both sexes. In a word, such an excellent and theophoric *politeia* has its own laws, which go against those of nature. These athletes without a body, as it were, lead a double life, as they also bring remedies to the bodies of those who live in the flesh.

To the best of my knowledge, this striking and important passage, which has no real parallel in monastic literature, has not yet attracted the attention it

---

[24] Inter alia, Eleutheropolis was also the birthplace of Epiphanius of Salamis.

[25] *prospoioumenos môrian.*

[26] The text was published by F. Nau in Jean Rufus, *Plérophories*, Appendice, PO 8, (Paris 1911): 178–79.

[27] Text in Parmentier and Bidez, tr. in Festugière.

[28] For possible (but indirect) Buddhist influences on early Christian monasticism, see G. G. Stroumsa, *Savoir et salut* (Paris 1992), 314–27, and chapter 16 of this volume.

deserves. It strikes me as describing, in so many words, the liminal search for androgyneity among the monks. This is what Evagrius calls the theophoric character of their behavior, a behavior that involves crossing the boundary between
human and divine nature. Having completely mastered their passions and overcome their gender, these monks have in fact become angels, not beasts. They are
now divine creatures, having returned to Adam's androgyneity before the fall,
an androgyneity described in different traditions, such as the Gnostic *Apocalypse of Adam,* or *Genesis Rabba,* a contemporary Midrashic text, edited in
fifth-century Palestine.

The *Life of Abba Daniel of Skete,* a text from the fifth century, offers another
example of a *salos* named Mark, who was a contemporary of Symeon of
Emesa.[29] Mark lived in Alexandria, together with other *saloi* (i.e., with real mad-
men) who survived by stealing at the market. When described as a madman, he
answered: "It is you who are mad *(saloi)*!" Here again, the saint mascarading as
a *salos* functions as a revealer of common madness, and of the inhuman character of common life. Only his shocking behavior can bring people to realize their
own distance from both human dignity and God's presence, and only a shock
can induce them to repent and convert. In this text, for the first time, repentance
for past sins is presented as the reason for his strange behavior.

We know of other instances of *saloi* in the sixth and early seventh century.
John of Amida (Diarbekyr) plays the clown. Priscus Vitalius, a poor stranger, is
surrounded by fire, and is happy in the city where he lives precisely because
people leave in peace someone they consider to be mad. Another *salos,* Vitalios,
lives at the convent of Abba Seridon, near Gaza.[30]

Another instance of an Alexandrian *salos* is found in John Moschus's *Spiritual Meadow,* a good witness of monasticism in the early seventh century (particularly in Judea). In the Alexandrian church of Theodosius, John and his friend
Sophronius meet a bald man who wears a sack *(phalakros)* to his knees and appears to be *salos.* As they give him some money, he accepts it without a word,
then, turning around, throws his right hand, with the money, toward heaven,
prostrates in front of God, deposits the money on the earth, and leaves. John
Moschus does not offer any comment on this story, which obviously presents the
apparently strange, irrational behavior of the *salos* as a clear sign of his holiness.[31]

---

[29] L. Clugnet, ed., (Paris 1901), ch.7, pp. 22–25. See also the text in *ROC* 5 (1900): 60–62.
[30] *Life of John the Almsgiver.* These texts are referred to by A. J. Festugière, and L. Rydén, *Léontios de Néapolis, Vie de Syméon le Fou et Vie de Jean de Chypre* (Paris 1974), 24–30.
[31] John Moschus, *Pratrum Spirituale* 111, PG 87, 2976 A-B.

3.

Evagrius Scholasticus is our first witness for Symeon of Emesa (today Homs), who lived in Syria and Palestine in the sixth century. Evagrius tells us quite simply that Symeon was playing the fool in the agora, but that with his close friends he did not act anymore.[32] Stressing the chasm between Symeon's private and public attitudes, Evagrius also mentions that Symeon usually lived in complete isolation, so that no one knew how he prayed or what he ate. Our hero, then, is the ultimate actor, a secret saint who, in a radical Christian transformation of Greco-Roman theatre, plays the role of the villain. Christians deeply mistrusted and disliked the stage. But in this new kind of tragi-comedy, Symeon takes the theatre to the street. His name is linked, in particular, to sexual scandals. In one case, a pregnant servant accuses him of having fathered her child, and she retracts the accusation only at the time of her delivery, as Symeon prevents her from giving birth until she reveals the name of the true father. Another story finds Symeon staying, for quite a long time, in a prostitute's booth. As suspicion grows, she is brought to the tribunal, where she swears that he had come only to feed her, since she had no money to buy food. Note that in both cases, Symeon does not really sin and break ethical or religious norms. The suspicion and accusations that his non-conformist behavior attracts are thus baseless.

It is thanks to the *Life of Symeon the Fool,* written in the seventh century by Leontius, bishop of Neapolis (today Limassol) that Symeon remains the most famous of all the "Fools for Christ's sake." This hagiography also ensured the "recuperation" by ecclesiastical authority of that liminal and potentially dangerous character. Through early Syriac, Arabic, and Georgian translations, Leontius's *Life* soon achieved wide recognition in the Christian Orient. This *Life* has attracted much attention in the last generation. Lennard Rydén and the late Father A. J. Festugière offered an excellent edition with commentary on the text. More recently, Derek Krueger and Vincent Déroche have published important monographs. To a great extent, a close reading of the *Life of Symeon the Fool,* which remains our major source on the figure of the Holy Fool, holds the key for a better understanding of the radical kind of self-transformation, through which a saint acts as a fool.[33]

Symeon's story begins with the meeting between two young Syrian pilgrims in

---

[32] Evagrius, *Hist. Eccl.* 4.34.

[33] In many ways, as Derek Krueger has shown, this *Life* conforms to the patterns for managing the lives of holy men in late antiquity. Krueger conludes his analysis (126) by noting that Diogenes and Christ are the two prototypes for the *Life of Symeon.* I use the edition of L. Rydén, in *Vie de Syméon le Fou et Vie de Jean de Chypre,* by A. J. Festugière, in collaboration with L. Rydén, (Institut français d'archéologie de Beyrouth, bibliothèque archéologique et historique, XCV; Paris 1974). I quote the English translation of Krueger, published as an appendix to his *Symeon the Holy Fool.*

Justinian's Jerusalem. Their dear ones have remained at home: John, the more sophisticated of the two, has left his young bride, and Symeon his elderly mother. Being both lonely, they become friends, and go together to Jericho and the Jordan river. On the way, Symeon, a guileless and innocent character, inquires (in Syriac, of course) about the monasteries in the Judean wilderness. Their dwellers are "angels of God," answers his friend, and only if we become like them will we be able to see them.[34] At the monastery of Abba Gerasimos they meet Nikon, a remarkable man whose name alludes to his personal victory over the "demonic battalions." Nikon, indeed, teaches them to fight the devil. A dream reveals to them that both Symeon's mother and John's bride have died. Freed from the bonds of this world, and in particular from the love of women, they are now free to stay together and become monks, i.e., to don "the angelic habit," and begin a life of ascetic practices as anchorites in the desert, "absolutely homeless," and eating the little grass to be found there, becoming "grazers," or *boskoi*. Symeon, the text says, "nearly exceeded the limits of human nature" in his mortifications. In the desert, then, he crosses the boundaries of humanity on both sides, behaving at once as an angel and as a beast.

After twenty-nine years of this regimen, Symeon tells his companion: "What more benefit do we derive, brother, from passing time in this desert? But if you hear me, get up, let us depart; let us save others. For as we are, we do not benefit anyone except ourselves, and have not brought anyone else to salvation." John, immediately suspecting a trick of Satan, tries to dissuade his friend, and warns him of the many dangers and temptations lurking in the world at large. Symeon rejects these words of caution, saying: "I will go in the power of Christ; I will mock the world *(empaizô tôi kosmôi)*." As we shall see, this sentence offers the key to Symeon's later behavior as a *salos*. "Beware, Symeon," John keeps repeating, "Be on your guard, brother, lest the delusion of worldly things corrupt the prudence of the monastic life." He lists the main dangers of the world: women and possessions. "Beware, lest you lose your compunction through laughter and your prayer through your carelessness. Beware, please, lest when your face laughs, your mind be dissolved." As is well-known, compunction *(penthos)* is one of the major virtues cultivated in Byzantine and eastern monasticism.[35] Monastic life should be a constant repentance of one's sinful nature. In such a cultural context, laughter is shocking, bearing a demonic character, as it were. Strikingly, Symeon will decide to use precisely such means in order to confront Satan's threat: he will enter the world, the lion's den, under the disguise of laughter, mocking the world, and in particular the prince of this world, Satan, who does not recognize him as his bitter enemy, under his disguise as a laughing

---

[34] The monk as an angel in this world: S. P. Brock, "Early Syrian Asceticism," *Numen* 20 (1973): 1–19.

[35] See I. Hausherr, *Penthos: The Doctrine of Compunction in the Christian East* (Kalamazo, Mich. 1982)

fool. Laughing ridicules the enemy, transforming him into a laughingstock, eventually disarming him.[36]

Symeon begins his new life by spending three days in prayer at the Holy Sepulchre, asking that his virtue remain hidden from now on and until his death, whether he cures possessed people, accomplishes miracles, prophecies, converts Jews, or brings prostitutes back to the path of virtuous life. It is precisely in order to remain incognito as a thaumaturge that Symeon decides to appear under the garb of an idiot. "Crazy abba!" cry the children as he walks the streets of Emesa, dragging the corpse of a dog attached to his leg. He indeed plays the fool so well *(ton salon poiei),* scandalizing the townsfolk so much that he soon has reason to fear for his life at the Emesans' hands.

Like a stylite saint, he is an eccentric, who does everything to attract attention, in the street rather than from the top of a pillar, as a godless madman, misbehaving in church, letting himself be accused as a rapist, eating meat in public when expected to show some restriction. "It was entirely as if Symeon had no body, and he paid no attention to what might be judged disgraceful conduct either by human convention or by nature."

All this he does "wishing to persuade (others) that he did this because he had lost his natural sense." He behaved as if he had no body, says Leontius; that is to say, precisely, and in paradoxical fashion, like a monk, who leads a *bios angelikos* (Syriac, *ḥayyei de-mal'akhei*). He relieves himself in the open, walks naked, enters the women's baths as if "it did not matter at all" (whence the women, of course, instantly and forcefuly kicked him out).

It would be a mistake to perceive this antinomian behavior as reflecting no more than a monastic version of *adiaphora,* indifferent matters in Stoic ethics. It rather expresses Symeon's total mastery of his body, his radical uprooting of the sexual instinct. When asked about this last adventure, he says: "Believe me, child, just as a piece of wood goes with other pieces of wood, this was I there. For I felt neither that I had a body nor that I had entered among bodies, but the whole of my mind was on God's work, and I did not part from Him." In other words, *unio mystica* at the sauna, or rather at the hammam. The complete disappearance of sexual instinct plays a major role in the description of Symeon's foolishness. He appears, of course, to behave in lewd and promiscuous fashion, while in fact nothing is further away from his acts, thoughts, and feelings.

The text gives us here a twofold justification of the saint's odd behavior, which has all the appearances of antinomianism: "Some of his deeds the righteous one did out of compassion for the salvation of humans, and others he did to hide his way of life." Actually, this twofold justification reflects Symeon's clearly thought-out decision that saving people by going into the world could be

---

[36] See T. Bakonsky, *Le rire des Pères* (Paris 1996), and I. Gilhus, *Laughing Gods, Weeping Virgins* (London 1997).

achieved only incognito, or rather through hiding under the cloak of madness. Precisely so as not to attract Satan's attention, not to awake his suspicion, as the saint is fighting him in his own kingdom. Not just anyone, however, can achieve anonymity through masquerading as a fool. Such a paradoxical behavior is reserved to those who have spent years in the desert and reached *apatheia,* the total insensitivity to passions (and in particular, of course, to sexual passions). In other words, only he who lives like an angel can seek to live like a beast.

There are two different, although related aspects of Symeon's behavior as a *salos*. On the one hand, he appears to be both completely devoid of human decency, as when he shows total bodily shamelessness. On the other hand, he seems to be quite out of his mind, and is called a madman or an idiot by everybody, children included. To such interjections, his standard answer is: "It is you who are the idiot!" Those who consider him to be mad are themselves prisoners of material reality, and unable to see truth. Symeon's "madness" also reflects his prophetic powers: one day, he starts whipping the pillars, saying: "Your master says, 'Remain standing!'" as he knows a large earthquake is about to seize the city. When the earthquake came, none of the pillars he had whipped fell. On another occasion, he goes around kissing some of the school children. To the teacher at each school, he says: "In God's name, idiot, do not thrash the children whom I kiss, for they have a long way to go." The saint alone knew that an epidemic which was coming to the city would kill these children. A somewhat similar story is found in Rabbinic literature: Rabbi Joshua ben Levi accompanies Elijah, who is the bearer of special knowledge. Elijah's behavior is perceived as odd, as its reasons remain misunderstood by everybody, including Rabbi Joshua.[37]

Symeon's behavior shocks monks as well as laymen. As ascetics from the Judean desert had come to Emesa to meet him, they were laughed at: "What do you want from him, fathers? The man is beside himself, and he abuses and jeers at all of us, particularly monks." Eventually, when they find him "eating beans like a bear," as the text has it, they ask him to bless them, saying: "Truly we have come to see a great sage *(gnostikos);* this man has much to explain to us." To which he answers: "You have come at a bad time, and the one who sent you is an idiot." He not only eats as a bear, but also gorges himself on Holy Thursday. Moreover, he "skips and dances in the middle of the whole circus." He plays, indeed, "all sorts of roles foolish and indecent," and is seen flirting with prostitutes, dancing naked and whistling with them, even being whipped by one of them. He remains undefiled throughout these ordeals, thanks to the level of purity and impassivity that he has reached.

Symeon's goal in all these actions is double: on the one hand, he intends to save souls, by both his "strange deeds" (cf. *ma'assim zarim* among the Sabba-

---

[37] See W. Bacher, *Die Agada der palästinensischen Amoräer* (Strasbourg 1892), 1: 187–94.

teans) and his puzzling words. On the other hand, he hopes, through his mask of *salos*, to retain the salvation of his own soul, which he has achieved by reaching *apatheia* through his ascetic endeavors during the long training in the desert of Jerusalem. For this, he must remain anonymous, or rather, keep his virtue hidden, in order to avoid the corrupting respect and honor.

Is it quite correct, then to speak of Symeon's self-transformation? There are two aspects to this question. From the point of view of Symeon's folly, the answer is negative. The transformation of the *gnostikos* into a *salos* remains only a *functional* self-transformation. The former ascetic has succeeded in wearing the mask of an antinomian fool and sinner, without giving up his real personality, that of a saintly ascetic. Indeed, his folly is only public. "But he behaved otherwise before the crowd," says the text, in a clear *imitatio Christi*.[38] With his close friend John, he retains his ascetic behavior, fasting and praying intensely. For his prayer and ascetic practices he usually retires to his hiding place, about which no one but John knows. Yet, he is once seen conversing with two angels at the baths. The man who saw him was a Jewish artisan, soon to be converted, together with his household. Those who believe his miraculous power are healed (or converted), while the others he calls "idiots!" "Where are you going, idiot?" he once asked a mule driver, "for he always had these words in the same way on his lips." "Fool," *salos*, has become more than his choice epithet, his nickname, to the extent that people invoke to their help "the God of the Fool." The various characters whom he meets, those possessed by demons, the onlookers, some thieves, a clairvoyant amulet maker, beggars, a Jewish glassblower, all call him "Fool," believing, somehow, that his folly will help him to accomplish miracles.

One day, John happens to see him praying in his cave: "And seeing him from afar stretching out his hands to heaven, he was afraid, not daring to approach the monk. For he swore that he saw balls of fire going up from him to heaven." In monastic literature, this vision of light going out of the monk's cell reflects the *unio mystica*. It is in that sense that we can speak of Symeon's self-transformation: the radical self-transformation of the saintly man into an angel – one should perhaps even say his transfiguration *(metamorphôsis)*. Here, it represents the acme of Symeon's life. At his death, too, the angels will be called to take part at his funeral. As two men were carrying his body silently to the plot of land reserved for foreigners, the converted Jewish glassblower heard "psalm singing, music such as human lips could not sing, and a crowd such as human lips could not gather." The Fool might have been a total stranger among men, but the angels themselves had come down from heaven to sing for him. The former Jew buried him with his own hands. When John searched for the body of his friend, he could not find it in the grave, "for the Lord had glorified him and

---

[38] See n. 33 above.

translated him." As with Enoch, Mary, and Christ Himself, Symeon's body had reached heaven. Like the balls of fire coming from his hut, the translation of Symeon's body is a clear sign of the Saint's glorification, or, in other words, of his *theiôsis,* divinization. "Truly human in face, but God in heart," concludes Leontius: he who was called a Fool, who behaved as a beast, seemingly leaving aside both divine and natural law, had in fact become a truly Christ-like figure. One could hardly imagine a more radical self-transformation, achieved by more paradoxical ways. It is only after his death that the Fool's real nature would be revealed to men, by the angels (and through the Jew). This revelation is also an *apotheôsis.* Incidentally, the translation of Symeon's body also functions as a final act of humility on his part: no cult will develop at his tomb.

4.

Acting as a fool, then, is not the last stage of the saint's self-transformation. The ultimate goal of the Christian holy man is to get as close as possible to God, even to become united with Him, or rather with the incarnate God. The *imitatio Christi* is known, in the East, mainly as the *theiôsis,* divinization, which awaits the saint at the end of his ascetic travail. A long Patristic and monastic literary tradition deals with the mystic's ultimate goal, from Gregory of Nyssa and Pseudo-Macarius in the fourth century to Symeon the New Theologian (died 1022).[39]

As the case of Symeon of Emesa shows, however, the *salos* may strive to appear like a beast, but what he really seeks is to become transformed into an angel and to belong to the divine world. In a paradoxical way, then, his case too represents a kind of divinization. By His incarnation, Christ had crossed the boundaries between the divine and the human world. The *salos,* who wants to become like Christ, seeks to descend in order to climb.

"Descending in order to climb": the phrase sounds as a translation from Hebrew: *"yerida le-tsorekh ʿalya,"* a major stance in Hassidism, associated with the Baʿal Shem Tov.[40] Besides the *Fortleben* of the Fool for Christ's sake in the Christian tradition, the history of religions provides some striking parallels to the phenomenon, which have not yet been seriously studied. The Hassidic movement is certainly one, and Christian influences at the very origins of the movement remain a tantalizing possibility, not yet explored. The Malamatia saints in medieval Islam offer another striking parallel.[41] Here, the direct influence from the

---

[39] See especially B. Krivochéine, *In the Light of Christ: Saint Symeon the New Theologian* (New York 1987). On divinization in Patristic thought, see for instance "divinisation," *DS* 3: 1370–97.

[40] See G. Scholem, *The Messianic Idea in Judaism* (New York 1971), 219.

[41] See Déroche, *Etudes sur Léontius de Néapolis,* and especially M. W. Dols, *Majnûn: The Madman in Medieval Islamic Society,* ed. D. E. Immisch (Oxford 1992), ch. 13, 366ff..

saloi are even more plausible. Alexander Syrkin has published what is perhaps the most interesting phenomenological analysis of the *salos*'s religious behavior.[42] Insisting on Symeon's systematic transgression of various human and ecclesiastical precepts, Syrkin seeks to understand the fool's behavior through a comparison with three semantic levels of religious behavior in Indian religions. For him, the *salos* represents a combination of sorts between the virtue of the *sannyasin,* who rejects the world, and the highest sanctity of the *arahant,* who strives on the *coincidentia oppositorum.* Despite the great interest provided by structural comparisons, however, it seems to me that it is the Christian and late antique context that holds the key to this phenomenon.

Such a social and religious contextual reading, precisely, is attempted in Teodor Bakonsky's recent monograph. Bakonsky compares the *saloi* to the holy mimes, who displayed their *parrhèsia* by playing as actors (a rather disreputable way of earning one's living, of course) at the theater.[43] Laughter is here perceived as a secondary effect of this *parrhèsia.* The *salos* is even more radical: for this Promethean character, the world is a stage, and through his acting he denounces and reveals the devil's sway over this world. But even this attempt to understand the *salos* as a late antique Christianization of traditional sacred madness, remains unsatisfactory. Although Bakonsky recognizes that the birth of the *salos* coincides with that of the monastic movement, his explanation does not perceive the close connection between the behavior of the *salos* and the monastic ideal of *theiôsis.* It is here, to my mind, that one can speak meaningfully of a *coincidentia oppositorum:* it is in order to remain an angel, in this world, that the saint has to appear as a beast: for him (or her), this exhibitionist kind of masquerading is, paradoxically enough, the best way to appear incognito, or rather to be taken for somebody else, and thus to hide his (or her) true identity.

According to a rather disturbing tradition, it was Simon of Cyrene who bore the cross on his shoulder and the crown of thorns upon his head, while Christ, from heaven, was laughing at the ignorance of those who did not realize what was happening.[44] This docetic story, reported by Irenaeus in the name of Basilides,[45] is repeated in the *Second Treatise of the Great Seth,* one of the Gnostic texts found at Nag Hammadi.[46] Christ's chilling laughter, which resounds deeply throughout the eons, presents a particularly disturbing image of the Savior, poking fun at his arch-enemies the archons, rulers of this world, in the great game of *Heilsgeschichte,* while remaining insensitive to the suffering of poor Simon cru-

---

[42] A. Syrkin, "On the Behavior of the 'Fool for Christ's Sake,'" *HR* 22 (1982): 150–71.

[43] T. Bakonsky, *Le rire des Pères* (Paris 1996).

[44] Cf. the important theme of the biblical prophets, the archons' vassals, as "laughingstocks" in the *Second Treatise of the Great Seth,* CG VII, 62–63.

[45] Irenaeus, *Adv. Haer.* 1.24.4.

[46] CG VII, 55.9–56.19.

cified in his place. Another Gnostic text tells us, even more brutally, that Jesus, rather than being crucified, himself "came crucifying the world."[47] Such powerful metaphors strike one as close in tone to Leontius of Neapolis's remark, in his *Life of Symeon the Fool,* that the shocking behavior of the *salos* was meant to poke fun at the world, *empaizein tôi kosmôi.*[48]

At first sight, the intellectual and religious milieus of Gnostics and *saloi* seem worlds apart. The Gnostics were radical deniers of the biblical God, at a time when Christianity was still in search of its own beliefs and identity. The *saloi,* on the other hand, belong to the elite of religious virtuosi, at a time when Christianity had become the official religion of the Empire. Christian virtuosi and ecstatics, however, while they certainly represented a Christian elite, remained in some ways liminal not only to Christian society, but also to Christian orthodoxy, from the Montanists in the second century to the Messalians in the fourth.

And yet, the *saloi,* in a sense, acted like the Gnostics, when they chose to "fool the world," i.e., to use the weapons of ruse against naked force in their fight with the evil archons or with their leader the devil. In both cases, one observes a radical behavior, on the verge of antinomianism: social and religious norms may, or even ought to be transgressed. As is now well-known, the Pakhômian documents found in the cardboard covers of the Nag Hammadi codices reveal a provenance from monasteries around Chenoboskion. Although a definitive explanation for this puzzling fact eludes us, it is plausible, or perhaps even probable, that some Egyptian monks were fond readers of the Gnostic texts.[49] Could it be that for such monks, the declared stance of the Gnostics as aliens in a threatening world which must be fooled and fought through ruse was perceived as a model for their own behavior?[50] After all, the monks, like the Gnostics, claim to live as foreigners in the world, from a social if not a metaphysical point of view. As Antoine Guillaumont has shown, *xeniteia,* the radical cultivation of one's sense of being a foreigner, was a major value among the early monks, in particular in Egypt.[51] Christian ascetics sought to practice asceticism abroad, far from their native soil, and they used all means to behave as total strangers, including through eccentric or strange behavior. An analysis of the evidence

---

[47] *Gos. Phil.,* CG II, 63:24. See J. Dart, *The Jesus of Heresy and History* (San Francisco 1988), ch. 13, 93–101.

[48] The characterization of Leontius's *Life of Symeon the Fool* as a highly puzzling text is that of the Bollandist H. Delehaye (quoted by Krueger, 1, n. 1).

[49] See, e.g., G. G. Stroumsa, *Savoir et salut,* ch. 8, 145–62.

[50] A similar use of ruse as a legitimate religious behavior is also found in later movements, in what might reflect a Gnostic influence. In Shi'ite Islam, in particular, it became known as *taqqyya*: as for the Gnostics, lying becomes justified in front of religious persecution.

[51] A. Guillaumont, "Le dépaysement comme forme d'ascèse dans le monachisme ancien," in his *Aux origines du monachisme chrétien* (Spiritualité orientale 30; Abbaye de Bellefontaine 1979), 89–116.

might enable us to ponder the tantalizing possibility that in doing so, the monks were following a pattern set earlier by the Gnostics, who had claimed to be *allogeneis,* coming from "another seed."[52]

These phenomenological parallels between *saloi* and Gnostics are perhaps genetic connections. Masquerading in order to enter this world, Satan's realm, and to challenge him and remain unhurt is a conception developed even before the birth of monasticism. Among religious virtuosi, the *salos* is super-virtuoso. Even in the desert, he feels the need to hide, since the desert has become a city, to use Athanasius's pregnant image in his *Vita Antonii*. Only thanks to his madness can he live in the city as if it were a desert. He travels through the world unharmed, saving men without being sullied by their impurity. Thanks to his feigned madness, he can remain in God's presence while staying in Satan's kingdom and waging war at him.

Ernst Benz has argued that the early *salos* was not a complete outsider to society, but only strove to keep his distance from the active, working world, remaining aloof from social responsibilities. A hippie, as it were, or perhaps a scholar.[53] Despite its rather apologetic tone, which seeks to tame a radical phenomenon, Benz's remark points into the right direction: far from being isolated by his behavior, the *salos* stands in an active, dialectical relationship with society at large. Some similarities between monks, *saloi,* and cynics have been duly pointed out.[54] There are however vast differences between the two types of behavior, as Déroche rightly insists. It is hard to present the cynic as a religious type, or as someone interested in interaction with society at large. Like the stylite saint, the *salos* is a magnetic pole for society, a kind of charismatic anti-leader, if I may risk this oxymoron. The *salos* is, first of all, a monk. Thanks to his ruse, he is able to come back to the world, poking fun at it, after having fled it to the desert.[55]

---

[52] See for instance G. G. Stroumsa, *Another Seed: Studies in Gnostic Mythology* (Nag Hammadi Studies 24; Leiden 1984), passim.

[53] Hebrew *batlan* [from Greek *scholè*]; as the Mishna states, any city, in order to justify its name, needs the presence of at least ten *batlanim*: scholars? *saloi*?

[54] By both Krueger, *Symeon the Holy Fool,* and Guillaumont, "Le dépaysement comme forme d'ascèse."

[55] Abba Or, fourth-century Nitria, *Apoph. Patrum,* Or 14, PG 65, 440c.

Part IV

Radical Dualism

Chapter 14

Gnostic Justice and Antinomianism:
Epiphanes' *On Justice* in Context

1. Law and Justice

In the mental world of the early Christians, the Law *(nomos)* was either Jewish or Roman. To varying degrees, the Christians rejected Jewish Law, since they did not for the most part accept its traditional validity (although they recognized the legitimacy of the concept of law). On the other hand, they were placed outside the pale of legality by Roman law. This deep ambiguity toward laws and the concept of law in early Christianity also reflects on the concept of justice *(dikaiosunè)*. Justice, indeed, is defined by legal criteria, and early Christian self-identity was shaped in opposition to the two main legal systems of thought then available. Despite various references to justice in early Christian literature, from the New Testament on, the problem of justice does not seem to have been of paramount importance to early Christian thinkers. Christian theologians did of course devote much of their efforts to the establishment of Christian ethics (and were known among Hellenic thinkers for their high ethical standards), but these ethics were built upon the presupposition (at least implicit) that law and justice as practiced in the world were objectionable. Early Christian ethics were thus mainly superogatory, and *dikaiosunè* mostly referred to Pauline "justification."[1]

Much more radically than other Christians, dualist and Gnostic thinkers under the early Empire strongly objected to the divinely revealed Law of Israel. While those who later became identified as "orthodox" Christians argued that Jesus had not come to abolish the Law, but to offer a new interpretation of it, the Gnostics saw this law, at the very least, as an impediment to salvation. With varying degrees of vehemence and with a series of arguments, they constructed their theologies and mythologies around their rejection of the Law revealed by

---

[1] One of the best articles dealing with the variety of meanings of *dikaiosunè* and *iustitia* in pagan and Christian antiquity is A. Dihle, "Gerechtigkeit," *RAC* 10 (1978): 233–60, with a detailed bibliography. See also the various articles under the general title "Gerechtigkeit" in *TRE* 12 (1984): 404–48. On early Christian ethics, see for instance E. Osborn, *Ethical Patterns in Early Christian Thought* (Cambridge 1976), or W. A. Meeks, *The Origins of Christian Morality: the First Two Centuries* (New Haven 1994). For a summary of the question and further bibliography, see E. Osborn, "Ethics," *EEC,* 1: 286–88.

God to Israel.[2] Moreover, some of the Gnostic communities were established upon the same principles, and the antinomian practices of some Gnostics – in particular some sexual "pornographic" practices – became the core of the Christian heresiologists' deep repulsion to the dualist heresy.[3]

In such contexts, the demiurge and Lawgiver was perceived as a lower heavenly figure who had rebelled against the higher God.[4] The Law that he imparted to Israel was meant to keep the human race in slavery. Such a drastic rejection of the Law and of its soteriological value entailed negative attitudes to the concept of justice. Law, indeed, is the locus of justice: there can be no justice without law. Marcion, for instance, calls the demiurge and lawgiver the *just* god, while the Father of Jesus Christ he calls the *good* God.[5]

What happens to the concept of justice in an antinomian thought which seeks to offer an interpretation of the Christian message deprived of its Hebrew roots? What follows will address this question, pointing out the tension between two very different conceptions of law and justice in Gnostic antinomianism.

As the Homeric *dikè,* the figure of Justice is present in Greek literature from its very beginnings. With the emergence of philosophical thought, however, we witness a new stage in the reflection upon the nature of justice. The very passage from *dikè* to *dikaiosunè* reflects a move to abstract thought, an internalization of sorts: justice is now perceived as a virtue.[6] Pythagoras defined *dikaiosunè* as the equal distribution among all, its principle being mutuality and equality, as expressed by Iamblichus in his *Life of Pythagoras.*[7] More than anyone else, however, Plato made strenuous efforts to understand the nature of justice, and placed its cultivation at the heart of the educational system he devised. No wonder, then, that he dedicated the ten books of his *Republic* to the clarification of

---

[2] See for instance H. Merkel, "Gesetz IV" (Alte Kirche) in *TRE* 13 (1984): 75–82, with bibliography. On the various attitudes to law in Christian thought, see J. Neumann, "Gesetz," *HrgG, 3* (1993): 9–17.

[3] See for instance G. W. MacRae, S.J., "Why the Church Rejected Gnosticism," in his *Studies in the New Testament and Gnosticism* (Good News Studies, 26; Wilmington, Del. 1987), 251–62. See further M. Tardieu, "Epiphane contre les gnostiques," *Tel Quel* 88 (1981): 64–91.

[4] See for instance G. Quispel, "The Origins of the Gnostic Demiurge," in *Kyriakon: Festschrift Johannes Quasten*, (Münster 1970), vol. 1, 271–76.

[5] See for instance Irenaeus, *Adversus Haereses*, 1. 27. 3 (350–53 Rousseau-Doutreleau). See further Tertullian, *Adversus Marcionem* 1. 11 and 1. 19 on the God of Israel and the separation of Law and Gospel (26–27 and 46–49 Evans), and Origen, *Hom. in Num.*, 9. 4: "deus legis non est bonus, sed iustus." The best study on Marcion remains A. von Harnack, *Marcion: das Evangelium vom fremden Gott: eine Monographie zur Geschichte der Grundlegung der katholischen Kirche. Neue Studien zu Marcion* (TU 45; Leipzig 1924). This classical work is now also available in English translation.

[6] On Greek justice, see in particular E. Havelock, *The Greek Concept of Justice, from its Shadow in Homer to its Substance on Plato* (Cambridge, Mass. and London 1978). For a recent discussion, see M. Nussbaum, "Equity and Mercy," *Philosophy and Public Affairs* 22 (1993): 83–125.

[7] The discussion appears in ch. 30.

the concept of *dikaiosunè*. In Plato's footsteps, Aristotle devoted much attention to the most important of the four cardinal virtues, mainly in the fifth book of
his *Nichomachean Ethics*. During the Hellenistic period, standard perceptions
of justice seem to have been a blend of the various philosophical schools. Judg-
ing from the example of Philo, at least, the importance of the Pythagorean criteria in the understanding of the nature of justice seems obvious.[8]

Building on the complex meanings of *dikaiosunè*, the semantic field of the
term in Jewish and Christian Greek is of course a rich one. In particular, however, it translates *tsedeq* and its cognates in the LXX.[9] The Hebrew conception
of justice is directly linked to the revealed Law. Man must be just because God is
just.[10] The Lawgiver, indeed, is conceived as *a just judge*:

> Then the heavens proclaimed His righteousness [*tsidqo; tèn dikaiosunèn autou*] for He
> is a God who judges. (Psalms 50: 6)

The figure of the Messiah, too, is perceived as that of a Just Man. The Messiah is
called a *tsadiq* in the few biblical texts which refer to him (Jer. 23:5, 6; 33:15;
Zech. 9:9); he is the incarnation of supreme justice. In post-biblical Jewish literature of the Second Commonwealth, righteousness is one of the marks of the
messianic times, as exemplified in *I Enoch* 38:2, 53:6. The importance attributed
to the figure of the just prophet or priest is also a central preoccupation of
various pious circles in the Second Commonwealth. The "Master of Justice,"
more ha-tsedeq (cf. Hosea 10:12), for instance, is a central figure in the *Damascus Covenant*, though the messianic dimension of this figure remains far
from obvious. In a few passages in Rabbinic literature appears the messianic
figure of the *kohen tsedeq*, a figure whose precise identity and function remain
much in the dark.[11]

The earliest layers of Christian literature stand in the Hebrew biblical tradition. The trend represented by the leaders of the Jerusalem church, and in particular by James, brother of the Lord, insists on the ways of justice to be followed
by both the individual, who must be just, and the community. Jesus is presented
as "the Righteous": in his last speech, Stephen calls Jesus "the Righteous" ([*ho
dikaios*, equivalent of *ha-tsadiq*] Acts 7:52), and so does Pilate's wife (Mat.
27:19). Such an epithet is a messianic one. The Ebionite conception of Jesus as
being at once king, priest, and prophet reflects the unification of the three messianic figures described for instance in I Macc. 14:41.[12]

James, the brother of the Lord and the leader of the Jerusalem community, is

---

[8] See for instance *Spec. Leg.* IV. 230–1, and cf. the discussion by J. Dillon, *The Middle Platonists* (Ithaca, N.Y. 1977), 148–50.

[9] See in particular D. Hill, *Greek Words and Hebrew Meanings: Studies in the Semantics of
Soteriological Terms* (Cambridge 1967), ch. 4, 82–162.

[10] For discussion and literature, see the articles of Dihle and Merkel, n. 1 above.

[11] See the entries "Messiah" in *EJ*, 11: 139ff.

[12] See D. Flusser, "Messiah," *EJ,* 11: 140–41.

also called "righteous." Here, for instance, is the testimony of Eusebius: "He was called 'the Righteous' by all men from the Lord's time to ours. ..." And a little further: "So from his excessive righteousness he was called 'the Righteous and Oblias,' that is in Greek 'Rampart of the people and righteoussness,' as the prophets declare concerning him."[13]

In some New Testament texts, moreover, it is the community of believers itself which is described as "the *dikaiosunè.*" In early Christian literature, "the way of righteousness *(hodos dikaiosunès)*" seems to refer to Christianity itself,[14] and the same expression occurs again in later Patristic literature.[15]

The perception of justice in early Christianity, however, owes much of its complexity to Paul's radical transformation of the concept of justice *(tsedeq/dikaiosunè)* through its internalization.[16] "The just shall live in his faith (cf. *tsadiq be-emunato yihye)*" becomes the leitmotiv of what is now justification of the sinner before God, an essential element of Paul's religious reinterpretation of the Jewish tradition. This internalized justice (in this context, *dikaiosunè* is usually rendered *righteousness* or *justification* in English) is directly related to Paul's view on the end of the Law's hegemony.[17]

2. Carpocrates

Of all the second-century Gnostic masters, Carpocrates is perhaps the one to have aroused the most vehement reaction from the side of the Church Fathers. What shocked the Christian theologians most were the antinomian sexual practices of the Carpocratians, who argued, among other things, for the community of women.[18]

Epiphanes, Carpocrates' son, devoted a treatise to justice, the very first treatise on the topic by a thinker at least nominally Christian. His *Peri dikaiosunès* is lost, but a rather detailed summary of at least some of its argument is preserved by Clement of Alexandria.[19] Oddly enough, the implications of this

---

[13] Eusebius, *Hist. Eccl.* 2. 24. 4, 7 (170–71 LCL).

[14] See for instance *Barnabas* 1. 4; V. 4 and *II Clement* 5.7. Cf. *Halakha*, or the Qur'anic *sirât*.

[15] See for instance Pseudo-Macarius, *Homilies* 16.1. Ps. Macaire, *Oeuvres spirituelles*, I (SC 275; Paris 1980), 178–79. See also A. Descamps, *Les justes et la justice dans les Evangiles et le christianisme primitif* (Louvain 1950).

[16] The literature is immense; see for instance Schrenck, "*dikaiosunè,*" *TDNT* 4:192–210, and K. Kertelge, "*dikaiosunè,*" *EDNT*, 1: 329–30. On the internalization of various concepts in Paul, see chapter 5 of this volume.

[17] On Paul and the Law, see the bibliography in G. Klein, "Gesetz," (Neues Testament) in *TRE* 3: 13, 58–75.

[18] On Carpocrates and the Carpocratians, see A. Monaci Castagno in *EEC, 1:* 145A. See further M. Smith, *Clement of Alexandria and a Secret Gospel of Mark* (Cambridge, Mass. 1973), ch. 4 and appendix 8; and especially W. A. Löhr, "Karpokratianisches," *VC* 49 (1995): 23–48.

[19] See *Stromateis* 3.2.8,3; 9.2–3. 1977,18–199,13 (199,29–200,4 Stählin). The text is reprodu-

well-known passage do not seem to have been fully analyzed. Only very recently was an article devoted to the topic.[20] The Gnostic attitude to justice, as reflected in Epiphanes' conception, seems to stand at the confluence of the Greek philosophical, Jewish, and early Christian traditions.

About Carpocrates and his son Epiphanes, we know only what is reported by the heresiological tradition. No Carpocratian text has been identified coming from Nag Hammadi. The two main testimonies are those of Ireneaus,[21] repeated, more or less, by Hippolytus[22] and of Clement of Alexandria.[23]

The heresiologists report that the Carpocratians (who seem to have originated in second-century Alexandria) called themselves *gnostikoi*. We are also told that they made cultic use of images of Christ, as well as of Greek philosophers such as Pythagoras, Plato, and Aristotle. The strong Hellenic influences upon their religious behavior contrasts with some other beliefs which they share with the Ebionites, for instance their claim that Jesus was the son of Joseph, and was not possessed of a divine nature. For the Carpocratians, what distinguished Jesus from other human beings, reports Hippolytus, is the fact that he was "more just" *(dikaioteron)* than other people. In other words, the Carpocratians retain, together with strong Hellenic syncretistic influences, the Jewish and Jewish-Christian conception of the Messiah as *tsadiq*.

Another related trait of Carpocratian theology, according to Hippolytus, was the belief that Jesus' soul kept the memory *(diamnèmoneusai; commemorata fuit)* of what it had seen above, "in the sphere of the unengendered God."[24] This memory of things seen before birth alludes to yet another of their beliefs: the transmigration of the soul. According to them, the souls are to undergo a series of reincarnations, until they achieve salvation, which is freedom from the body, i.e., the soul's prison, and from the powers of the demiurgic angels. The motif of transmigration is probably inherited from the school of Pythagoras, while the mention of *sôma/sèma* refers to a common theme of Orphic origin.[25]

This salvation from transmigration will happen only when the soul has accom-

---

ced in W. Völker, *Quellen zur Geschichte der christlichen Gnosis* (Tübingen 1932), 33–36. For a German translation and commentary, see H. Leisegang, *Die Gnosis,* 4th ed. (Stuttgart 1955), 261–70. I am using the translation in J. E. L. Oulton and H. Chadwick, *Alexandrian Christianity* (Library of Christian Classics; Philadelphia 1954), 42–45.

[20] W. H. Löhr, "Epiphanes' Schrift 'Peri dikaiosunès' (= Clemens Alexandrinus, Str. III,6,1–9,3)," in *Logos: Festschrift für Luise Abramowski,* eds. H. C. Brennecke, E. L. Grasmück and C. Markschies (Beihefte zur Zeitschrift für die neutestamentliche Wissenschaft, 67; Berlin and New York 1993), 12–29.

[21] *Adversus Haereses* 1. 25.

[22] *Elenchos* 7. 32.

[23] *Stromateis* 3.5–11.

[24] *Elenchus,* 7. 32.

[25] Cf. Diels, *Fragmente*, 11b. 7 (Xenophanes). On the belief in transmigration in early Christian thought, see K. Hoheisel, "Das frühes Christentum und die Seelenwanderung," *JAC* 27–28 (1984–1985): 24–46.

plished all possible actions, all possible ways of life. Such a requirement entails a strong antinomianism, or behavior in radical opposition to the requirements of the law, and its correlate belief that no action is evil in itself, since there is nothing inherently evil in human nature. Acts are thus in themselves beyond good and evil, or *indifferent (adiaphora)*, to use Stoic terminology, while only faith and love are significant toward salvation. Our sources add that these beliefs were transmitted by Carpocrates to his disciples as esoteric teachings.[26]

One obvious consequence of such antinomian teachings is the belief that Jesus, though he had been raised in the Jewish practices, despised them.[27] To such details Tertullian adds that that Carpocrates' disciples considered themselves to be equal to Christ.[28] Referring to *anamnèsis,* moreover, he points out the deep Platonic roots of the Gnostic heresies. Tertullian is obviously on the right track, although Orphic, Pythagorean, and Stoic elements can also be easily identified in his doctrines, as reported by Irenaeus.

3. Epiphanes

According to Clement, Epiphanes, who was Alexandrian on his father's side and Cephallenian on his mother's side (Clement reports that she was called Alexandria), died when he was seventeen. After his death, a cult was offered to him on Cephallenia, where he was "honored as a god." Clement gives rather substantial quotations from his *Concerning Righteousness*, a work which has been uncharitably described as consisting "of the scribblings of an intelligent but nasty-minded adolescent of somewhat pornographic tendencies."[29] "The righteousness of God, says Epiphanes, is a kind of universal fairness and equality *(tèn dikaiosunèn tou theou koinônian tina einai met' isotètos)*. Equality is a quality of the cosmos; "the sun shines equally upon all." But it also reflects upon people: "there is no distinction between rich and poor, people and governor, stupid and clever, free men and slaves." God thus "establishes His righteousness to both good and bad." In other words, "the universal righteousness is given to all equally *(dikaiosunès te tès koinès hapasin ep' isès dotheisès)*." Cosmic order, which he calls "the manifest universality of God's fairness," "is regulated by no law *(oudeni nomôi kratoumenè)*."

This seems to be the kernel of Epiphanes' thought: the opposition he makes between *dikaiosunè* and *nomos*. "And for birth, there is no written law *(all' oude*

---

[26] On Gnostic esotericism, see G. G. Stroumsa, *Hidden Wisdom: Esoteric Traditions and the Roots of Christian Mysticism* (SHR 70; Leiden 1996), ch. 3, 46–62.

[27] Hippolytus, *Elenchos,* 7. 32.

[28] *De anima,* 23.35.

[29] Oulton and Chadwick, *Alexandrian Christianity* (Library of Christian Classics; Philadelphia 1954), Introduction, 25.

ta tès geneseôs nomon echei gegrammenon)." The Creator and Father of all with his own justice appointed all this...with a single command."[30]

First of all, says Epiphanes in an argument that sounds like a prefiguration of Rousseau's *Discourse on the Origin of Inequality,* laws are multiple, in opposition to this divine fairness and righteousness. Moreover – and this in his opinion represents their cardinal sin – they presuppose the existence of private property. The original partaking of goods has disappeared in the present world, and the laws are at the origin of the current state of inequality and injustice. The original communism was God's will: "God made all things for man to be common property *(koinè toinun ho theos hapanta anthrôpôi poièsas)."*[31] According to Epiphanes, laws, i.e., human laws, are pitted against "divine law," or "universal fairness and equality." Although Epiphanes does not use the term, it is safe to assume that this divine law is identical with what is usually referred to in Greek thought as natural law, *phusikos nomos.*[32]

For Paul the soteriological impotence of the Law meant the internalization of justice into "justification" through faith. With Epiphanes, however, we can follow the passage from the Jewish conception of Revealed Law to the Greek conception of Natural Law. It is only within the parameters following this transformation that we can understand the new meaning given by Epiphanes to *dikaiosunè.*

One of the consequences of this natural law advocating the community of goods is the argument for the community of women. Clement sees here the open rejection of "both law and gospel," quoting Ex. 20:14 and Mt. 5:28 On this ground, Clement argues that Epiphanes should by no means be considered a Christian. Clement further claims that although Plato had already argued for the community of women in the *Republic,* Epiphanes has clearly misunderstood him, since Plato's intention was that only unmarried women should be common.[33]

4. Gnostic Justice

According to the Carpocratians, as we have seen, Jesus is a Righteous Man. Various indices in Gnostic texts and traditions lead us to postulate some close

---

[30] Clement, *Strom.* 3.7.1 (198, 20–26 Stählin).

[31] Ibid., 3.8.1 (199,4 Stählin).

[32] On *phusikos nomos* in early Christian context, see for instance H. Koester, "NOMOS PHYSEOS: the Concept of Natural Law in Greek Thought," in *Religions in Antiquity: Essays in Memory of E. R. Goodenough,* ed. J. Neusner (SHR 14; Leiden 1968), 521–41.

[33] *Strom.* 3. 10. This is also how Plato is understood by Epictetus, 2, 4: 8–10 (see Oulton-Chadwick, p. 45, n. 24). For an analysis of Epiphanes' ideas in a comparative perspective, and for their possible influence on heretical movements in Sasanian Iran, see P. Crone, "Zoroastrian Communism," in *Comparative Studies in Society and History* 36 (1994): 447–62, esp. 461–62.

connections between Jewish-Christian and Gnostic theologoumena.[34] One of the most obvious such indices is the importance of the figure of James the Just, the Lord's brother, among the Gnostics. His figure is present, for instance, in the *Gospel of Thomas*,[35] or in the *Second Apocryphon of James*, which begins: "This is the discourse that James the Just spoke in Jerusalem."

The usual perception of "justice" in Gnostic texts and traditions, however, is much less positive, and is ambiguous at best. In his *Epistle to Flora*, for instance, the Valentinian teacher Ptolemaeus describes the creation of the world as that of a just God, who hates evil *(dikaiou kai misoponèrou)*.[36] This God, who is the "umpire of justice" *(tès kat' auton dikaiosunès ôn brabeutès)*, is located between the perfect God and the devil: neither good nor evil or unjust.[37]

According to another Valentinian text, the *Extracts of Theodotus*, "Among the offspring of Adam, some, the righteous *(hoi men dikaioi)*, going their way amidst created things, were retained in the Place *(para tôi topôi)*."[38] The Place, *ho topos* (Hebrew *ha-maqom*) refers to the God of the Old Testament.

For Marcion, these just men of the Old Testament, such as Abel, Enoch, Noah, and their likes *(et reliquos iustos)* do not partake in salvation, since they did not believe the message of Jesus.[39] Justice also plays a role in the thought of Basilides, for whom it is part of the *ogdoad*.[40]

5. Elchasai

"Callistus brought to Rome the book that 'a certain righteous [man], named El-chasai *(tina andra dikaion Elkhasai)*' had received from the Seres of Parthia," and which advocated a new remission of sins. So Hippolytus.[41] The expression makes it clear that Elchasai was called "a righteous [man]."[42] Another testimony about the same self-designation of Elchasai as *diakios* is found in the *Cologne Mani Codex*. The "image of a man" appears to Elchasai in the water, asking him:

---

[34] On the possible relationships between Jewish-Christianity and Gnosis see for instance G. G. Stroumsa, *Savoir et salut* (Paris 1992), 91 and the bibliography adduced in the notes.

[35] Logion 12 (cf. logion 13, where Simon Peter compares Jesus to "a righteous angel").

[36] *Letter to Flora* 3. 6 (52–53 Quispel).

[37] Ibid., 7. 5 (70–71 Quispel).

[38] *Extr. Theod.* 37 (140–41 Sagnard).

[39] Irenaeus, *Adv. Haer.* 1. 27. 3 (350–53 Rousseau-Doutreleau).

[40] For other members of the *ogdoad,* see Clement of Alexandria, *Strom.*, 4 162. 1, and Irenaeus, *Adv. Haer.* 1. 24. 3.

[41] *Elenchos* 9. 13. 1 (114–15 Klijn-Reinink).

[42] According to Henrichs and Koenen's commentary on the *Cologne Mani Codex* (*ZPE* 32 (1978): 188–89, n. 278), *dikaios* represents here "möglicherweise nicht *tsadiqa* sondern *qushi-ta.*"

"Why did you not respect me, you who claim to be a servant of God and a just [one] *(su ho phaskôn latrès einai kai dikaios)*?[43]

Elchasai, who claimed to live "according to the Law,"[44] is portrayed as the leader of a Jewish-Christian baptist sect. It should be noted in this context that new members of the Elchasaite community had to swear, among other things, not to be guilty of injustice.[45] Thanks to the *Cologne Mani Codex,* we now know a little more about the community in which Mani grew up. The epithet "just" was important in Elchasaite theology, since it was used as a self-designation not only by Elchasai, but also by the members of his sect. When, for instance, the baptist Sabbaios wanted to bring vegetables to the city elder, one of the vegetables cried, and asked him: "Are you not a Righteous [one]? Are you not a Pure [one]? *(ouk ei dikaios? ou katharos tugkhaneis?)*"[46]

6. Mani

The self-identification of the baptist sectarians as "righteous" was passed on to the new religion established by Mani. The inner circle of the believers, the Manichaean monks, are called *tsadiqin* in the Syriac sources (*ardavan* in Middle Persian; cf. *electi* in the Latin sources), in contradistinction to the *shemuʿin* (*niyoshagan*; *auditores*).[47] See also, for instance *Psalm Book* 99. 38: "O virtuous assembly of the righteous [*dikaios*]...gathered, full of hymns," where "the assembly of the righteous" seems to refer to the community of the believers.

The importance of the concept of justice in Manichaeism is further established by the multiple references to a *judge (kritès)* in Manichaean theological and mythological texts.[48] Perhaps the clearest mythological development of the judge figure presents, in *Kephalaion* 28, "the twelve judges of the Father." These "judges" are mythological figures of the Manichaean pantheon: the Primal Man, the Great King of Honor, the Third Envoy, Yeshu Ziwa, the Virgin of Light, etc... Mani ends his speech by mentioning that the believers are following

---

[43] *CMC* 94. 9–95. 14. I use the text in L. Koenen and C. Römer, *Der Kölner Mani-Kodex: über das Werden seines Leibes* (Papyrologia Coloninsia 14; Oplade 1988). In *CMC* 58. 8ff., Enoch is called *dikaios*.

[44] *CMC* 14.1.

[45] *ouk adikèsô*; *CMC* 15. 6.

[46] *CMC* 97. 18–99. 3.

[47] See G. Widengren, *Mani and Manichaeism* (New York, Chicago, and San Francisco1965), 96.

[48] For a list of all passages in the Coptic sources – although without any detailed analysis of their meaning – see P. Van Lindt, *The Names of Manichaean Mythological Figures* (Studies in Oriental Religions 26; Wiesbaden 1992), 190–95.

"the path of justice *(dikaiosunè),*" and asking them "to judge according to true law as 'judges of justice' *(kritès nte tdikaiosunè).*"[49]

Like the first Christian community, the Manichaean community itself is called "justice." This denomination is reflected in the very title of *Kephalaion* 80: "the Chapter of the Commandments *(entolè)* of Justice *(dikaiosunè).*" The meaning of justice is further clarified in the text, when the *Phôstèr* tells his disciples that "the first justice *(dikaiosunè)* that a man must do in order to be righteous *(dikaios)*" is the practice of encratism *(egkrateia)* and purity. Further, he adds that "the first justice" is the abstention from meat *(sarx)* and eating blood, thanks to which a man can be recognized as "righteous *(dikaios)*" by everybody.[50]

Religious ascetic practices, thus, are the criterion through which a member of the community is identified as "just." Man is just when he follows God's commandments. As we have seen, God himself is called a judge. This denomination of God is perhaps nowhere more clear than in the discussion between a Nazorean and Mani reported in *Kephalaion* 89.[51] The Nazorean *(nazoraios*; a Jewish-Christian of sorts)[52] asks Mani about the nature of his God: is He good or evil? To which Mani answers: "My God is a judge *(kritès).*"[53]

In his turn, the Nazorean answers that there is no such thing as a good judge. All judges are evildoers, since they use cruel punishments; wherever there is a judge, one finds leather whips *(taurea),* with which he strikes people. To which Mani points out that his God is no evildoer; on the contrary, his role is to extirpate evil. Hence, it is the souls of those who have been seduced by Satan and listen to him that he judges. God thus rewards and punishes just and evil deeds, and this is the precise meaning of His being called a judge.

7. Conclusion: antinomianism in context

With the exception of Epiphanes, Lactantius is the first Christian writer, in the wake of the Constantinian revolution, to offer a detailed analysis of justice.[54] For him, law entails justice, and after the abolition of the Law, justification passes through Christ. Indeed, the Christian can be righteous only in Christ. But besides this rather general statement, Lactantius conceives of *iustitia* in Ciceronian rather than in biblical terms and his discussion of justice is directly influenced by Cicero's argument in the *De Officiis.* Lactantius makes very few ref-

---

[49] *Kephal.* 81. 13ff Polotsky-Böhlig.

[50] *Kephal.* 80, 192–93 Polotsky-Böhlig.

[51] *Kephal.* 221–23 Polotsky-Böhlig.

[52] See J. De Menasce, ed., tr. *Skand Gumanic Vicar* (Collectanea Friburgensia 30; Fribourg 1945), 206–207, 230; Augustine, *Contra Faustum* 19. 4.

[53] On God as a judge, cf. Shaked, "Mihr the Judge," *JSAI* 2 (1980): 1–31.

[54] In the fifth book of his *Divine Institutions* (P. Monat, ed., trans., SC 204, 205; Paris 1973).

erences to Christian doctrine in his discussion, and the editor of the text can point out that he "does not recognize the paradox of Christian justice."[55] *Aequitas*, the deep sense of justice, is the conscience of the equality of all men before God, but Lactantius' interpretation of the evangelical dictum "Render to Caesar what belongs to Caesar and to God what belongs to God" entails the neutralization of the demand for political and social reform. The conversion of the Empire had also meant the Romanization of Christianity.

Both a revolutionary and a conservative trend can be detected in early Christian thought, as Ernst Troeltsch argued in his seminal study on *The Social Teachings of the Christian Churches*.[56] As is well-known, for Troeltsch the development of the Catholic Church up to the fourth century reflects the victory of the conservative trend. According to him, it is partly due to their strongly revolutionary tendency that the Gnostics, as well as the Manichaeans, lost the battle.

Despite their strong objections to the just demiurge and to his law, the early Christian antinomian thinkers, as we have seen, could not completely reject the idea of justice/justification. The case of Epiphanes' *Peri dikaiosunès*, however, is remarkable in that it insists upon the primordial importance of law and justice within a system which denies the validity of the revealed Law and of the justice it enhances. The concepts of *nomos* and of *dikaiosunè* are central for Epiphanes, but in his tractate the terms have undergone two radical changes from their original biblical, Jewish, and early Christian meaning.

Moreover, Epiphanes' understanding of *nomos*, although it is *in bonam partem*, remains quite alien to the Jewish and Christian meaning of the term. Namely, it refers not to the heavenly revealed Law, but the Greek natural Law *(phusikos nomos)*. From this, as we have seen, results a new meaning of *dikaiosunè*, a deeply internalized form of "justification" as it had been first developed by Paul. This new meaning is reflected, for instance, in Epiphanes' quotation from Paul.[57]

In other words, Epiphanes developed a theology that brought together central elements of two fundamentally different systems. He attempted to offer a radical reinterpretation of the Jewish and Christian concepts of law and justice, rather than discarding them, as other Gnostic thinkers did. By doing so, he rejected the revealed Law, but not the Jewish and Christian system of reference. The result of this mix-up is, precisely, the antinomianism of Carpocratian Gnosticism, which not only understood acts to be *adiaphora*, but also encouraged the reversal of all values, by transforming what was forbidden into religious duties.

If my analysis is correct, the example of Epiphanes offers us an insight into the nature of antinomianism. Indeed, not every rejection of law involves antino-

---

[55] Monat, *Divine Institutions*, introduction.
[56] *Die soziallehren der christlichen Kirchen und Gruppen* was first published in 1912.
[57] *Rom.* 7:7, quoted in *Strom.* 3.2.7.

mianism, as the case of Mani shows. Mani rejected the legal system of the baptist community of his youth, including food taboos and ritual purity. But he did not reject the idea of *God's justice,* that is to say, of providence. Therefore, his rejection of the biblical tradition, far from entailing an antinomian behavior, brought him to promote the strictest encratism.

Two opposite attitudes, indeed, can stem from the rejection of the divine law. Within the dualist movements of the first Christian centuries, both encratic and antinomian attitudes can be detected. It seems that the development of these two attitudes answers to a different logic.[58]

---

[58] On the two different attitudes which can result from the despise of the world and of its creator, see G. G. Stroumsa, *Savoir et Salut* (Paris 1992), ch.4, 145–62.

Chapter 15

Jewish and Gnostic Traditions among the Audians

The borders of the Holy Land have always been disputed. What is true of geography and political power seems to be also true of religious history. Indeed, one of the main problems confronting the historian of religion in the Holy Land is that of boundaries. These are, first of all, boundaries between religious communities, but not only. Spacial and chronological boundaries are certainly not easier to delimit. How are we to distinguish "the Holy Land" from the larger geographical area to which it belongs? Is anything specific in the religious history of Palestine that differentiates it from that of Arabia or al-Shâm? And should the periodization necessarily be one that fits the passing of political power from one religion to another? Doctrinal boundaries, moreover, do not necessarily follow closely those of the religious communities with which they are usually associated. It is a banality to remark that the same beliefs, or closely similar ones, can be partaken by members of different communities. Such cases can be analyzed as reflecting influences, syncretistic phenomena, or patterns of "popular religion" (at best a slippery concept, to be used with care).[1] It is perhaps less trivial to point out that the very boundaries of the religious communities, which are usually defined by the winners, i. e., the "orthodox" parties, may sometimes be inadequate to describe the religious situation. In other words, it would appear that the boundaries are sometimes rather flexible, and that phenomena which may appear prima facie to be rather marginal, are of major importance in the attempt to draw the map.

The following remarks will deal with such a marginal phenomenon. The Audians, who have drawn very little attention on the part of scholars, have never been studied as a significant group in the context of the religious history of Palestine. As far as I know, only two articles have been devoted to them in this century.[2] It is impossible to point to fixed geographical or chronological boundaries of the Audians. Not only their beliefs, but also their very identity remains elusive. Very few sure facts are known about them. Audi, or ,Odi, their founder,

---

[1] See C. Colpe, "Syncretism," *ER* 14: 218–27, and C. Long, "Popular Religion," ibid., 11: 442–52. On relationships between religious communities in the Holy Land in late antiquity, see chapter 7 of this volume.

[2] H.-C. Puech, "Audianer," *RAC* 1 (1950): 910–15. The following pages owe much to Puech's article. See also J. Jarry, "Une semi hérésie syro-égyptienne: l'Audianisme," *Bulletin de l'Institut Français d'Archéologie Orientale* 63 (1965): 169–95.

who may have come from Edessa, as reported by Agapius, lived during the fourth century ("at the time of Arius," Epiphanius tells us).[3] The Audians seem to have been, at least during the early stages of the movement, schismatics rather than heretics. They established communities in various countries, including in the Holy Land; it remains unclear whether these were only monastic, male communities. In the early sixth century, Philoxenes of Mabbug still regards the Audians as almost orthodox.[4] What we know of their doctrines gives the impression of some syncretism. In some ways, they appear to have been close to Gnostic groups, while other traits of their teachings, as we shall see, recall certain Jewish-Christian doctrines. Finally, a few sources allude to a possible Manichaean influence.[5]

I shall try here to analyze some of our sources on the Audians which point to their possible connections with other religious groups. All in all, and notwithstanding the paucity of sources, a better understanding of the Audian's identity and presence in the Holy Land in late antiquity should add to our knowledge of the religious scene, from the point of view of the history of ideas as well as from that of sociology.

1. A Jewish context of the Audians?

No text redacted among the Audians has reached us. For our information, we must rely solely on secondary sources, i.e., on reports from the Christian heresiologists. In other words, the greatest caution is *de rigueur*. It would seem, however, that we can extract from the heresiological reports some authentic traits of Audian history and theology. The two main reports on the Audians are found, respectively, in the *Panarion* of Epiphanius of Salamis in the late fourth century (in Greek) and in the *Book of Scholies* written by Theodore bar Khoni in the eighth (in Syriac).[6]

Epiphanius was born c. 315 in Besanduch, near Eleutheropolis. Throughout his long life, and also after he became bishop of Salamis (Constantia) in Cyprus in 365, he remained very active in Palestinian ecclesiastical affairs. In his youth, upon his return from a pilgrimage among the monks of Egypt, he established a

---

[3] Epiphanius, *Pan.*, 70.1.1. (Holl, 233). Audi's name is written in different ways in our sources. See Puech, "Audianer," 910.

[4] See J. Lebon, "Textes inédits de Philoxène de Mabboug: Lettre à tous les moines orthodoxes qui sont en Orient," *Le Muséon* 43 (1930): 211, n. 1.

[5] This is an explicit accusation only in Theodoretus, *Hist. Eccl.* 9, (PG 82, 1141 B.), but some similarities with Manichaean teaching appear in the reports of Agapius and of Bar Hebraeus (see below). On Gnostics and Manichaeans in the Holy Land, see G. G. Stroumsa, "Gnostics and Manichaeans in Byzantine Palestine," in *Studia Patristica* 18 (Kalamazoo, Mich. 1985), 1: 273–78 (= Stroumsa, *Savoir et salut* [Paris 1992], 291–98).

[6] For a full listing of the sources, see Puech, "Audianer."

monastery near Eleutheropolis. We know Epiphanius to be a trustworthy witness of various religious movements in fourth-century Palestinian Christianity
(for instance of Origenism among the monks of the Judean wilderness, or of
some Gnostic groups on Palestinian soil).[7] To the Audian schism *(peri tou skhès-
matos tôn Audianôn)* he devotes Chapter 70 of his *Panarion*. The text begins
thus:

> Audians, or Odians, are a body *(tagma)* [of laity]. They have withdrawn from the world
> *(anakhôrountes)* and reside in monasteries – in deserts and, nearer the cities in suburbs,
> and wherever they have their residences, or "folds." Audius became their founder in
> Arius' time, when the council of those who pronounced his sentence of deposition was
> convened against Arius [i.e., around 325].
>
> Audius was from Mesopotamia and eminent in his homeland for the purity of his life,
> for godly zeal, and for faith.[8]

Epiphanius thus announces at the onset his respect for the ethical stand of Audi,
who launched an ascetic movement of return to the lost pristine purity of the
Church. The single reference to the presence of the Audian movement in Palestine appears at the end of the chapter (15.5):

> Many Audian refugees from Gothia came even here [to] our country [i.e., Cyprus], and
> lived as resident aliens for four years after that time. But they also withdrew once again
> [to] their Audian monasteries in the Taurus mountains, and in Palestine and Arabia.
> For now they are widely dispersed by now but are still very few in number, and have
> few monasteries.

All this does not amount to very much, yet there is no reason to discard this fac-
tual statement. As we shall see below, moreover, some circumstantial evidence
corroborates Audian presence in fourth-century Palestine.

For Epiphanius, the Audians represented originally a schism rather than a
heresy. Audi was an ascetic who launched a purification movement within the
Church. Epiphanius does not hide his respect for Audius's courage and orthodoxy: "It was not by any divergence from the faith [that they separated from the
Church]; he and his companions were entirely orthodox."[9] On this point, it
would seem that asceticism remained an essential trait of the sect: a later source

---

[7] The only monograph on Epiphanius is that of J. Dechow, *Dogma and Mysticism in Early
Christianity: Epiphanius of Cyprus and the Legacy of Origen* (Macon, Ga. 1988).

[8] *Pan.* 70.1.1. (K. Holl [Epiphanius, *Panarion,* GCS 37; Leipzig 1931], 232–48). I quote the
new translation by F. Williams, *The Panarion of Epiphanius of Salamis* (Nag Hammadi and Manichaean Studies 35–36; Leiden, New York, and Köln 1987 [Book I, sects 1–46], and 1994
[Books II and III, sects 47–80 and *De Fide*]). Sect 70 is in vol. II, pp. 402–18. See also the incomplete translation of *Pan.* 70, by Ph. R. Amidon, S.J., *The Panarion of St. Epiphanius, Bishop of
Salamis* (New York 1990), 271-78. Unfortunately, this translation omits Epiphanius's discussion and refutation of the various heresies, for instance about the Audians' anthropomorphic
doctrines.

[9] Epiphanius, *Pan.* 70.1.5 (Holl, 233).

relates that among the Audians "some pray and some fast."[10] Yet, some traits of their doctrines and practices point to what can at least be defined as a certain lack of orthodoxy. For instance, "they prefer to celebrate Easter with the Jews." (9.1). Epiphanes also quotes a passage dealing with Easter from one of the works of dubious authority which they read, the *Regulation of the Apostles* (*tén tôn apostolôn diataxin,* probably some version of the *Didascalia Apostolorum*): "but act when your brothers from the circumcision do; act together with them." In other words, the Audians were Quartodecimans. To be sure, Quartodecimans were, as a rule, neither Jewish-Christians nor directly influenced by Jewish-Christian theology.[11] The quotation from the *Regulation of the Apostles*, however, bears a certain Jewish-Christian "flavor." Other traits of Audian theology, as we shall see, point in the same direction.

The most significant aspect of this theology, according to Epiphanius, is their anthropomorphic conception of God. To this aspect, in any case, he devotes the greater part of his discussion, sections 2 to 8 of the chapter.[12] According to Epiphanius, the Audians thought that God had a human shape. When the Bible says that man was created "in the image of God" (Gen. 1: 26), it means exactly this: man's body is God's image. Epiphanius argues at length against this view, which he finds clearly heretical, and he also points out some of its implications.[13] For instance, an anthropomorphical conception of God entails a certain "concrete" mysticism. Speaking of the vision of God in this context is not the simple use of a metaphor, but rather the reference to a real possibility, and the term "visionof God" *(ophthè theou)* should be understood literally. If God has a body, He is visible. The Audians interpret literally Isaiah's vision of God Sabaoth sitting on His throne (Is. 6: 5). "He did not say with his mind, or with his intelligence, but with his eyes"(7.5). A similar conception is related by Theodoret.[14] Epiphanius argues at length, against the Audians, that God is invisible *(aoraton)* and incom-

---

[10] Abû l' Barakât, *La lampe des ténèbres,* 1.7 (PO 20, 4., p. 688).

[11] On the Easter controversy, see for instance the entry "Easter" in *EEC,* 1: 259. For the latest discussion of Jewish-Christianity in Palestine of the first Christian centuries, see J. E. Taylor, *Christians and the Holy Places: The Myth of Jewish-Christian Origins* (Oxford 1993), esp. ch. 2, 18–47. Taylor offers a systematic refutation of the "Bagatti-Testa Hypothesis" about the Jewish-Christian community in Palestine and of its dubious intellectual presuppositions. Her critique, however, is more convincing than her own vision of the emergence of the Christian Holy Land. This is not the place to discuss the book's thesis. Let us only point out that there is no reason ignore the continuous existence of Jewish-Christians communities with a theology of their own in Roman Palestine.

[12] Epiphanius, *Pan.* (Holl, 233–41).

[13] For the broader context of this polemics, see G. Gould, "The Image of God and the Anthropomorphite Controversy in Fourth Century Monasticism," in *Origeniana Quinta,* ed. R. Daly (Leuven 1992), 549–57. Cf. E. A. Clark, *The Origenist Contorversy: The Cultural Construction of an Early Christian Debate* (Princeton 1992), ch. 2. Despite her very solid argument and documentation, Clark does not perceive possible links between monastic and Jewish anthropomorphite doctrines.

[14] Theodoret, *Haeret. fabularum compendium,* 10 (PG 83, 428)

prehensible *(akataleptos),* and that the visible cannot see the invisible (7.9). Therefore, the various allusions in the Bible (Old and New Testaments) about the prophets' vision of God should be understood in a metaphorical way.[15] One should point out that the belief in a corporeal God may have been more common than usually thought.[16] The origins of such an anthropomorphism, however, seem to go back to Jewish conceptions.

A similar conception of a visible, embodied, God, possessed of "a beautiful form *(morphè),*" is to be found in some other early Christian texts, particularly in the *Pseudo-Clementine Homilies* (chapter 17), a fourth-century text known to reflect early Jewish-Christian, Ebionite traditions.[17] Attention has been called to the anthropomorphic God of the *Pseudo-Clementines* and its probable Jewish origins, which may reflect mystical and esoteric conceptions of a macrocosmic God.[18] Irenaeus reports about another similar description of the macrocosmic body of God, made up of the letters of the alphabet, propounded by Marc the Gnostic, a second-century disciple of Valentinus. The striking similarities between such doctrines and the *Shi'ur Qoma* texts of late antiquity were pointed out long ago.[19] It is surprising that the doctrines of the Audians on this point seem to have elicited no attention. These similarities may help in determining the age of the Jewish anthropomorphic conceptions more precisely than has been done until now.

True, anthropomorphic doctrines or Quartodeciman practices alone do not tell us much. It is their combination as the two main shibboleths by which the Audians differ from orthodox Christians which points to the possibility of a Jewish-Christian source for these views. In the following section, I shall seek to buttress this hypothesis.

2. Gnostic elements in Audian sources

Henri-Charles Puech is the only scholar to have devoted any serious attention to the Audians in this century. His splendid entry "Audianer" in the *Reallexikon für*

---

[15] Epiphanius, *Pan.* (Holl, 239). The discussion and refutation of Audian anthropomorphism (70.3.1 to 70.8.9) occupies more than one third of the whole chapter.

[16] See for instance D. L. Paulsen, "Early Christian Belief in a Corporeal Deity: Origen and Augustine as Reluctant Witnesses," *HTR* 83 (1990): 105–16.

[17] See in particular H. J. Schoeps, *Theologie und Geschichte des Judenchristentums* (Tübingen 1949); passim, cf. esp. 165, n.1.

[18] See, for instance, Sh. Pines, "Points of Similarity Between the Exposition of the Doctrine of the Sefirot in the Sefer Yezira and a Text of the Pseudo-Clementine Homilies: the Implications of this Resemblance," *Proceedings of the Israel Academy of Sciences and Humanities,* 3, no. 3 (Jerusalem 1989): 63–142.

[19] In the late nineteenth century, Moses Gaster had already pointed out these similarities, emphasized anew by G. Scholem; see for instance his *Jewish Gnosticism, Merkabah Mysticism and Talmudic Tradition* (New York 1965).

Antike und Christentum had been preceded by a seminal paper published in 1936. The discovery of the Coptic library in Nag Hammadi offered, after the Second World War, a decisive confirmation of Puech's hypothesis.[20]

On the basis of Theodore bar Khoni's discussion of Audian doctrines, Puech had postulated that some quotations from various books in use among the Audians were in fact coming from early Gnostic texts (dating from the second century). The existence of these texts was known thanks to a few references, in particular by Porphyry (*Vita Plotini* 16), where he alludes to various apocryphal texts read by Plotinus's Gnostic opponents. Porphyry refers to a certain *Apocalypse of the Strangers (Apokalupsis Allogenous)*. Puech identified some short quotations given by Theodore as stemming from this *Apocalypse.* Theodore bar Khoni also mentions various texts in use among the Audians. He mentions an *Apocalypse of Abraham (gelyona dabshem Abraham),* an *Apocalypse of John (gelyona dabshem Iohanan),* a *Book of Questions (sefar shelata)* and to a *Book* as well as an *Apocalypse of the Strangers.*[21] In the few sentences quoted from these sources, the demiurge and the powers or archons *(shalitane)* who are with him rape Eve, so that her progeny remains under their dominion.

Similar conceptions are referred to, in some detail, by Agapius of Menbij in the tenth century and by Bar Hebraeus in the twelfth century.[22] These two ecclesiastical writers quote similar sentences from works in use among the Audians, but do not mention their titles.

The three oriental writers who refer to Eve's rape by the demiurge, Theodore bar Khoni, Agapius, and Bar Hebraeus, are all late sources. One could therefore argue that these books reached the Audians at a late stage, and only in the East. There is, however, reason to believe that similar books were already known in fourth-century Palestine.

In his *Panarion* (Chapter 40), Epiphanius writes in detail about a Gnostic sect, the Archontics, or *archôntikoi,* established in Palestine by a certain "elder" [*gerôn,* i.e., a monk] named Peter. This Peter, who wore a sheepskin, lived as an anchorite in a cave near Kaphar Barikha, a village three miles south-west of He-

---

[20] Puech, "Fragments retrouvés de l' Apocalypse d'Allogène," *Annuaire de l'Institut de philologie et d'histoire orientales et slaves, IV (Mélanges Franz Cumont),* (Bruxelles 1936), 935–62. This essay has been republished in H.-C. Puech, *En quête de la gnose,* vol. 1(Paris 1978), 271–300. The origin of the argument in my *Another Seed: Studies in Gnostic Mythology* (NHS 24; Leiden 1984) owes a great deal to this article.

[21] These last two titles may refer to the same work, since the single quotation from each one is very similar to the quotation from the other. Text in A. Scher, ed., *Théodore bar Koni, Liber Scholiorum,* vol. 2, 2nd. ed. (CSCO 69; Louvain 1954) 319–20. R. Hespel and R. Draguet, trs., *Théodore bar Koni, Livre des scholies* (CSCO, *Scriptores Syri,* 188; Louvain 1982), 238–39. On some points, one should prefer the text and tr. of H. Pognon, *Inscriptions mandaïtes des coupes de Khouabir* (Paris 1898), 132–33 and 194–96.

[22] Agapius, *Kitab al-'Unvan* (PO 7, 4), 562–64. Bar Hebraeus, *Sur les hérésies* (PO 13, 2), 259–60. On these texts, see further J. C. Reeves, *Heralds of that Good Realm: Syro-Mesopotamian Gnosis and Jewish Traditions* (Leiden, New York, and Köln 1996), 115–17.

bron, near the border between the districts of Jerusalem and Eleutheropolis (according to Jerome, this was the place to which Abraham had escorted the angels on their way to Sodom). "He gathered many for the ascetic life, if you please; and he was called 'father', of all things, because of his age and his dress." Peter seems to have obtained a certain success in propagating his views. Epiphanius reports that shortly before Constantius's death (which occurred in 367), Eutactus, an Armenian on his way back from a visit to Egypt, had learned the nefarious doctrine from Peter, and brought it back to his native land.

"Peter had distributed his possessions to the poor, and he gave alms daily," adds Epiphanius.[23] In other words, he was a saintly man, rather similar in his behavior to other holy men, such as Audi. Peter had been accused by bishop Aetius – probably the bishop of Eleutheropolis in the forties and fifties of the fourth century – of belonging to the heresy of the *gnôstikoi* and was banished by him to Arabia, i.e., Transjordan. There he stayed in Kokhave (a village whence both Ebionites and Nazoreans stemmed) located in an area where various heresies flourished.[24] Years later, as an old man, he came back incognito to Judea, secretly retaining the Gnostic poison. Epiphanius prides himself in having unmasked the dangerous heretic, who was then deserted by most of his disciples and left to die in isolation. Epiphanius reveals in this remark how close he was to such heretics (or how close these heretics were to ecclesiastical or monastic milieus). Indeed, about the *gnôstikoi,* for instance, Epiphanius tells us that he had direct and personal knowledge of the details of their teachings.[25]

Epiphanius then goes into a detailed description of Peter's doctrines. These doctrines show very close links with those of the Sethians, or *sèthianoi,* the Gnostics whom Epiphanius remembers having met in Egypt (their views are discussed by Epiphanius in the preceding chapter). This is not the place to deal with the thought of these Archontics (who owe their name to the importance of the powers, or archons, in their mythology).[26] What interests us in the present context is the books read by these heretics. Epiphanius mentions works such as the *Little Symphonia* and *Great Symphonia,* and an *Anabatikon Isaiae,* which might be identical with the known *Ascension of Isaiah.* The origin of this last text is still being debated. For the traditional view, it represents the Christianized version of a Jewish apocalyptic text which shows similarities with works known at Qumran. According to a new, alternative hypothesis, however, the whole text

---

[23] *Pan.* 40.1.4. I quote Williams, *Panarion,* vol. 1, 262.

[24] Puech, "Audianer," *RAC* 1:, 641 simply concludes that Peter spent some time "in a Jewish-Christian milieu." On the Jewish-Christian connections of Kokhave, see Stroumsa, "Gnostics and Manichaeans," 277, n. 12. For a fresh discussion of the various locations called Kokhave/ Kokaba, see Taylor, *Christians and the Holy Places,* 36–38.

[25] *Pan.,* 26.17.4. He does not say, however, where he met them.

[26] See H.-C. Puech, "Archontiker," *RAC* 1: 633–43.

would have been a Jewish-Christian composition.[27] In any case, it is significant for our discussion to note that the *Ascension of Isaiah* insists upon the possibility of the vision of God:

> And Isaiah himself has said, "I see more that the prophet Moses." Now Moses said, "There is no man who can see God and live," but Isaiah has said, "I have seen God and behold I live.[28]

It should be pointed out that the *Ascension of Isaiah* seems to have been a favorite text among various heretics, including Manichaeans, and even medieval Cathars. Whether the insistence on the possibility of the vision of God was also part of the *Anabatikon Isaiae* read by the Archontics cannot be proven, but it remains a tempting possibility. A confirmation of the Jewish-Christian nature of the *Ascension of Isaiah* would be very significant for the possible relationships between Jewish-Christians and Gnostics in Roman Palestine.

The Archontics also knew books attributed to Seth, as well as books of the *Allogeneis,* the mythical sons of Seth, having come, like him, from "the other seed" (Gen. 4:25), and foreigners to the evil powers who made and rule this world.[29]

The similarities between Archontics and Audians have already been pointed out by Puech.[30] If books of the *Allogeneis* were known to the Archontics in fourth-century Palestine, and books bearing the same title were known to the eastern Audians at a later date, it is a safe assumption that the Audians already knew these texts in fourth-century Palestine.

This hypothesis is highly plausible, since the few quotations from these texts given by Theodore bar Khoni are strikingly similar to mythologoumena from some of the Nag Hammadi texts, such as the *Apocryphon of John* and the *Hypostasis of the Archons,* the *Vorlage* of which was presumably redacted in the first half of the second century.

If the *Apocalypse* and *Book of the Strangers,* as well as the *Book of Questions* mentioned by Theodore bar Khoni were already known to the fourth-century Palestinian Audians, the same may hold true for the two other works mentioned by him – the *Apocalypse of Abraham* and the *Apocalypse of John.* Now in the first of these works, its is said concerning one of the representations of the creators *(beparzuf ḥad men 'abude)* that the world was created by Darkness *(ḥeshoka)* and six other Powers *(ḥailin),* while the second of these texts gives the names of the seven Powers *(shalitane),* or Holy Creators *('abude qedoshe)* of the human body. "My Wisdom *(ḥakimuti),* Understanding *(binta),* Elohim, my Kingdom *(mal-*

---

[27] This new theory is propounded by Enrico Norelli, ed., *Ascensio Isaiae,* 2 vols. (*Corpus Christianorum: Series Apocryphorum,* 7–8; Turnhout 1995).

[28] *Ascension of Isaiah* 3.8–9, In *New Testament Apocrypha,* ed. W. Schneemelcher, tr. R. McL. Wilson, vol. 2 (Cambridge and Louisville, Ky. 1992), 607. On the text itself, see C. D. G. Müller, ibid., 603–605 (with bibliography).

[29] See Stroumsa, *Another Seed,* passim, esp. ch. 2.

[30] See for instance "Fragments retrouvés," 281 ff.

kuti), Adonai, Zeal *(qeneta),* and Thought *(maḥshabta)."* Theodore comments: "And this he [sc. Audi] has borrowed from the Chaldeans." Indeed, even the most superficial perusal of this text calls immediately to mind the *Amesha Spentas* of Zoroastrianism, the six abstract superior entities which stand near the good God, Ahura Mazda, and which constitute with Him a holy hebdomad.

At the same time, the names of the seven Powers *(ḥeilin)* in the *Apocalypse of Abraham* known by the Audians are reminiscent of some of the kabbalistic *sefirot,* as well as of other central terms of Kabbalah, such as the *ḥeilin* or the divine *parzuf.* To be sure, the Kabbalistic texts within which these terms appear are all much later. At the same time, students of Kabbalah usually speculate that the origin of such terms is much earlier than their first literary appearence. As we have seen, various elements point to possible connections between the Audians and Jewish traditions. In this context, an apocryphal text reflecting the early existence of seven entities that later could have developed into seven *sefirot* is not altogether surprising. I cannot elaborate this point here, but I have argued elsewhere about an early (more precisely a Zoroastrian) origin of the *sefirot.*[31]

Let us summarize some implications of the evidence about the identity of the Audians and the nature of their beliefs:

1. We have seen the presence, among the Audians, of both Jewish-Christian and Gnostic traditions. Although Puech convincingly argued the Gnostic connection of the Audians, he completely overlooked the plausibility of a Jewish (or Jewish-Christian) connection as well. As a matter of fact, it is almost impossible to differentiate clearly between these traditions. The so-called "Gnostic" traditions, for instance, clearly carry various important Jewish elements. This, too, should not come as a total surprise, since the genetic proximity between Jewish-Christianity and Gnosis has been argued or suspected for a long time, at least since the discovery of Nag Hammadi.[32] As to the identity of the Audians, however, we still know very little. We thought that the Audians were an ascetic group seeking to restore lost Church discipline. Now, despite their orthodoxy, their thought also reflects some intriguing parallels with Jewish-Christian conceptions. It is not inconceivable that the Audians themselves (who were not Jewish-Christians, since they opposed baptism, as Epiphanius reports) could also have had some contacts with Jewish-Christians communities.

2. The Audians, moreover, may have been cognizant of some esoteric Jewish conceptions on the nature of God, both His bodily appearance and the complex structure of the divine "persons" which were to become the *sefirot* of medieval Kabbala.

---

[31] See G. G. Stroumsa "A Zoroastrian Origin to the Sefirot?," in *Irano-Judaica III,* eds. Sh. Shaked and A. Netzer (Jerusalem 1994), 17–33; on the texts quoted by Theodore bar Khoni, see addendum, p. 33.

[32] For some bibliographical elements, see Stroumsa, "Gnostics and Manichaeans," 277, n. 13.

3. We end, thus, where we began: from the little we know of Audian beliefs, a strong impression of syncretism emerges. It is a common mistake to study religious syncretism only in the context of "popular religion." As the case of the Audians shows, syncretistic patterns of thought can also appear among elite groups, such as groups of ascetics, or religious *virtuosi*, as Max Weber called them. These groups often cross the traditional boundaries of religious identity, as they cross geographical and political borders.

4. The Audian ascetics, who read texts containing Jewish and Gnostic teachings, appear to have been closer to Christian monks than to a Jewish-Christian or a Gnostic sect. As is well know, material from Christian monasteries in the neighborhood of Nag Hammadi was found in the bindings of some of the Coptic codices discovered there. A plausible explanation for this puzzling fact assumes that these texts were read by monks in a Chenoboskion monastery, perhaps in secret. Do the Audians represent another case of Christian monks, apparently orthodox in their beliefs and praxis, but who are the carriers of radical, heretical teachings?

5. Finally, one should read anew some sources dealing with the anthropomorphist monks of Egypt (about which an Audian origin has been argued, to begin with by Epiphanius himself, who assumes links between the Melitians of Egypt and the Audians).[33] It is a distinct possibility, upon which I intend to elaborate elsewhere, that the anthropomorphism of these monks does not reflect a simplistic conception of the divinity, as is usually thought. Rather, this anthropomorphism might preserve an archaic Christian conception of the Divinity, and of the mystical *visio Dei,* directly received from early Jewish esoteric traditions.[34]

6. There are, indeed, no clear boundaries to the Holy Land, certainly not from the point of view of religious history. In late antiquity as in other periods, Palestine remains – between Syria and Egypt – a spiritual magnet rather than a defined, closed entity. Just as there are no fixed borders to the land, the boundaries between the religious communities in the land itself are not always clear. Like nomads, theologoumena seem to move at ease, ignoring the artificial and rigid definitions that we, sedentary scholars, try to impose on them.

---

[33] Epiphanius, *Ancoratus* 14, 1–3 (K. Holl, ed., *Epiphanius Werke* vol. 1 (GCS 25; Leipzig 1915), 22. See E. Drioton, "La discussion d'un moine anthropomorphite audien avec le patriarche Théophile d'Alexandrie," *ROC* n.s. 10 (1915–1917), 92–128.

[34] For a preliminary discussion of such originally Jewish conceptions, in monastic literature, see G. Quispel, "Sein und Gestalt," in *Studies in Mysticism and Religion presented to Gershom G. Scholem,* eds. E. E. Urbach, R. J. Z. Werblowsky and Ch. Wirszubski (Jerusalem 1967), 191–95. See further G. G. Stroumsa, *Hidden Wisdom: Esoteric Traditions and the Roots of Christian Mysticism* (SHR 70; Leiden 1996), esp. ch. 7, 92–108.

Chapter 16

Purification and Its Discontents:
Mani's Rejection of Baptism

Introduction

What happens when the means of purification from defilement that had been in use in a given religious system break down, when they are not believed to function anymore? No religious community can survive without easy reach of ways of purification, which alone permit the reintegration within the community of members declared impure, for either cultic or moral reasons. Hence the centrality for the very identity of religious communities of some means of purification.[1]

The example of Mani is topical, and will serve us here to understand the central function of conceptions of purity – and hence of purification – in the transformation process of religious beliefs.[2] Mani, who had grown up among a Jewish-Christian baptist community, the Elkasaites, rejected in his youth the validity of the baptists' ritual, and in particular of their daily purifying ablutions.[3] The young Mani turned against both the practices and the underlying beliefs of the baptist sect, and soon offered an alternative to their cultic behavior as well as to their articles of faith. This alternative not only took the form of a new cult, but offered a complete system of the universe, which integrated cosmogony, cosmology, and world history into a complex web of myths. Indeed, it is the very birth

---

[1] For one of the few attempts to tackle the problem from different point of view, see *Guilt or Pollution and Rites of Purification* (*Proceedings of the XIth International Congress of the International Association for the History of Religions,* vol. 2; Leiden 1968). From a comparative perspective, see also "Purification," *ER* 12: 91ff; "Reinigungen," *RGG* 5: 946ff.; and especially "Pureté et impureté; I. L'histoire des religions," *Supplément au Dictionnaire de la Bible* 19: 398–430.

[2] Oddly enough, it seems that little has been done on the topic. For a rather general statement of the problem, see the abstract by L. J. R. Ort, "Guilt and Purification in Manichaeism," in *Guilt or Pollution,* 69.

[3] See A. Henrichs, "Mani and the Babylonian Baptists: A Historical Confrontation," *HSCP* 77 (1973): 23–59. On the Elkasaites, see L. Cirillo, *Elchasai e gli Elchasaiti: un contributo alla storia delle comunita giudeo-cristiane* (Cosenza 1984), and G. P. Luttikhuizen, *The Revelation of Elchasai: Investigations into the Evidence for a Mesopotamian Jewish Apocalypse of the Second Century and its Reception by Judeo-Christian Propagandists* (Tübingen 1985). Both works provide detailed analyses of the heresiological sources (Luttikhuizen does not refer to Cirillo's study).

of the Manichaean religion that can be observed hatching out of a polemic focusing precisely upon the concepts of purity, impurity, and purification. An inquiry focusing upon Mani's rejection of baptism should then help us understand better the nature of his new approach. Mani offered nothing less than a religious *revolution,* which is sometimes (as in the so-called *Cologne Mani Codex* [=*CMC*]) framed in terms of a radical *reformation* of the cult, advocating a return to the original teaching distorted by mistaken believers.

To a great extent, however, the attempt to dissociate between beliefs and praxis is misleading. Mani did not reject the cultic practices of the Elkasaites while retaining their fundamental beliefs – although this is what some of the texts would seem to suggest. He rejected their religious praxis precisely because it entailed some anthropological presuppositions that he did not accept. Hence, it is the very validity of the Elkasaites' religious system that the young Mani radically questioned.

1. The Text

With the discovery and publication of the *CMC,* we are fortunate to possess now a detailed and impressive testimony of the deep crisis into which Mani threw the community when he expressed serious doubts as to the value of Elkasaite "law."[4] I propose to reflect here on a particularly pregnant passage concerning the validity of the washings. The text is here put under the name of Baraies the Teacher, a Manichaean leader of the first generation.

> My lord (Mani) said: "I have had enough debating [with] each one in that Law, rising up and questioning them [concerning the] way of God, [the] commandments of the Savior, the washing *(peri tou baptismatos),* the vegetables they wash, and their every ordinance and order according to which they walk.

> Now I destroyed and [put to nought] their words and their mysteries, demonstrating to them that they had not received these things which they pursue from the commandments of the Savior; some of them were amazed at me, but others got cross and angrily said: "does he not want to go to the Greeks?" But, when I saw their intent, I said to [them] gently: "[This] washing *(to baptisma)* by which you wash your food is of [no avail] *(ouden tugkhanei).* For this body is defiled *(miaron)* and molded from a mold of defilement ... [79,13–80,3]

---

[4] *nomos,* e.g., 89, 12. Cf. "their every ordinance and order according to which they walk *(kath' hèn poreuontai)*" (80,3–5; the expression reflects a linguistic calque of Hebrew *halakhah,* i.e., the legal system of religious duties). I quote *CMC* according to the translation of R. Cameron and A. J. Dewey, *The Cologne Mani Codex (P.Colon. inv. nr. 4780) "Concerning the Origin of his Body"* (Missoula, Mont. 1979). See also the *editio princeps* and commentary of L. Koenen and A. Henrichs in *ZPE* 32 (1978): 87–199 (for *CMC* 72,8–99,9). For a critical edition, see L. Koenen and C. Römer, *Der Kölner Mani-Kodex* (Abhandlungen der rheinisch-westfälischen Akademie der Wissenschaften; Opladen 1988).

Mani then justifies his statement about the uselessness of the washing of vegetables through the intestinal transformation of food.

> Likewise, the loathsomeness and dregs of both [types of food] are seen as not differing
> from each other, so that what has been washed, which [it (the body) rejected] and
> sloughed off, is not at all distinguishable from that [other] which is unwashed. [81,13–
> 24]

Mani goes on to submit the daily washings of the baptists to the same scathing
critique:

> Now the fact that you wash in water *(baptisesthe en hudasin)* each day is of no avail. For
> having been washed and purified once and for all, why do you wash again each day? So
> that also by this it is manifest that you are disgusted with yourselves each day and that
> you must wash yourselves on account of loathsomeness *(dia tèn bdelurotèta baptises-*
> *thai)* before you can become purified. And by this too it is clear most evidently that all
> the foulness is from the body. And, indeed, [you] have put it (i.e., the body) on.
>
> Therefore, [make an inspection of] yourselves as to [what] your purity *(katharotès)* [re-
> ally is. For it is] impossible to purify your bodies entirely *(adunaton gar ta sômata*
> *humôn pantelôs katharisai)* – for each day the body is disturbed and comes to rest
> through the excretions of feces from it – so that the action comes about without a com-
> mandment from the Savior. The purity, then, which was spoken about, is that which
> comes through knowledge *(dia tès gnoseôs)* a separation *(khorismos)* of light from
> darkness, of death from life, of living waters from turbid, so that [you] may know [that]
> each is...one another and...the commandments of the Savior, [so that ...] might redeem
> the soul from [annihilation] and destruction. This is in truth the genuine purity *(hè kat'*
> *alètheian euthutatè katharotès),* which you were commended to do; but you departed
> from it and began to bathe, and have held on to the purification of the body, (a thing)
> most defiled and fashioned through foulness; through it (i.e., foulness) it (the body)
> was coagulated and having been founded came into existence. [82,23–85,12]

The text goes on to state that it is precisely these words of the young Mani which
sparked the split within the community: while some were deeply impressed and
regarded him as "a prophet and teacher," others became "filled with jealousy and
rage, some of whom were voting for (my) death." Mani was summoned and accused of destroying "the washing of our Law and that of the fathers," as well as the
commandments of the Savior. Of course, he denied doing this last thing, claiming
on the contrary that he was the real follower of the Savior, i.e., Jesus. [90–91].

To be sure, this extremely rich text should not be understood as quoting
Mani's *ipsissima verba*. We deal here with a later reconstruction, written by a
Manichaean author, perhaps one generation after Mani, describing the beginning of his teaching. In many ways, indeed, the *CMC* can be considered to be an
official biography of the prophet. In that sense, we cannot expect our text to reveal the true motifs of Mani's break with the baptists. But it does offer us a very
important insight about the justification of this break for the first generation of
Manichaean teachers, perhaps for the later Mani himself.

2. Elkasaite baptism

In order to better understand the nature of Mani's stance, we must assess with some precision that which he rejects. What do we know about Elkasaite baptism? From our sources, mainly a few reports by Patristic heresiographers, we know that the Elkasaites practiced various kinds of purifying ablutions: side by side with the washing of vegetables, they practiced an initiatory sacramental baptism, which was meant for the remission of sins, as well as daily baths.[5]

Although various features distinguished the Elkasaites from the other baptist groups swarming in the Near East in the second and third centuries, including the Mandeans, they can quite safely be identified as a rather special branch of Jewish-Christians.[6] Their religious way of life is called *nomos* in *CMC*, which refers to the baptists' "ancestral traditions." As pointed out by Gerard P. Luttikhuizen, "these features suggest that the ritualistic piety of the baptists had developed from Jewish roots."[7] On the other hand, some Christian elements are clearly present. They shared the practice of daily baths with other Jewish-Christian groups, such as the Hemerobaptists and the Ebionites (who also practiced a sacramental baptism). Indeed, one can say, with Luigi Cirillo, that Elkasaism represents one of the most important manifestations of the Baptist movement stemming from Palestine, and also its most northern branch.[8]

The reference to the purifying role of the various ablutions does not in itself make clear that the various baptismal rites were used as a therapy against both spiritual and physical evils. This fact emphasizes an important characteristic of their anthropology (which was, of course, not only their own, but was widely spread across the spectrum of highly diverse religious and cultural groups): there is a continuum between the body and the spirit, and hence there is no hiatus between physical and ethical or spiritual purity.[9]

The development of the *paenitentia secunda,* or the second baptism, meant to cleanse the sinner, one of the most notoriously complex questions in early Chris-

---

[5] See Henrichs, "Mani and the Babylonian Baptists," esp. 46–47, on the concordance between the data of the heresiologists and those of *CMC.*

[6] On the various baptist groups, see K. Rudolph, *Antike Baptisten: zu den Überlieferungen über frühjüdische und christliche Taufsekten* (Sitzungsberichte des sächsichen Akademie der Wissenschaften zu Leipzig, Phil.-hist. Klasse, 121.4; Berlin 1981). See further Rudolph, "Jüdische und christliche Täufertraditionen im Spiegel des CMC," in *Codex Manichaicus Coloniensis: Atti del Simposio Internazionale,* ed. L. Cirillo (Cosenza 1986), 69–80, and G. Strecker, "Das Judenchristentum und der Manikodex," ibid., 81–96.

[7] *The Revelation of Elchasai,* 164.

[8] "Elchasaiti e battisti di Mani: i limiti di un confronto delle fonti," in *Codex Manichaicus Coloniensis,* ed. L. Cirillo, 111.

[9] Jean Daniélou suggests that Elchasaite baptism might also have been an act of reconciliation, which could, however, have been suppressed later because of the ambiguity with the first, initiatory baptism; see his *Théologie du Judéo-Christianisme,* 2nd. ed. (Paris 1991), 100.

tianity, cannot be discussed here.[10] Such a second baptism, for the forgiveness of sins, was also known to the Elkasaites – an oddity, it would seem, since there was no dearth of opportunities for cleansing ablutions in their religious system. According to Hippolytus, the *Book of Elchasai* mentioned seven witnesses to the second baptism, intended for the remission of sins. [*Ref.* 9.15.1–2]:

> If therefore, children, someone has had intercourse with any animal or with a male or a sister or a daughter, or if he has committed adultery or fornication, and wishes to receive remission of his sins, let him, as soon as he has heard this book, be baptised a second time in the name of the great and most high God and in the name of his Son, the Great King. Let him purify and cleanse himself *(katharisatô kai agneusatô)* and let him call to witness the seven witnesses written in this book: the heaven and the water and the holy spirits and the angels of prayer and the oil and the salt and the earth.

This text reveals clearly that the sins for which one needs to be cleansed through immersion are all of a sexual nature. Epiphanius too mentions Elxai's seven witnesses for oaths.[11] The seven witnesses do not seem to appear elsewhere. From ancient Near Eastern literature, however, we know that heaven and earth can often be called to witness solemn oaths.[12] Moreover, the seven witnesses to the baptismal rite recall the five seals *(sphrageis)* to Gnostic baptism as described in the *Apocryphon of John*.[13] In the various literatures of the ancient Near East, "seal" usually refers to an attestation, an authentification.[14] Hence, one can say that "seal" and "witness" perform similar functions on the solemn occasion of an oath or a lustration. One may speculate that the origin of the Manichaean conception of seals *replacing* baptism may find its origin in the witnesses/seals *accompanying* solemn baptism among Elkasaites and various Gnostic groups.

3. Mani's rejection of baptism and its Gnostic background

It is to the repeated ablutions, as well as to the washing of the food, that Mani objects. Our text does not mention the initiatory baptism, but from Mani's arguments, it is hard to believe that it would have fared any better than the others. According to him (or more precisely, to the words put into his mouth by Baraies), these ablutions do not work, since water is incapable of purifying either the food or the body. The reason given is the same in both cases: the digestion process shows the body to be irremediably impure. But Mani does not reject the

---

[10] See chapter 9 of this volume.

[11] *Pan.* 19.6, on the Osseans. See Luttikhuizen, *Revelation of Elchasai,* 126, 199–200.

[12] See M. Delcor, "Les attaches littéraires, l'origine et la signification de l'expression biblique 'prendre à témoin le ciel et la terre,'" *VT* 16 (1966): 8–25.

[13] *NHC* II: 31:11–27; see J.-M. Sevrin, *Le dossier baptismal séthien: études sur la sacramentaire gnostique* (Bibliothèque copte de Nag Hammadi; Québec 1986), 31–37.

[14] See G. G. Stroumsa, *Savoir et salut* (Paris 1992), 275–88.

very notions of purity and impurity, and hence of purification. In that sense, what he proposes appears prima facie more like a reform: going back to the real intentions of the Savior, which were forgotten in the baptists' mistaken conceptions. Purification is necessary, and also possible, provided one does not try to purify the body, through water, but rather the soul, through what the text calls *gnosis*, salvific knowledge. Incidentally, Mani's rejection of physical baptism also meant that he denied Jesus's baptism; according to our sources, indeed, such a baptism would have indicated his sinfulness.[15]

What is the nature of this *gnosis*? Although our text is not explicit here, it stands to reason to assume that it is the knowledge of Manichaean mythological theology, for which impurity lies in the very mixture of light particles with matter in the physical, created world. Hence, real purification would mean understanding the cause of impurity, and the attempt to restore the original separation *(chorismos)* between the elements of light and those of matter. The whole Manichaean religion, indeed, its cult as well as its mythology, is precisely aimed at dismantling the impure *mixis* through which our world came to be.

In Manichaean doctrine, there are two ways of speaking of impurity. On the one hand, impurity is the very *mixis* between the two realms, the realm of light and the realm of darkness. In a more basic sense, however, the realm of darkness, by itself, is impure. Purification, therefore, will essentially consist in the separation of the two realms, achieved through *gnosis*, i.e., the purification of the light elements. This is not attained though a purely intellectual process of knowledge, but also through Manichaean cultic practices: Manichaeism is a full-fledged religion, not a philosophical system.

Mani's radical rejection of baptism and its replacement by *gnosis* should be understood within the context of Gnostic traditions. There are indeed some quite striking Gnostic parallels to Mani's rejection of baptism. In the earliest strata of Gnosticism, moreover, there seems to have been an obsession with purity and purification from pollution. The centrality of "saving knowledge" probably developed at later stages of the movement.[16]

In a seminal study, Ludwig Koenen was able to show that the theme of the metaphorization of baptism is widespread in various Gnostic texts from Nag Hammadi as well as in traditions in the heresiological literature.[17] His analysis also reflects the strong vitality of baptismal rites, even among Gnostic groups. It is precisely with the background of this vitality that the movement of reaction can be understood. There is no need to repeat here Koenen's results. Let us only

---

[15] *Acta Archelai* 60.11; Augustine, *Contra Faustum* 23.3; references in Henrichs-Koenen, *ZPE* 32 (1978): 143, n. 204.

[16] See the conclusions of G. G. Stroumsa, *Another Seed: Studies in Gnostic Mythology* (NHS 24; Leiden 1984).

[17] L. Koenen, "From Baptism to the Gnosis of Manichaeism," in *The Rediscovery of Gnosticism, II: Sethian Gnosticism*, ed. B. Layton (SHR 41; Leiden 1981), 734–56.

refer to texts such as the *Paraphrase of Shem,* the *Testimony of Truth,* the *Exegesis of the Soul* (which understands the Biblical baptism of repentance in a metaphorical way), as well as the rejection of baptism by the Valentinians, or the reference to "dark and filthy waters" by Hippolytus's Sethians.

4. Christian origins of Mani's attitude?

In their detailed commentary to the *CMC,* Henrichs and Koenen state that Mani's reinterpretation of baptism into *gnosis* stands at the end of a long historical evolution. According to them, the rejection of baptism by various Gnostic thinkers finds its ultimate origin in Jesus' polemic against the Pharisaic purity rites.[18]

Henrichs and Koenen state that Mani's claim that the daily washings only emphasize the uselessness of the first baptism finds its origin in the Letter to the Hebrews 10: 1–4, esp. 10: 2:

> For then would they [i.e., the sacrifices] not have ceased to be offered? because that the worshippers once purged *(hapax kekatharismenous)* should have had no more conscience of sins *(suneidèsin hamartiôn).*

In Hebrews, the yearly sacrifices are replaced by the single sacrifice of Christ, whose blood purifies the conscience of the believers, rather than their flesh (Heb 9: 12–14: *kathariei tèn suneidèsin hèmôn*) of dead works.

There are some other New Testament parallels to Mani's objection to the washings. One may think of Peter's vision of the impure food (Acts 10: 9–16): "What God has cleansed, that call not thou common *(ha ho theos ekatharisen, su mè koinou).*" Similarly, Paul states (Rom. 14: 14) that "nothing is in itself impure *(koinon).*"[19]

Such positions would appear to be directly related to the famous words of Jesus in his polemic against the Pharisees' purity laws (Mark 7: 14–23; Matt. 15:10–20):

> There is nothing from without a man, that entering into him can defile *(koinôsai)* him: but the things which come out of him, those are they that defile that man. (Mark 7:15; cf. Matt. 15: 11, 20).

The reason given by Jesus to the lack of defiling power of food is based upon the fact of digestion:

---

[18] *ZPE* 32 (1978): 142, n. 198; 145, n.206; see further Koenen, "From Baptism to the Gnosis of Manichaeism," esp. 749ff.

[19] *koinon* renders the Hebrew *ḥulin.* On Mani and Paul, see H.-D. Betz, "Paul in Mani's Biography (Codex Manichaicus Coloniensis)," in *Codex Manichaicus Coloniensis,* ed. L. Cirillo, 215–34.

And he saith unto them, Are ye so without understanding also? Do ye not perceive, that whatsoever thing from without entereth into the man, it cannot defile him; because it entereth not into his heart, but into the belly, and goeth out into the draught. ... (Mark 7: 18–19; cf. Matt. 15: 16–18)

The similarity is indeed striking between this argumentation and that buttressing Mani's claim that baptism by water cannot cleanse, since the body remains bound to perform the same activity of defecation, with or without ablutions. It is this similarity which has brought the learned editors of *CMC* to relate Mani's claim that the body cannot be cleansed to Jesus's words.

What *does* defile man are the evil thoughts which come out of his heart, as well as "adulteries, fornications, murders, thefts, covetousness, wickedness, deceit, lasciviousness, and evil eye, blasphemy, pride, foolishness" (Mark 7: 21–22; cf. Matt. 15: 19–20).

Together with its parallel in Matthew, this passage of Mark is usually considered as the *locus classicus* of Jesus's radical rejection of the very foundations of "Mosaic Law," of the entire Jewish halakhic system.[20] Similarly, Herbert Braun can claim: "Das extrem Unjüdische dieser Position sichert die Echtheit eines Jesuswortes wie Markus 7,15."[21] For the New Testament scholars who share this opinion, the fact that these words can plausibly be considered as Jesus's *ipsissima verba* is highly significant, since it emphasizes Jesus' "souveräne Stellung ... zur Thora," in Kümmel's words. Although this perception is fairly common, it is highly inadequate, as we shall see.

The hypothesis according to which the rejection of baptism finds it ultimate origins in Jesus' doctrine seems to have been accepted without question. It is, however, rather puzzling, if not altogether paradoxical: after all, Jesus is at the origin of the exportation of baptismal rites from Judea to the world at large. Some serious arguments may be adduced against it.

First of all, the hypothesis does not take into account the fact that the critique of Israelite ritual and doubts upon its value when it is not accompanied by the right attitude of mind, is known already from the Hebrew Bible, and is well-attested in the Prophets and in the Psalms. Psalm 51, for instance, deals with the impossibility of expiation for a sin through the normal method of sacrifice when the Temple is destroyed.[22] Philo, too, insists upon the need for unity between body and soul with respect to the pure intention accompanying sacrifices.[23] The

---

[20] "Nirgendwo aber zeigt sich die Radikalität von Jesu Einstellung zur Tora deutlicher als im Streit um das Reinheitsgesetz," Günter Klein, in "Gesetz, III," *TRE* 13: 59.

[21] Quoted by W. G. Kümmel, "Äussere und innere Reinheit des Menschen bei Jesus," (1973), reprinted in his *Heilsgeschehen und Geschichte,* vol. 2 (Marburger Theologische Studien 16; Marburg 1978), 117–29.

[22] See A. Caquot, "Ablution et sacrifice selon le Psaume LI," in *Guilt or Pollution and Rites of Purification,* 74–77.

[23] See H. Wenschkewitz, *Die Spiritualisierung der Kultusbegriffe: Tempel, Priester und Opfer im Neuen Testament* (Angelos 4; Leipzig 1932), ch. 3.

necesity for moral cleanliness together with ritual purity is emphasized in various Jewish texts from the Second Temple period.[24] Jacob Neusner has argued convincingly that the most important point for understanding the idea of purity in ancient Judaism is the relationship between physical and moral purity.[25]

The same is true at Qumran, where the scrupulous observance of ritual laws concerning purity and impurity is directly related to the obsession by the members of the sect of the idea of physical defilement produced by moral fault.[26] As David Flusser has argued, a similar relationship between ritual and ethical purity is found at Qumran and in John the Baptist.[27] This Jewish traditional attitude is the background of Jesus' attack against the inadequacy of Jewish ritual purity laws:

> And the Lord said unto him: "Now do ye Pharisees make clean the outside of the cup and the platter; but your inward part is full of ravening and wickedness." (Luke 11: 39 cf. Matt. 23: 25–26).

Obviously, such a text does not deny the legitimacy of the purity rules, but insists that their validity is conditioned upon a complete conjunction between inner intention and cultic action. Such a demand is similar to that of the prophets, who "had nothing to object to sacrifice, provided it was carried out with a clean mind and with due esteem for law and justice."[28] It may be noted here that a similar trend is found in classical Greece with regard to rituals of purification. As emphasized by Walter Burkert, Plato's statement: "The impure man is whoever is wicked in his soul," or the inscription over the entrance of the Asclepios sanctuary at Epidauros: "Purity is to think pious things" "were regarded not as devaluing the outer forms of piety, which were still rigorously upheld, but as adding a deeper dimension. In the sphere of purification, ritual and ethical reflection could therefore emerge without a break."[29]

From the prophets on, this insistence upon inward, moral purity, side by side with the continued development of the ritual washings which have their ulti-

---

[24] See for instance A. Brody, "On the Development and Shifting of Motives in the Israelitic-Jewish Conceptions of Clean and Unclean," in *Ignace Goldziher Memorial Volume,* eds. S. Löwinger, A. Scheiber, and J. Somogyi, vol. 2 (Jerusalem 1958), 111–26.

[25] J. Neusner, *The Idea of Purity in Ancient Judaism* (Studies in Ancient Judaism 1; Leiden 1973), esp. 125.

[26] See A. Dupont Sommer, "Culpabilité et rites de purification dans la secte juive de Qumran," in *Guilt or Pullution,* esp. 79. See further F. Garcia Martinez, "Les limites de la communauté: pureté et impureté à Qumran et dans le Nouveau Testament," in *Text and Testimony: Essays in Honor of A. F. J. Klijn,* eds. T. Baarda et al., (Kampen 1988), 11–122.

[27] "John's Baptism and the Dead Sea Sect," in D. Flusser, *Judaism and the Origins of Christianity* (in Hebrew) (Tel Aviv 1979), 81–112, esp. 87.

[28] Brody, "On the Development and Shifting of Motives," 122. For some reflections on the "purity of the heart" for Jesus, see H. D. Betz, "Jesus and the Purity of the Temple (Mark 11: 15–18): a Comparative Religion Approach," *JBL* 116 (1997): 455–72.

[29] *Leg.* 716e; cf. Eur., *Or.* 1604, Aristoph. *Ram.* 355. These texts are quoted by W. Burkert, *Greek Religion in the Archaic and Classical Period* (Cambridge, Mass. 1984), 77.

mate roots in Leviticus, is found time and again in Jewish texts.[30] From apocryphal literature, through Philo, and up to Targumic and Rabbinic literature, we can follow a continuous trend "spiritualizing" the cultic concepts, and insisting upon inward purity as a *conditio sine qua non* for the legitimacy and functioning of the ritual purity laws.[31]

Moreover, the New Testament texts nowhere allude to a possible rejection of baptism itself. On the contrary, the importance of Jewish baptismal practices is much enhanced in their reinterpretation in early Christian baptism.[32] As we have already seen, what we have in Jesus' polemic with the Pharisees is rather a demand that cultic practices not be disconnected from an interior, ethical, purified mind. One cannot therefore simply speak of a clear, radical opposition to external purification rituals in the New Testament. In the conclusion of a careful study of Jesus and the purity laws, Roger Booth states: "Jesus did not deny the concept of cultic purity absolutely, but only relatively in comparison with ethical purity." In other words, Jesus "did not deny the fact of cultic impurity,... but only treated it as of less gravity than moral impurity."[33] Similarly, analyzing the idea of purity of the heart in the Beatitudes, Jacques Dupont concludes that there is no opposition between ritual and moral purity.[34] Hence, in different ways, and from various points of view, a great number of scholars seem to reject the traditional perception of a Jesus in direct and radical opposition to the Jewish ritual system.

The same trend of insisting upon the internalization of cultic behavior is found later, in Patristic literature. At the end of the second century, for instance, Tertullian insists that the purification of the soul must be parallel to bodily purification: "Is it reasonable to pray after having washed one's hands, but with a defiled mind?"[35]

---

[30] On the common roots of Jewish and Christian baptism, see A. Yarbro Collins, "The Origin of Christian Baptism," in her *Cosmology and Eschatology in Jewish and Christian Apocalypticism* (Suppl. to the *Journal for the Study of Judaism* 50; Leiden 1996), 218–38.

[31] See esp. Wenschkewitz, *Die Spiritualisierung der Kultusbegriffe,* passim. Let us mention here, at least, Philo, *Vita Mosis* II.24; see also the references in Strack-Billerbeck I s.v. Matt. 15: 11, 719ff. esp. R. Meir, in *Berakhot* 17a: "Keep thy mouth from every sin, and purify thyself from all sin and guilt; for I shall be with thee everywhere," cf. *Sanhedrin* 65b, "spirit of purity, not of impurity."

[32] See Yarbro Collins, "The Origin of Christian Baptism."

[33] R. P. Booth, *Jesus and the Laws of Purity: Tradition History and Legal History in Mark 7* (JSNT, Suppl. Series 13; Sheffield 1986), 211.

[34] J. Dupont, *Les Béatitudes,* vol. 3 (Etudes Bibliques 56; Paris 1973), 590. See also C. Spicq, O.P., *Théologie morale du Nouveau Testament* (Etudes Bibliques 51.1; Paris 1965), 202–203, on the purification of conscience from sin in the New Testament. For an excellent overview of the problem, see E. Cothenet, "Pureté et impureté, III Nouveau Testament," *Suppl. au Dictionnaire de la Bible* 19: 508–54.

[35] *On Prayer,* 13.1. On interior *katharsis,* which is identical with *metanoia,* cf. Clement, *Strom.,* IV.22.143.1. Both texts are quoted in H. Karpp, *La pénitence* (Neuchatel 1970), 166–77 and 138–39. For Origen's discussion of ritual purity, see F. Cocchini, "La normativa sul culto e sulla purita rituale nella interpretazione di Origene," *Annali di Storia dell'Esegesi* 13 (1996):

In other words, and in radical contrast with Mani, Jesus does not demand a radical separation of the elements of light from those of darkness, of soul from body. On the contrary, he asks for purification of conscience, i.e., a unification of the person, soul and body, in order to avoid *dipsukhia,* the disconnection between beliefs and behavior.

Moreover, contrary to the *opinio communis,* the idea of ritual impurity was retained in early Christianity, as Marcel Simon convincingly argued.[36] In the early Christian context, *porneia* involved a defilement that was ritual in nature, rather than moral. The Christian insistence on the essential unity of the human composite presented a new anthropology, but more within the Greco-Roman world than in Jewish context.[37] This new anthropology was reflected also in the new Christian practice of burying the dead *intra muros.*[38] A similar revolution in the attitude to the dead body was reflected in the Christian practice of burial *ad sanctos,* which represented a radical break with old habits in the various Mediterranean societies.[39]

Mani, on the other side, did not conceive the possibility of unification between soul and body. Since the human composite is an unnatural *mixis,* due to evil archons, the only possible salvation entailed a complete separation of body from soul. We have here an anthropology established on a quite different basis. The radical encratism reflected in this kind of anthropology is usually explained, genetically, as the end of a radical evolution originally stemming from some elements within the biblical (Jewish and early Christian) traditions. Yet, it may also reflect an influence from a quite different source.

7. A Buddhist origin?

I wish here to call here attention to an early Buddhist text, which offers a striking parallel, as yet unnoticed, to Mani's objections to baptism:

> Thus have I heard: On a certain occasion the Exalted One was staying near Gayâ, on Gayâ Head. Now on that occasion a great number of ascetics, on the cold winter be-

---

143–58. On Clement, see further A. Baumgarten, "Josephus and Hippolytus on the Pharisees," *HUCA* 55 (184): 12–13.

[36] M. Simon, "Souillure morale et souillure rituelle dans le Christianisme primitif," in *Guilt or Pollution*, 87–88.

[37] See Stroumsa, *Savoir et salut,* 199–223.

[38] See G. Dagron, "Le christianisme dans la ville byzantine," *DOP* 31, (1977): 11–19, who states: "La levée de l'interdit religieux sur la sépulture *intra muros* vieux d'un millénaire...est le signe d'une véritable mutation historique," (quoted by P. Brown, *The Cult of the Saints: its Rise and Function in Latin Christianity* (Chicago 1981), 133, n.16.

[39] R. Parker, *Miasma: Pollution and Purification in early Greek Religion* (Oxford 1983), 71, who refers to. Ph. Ariès, *The Hour of our Death,* 30–40, for the origins of the *depositio ad sanctos.*

tween the eighths in time of snowfall,[40] were plunging up and down [in the water] and sprinkling and burning sacrifice, thinking: This way comes purity.

Now the Exalted One saw that great number of ascetics so doing, and at that time, seeing the meaning of it, gave utterance to this verse of uplift:

Not by water is one pure, tho' many folk bathe here. In whom is truth and dhamma, he is pure and he's a brâhmin.

This Pali text, which I quote in F. L. Woodward's translation, is taken from the *Udâna,* the third book (of fifteen) of the *Khuddaka-nikaya,* which is the fifth collection of the Pali *Sutta Pitaka.*[41] It is a collection of eighty inspired verses reportedly uttered by the Buddha himself. Each verse is preceded by a short anecdote that more or less sets forth the occasion for the utterance.

In other words, we have here, at least from a phenomenological point of view, a rather precise parallel to Mani's argument against the purifying capacity of water in *CMC.* Like Mani, Buddha rejects the ablutions of the ascetics around him, claiming that water cannot purify the body. This parallel strikes me as much closer to any of Jesus' *logoi.* None of these, after all, refers to the cleansing power of water. To be sure, Buddha's utterances in this text can no more be considered *ipsissima verba* than Mani's in *CMC.* But the real question is whether we have here more than a phenomenological parallel, namely a possible source for the early Manichaean rejection of baptism. Although they cannot be dated with precision, the texts of the Pali canon are early. They were certainly in existence before the third century C.E., and Mani might well have heard similar arguments when he spent time in Buddhist kingdoms of Northern India. Al-Biruni, who is generally an accurate and well-informed writer, tells us that Mani had gone to India after having been exiled from the Sasanian empire, adding that he learned there, from the Hindus, the doctrine of metempsychosis, which he then adapted to his own system.[42] Al-Biruni mentions the Hindus, but Mani could of course have heard about metempsychosis from the Buddhists as well, in whose system *samsara* plays a major role. Although his trip took place after his break with the community of his youth, he may have found there also a theoretical justification for his opposition to the baptist practices of the Elkasaites.

The once-fashionable view that Mani's syncretism amalgamated elements taken from Zoroastrianism and Buddhism as well as from Christianity has long

---

[40] I.e., the eighth day before and after the full moon of the months equivalent to January and February.

[41] I quote the translation of F. L. Woodward, *The Minor Anthologies of the Pali Canon, II: Udâna: Verses of Uplift* (London 1948), 7–8. On the *Udâna,* see further F. E. Reynolds, *A Guide to the Buddhist Religion* (Boston 1981), 102, and K. R. Norman, *Pâli Literature* (Wiesbaden 1983), 60–61. In a different context, our passage was already quoted by I. Scheftelowitz, "Die Sündentilgung durch Wasser," *ARW* 17 (1914): 353–412; see 369.

[42] References given by S. N. C. Lieu, *Manichaeism in the Later Roman Empire and Medieval China: A Historical Survey* (Manchester 1985), 56.

ceased to be popular. With good reason, most scholars focus today upon the Jewish-Christian and Gnostic texts, which provide Mani's immediate religious background. Despite the few mentions of the Buddha in the Coptic *Kephalaia* (*Keph.* I, p. 33, l. 17; the text was probably written in the first generation after Mani), the scholarly consensus today is that "Buddhist elements [in Manichaeism] were acquired in the course of mission, and were not fundamental to Manichaeism."[43]

In itself, the striking parallel on the powerlessness of water is insufficient to break this consensus. However, it is worth calling attention to yet another similarity between the earliest stages of Manichaean doctrine and Buddhist traits, side by side with metempsychosis and the denigration of the cleansing power of water. I am referring to the idea and practice of monasticism, and, more specifically, to the monastic community perceived as the real nucleus of the religious community, the *samgha*, while married people are looked upon as supporters, "fellow travelers," rather than first-class members of the community. Years ago, I argued that, since we know of the existence of Manichaean monasteries in Egypt a few decades before the first appearance of Christian monasticism, the former might well have provided a catalyst for the emergence of the latter. Furthermore, I postulated a Buddhist influence, acquired by Mani himself during his stay in northern India, upon the idea of *electi* and *auditores*.[44] There seems, therefore, to be mounting circumstantial evidence, calling for a revision of the consensus denying any serious Buddhist (or perhaps also Jain) influence upon nascent Manichaeism.[45]

The history of religions offers many examples of sects emerging from broad religious traditions. Since Troeltsch, sociologists of religion have learned to analyze the conditions within which sects are born and can grow. What is much less common, however, is the mutation through which, out of a sectarian milieu, emerges a full-fledged religion, with ecumenical ambitions. This is exactly what the birth of Manichaeism offers: a very special case study for historians of religions. In her well-known thesis, propounded a generation ago,[46] Mary Douglas

---

[43] Ibid., 53–54. For a synthetic study of the question, see H.-J. Klimkeit, *Die Begegnung von Christentum, Gnosis und Buddhismus an der Seidenstrasse* (Opladen 1986).

[44] Stroumsa, *Savoir et salut,* 299–327.

[45] The best study of the topic is W. Sundermann, "Mani, India and the Manichaean Religion," *South Asian Studies* 2 (1986): 11–19. See further, W. Sundermann, "Manichaeism Meets Buddhism: The Problem of Buddhist Influence on Manichaeism," in *Bauddhavidyasudhakarah, Studies in Honor of Heinz Bechert*, eds. P. Kiefer-Pülz and J.-U. Hartmann (Swisttal-Odendorf 1997), 647–56. Sundermann remains skeptical as to the possible Buddhist influences upon Mani, and thinks that during his stay in India, Mani taught rather than learned. See also J. Ries, "Buddhism and Manichaeism, the Stages of an Inquiry," *Buddhist Studies Review* 111 (1986): 108ff (= "Bouddhisme et manichéisme, les étapes d'une recherche," in *Indianisme et bouddhisme, Mélanges Etienne Lamotte* [Louvain la Neuve 1980], 281–95).

[46] M. Douglas, *Purity and Danger: An Analysis of Concepts of Pollution and Taboo* (London 1966).

argued that rules of purity and impurity (and hence rituals of purification) develop especially in societies which must avoid contacts with the world at large in order to survive. Mani's rejection of Elkasaite baptismal practices tends to sharpen Douglas's underlying thesis. Indeed, rituals of purification seem often to be central in the self-definition of religious groups, and calling the value of these rituals into question may bring about a radical transformation of the group's identity.

Chapter 17

The Two Souls

> "Zwei Seelen wohnen, ach, in meiner
> Brust."
>
> Goethe, *Faust I*

> Since they say that every living being has two souls, one of the race of light, and the other of the race of darkness, is it the case that the good soul leaves at death, while the bad soul remains?

Thus Augustine wrote in his *Contra Faustum*.[1] This is not the only reference to this strange doctrine in his writings. On various other occasions, Augustine polemicizes against the Manichaean belief in the two souls, one good and one evil, present in each human being, and tries to show the absurd implications of such a belief.[2] In the *Confessions,* for instance, Augustine says:

> Let them no more say, therefore, that since they perceive two wills to be contrary one to another in one man, that there be two contrary souls, made of two contrary substances, one good, and the other bad, contending one with another.[3]

According to this text, the serious problem which the Manichaean doctrine of the two souls attempts to solve is that of two opposite wills in man, a problem which, as is well known, remained a serious preoccupation for Augustine throughout much of his adult life.

But Augustine did not satisfy himself with a few references to this Manichaean doctrine. He also devoted a whole treatise to its refutation, the *De duabus animabus,* a text probably written in or around 391.[4] There is no such thing as an evil soul, contends Augustine, since all souls come from God, and Manichaean doctrine directly contradicts common sense. It is through our will that we sin, not by the nature of our soul.

---

[1] "Deinde cum duas animas esse in uno animantis corpore adfirmant, unam bonam de gente lucis, alteram malam de gente tenebrarum, numquid, cum occiditur animal, bona anima fugit et mala remanet?" *Contra Faustum* 6. 8 (297–98 Zycha).

[2] See for instance *De vera religione* 9. 16, *De haeresibus* 46, *Op. Imperf. contra Iul.* 3. 172.

[3] (8. 10. 22). "Iam ergo non dicant, cum duas voluntates in homine uno adversari sibi sentiunt, duas contrarias mentes, de duabus contrariis substantiis, et de duobus contrariis principiis contendere, unam bonam, alteram malam."

[4] See J. Jolivet and M. Jourjon, *Six traités anti-manichéens,* Introduction (Bibliothèque augustinienne 17; Paris 1961), 41.

It is beyond dispute that Augustine knew Manichaean doctrines well. He had been an *auditor* in the sect for about ten years, after all, an intellectual "fellow traveler," as it were, who had been seduced as a young man by the sect's mythical cosmology and anthropology. Yet he is our only direct source on such a doctrine, and the idea of the two souls in man cannot be confirmed from primary Manichaean sources. Thus various scholars, from Ferdinand Christian Baur to Henri-Charles Puech, have often reiterated that Augustine was mistaken when speaking of two "souls," when in fact the Manichaeans speak of two natures – but, it is implied, of only one (good) soul. It should be pointed out, however, that the father of modern Manichaean studies, Isaac de Beausobre, in the seventeenth century, followed by Mosheim in the eighteenth, and Alfaric in the twentieth, did accept as a fact that the Manichaeans believed in two souls.[5] It is a matter of regret that this trend of research seems to have been ignored in more recent scholarship. In Puech's terms: "En réalité, pour les manichéens, il n'y a pas deux âmes, il y a une seule âme qui ne peut être que bonne en soi et par nature ... ."[6] For Puech, then, Manichaean cosmological dualism is reflected in anthropology through the radical duality of the soul, which belongs to the realm of good, light, and spirit; and of the body, which belongs the realm of evil, darkness, and matter. Twelve years ago, the same view was reiterated by R. Ferwerda, in what seems to be the last treatment of the topic.[7]

For Puech, and to some extent for Ferwerda in his footsteps, Augustine mixed up the idea of the two souls, which does in fact exist elsewhere in ancient thought, with similar but not identical arguments in the Manichaean doctrine about the two natures. Both cite various traditions, mainly from Greek philosophical texts, which allude to the same doctrine. Following Puech, Ferwerda cites as the first of these traditions a passage from Xenophon, according to which the Persian sage Araspas argues, in conversation with Cyrus, that man is endowed of two souls:

but it is obvious that there are two souls, and when the good one prevails, what is right is done; but when the bad one gains the ascendancy, what is wrong is attempted.[8]

[5] Baur, *Das manichäische Religionssystem* (Göttingen 1928), 163, quotes de Beausobre and Mosheim. P. Alfaric, *L'évolution intellectuelle de saint Augustin,* vol. 1 (Paris 1918), 117 and notes 6, 7.

[6] H.-C. Puech, *Les sources de Plotin* (Entretiens Hardt sur l'antiquité 5; Vandoeuvres, Genève 1957), 39. Puech partially retracts here what he had written in 1934 in "Numénius d'Apamée et les théologies orientales," where he had argued for a close parallel between Numenius and Manichaeism. He now says: "C'était trop me fier aux affirmations de Saint Augustin...."

[7] R. Ferwerda, "Two Souls: Origen's and Augustine's Attitude towards the Two Souls Doctrine: Its Place in Greek and Christian Philosophy," *Vigiliae Christianae* 37 (1983): 360–78. I wish to thank Dr. Ferwerda for having first called my attention to this topic in 1982.

[8] "*alla dèlon hoti duo eston psukhai, kai hotan hè agathè kratèi, ta kala prattetai, hotan de ponèra, ta aisxra epikheireitai,*" Xenophon, *Cyropaedia* 6. 1. 41 (II, 140–43 LCL). This text is in fact already quoted by Baur, *Das manichäische Religionssystem*, 175.

This doctrine, Iranian in origin, would then have infiltrated Greek philosophy, as it reappears not only in Plato's *Laws*,[9] but up to such late representatives of the Platonic tradition as the fragments of Numenius or the *Chaldaean Oracles*.[10] As is well known, and as was most recently emphasized anew by Shaul Shaked, the conception of multiple souls is indeed "so typical of the Zoroastrian mode of thinking."[11] Shaked's study, which points out the existence of different schools of thought on this issue in Sasanian Iran, does not refer to a *duality* of the human soul in Sasanian theology.[12] Shaked himself, however, has elsewhere analyzed some notions, such as *axw* (or *akw, okh*), which appear, in particular, at the beginning of *Denkard* VI, and which point to a division of the human soul into two camps, ruled by two impulses, one toward the good, and the other toward evil.[13] As Carsten Colpe has suggested, moreover, it is possible that a conception of the soul as reflecting cosmic dualism was held by the Zoroastrian Magians in the Hellenistic world.[14]

Ferwerda seeks to offer an interpretation of what he, together with Puech, considers Augustine's odd mistake. According to him, he would have mistaken for being Manichaean a doctrine widespread not among them, but among the Gnostics. In order to prove his argument, Ferwerda refers to Plotinus, who accused the Gnostics of being "senseless" for having introduced a second soul.[15] Moreover, he quotes a text from Clement of Alexandria, for whom Isidorus (Basilides's son) believed, like the Pythagoreans, in two souls[16]; and the *Excerpta ex Theodoto,* which refer to two souls, one irrational and the other divine.[17] Ferwerda, moreover, points out Origen's references to two souls as reflecting a Gnostic background.[18]

The solution is ingenious, and yet I must confess that I remain unconvinced. Ferwerda, a student of Greek philosophy, understandably relies upon Puech's opinion that there was no Manichaean doctrine of the two souls. It is hard, however, to accept easily that Augustine was simply mistaken. While he did not have

---

[9] *Laws* 10, 896 d-e: there are at least two souls, one doing the good and the other one its opposite.

[10] Numenius, fragment 44 (91 Des Places), speaks of two souls, one rational *(logikèn)* and the other irrational *(alogon)*.

[11] For a study of Zoroastrian, and in particular Sasanian, anthropology, see Sh. Shaked, *Dualism in Transformation: Varieties of Religion in Sasanian Iran* (Jordan Lectures, 1991; London 1994), 58; Shaked points out that this Zoroastrian conception was borrowed by Mani (57). See also Appendixes B and C.

[12] See esp. ibid., 56–59.

[13] See Sh. Shaked, "Some Terms relating to Man in Pahlavi: I. *axw* (ox)," in *Mémorial Jean de Ménasce* (Louvain 1974), 319–26.

[14] See C. Colpe, "Geister," *RAC* 9 (1974): 585–98, esp. 93.

[15] Plotinus, *Enneads* 2. 9. 5. 16; cf. ibid., 4. 3. 27. 1–6.

[16] Clement, *Strom.* 2. 20. 113. 3.

[17] *Exc. Theod.* 50. 1; cf. 51. 3.

[18] See for instance *De Principiis* 3. 4. 1.

a first-hand knowledge of second-century Gnostic doctrines, he certainly had such a knowledge of Manichaean doctrines. I shall argue in what follows that it stands to reason to postulate that the Manichaeans could have believed in the doctrine of the two souls.

As we have seen, the Iranian tradition reported by Xenophon is presented in the history of scholarship as being at the origin of the Greek conceptions about the duality of the human soul. Oddly enough, however, scholars of Manichaeism do not seem to have recalled in this context that since the Hellenistic period, Iranian anthropological ideas also had a strong influence upon Jewish conceptions. Indeed, neither Baur nor Puech seem to have taken the Jewish sources into account in this context, except for Philo, who represents the Platonic tradition when he states, for instance, that "in every soul at its very birth there enter two powers *(dunameis),* the salutary and the destructive."[19]

The *Community Rule* found at Qumran is probably the most obvious Jewish text emphasizing anthropological duality.

> He has created man to govern the world, and has appointed for him two spirits in which to walk until the time of His visitation: the spirits of truth and falsehood.[20]

This well-known text remains, however, rather mysterious, and it is not quite clear whether every man shares in both spirits, although this is certainly a possibility.[21] Indeed, the two spirits, which are engaged in a constant struggle, seem to be living together within every man, and not only to rule each upon a different category of men. An Iranian influence upon such an anthropology is more than plausible. In the careful words of Shaul Shaked, who argued for such an influence, mainly from structural arguments: "It may be imagined that contacts between Jews and Iranians helped in formulating a Jewish theology which, though continuing traditional Jewish motifs, came to resemble fairly closely the Iranian view of the world."[22]

---

[19] *Qaest. in Ex.* 1. 23 (32–34 LCL). Here again, the remarkable intuitions of de Beausobre should be noted. More clearly than many scholars after him, he was able to perceive the fundamental importance of Jewish pseudepigraphical literature for understanding the background of Mani's thought (such as his *Book of Giants*). On this issue, see J. C. Reeves, *Jewish Lore in Manichaean Cosmogony: Studies in the Book of Giants Traditions* (Cincinnati 1992). For an evaluation of De Beausobre's opus, see G. G. Stroumsa, "Isaac de Beausobre Revisited: The Birth of Manichaean Studies," in *Proceedings of the Third International Conference of Manichaean Studies,* ed. W. Sundermann (Berlin, forthcoming).

[20] *"va-yasem lo shtei ruḥot lehithalekh bahem, ruaḥ ha-emet ve-ruaḥ ha-avel,"* *Community Rule* III. 18ff.

[21] See for instance M.-E. Boimard, O.P., "The First Epistle of John and the Writings of Qumran," in *John and the Dead Sea Scrolls,* ed. J. H. Charlesworth (New York 1991), 156–65. See also, in the same volume, J. H. Charlesworth, "A Critical Comparison of the Dualism in IQS 3: 13–4: 26 and the "Dualism" contained in the Gospel of John," 76–106.

[22] Sh. Shaked, "Qumran and Iran: Further Considerations," in *Israel Oriental Studies* 2 (1972): 432–46.

As is well known, the *Testaments of the Twelve Patriarchs* are in their present form early Christian texts that reflect the dualism found in the Qumran texts. The *Testament of Judah* reads:

> So understand, my children, that two spirits await an opportunity with humanity: the spirit of truth and the spirit of error. In between is the conscience of the mind which inclines as it will. The things of truth and the things of error are written in the affections of man, each one of whom the Lord knows.[23]

In the *Testament of Asher*, we read:

> God had granted two ways to the sons of men, two mind-sets, two lives of action, two models, and two goals.... The two ways are good and evil, concerning them are two dispositions within our breasts that choose between them.[24]

Although there remains some uncertainty as to terminology, the juxtaposition of these two texts shows clearly that the two spirits are located in everybody. In the words of Albrecht Dihle, "man finds himself placed between two spirits, a good and an evil one. These are spoken of either as faculties and inhabitants of the human soul or as cosmic powers. They are called instinct, impulse, spirit, intention, angel and the like .... The human intellect chooses – namely the objective of action – and turns itself – namely to one of the two angels or spirits."[25]

A similar duality in the soul is reflected in the Rabbinic idea of the two basic instincts of good and evil in man's soul (*yetser ha-raʿ* and *yetser ha-tov*).[26] It also reappears in various early Christian texts, which all seem to show in some way or another a relationship to the Jewish and Jewish-Christian conceptions.[27] The most representative of these texts should be at least briefly reviewed here.[28]

As has often been pointed out,[29] the *Shepherd of Hermas* offers the clearest

---

[23] ...*hoti duo pneumata skholazousin en tôi anthrôpôi, to tès alètheias kai tès planès. Test. Judah* 20. 1–3 (transl. II, 800 Charlesworth). For the text of the *Testaments*, see the edition by M. de Jonge, H. W. Hollander, and Th. Korteweg (Leiden 1978).

[24] *Test. Asher* 1. 3–9 (transl. vol. 1, 816–17 Charlesworth).

[25] A. Dihle, *The Theory of Will in Classical Antiquity* (Sather Classical Lectures 48; Berkeley, Los Angeles, and London 1982), 77.

[26] See for instance *b. Yoma* 69b, *b. Baba Bathra* 16a, *Gen. Rabba* 9.9. See further the discussion in E. E. Urbach, *The Sages* (in Hebrew) (Jerusalem 1967), 415–27.

[27] See O. J. F. Seitz, "Antecedents and Signification of the Term *dipsukhos*," *JBL* 66 (1947): 211–19. Seitz states that "it becomes highly probable that the real antecedent of the notion expressed by the Greek term *dipsukhos,* which James, I and II Clement, and Hermas appear to have derived from a single source, is to be found in the Rabbinic conception of a double heart or two hearts, which is generically related to the idea of the two *yetsarim*. ..." (214). This was written, of course, before the Dead Sea Scrolls were made available.

[28] For a series of Jewish and early Christian texts on the two spirits in man, see also Dihle, *Theory of Will*, 100, n. 42.

[29] See for instance P. Lluis-Font, "Sources de la doctrine d'Hermas sur les deux esprits," *Revue d'Ascétique et de Mystique* 39 (1963): 83–98, who states that this doctrine comes from Essene theology. Referring to the (misleading) patterns of thought developed by Jean Daniélou, he concludes on the "outillage mental surtout sémitique" of early Christianity (98). See further J.

parallel in Apostolic literature to the two spirits from Qumran: "For if you are courageous the Holy Spirit which dwells in you will be pure, not obscured by another evil spirit...."[30] The presence of both spirits in the same person is made quite specific further: "If therefore, both spirits dwell in the same place it is unprofitable and evil for that man in whom they dwell."[31] To be sure, this is not a necessary or ideal state of affairs:

> For when these spirits dwell in one vessel, where also the Holy Spirit dwells, there is no room in that vessel, but it is overcrowded. Therefore, the delicate spirit which is unaccustomed to dwell with an evil spirit, or with hardness, departs from such a man, and seeks to dwell with gentleness and quietness.[32]

The clearest testimony from Hermas, however, relates specifically the existence within man of two angels, one good and the other evil (note the fluidity of the terminology: *aggeloi* seem to be identical with *pneumata*):

> Hear now, said he, concerning the faith. There are two angels with man, one of righteousness and one of wickedness.[33]

The *Epistle* of Barnabas has often been referred to in the same context. This last text, however, presents a rather different kind of dualism, identical to the one found in the *Didachè*: the two ways of teaching and power (of Light and of Darkness), as well as their pomps of angels remain distinct and separate.

> And there is a great difference between the two ways. For over the one are set light-bringing angels of God *(phôtagogoi aggeloi tou theou)*, but over the other angels of Satan *(aggeloi tou satanas)*.[34]

A different conception, which posits a hierarchy of two souls, one above the other – rather than two parts of the soul opposite to one another – was held in the second half of the second century by Tatian, the encratite Apologist "from the land of the Assyrians."[35] As we shall see, the Eastern origin of Tatian is of some significance, since similar conceptions reappear later, also from Eastern provenance. It hs often been pointed out, moreover, that Tatian's thought often seems to reflect early or "archaic" Jewish-Christian conceptions. On the soul, Tatian says:

Paramelle and P. Adnès, "Hermas," *DS*, 7: 315–34, esp. 322, who point out the parallels with the *Didachè* and present the angel of iniquity as a supporter or an emanation of the devil.

[30] *heteron ponèrou pneumatos. Mandates*, 5.2.

[31] *amphotera oun ta pneumata epi to auto katoikounta, asumphoron estin kai ponèron tôi anthrôpôi ekeinôi, en hôi katoikousin. Mandates*, 5.4.

[32] Ibid., 6.5–6.

[33] *Aggeloi meta tou anthrôpou, eis tès dikaiosunès kai eis tès ponèrias. Mandate* 6.2.1.

[34] *Ep. Barnabas*, 18.1–2. On the dualistic trends in early Christian literature and their influence on Augustine, see J. van Oort, *Jerusalem and Babylon: A Study into Augustine's* City of God *and the Sources of his Doctrine of the Two Cities* (Suppl. to V.C.; Leiden 1991), esp. 286ff.

[35] Tatian, *Oratio ad Graecos*, 42.

We have knowledge of two different kinds of spirits, one of which is called soul, but the other is greater than the soul; it is the image and likeness of God. The first men were endowed with both, so that they might be part of the material world, and at the same time above it. This is how things are.[36]

A view closer to the one which we have sought to follow until now, and which speaks about two opposite powers dwelling together in the soul is preserved by Origen, in his *Homilies on Luke*:

> Everyone is assisted by two angels, one of justice and one of iniquity. If good thoughts dwell in our heart, and if justice brings forth many fruits in us, there is no doubt that it is the angel of the Lord which speaks to us. But if it is evil thoughts which agitate our heart, then it is the angel of the devil which speaks to us.[37]

It should not come as a surprise that this view is quite similar to that presented by the *Shepherd of Hermas*. In the *Peri Archôn,* indeed, Origen expresses his debt to Hermas (*PA*, 3.2.4). The opposition of the two angels within man reflects the stakes of the spiritual fight between darkness and light. Therefore, discerning between the two spirits is a task of importance, as emphasized by Origen in the *Peri Archôn*.[38]

This idea, which reappears in Cassian, was picked up by Gregory of Nyssa:

> The Divine providence ... has placed next to each of us, in order to help him in life, an angel, incorporeal in nature, while the "corruptor of our race," seeking to hurt man, used the same procedure through the means of an evil and evildoing demon.[39]

As mentioned above, the "two souls" theory is propounded also by various dualist and Gnostic texts. From our scarce evidence, the two souls mentioned by the Gnostics are not two opposite souls, one good and one evil. Rather, they seem to be hierarchically ordered, one being higher than the other, "one more divine and heavenly and the other inferior."[40] As we have seen, such a conception, far from being exclusive to the Gnostics, seems to have been fairly widespread, since we find it also expressed by different early Christian authors, such as Tatian. It should be noted that this conception is different from the one that

---

[36] *Duo pneumatôn diaphoras ismen hèmeis, hôn to men kaleitai psukhè, to de meizon men tès psukhès...Oratio ad Graecos*, 12.1 (22–23 Whittaker; Oxford 1982).

[37] Unicuique duo assistunt angeli, alter iustitiae, alter iniquitatis. Si bonae cogitationes in corde nostro fuerint et in animo iustitia pullulaaverit, haud dubium, quin nobis loquatur angelus Domini. Si vero malae fuerint in nostro corde versatae, loquitur nobis angelus diaboli. *Hom. Luke* 12.4 (202–203 Crouzel, Fournier, Périchon; SC 87; Paris 1962).

[38] See F. Marty, "Le discernement des deux esprits dans le *Peri Archon*," *Revue d'Ascétique et de Mystique* 34 (1958): 147ff. See further Crouzel et al., eds., *Hom. Luke*, 202, n. 2; see further Daniélou, "Démon," *DS*, 3.163–67.

[39] *all' aggelon tina asômaton eilèkhotôn phusin....dia ponèrou tinos kakopoiou daimonos.* Gregory of Nyssa, *Vita Mosis* 2.45 (131–33 Daniélou; SC 1ter; Paris 1968). Cf. John Cassian, *Conferences* 8.17 (54 SC); see the discussion in J. Daniélou, *Les anges et leur mission* (Paris 1990[1952]), 120–123.

[40] See the discussion in Ferwerda, "Two Souls," 362.

posits two opposing spirits, or else two forces, instincts, or angels fighting within the soul.

We must acknowledge that in our cursory review of the evidence, we have encountered no clear reference to *two souls* in ancient Jewish or Christian texts. Philo mentions two powers *(dunameis)* in the soul; Tatian speaks of two spirits *(pneumata),* and the same is true for the *Testament of Judah* and for Hermas. All these texts reflect a basic conception that we find expressed most clearly in the *Manual of Discipline.* Moreover, those authors, such as Barnabas, Origen, and Gregory of Nyssa, who mention two angels fighting within the human soul seem to follow the same basic pattern of thought.[41]

Although Augustine remains rather vague when he objects to the Manichaean doctrine of the two souls, he seems clearly to refer to an anthropology in which two opposing forces are contesting one another within man, and *not* of the hierarchical conception of two souls. He can speak, for instance, of "duas animas, vel duas mentes, unam bonam, alteram malam." Elsehere, he writes: "Duas simul animas in uno homine esse delirant, unam malam, alteram bonam, de suis principiis emanantes."[42] The same view is expressed by Titus of Bostra in his *Adversus Manichaeos,* when he states that the Manichaeans believe that there are two opposite natures *(duo phuseis enantias)* within man, one good and one evil.[43] No other sources, however, speak of the two opposite souls *within man.* Shaharastani's testimony refers indeed to the soul of the kingdom of light, which is "good, noble, wise, acting the good and knowledgeable," while the soul of darkness is "evil, low, stupid, evildoing and ignorant."[44]

The evidence produced until now does not allow us to show clearly the existence of the two souls doctrine in Manichaeism. The circumstantial evidence, however, does point to a long tradition, from Qumran on, of a duality of opposing forces within man. We have seen, moreover, the existence of another conception, represented by Tatian in the East, of a hierarchy of souls.

What does not seem to have been pointed out in this respect, however, is the fact that another Manichaean conception of the duality of the soul is well-attested, and that there might have been a conflation of the two conceptions. I am

---

[41] For a similar conception developed in Syriac, see also Aphrahat, *Demonstrationes*, PS I.416.17f., 744.4ff., 848.20ff., cf. Vööbus, in *JAC* 3 (1960): 152–55.

[42] *De haeresibus,* 46 and *Opus Imperfectum contra Iulianum*, III.172 (last text quoted by Baur, *Manichäische Religionssystem*, 165).

[43] Titus of Bostra, *Adv. Manich.,* II.6 (*PG* 18, 1144B). On Titus' anti-Manichaean polemics, see G. G. Stroumsa, *Savoir et salut* (Paris 1992), 329–40.

[44] Text in Shahrastani, *Book of Religions and Philosophical Sects*, ed. W. Cureton (London 1848), 189; tr. D. Gimaret and G. Monot, Shahrastani, *Le livre des Religions et des Sectes* (Louvain and Paris 1986), 656. For another fourth-century refutation of Manichaean psychology, see Numenius of Emesa, *de Natura Hominis*, 18 (tr. W. Telfer, *Cyril of Jerusalem and Nemesius of Emesa,* [LCC 4. London 1955, 286–87]; Nemesius speaks of a single world soul, which can be divided up).

referring to Mani's belief that he had a heavenly double, his Twin *(tauma),* an alter ego of sorts, a belief known from different sources, and in particular from the Cologne Mani Codex. This heavenly Twin, who, as Mani's guardian angel, brings him the Revelation, also functions as the Paraclete, the Holy Spirit.[45] Now it has been pointed out long ago, in particular by Erik Peterson, that this conception of the Twin seems close to that of Tatian, for whom the soul forms a couple, or *suzugia,* with the Spirit, which leads her to heaven. According to Gilles Quispel, Mani's conception of his heavenly Twin represents a transformation of the "Jewish-Christian concepts of the Angel of the Spirit" which appears, for instance, in the *Shepherd of Hermas* and in the *Ascension of Isaiah.*[46] In a sense, then, the Twin can be considered as identical to the heavenly, superior soul. The same conception, which was already known in Iran,[47] clearly reflects shamanistic thought patterns, according to which the soul can go out of the individual under certain conditions. It reappears in some Gnostic texts, such as the *Pistis Sophia:* "This man is me and I am this man."[48] It is probably also in the same light that logion 108 of the *Gospel of Thomas* must be understood:

> Jesus said: "He who will drink from my mouth will become like Me. I myself shall become he, and the things that are hidden will be revealed to him.[49]

The conception of the *suzugia* expressed here is rather different from that well known from the Pseudo-Clementine literature, where the members of the pairs appear in chronological succession, for example, of a false prophet preceding a true one: "God has appointed for this world certain pairs; and he who comes first of the pairs is of evil, he who comes second, of good."[50]

We must conclude that two different conceptions of the duality of the soul coexisted in Manichaeism from its earliest stages, the one horizontal, as it were, (a good *versus* an evil soul), and the other vertical (the soul and its heavenly

---

[45] See A. Henrichs and L. Koenen, "Der Kölner Mani-Kodex (P. Colon. inv. nr. 4780) *peri tès gennès tou sômatos autou*; Edition der Seiten 1–71," *ZPE* 19 (1975): n. 39*, pp. 75–76 (on CMC 69–70). For a detailed discussion of Twin figure in the Mani Codex and in other sources, see Henrichs and Koenen "Ein griechicher Mani-Codex," *ZPE* 5 (1975): VI: "Manis himmlischer Zwilling." Evodius, too, identifies Mani's Twin as the Holy Spirit: "a gemino suo, hoc est spiritu sancto." (*De Fide contra Manich.* [CSEL 25, 961]). See now W. Fauth, "Manis anderes Ich: Gestalthafte Metaphysik im Kölner Mani-Kodex," in *Gnosis und Philosophie,* eds. R. Berlinger and W. Schrader (Elementa 59; Amsterdam and Atlanta 1994), 75–139.

[46] This is developed further, in particular, by G. Quispel, "Genius and Spirit," in *Essays on the Nag Hammadi Texts in Honour of Pahor Labib,* ed. M. Krause (NHS 6; Leiden 1975), 155–69, esp. 166.

[47] See J. Russell, "Kartir and Mani: a Shamanistic Model of their Conflict," in *Iranica Varia: Papers in Honor of Professor Ehsan Yarshater (Acta Iranica* 30 [1990]: 191, n.16).

[48] *Pistis Sophia,* 2.96 (231 Schmidt, McDermot [NHS 9; Leiden 1978]).

[49] See the discussion by H.-C. Puech, *En quête de la gnose,* vol. 2 (Paris 1978), 210ff.

[50] Ps. Clement, *Recognitiones,* 3.59; cf. Hom., 2.15, 3.23. Cf. the discussion of W. Bousset, *Hauptprobleme der Gnosis* (FRLANT 10; Göttingen 1907), 152: the first member of a pair to appear is feminine, the second is masculine.

counterpart). Even if the nomenclature did not always speak about "souls," it would seem that Augustine's references to "two souls" most probably reflect a known reality.

This is not all, however. There seems to have been another conflation of terms in antiquity, this time between a Jewish and a pagan conception. As was shown by Robert Schilling, an osmosis occurred at some point between the Greek idea of *daimôn* and the Jewish concept of angel.[51] In particular, Schilling refers to the dualist theory of a *daimôn agathos* and a *daimôn kakos*, also considered in Greek literature as a sort of guardian angel.[52] According to him, this would have conflated with the Jewish theory of a guardian angel, a conflation already clearly visible in Philo, and reflected later in the doctrines of Origen and Gregory of Nyssa on the two angels assisting every man.

To conclude, the belief in the two souls, which in all probability originates in Iran, reappears in various Jewish garbs, but also in pagan contexts as well as in Platonic teaching. From this multiple background, two different ideas of the two souls ("horizontal" and "vertical") appear in early Christian literature, including Jewish Christian and Gnostic texts. This forms the proximate channel through which these conceptions reached Manichaeism and were reinterpreted and radicalized in the light of Manichaean dualist cosmology. Augustine, therefore, knew what he was speaking about when he refuted the Manichaeans on their two souls theory. But if their solution was to be rejected as childish, the problem of the divided will, which preoccupied Augustine so much, could not disappear. The recognition of the divided will was not Paul's privilege. It was much wider, as Ovid's verse testifies: "Video meliora proboque, deteriora sequor."[53] It was, however, analyzed by no one so well as by Augustine.[54]

---

[51] R. Schilling, "Genius," *RAC*, 52–83. I am quoting according to the original version, in his *Rites, cultes, dieux de Rome* (Paris 1979), 415–43.

[52] See Andres, *"Daimôn," PW*, Suppl. III, 287–90 (1918).

[53] Ovid, *Metamorphoses*, VII.21.

[54] On this, see G. G. Stroumsa and P. Fredriksen, "The Two Souls and the Divided Will," in *Soul, Self, and Body in Religious Experience*, ed. A. Baumgarten, J. Assmann, and G. G. Stroumsa (SHR 78; Leiden 1998), 198–217.

Envoi

Chapter 18

Mystical Jerusalems

Vincet pax et finietur bellum. Quando
autem vincet pax, vincet illa civitas
quae dicitur visio pacis

Augustine, *Enar. in Psal.*, 64.4.

In his book on the *Martyrs of Palestine,* Eusebius reports the following conversation between the Roman Governor of Palestine and the Christian Pamphilus, in late third-century Caesarea:

> "Where do you come from?", asks the Governor.
> "From Jerusalem," answers Pamphilus.
> "Where is that?"
> "It lies toward the Far East and the rising sun."[1]

This exchange is revealing on two accounts. Not only does it show that the Roman Governor in Caesarea could ignore the former name of Aelia Capitolina. It also reflects Pamphilus' intention to describe the heavenly Jerusalem, rather than the earthly one, as his true homeland – a characteristic Christian attitude in the pre-Constantinian period.[2] Incidentally, the governor was not the last person to be ignorant of the geographical location of Jerusalem. Some twenty years ago, when my wife and I told a major American poet that we came from Jerusalem, she asked: "Is it far from Israel?"

The idea of a heavenly Jerusalem as a model of the earthly city is of course originally a Jewish idea, which owes its centrality in Christian literature to the fact that it was picked up and developed in the book of Revelation. This text, as well as the Letter to the Hebrews, propounded a conception of the heavenly Jerusalem as the perfect model of which the earthly Jerusalem was, at best, a pale reflection.[3] In Christian thought patterns, the heavenly or new Jerusalem

---

[1] Eusebius, *Martyrs of Palestine* 11.9–12.

[2] P. Walker, "Jerusalem and the Holy Land in the Fourth Century," in *The Christian Heritage in the Holy Land,* eds. A. O. Maloney et al. (London 1995), 23–24. Cf. E. D. Hunt, *Holy Land Pilgrimage in the Later Roman Empire, A.D. 312–460* (Oxford 1984), 4–5.

[3] On the Heavenly Jerusalem, see E. Lamirande, "Jérusalem céleste," in *DS* 8 8: 944–58, with bibliography; W. D. Davies, "Jerusalem and the Land in the Christian Tradition," in *The Jerusalem Colloquium on Religion, Peoplehood, Nation and Land,* eds. M. A. Tanenbaum and R. J. Z. Werblowsky (Jerusalem 1972), 115–57; W. D. Davies, *The Gospel and the Land: Early Christianity and Jewish Territorial Doctrine* (Sheffield 1994).

soon achieved autonomous status, as it were, from the earthly Jerusalem, a phenomenon that has no parallel in Jewish representations.

The noble status of Jerusalem did not only stem from its having been the home of the first Christian community, the "Mother Church." It soon achieved mythical status. In various strata of early Christian literature, for instance in some New Testament Apocryphal texts, the Mount of Olives, in particular, became the mythical site of dialogues between the resurrected Christ and his disciples. Since its appearance in Zachariah 14: 4 (a radically eschatological passage, and the only time it is mentioned in the Hebrew Bible) the Mount of Olives had achieved eschatological importance; in Christian consciousness, it was not affected by the curse on Jerusalem.[4] So, too, Golgotha was not simply the place where Jesus had been crucified, but it soon became identified with the burial place of Adam in an adaptation of Jewish traditions regarding Mount Moriah. Like its Jewish antecedent, the early Christian conception of Jerusalem as the *omphalos* did not only imply that it was the center of the inhabited earth, the *oikoumenè* (as represented in medieval maps), but also the locus of a direct connection between heaven and earth. Fifth-century Christian Jerusalem, for instance, was a place where letters could fall from heaven, offering the possibility of new divine revelations.[5]

The singing of the praises of *Urbs beata Hierusalem* in medieval hymns and religious poetry refers to the heavenly city, not to its earthly *figura*. This dual nature of Jerusalem, and more specifically the dialectical relationship between the earthly and the heavenly Jerusalem, is crucial for any understanding of medieval attitudes to the holy city.[6]

In contradistinction to the heavenly Jerusalem, the earthly city was charged with a deep ambivalence in early Christian literature.[7] Indeed, Jerusalem in New Testament writings left a powerful yet ambivalent impact upon the early Chris-

---

[4] See O. Limor, "The Place of the End: Eschatological Geography in Jerusalem," in *The Real and Ideal Jerusalem*, ed. B. Kühnel (forthcoming).

[5] See M. van Esbroek, "La lettre sur le dimanche, descendue du ciel," in his *Aux origines de la dormition de la Vierge* (London 1995), xiii.

[6] See K. L. Schmidt, "Jerusalem als Urbild und Abbild," *Eranos Jahrbuch* 18 (1950): 207–48. See further the important work of B. Kühnel, *From the Earthly to the Heavenly Jerusalem: Representations of the Holy City in Christian Art of the First Millenium* (Römische Quartalschrift für christlische Altertumskunde und Kirchgeschichte 42. Supplementheft; Rome, Freiburg, and Vienna 1987).

[7] On Jerusalem in earliest Christian thought, see especially N. Brox, "Das 'irdische Jerusalem' in der altchristliche Theologie," *Kairos* 28 (1986): 152–73. Brox rightly emphasizes the theme of the Mother Church in Jerusalem as a regulating model in Patristic literature and its importance, also for the construction of the monastic ideal. See also P. C. Bori, "La référence à la communauté de Jérusalem dans les sources chrétiennes orientales et occidentales jusqu'au cinquième siècle," *Istina* 19 (1974): 31–48. See further P. Fredriksen in *City of the Great King: Jerusalem from David to the Present,* ed. N. Rosovsky (Cambridge, Mass. 1996). On the ambivalent status of Jerusalem in Early Christian thought, see. G. Stroumsa, "Which Jerusalem?" (in Hebrew), *Cathedra* 11 (1979): 119–24. See further K. Thraede, "Jerusalem II (Sinnbild)", *RAC* 17, 718–764.

tian mind. In the gospels, Jesus had predicted the destruction of the Temple. Paul's career, moreover, symbolized the passage of the new religion from Jerusalem to Rome, from a marginal, provincial city to the Empire's capital – in a movement that has been described as "elliptical" by Henry Chadwick.[8] In the first centuries, indeed, we can detect in the main a trend of de-territorialization, which denies any central importance – at least implicitly – to earthly Jerusalem. The City of David retained in Christian consciousness a deeply ambiguous position: its inhabitants had been guilty of Deicide. The destruction of the Temple, predicted by Jesus, was soon perceived as a divine punishment inflicted on the city for this crime.

An indication of the permanence of this ambivalence of Jerusalem in Christian consciousness, perhaps, is reflected by the fact that although there are at least five Bethlehems in the United States, the only other Jerusalem I could find in the atlas is located in Olutanga, a small, remote island in the South Philippines.

The Constantinian revolution brought with it the reconstruction of Jerusalem as a sacred city, its *renovatio,* mainly through the building of the Basilica of the Anastasis. During three centuries, until the Islamic conquest, Byzantine Jerusalem would be invested with earthly as well as heavenly glories, adorned with churches and sanctuaries; the city had become the recipient of much respect and the source of some spiritual influence. Holy Places were discovered not only in Jerusalem, but also throughout Palestine, soon transforming the latter into a *terra sancta,* a "Holy Land," during the fifth and sixth centuries – a process well-described by Robert Wilken.[9]

And yet, the Temple Mount remained barren until the end of the seventh century, when the *Kubbet a-Sahra,* the Dome of the Rock, was built. This building is the first extant architectural monument of Islamic civilization, and remains to this day the most majestic structure in Jerusalem. According to the theology first propounded in the Letter to the Hebrews, Jesus was both the High Priest and the Sacrifice. His body was the new Temple. Hence the theological central position of Constantine's Church of the Anastasis which was meant to replace the Temple.[10]

As is well known, even the birth of Christian pilgrimage to the Holy Land and Holy City in the fourth century took place despite reticence or objection by some of the leading teachers of the Church.[11] In a dialectical way, it is this movement back to Jerusalem that led the way to the reproductions of Jerusalem –

---

[8] H. Chadwick, "The Circle and the Ellipse: Rival Concepts of Authority in the Early Church," in his *History and Thought of the Early Church,* ch. 1 (London 1982).

[9] See R. Wilken, *The Land Called Holy: Palestine in Christian History and Thought* (New Haven 1992), 149–72.

[10] See J. Z. Smith, *To Take Place* (Chicago 1986).

[11] See E. D. Hunt, *Holy Land Pilgrimage,* above n. 2.

more precisely, of its heart for Christians, the Holy Sepulchre – in various cities of western Europe throughout the Middle Ages. Often built by personalities, such as bishops returned from Holy Land pilgrimage, the reproductions permitted those who could not go on pilgrimage themselves to experience it without leaving home, as it were: "abroad at home," to use the motto of a *New York Times* columnist. The Holy Sepulchre, then, can be said to represent the core of the emerging "cultural memory" of the Christian people. Its symbolic reproduction throughout Europe reflects the organization and institutionalization of this memory.

In a sense, both the reproductions of Jerusalem and the idea of a heavenly Jerusalem represent two different metamorphoses of Jerusalem, which run parallel to the Church understanding of itself as *verus Israel*: if the name "Israel" refers to believers in Christ, this entails the expropriation of its earlier owners from their identity. If the true Jerusalem is located in heaven or elsewhere upon earth, the old city upon the hills of Judea has lost its unique significance. The desacralization of the Judean space, however, can also be seen as the reverse of the sacralization of the European soil: Jerusalem is now not only elsewhere, to use Oleg Grabar's term, but everywhere. There is, then, another side to the radical metamorphosis of Jerusalem: the multiple senses and references to the name also reflect the spiritual conquest of a whole continent by the faith born in Judea.

In the following pages, I shall focus upon the connections between two strikingly different phenomena, the reproductions of the Holy Sepulchre and the metaphor of the heavenly Jerusalem. Both reflect central aspects of the metamorphosis of Jerusalem in medieval consciousness, or what the French call "l'imaginaire médiéval." To be sure, both phenomena have been studied often and well. Oddly enough, however, they seem never to have been approached simultaneously in their possible relationships. I shall first refer to the intriguing phenomenon of the duplication of the sacred places, the medieval *translatio* of Jerusalem to various European cities. I shall then discuss the idea of a new or heavenly Jerusalem, and the spiritual metaphors of Jerusalem, which have been prominent in Christian spiritual and mystical literature since the Patristic period. Prima facie, these two ways of "uprooting" Jerusalem do not seem to be connected to one another; one reflects an "overdose," as it were, of the spatial, earthly dimension of Jerusalem while the other represents its very negation. I shall argue that both phenomena dialectically complement one another, functioning like a pendulum of sorts in medieval thought patterns. In other words, the way to the heavenly Jerusalem does not pass as much through the earthly Jerusalem as through the multiple Jerusalems disseminated throughout Western Europe. It should be noted here that these phenomena have no real counterpart in Byzantium, for complex reasons that reflect the vast difference between Eastern and Western Christendom. In particular, the status of Constantinople as the new Jerusalem has no equivalent in the West. In the fourth century, Rome in a sense came to be considered a *nova Hierusalem*. Santa Croce in Gerusa-lemme was built as early as the second half of the fifth century.[12] The Hieroso-lymitan influence was not only architectural, but also liturgical, especially dur-ing the paschal period. However, when Rome was sacked by Alaric in 410, Au-gustine could explain the collapse of the Empire's capital precisely, by recalling its pagan past and contrasting it in radical fashion to the *Civitas Dei* – another name for the heavenly Jerusalem. Indeed, the Crusaders' *Iter Hierosolymae* did not have a Byzantine equivalent either. In a sense, then, this will be an investiga-tion into the mythopoieic power of Jerusalem in European religious imagin-ation.

1.

The idea of a Christian *translatio Hierosolymae* seems to occur for the first time with Montanus who, according to the testimony of Eusebius, "gave the name of Jerusalem to Pepuza and Tymion, which are little towns in Phrygia."[13] As con-firmed by Tertullian, who knew Montanist beliefs as an insider, this probably means that the heavenly Jerusalem was thought to have descended upon Pepuza and Tymion. The heretic status of the Montanists in the third century, and the Christian invention of the Holy Land in the fourth century probably prevented the *translatio Hierosolymae* from becoming implanted in Patristic literature. Nevertheless, this conception never quite disappeared, remaining an endemic expression of sectarian eschatology throughout Christian history, from the Hussite reconstruction of the Holy Land in Bohemia, and the Taborites' Tabor, up to nineteenth century Russia, for instance, where the sectarians of New Zion were expecting the descent of the Heavenly Jerusalem.[14]

If the new Jerusalem can descend from heaven on Pepuza, a small town in Asia Minor, who needs the city of David anymore?[15] To be sure, new Zions exist in various cultural surroundings. A famous case is that of the churches carved in the rock in Lâlibalâ, Ethiopia. This new Jerusalem became a major goal of pil-grimages at times when Axum was inaccessible.[16] In the modern world, we think mainly of Baptist churches in the south of the United States or in sub-Saharan

[12] See Ch. Auffarth, ""Himmliches und irdisches Jerusalem: ein religionswissenschaftlicher Versuch zur 'Kreuzzugseschatologie,'" *Zeitschrift für Religionswissenschaft* 2 (1993): 101–104.
[13] *Historia Ecclesiastica* 5.18.2; II, 486–7 LCL. On Pepuza and Tymion, see C. Trevett, *Mon-tanism: Gender, Authority and the New Prophecy* (Cambridge 1996), 15–26.
[14] See P. Kovalesky, "Messianisme et millénarisme russes?," in *Archives de Sociologie des Religions* 5 (1958): 47–70.
[15] On Montanist conceptions of the heavenly Jerusalem, see P. de Labriolle, *La crise monta-niste* (Paris 1913), 86–95, 330–32.
[16] See, e.g., M. Heldman, "Legends of Lâlibalâ: the Development of an Ethiopian Pilgrimage Site," *Res* 27 (1995): 25–38.

Africa, or the Swedenborgian churches"of the New Jerusalem."[17] It should be pointed out that the idea of *translatio* from the Holy Land to Europe was not limited to the Holy Sepulchre and to Jerusalem. In the last decade of the thirteenth century, for instance, the house of the Blessed Virgin Mary was transposed from Nazareth to Tersatz in Dalmatia, and from there to Loreto, near Ancona.[18]

Since Carolingian times, the symbolic transference of shrines from the Holy Land could bring considerable prestige and charisma to spiritual and political centers in the West.[19] The clearest and earliest example, perhaps, is Aachen (Aix-la-Chapelle), where the political stakes were particularly high. Charlemagne wished Aachen to be perceived in the sequence of Jerusalem, Rome, and Constantinople. The *Libri Carolini* call the city *sedes davidica* and New Jerusalem. The *translatio* here directly reflects the political claim of Charlemagne to be Constantine's, and ultimately Solomon's, successor.[20] Moreover, in his competition with the Byzantine emperor, he had succeeded in being granted by Harun al-Rashid a kind of protectorate over the Christian Holy Places in Jerusalem, with the right to build *xenodocheia* for western pilgrims.[21] Eusebius had specified that the dome of the Anastasis should "make conspicuous an object of veneration to all" the Holy Sepulchre. So the Rotunda Church of Aachen, Charlemagne's Capella Palatina, was perceived in typological association with the church of the Holy Sepulchre.[22] Let us also mention, among others, the case of Orléans, where a crucifix was seen weeping on the eve of the year 1000. Within the context of the changing religiosity at the turn of the millenium, such a prodigy was thought by some to foretell "far greater matters, some kind of *translatio Hierosolymae*, in which Orléans would play the role of the New Jerusalem."[23]

The most sustained effort to concretize such a *translatio* was the actual building of a city according to the ideal plan of Jerusalem. The heavenly Jerusalem

---

[17] For the meaning of "the heavenly Jerusalem" in the thought of Emmanuel Swedenborg, see e.g., his *The True Christian Religion*, § 782. The *Book of Mormon* offers another self-understanding of a modern religious movement issuing from Protestant Christianity as "the New Jerusalem."

[18] For a similar contemporary puzzling phenomenon, note the exact replica of the late Lubavitcher Rebbe Menaham Schneersohn's house in Brooklyn recently built in Kfar Chabad, Israel.

[19] S. Nichols, *Romanesque Signs: Early Medieval Narrative and Iconography* (New Haven, Conn. 1983), 75, who points out that renovation and translation are closely associated with artistic creation.

[20] On Orléans, see R. Landes, *Relics, Apocalypse and the Deceits of History* (Cambridge, Mass. 1995), 304, and Nichols, *Romanesque Signs*, 75.

[21] Nichols, *Romanesque Signs,* 70.

[22] Ibid., 70.

[23] R. Landes, *Relics, Apocalypse and the Deceits of History*, 304.

was often represented as *urbs quadrata* – but also as a circle[24] – and the sacral topography of the city could be perceived as a mental map, a mandala of sorts, reminding one of Christianity's central belief, and offering an immediate object for meditation.[25] A clear example is that of Constance, mentioned by Christoph Auffarth in his study of the significance of Jerusalem in the realized eschatology in the wake of the Crusades. Auffarth points out that such mental maps also became mental time-tables, as loci of pilgrimages.[26]

From the early ninth to the early twelfth century, at least nineteen churches were built in western Europe, which were meant to be copies of the Holy Sepulchre, imitating its main characteristics.[27] The first such constructions were built on a smaller scale than the original. So, for instance, Saint Maurice of Constance was built between 934 and 976, following that of Saint Michael of Fulda, built in 820 as a copy of the Anastasis. Bishop Konrad of Constance had gone on pilgrimage to the holy city; in his *Vita* (dating from 1123), mention is made of the reconstruction of the Holy Sepulchre with wonderful goldwork, *mirabili aurificis opere.*[28] The church in Paderborn, built between 1033 and 1036, was the first to be built "ad mensuras ejusdem ecclesiae et sancti Sepulchri." The oldest such church, however, seems to be the Narbonne Holy Sepulchre, built in white Pyrennean marble in the fifth century. The first real reproduction of the tomb in Jerusalem, complete with antechamber, was built in Eichstatt, Walbrun around 1160. Examples of similar churches from the twelfth century are numerous, from Northampton and Cambridge to Augsburg. Moreover, there exist ten round churches built by the Templars and the Hospitallers, as well as the Pisan baptistery.[29] These churches, which evoke the image of the Holy Sepulchre, express a devotion to the first shrine of Christendom.

One striking example of a new Zion in Europe was the Chiesa di Santo Stefano in Bologna, also called Sancta Jerusalem Bononiensis, one of the earliest and certainly the most famous of the many similar churches in western Europe. The Santo Stefano rotunda was conceived as a reproduction of the church of the

[24] See B. Narkiss, "Round is Perfect: Ideal Jerusalem as a Circle," forthcoming.

[25] Auffarth, above n. 12, 25–49 and 91–118. See also 98–100. The main thrust of Auffarth's learned study is to insist on the importance of the medieval "realized eschatology" and of the image of Jerusalem in the genesis of the Crusades.

[26] Ibid., 104.

[27] For various other copies of the Holy Sepulchre in Italy, see D. Neri, *Il Santo Sepulcro riprodotto in occidente* (Quaderni de "la terra santa"; Jerusalem 1971), ch. 10–12, where references are made to churches in Rome, in Toscana, in Florence, etc., and also in Granada.

[28] See L. Kötzsche, "Das Heilige Grab in Jerusalem und seine Nachforge," in *Die Reise nach Jerusalem: eine kulturhistorische Exkursion in die Stadt der Städte – 3000 Jahre Davidsstadt,* eds. H. Budde and A. Nechama (Berlin 1995), 65–66.

[29] G. Bresc-Bautier, "Les imitations du Saint-Sépulcre de Jérusalem (9e-15e s.): archéologie d'une dévotion," *Revue de l'Histoire de la Spiritualité* 50 (1974): 319–42, passim. See now H. Brandenburg, *Die Kirche S. Stefano Rotondo in Rom* (Hans-Lietzmann-Vorlesungen 2; Berlin, New York, 1998).

Anastasis, but at the same time, was also meant to refer to the to *Hierusalem coelestis,* and to Santa Maria Rotonda in Rome, i.e., the Pantheon. According to some traditions, Petronius, bishop of Bologna circa 431–450, upon returning from a Holy Land pilgrimage, had a replica of the Holy Sepulchre built in his city and consecrated to the protomartyr Saint Stephen. This reproduction is, in a sense, an *eidolon* of Jerusalem, a portable Jerusalem, as it were, whose function was to remind one of the great and original shrine, the *omphalos*.[30] A representation of Petronius, Bologna's patron saint, represents him holding the city in his hands. Bologna itself is thus represented as a *forma orbis*, similar, in a way, to Jerusalem.[31] The first testimony for the name of Jerusalem granted to the Petronian Church in Bologna, it would seem, is found in a document by Charlemagne, dated to 887; it confirms to Wibodus, bishop of Parma, the acquisition of various churches in Bologna, including that of "Sanctum Stefanum qui dicitur sancta Hierusalem."[32] The earliest mention of a *Hierusalem* in Europe would seem to go back to a document dating from 716 where mention is made of the church "Sancti Andrae, ubi est baptisterium, una cum ecclesia Sancte Hierusalem."[33]

The numerous scholars who have studied the impressive compound, its architecture, and its history, agree that it is quite distinct from the many other round churches, imitations, or copies of the rotunda of the Holy Sepulchre (or rather, copies of an idealized Holy Sepulchre). The church as it exists today seems to have been erected upon the ruins of an earlier Roman building, which may date from Saint Petronius's time. As is well known, Constantine X Monomachos had rebuilt in 1048 the Church of the Anastasis, which had been destroyed by the Caliph Al-Hakim in 1009. The Crusaders, in turn, launched extensive rebuilding activities at the Holy Sepulchre, from 1099 to 1161. The plan of S. Stefano relies on the arrangement that existed in Jerusalem prior to the Crusaders' extensive rebuilding of the Holy Sepulchre. The Bologna church thus remains to this day the only concrete testimony to the original form of the Anastasis, after the radical changes made in the Jerusalem sanctuary itself in the eleventh century. This original form was known accurately, since plans of the Holy Sepulchre, similar to

---

[30] See R. G. Ousterhout, "The Church of Santo Stefano: a 'Jerusalem' in Bologna," *Gesta* 20 (1981): 311–21, esp. 312.

[31] See F. Filippini, *S. Petronio, vescovo di Bologna* (Bologna 1948), 48, on the religious meaning of the Petronian Jerusalem.

[32] See I. B. Supino, *L'arte nelle chiese di Bologna*, vol. 1 (Arnaldo Forni 1990; 1st. ed. 1932), 45. See further M. Fonti, in *Il Carrobio* 10 (1984): 122–31, on the transformation of symbols. The name "Jerusalem," may even go back to the Lombardian kings Liutprand and Ildebrand (736–744), as pointed out by F. Lanzoni, *San Petronio, vescovo di Bologna* (Roma 1907), 104–18.

[33] See A. Sorbelli, "La 'Sancta Jerusalem' Stefaniana," *L'archiginnasio* 35 (1940): 14–28, esp. 15. I should like to express my thanks to Saverio Marchignoli, who sent me important material from Bologna.

those drawn by the seventh-century pilgrim Arculf, had been brought back to Europe by the Crusaders.

But the church did not stand by itself. It seems that originally, Sancta Hierusalem on the eastern side of Bologna consisted of a reproduction of the various holy places in Jerusalem. As early as the tenth century, mention is made of San Giovanni in Monte Oliveti; as well as a church of S Tecla, built as a *similitudo* of the Valley of Josaphat, whose identification with the Qidron valley was attested by Eusebius in his *Onomasticon*. This "Valle di Giosafat" is located between the Oliveti and Sancta Hierusalem – corresponding, in other words, to the topography of Jerusalem. To be sure, the claim that the distances between the different loci reproduce precisely those between their models in Jerusalem is not quite accurate. The distance between S. Giovanni in Monte Oliveti and S. Stefano differs by almost a kilometer from the distance between the Anastasis and the Mount of Olives in Jerusalem itself. The field of Aceldama and the Pool of Siloam are also mentioned in the medieval sources, although their location remains undetermined. The whole complex, then, was created as a "theme park" of sorts, the first Eurodisney, offering a reproduction of Jerusalem's hills and valleys, and permitting a short escapade to the mythical Holy Land without the vagaries of the voyage. This was a new Jerusalem, neither a faithful reproduction of the earthly Jerusalem nor a completely mythic one. Actually, neither "reproduction" nor "myth" quite fits the nature of this reconstructed Jerusalem, no more than either fits the maps of Jerusalem drawn by pilgrims and travelers throughout the centuries. Rather, its most obvious characteristic lies in what can be called the *actualization* of the Holy City.

The church of Saint Stephen itself did not originally possess a precise symbolism as did the Holy Sepulchre. This was added later, by the Benedictine monks who rebuilt the original church in the Middle Ages. It is reasonable to postulate that the First Crusade offered the impulse for the reconstruction of Sancta Hierusalem. We know of the great enthusiasm generated by the First Crusade among the Bolognese.[34] With the first crusaders returning from the liberated holy city, the times were ripe for a new symbolism, more powerful and more complex than the earlier tradition, itself inherited from the late antique pilgrimages to the Holy Land.

The Nuova Gerusalemme, however, was meant to be more than just a souvenir reproduction of the holy city. It had obvious liturgical dimensions that are referred to in our sources. In the twelfth century, we know of processions from S. Stefano to S. Giovanni in Monte that were organized by the returning crusaders. In the Middle Ages, S. Stefano was also the site of Easter week ceremonies, and of an *adoratio crucis* copied from the cult of the Holy Cross observed in Jerusalem. In its twelfth-century form, S. Stefano offered a clear and

---

[34] See Ousterhout, "The Church of Santo Stefano."

specific link to Jerusalem and to its holy sites. Through its architectural and liturgical imitations, it gave the citizens of Bologna a visible connection to Jerusalem,
both the holy city and the heavenly vision.

The liturgical dimensions of Jerusalem's *memoriae* permitted the performance of the sacred drama of Christ's Passion. Here too, the developments reflect
a deep ambivalence. In the mid-thirteenth century, Urban IV established the
Feast of Corpus Christi in order to express his own interest for the Holy Sepulchre.[35] Already in ninth-century Carolingian France, one could observe
various liturgical connections to Jerusalem, such as processions with palm branches. In Santa Croce in Bologna, we can recall the facsimile of the Holy Cross
kept at a special locus called "Golgotha." This may have been the setting for an
adoratio crucis, similar to the Exaltation of the Holy Cross on Holy Thursday described by Egeria, when the relic of the True Cross was presented to the faithful
to be kissed.[36] In the tenth century, tropes of the *visitatio sepulchri* were chanted
in places such as Saint Gallen or Limoges.[37] Altogether, Christian liturgy recognizes a direct relationship between the spacial and the temporal dimensions of
cultic behavior. It might be worth noting that the liturgy commemorating events
such as the Annunciation or the Birth of Jesus, which are usually celebrated
once a year, can be celebrated *at any time* on the spot itself.[38]

In the same context, one may also understand the development of the Passion
mystery plays: Jerusalem is everywhere; the reconstitution of its central shrine
performs a role similar to the re-enactment of the events which it is intended to
recall. Plays about visitation to the Holy Sepulchre were common in Western
Europe.[39] There is no doubt that the dissemination of such churches reflected
the new interest in the earthly Jerusalem inspired by the crusades. Moreover, the
movement for the construction of these churches came to a halt with the conquest of Jerusalem by Saladin. No wonder, then, if there is no similar phenomenon in Byzantium. The question remains, however, of the extent to which the
cult in these churches strengthened or weakened the believers' bonds to the
holy city. The Holy Sepulchre venerated in western Europe was no longer lo-
calized in Jerusalem, and the Passion of Jesus Christ, the *Via Crucis,* could be re-
enacted everywhere.[40]

---

[35] On the emergence of the medieval festival of Corpus Christi, see M. Rubin, *Corpus Christi* (Cambridge 1991).

[36] Ousterhout "The Church of Santo Stefano," esp. 316–17. The ritual of the Exaltation of the Holy Cross, celebrated on September 14, had been initiated in Constantinople in 614, and the rite became popular elsewhere in the seventh century. This appears clearly, for instance, from Leontius of Neapolis' *Life of Symeon the Fool.* See D. Krueger, *Symeon the Holy Fool: Leonti-us' Life and the Late Antique City* (Berkeley 1996), 17.

[37] See Bresc-Bautier, "Les imitations du Saint Sépulchre," 323.

[38] I should like to thank Laurence Vianès for calling my attention to this fact.

[39] Ousterhout, "The Church of Santo Stefano," 317.

[40] Bresc-Bautier, "Les imitations du Saint-Sépulchre," 321.

The idea of the Via Dolorosa itself is a medieval invention of the Franciscans which had been imported to Jerusalem from Europe. So was the rite of the Deposition, which reached Jerusalem only in the sixteenth century. In a sense, therefore, it is the very recovery of Jerusalem in medieval Christendom that brought, in a dialectical way, to its *Aufhebung,* and to the transformation of religious memory. Paradoxically, then, the *memoriae* of Jerusalem played a role in limiting the significance of the actual Holy City in Christian religious consciousness.[41]

In "Calvaries of Convenience," a chapter of his recent *Landscape and Memory*, Simon Schama focuses on a number of mounts transformed into symbolic Golgothas in the Middle Ages.[42] Schama begins his analysis with Monte Verna, the Piedmontese mount chosen in 1224 by Saint Francis as an alternative Calvary and where he received the stigmata; "And this, God willed, should manifestly appear on Mount Verna because there the Passion of our Lord Jesus Christ was to be renewed through love and pity in the soul of Saint Francis." In the following centuries, the Franciscans would continue converting mountains into inspirational theatres. Schama mentions the case of the Franciscan Friar Bernardino Caimi who, having seen the real Mount Zion while acting as patriarch of the Holy Land, determined in 1486 to create on Monte Verna a more readily available version. On the mount, various chapels were built, called by names such as "Nazareth" or "Bethlehem," and adorned with paintings from the "parallel lives" of Jesus and Francis. At these chapels, the pilgrim would pause for prayer and contemplation during his (or her) ascent. Monte Verna, therefore, was not only transformed into a new Golgotha, but into a new, symbolic Holy Land – a fact that emphasizes the abstract nature (or spiritualization) of the idea of the Holy Land in the Middle Ages.[43]

The piety that encouraged the development of the Via Dolorosa went against the grain of the *Iter Sancti Sepulchri* and Crusader piety.[44] Inspired by their love of the heavenly city, pilgrims and Crusaders came to the earthly Jerusalem: "Ter-

---

[41] For a wonderful description of the ways in which memory uses mental images (in a different period), see J. Spence, *The Memory Palace of Matteo Ricci* (New York 1984).

[42] S. Schama, *Landscape and Memory* (New York 1995), 436–42.

[43] See G. Constable, "Opposition to Pilgrimage in the Middle Ages," *Mélanges G. Fransen,* (Studia Gratiana 19; Rome 1976), 125–46 (= G. Constable, *Religious Life and Thought [11th-12th Centuries] [London 1979]*). For phenomenological parallels, see Rocamadour, which to this day pilgrims climb on their knees, or, further away, the Buddhist temple at Borobudur. Schama deals at some length with the case of the Mont Valérien near Paris. Referring to its disaffectation in "martyrized Europe" at the end of the World War II, he oddly enough forgets the last transformation of Mont Valérien. The fortress built there in the nineteenth century had become during the war an execution ground for underground fighters and hostages caught by the Wehrmacht. It hence received, as it were, a new legitimation as Calvary, becoming after the war a place of annual pilgrimage by the French chief of state (Schama, above n. 41, p. 444).

[44] See B. McGinn, "*Iter Sancti Sepulchri*: the Piety of the First Crusaders," in *Essays on Medieval Civilization,* eds. B. K. Ladner and K. R. Philp (Austin, Tex. 1978), 33–71.

restram celestis amore Jerusalem cum aliis currens".[45] As pointed out by Bernard McGinn, we cannot recapture the power evoked by the name "Jerusalem" at the time of the first crusades if we ignore the full scope of the name's meaning. In the piety of the Crusaders, engaged in a mixture of holy war and pilgrimage, there was also room for *concordia*, the peace of the heart necessary for a pilgrimage of penance.

This kind of piety, however, did not go unchallenged. The growth of a new, local religiosity in western Europe tended to belittle or even ignore the significance of – or the need for – Holy Land pilgrimage. One can also follow a trend of opposition to the Crusades during the Middle Ages.[46] After their final failure, the reconquest of the earthly Jerusalem had paved the way, as we have seen, for a radical spiritualization of the *Iter Sancti Sepulchri*.

2.

The failure of early Christian apocalyptic movements, illustrated by the perception of the Montanists as heretics, and the postponement *sine die* of the *parousia*, had direct implications on the representations of Jerusalem. Rather than earthly alternative locations, or the idea of an eschatological *renovatio*, it is the metaphor of a *spiritual* Jerusalem that became prevalent in the early Christian mind. This Jerusalem was the Christian's true fatherland, and it was in heaven. To be sure, the early Christian writers were here following in the footsteps of Jewish apocalypticism: in the book of Revelation, the new Jerusalem was to descend from heaven (Rev. 21: 1–5). For IV Esdras (a Jewish text redacted at the end of the first century C.E.), the eschatological element is still prominent: Jerusalem would be established by God in messianic times. The Syriac *Apocalypse of Baruch* weakens this element, by pointing out the direct relationship between *Urzeit* and *Endzeit*: the heavenly Jerusalem had been prepared by God since the origin of the world.

The transformation of the ideal city is completed in the late second century with Clement of Alexandria, who recalls that the Stoics referred to the heavens as to the true city.[47] For him, as a Christian, the obvious parallel to the heavenly city of the Stoics was heavenly Jerusalem, which he calls "my Jerusalem."[48] We touch here the roots of the mystical meaning of Jerusalem. For Origen, who follows and develops Clement's views on the *polis,* Jerusalem, whose Hebrew name means "vision of peace," could mean the Church, but also, in the tropo-

[45] This text is quoted by Kühnel, above n 23), 114.
[46] Constable, "Opposition to Pilgrimage" 134–38.
[47] *Strom.* 1.72.2ff. This text is quoted by Schmidt, "Jerusalem as *Urbild und Abbild*," 239.
[48] For a discussion of Clement's attitude, see K. Thraede, "Jerusalem II (Sinnbild)," *RAC* 17 (1995): 718–64, esp. 729–31.

logical sense, the soul.[49] A similar allegorical interpretation is found in the fourth-century Origenist, Didymus the Blind. For him, too, Jerusalem can be understood in a threefold way: it is at once the virtuous soul, the Church, and the heavenly city of the living God. We shall return to the *visio pacis* metaphor of Jerusalem, which runs like a thread throughout the centuries.[50] One should at least mention here another formative metaphor, stemming directly from Paul: the Jerusalem above, the Christians' mother, is also called free, *eleuthera* (Gal. 4: 26). "Caelestis Hierusalem, quae est mater libertatis, chorus libertatis": this is a leitmotif of medieval Latin Christian literature.[51]

As is well known, the Augustinian typology of the two cities finds its roots in Tyconius, whose *Commentary on the Apocalypse* refered to two *civitates,* Babylon *versus* Jerusalem.[52] It is impossible here to offer even a brief overview of Augustine's perception of the spiritual Jerusalem, whose praise he sings: "Quando de illa loquor, finire nolo."[53] For him the heavenly Jerusalem represents the Church, bride of Christ, while Babylon represents power and politics. In his *De Civitate Dei*, the *civitas dei* is also called "Jerusalem." It is needless to dwell upon the major formative influence of this typology on medieval perceptions.[54] Augustine's most interesting developments on Jerusalem, perhaps, occur in his *Enarrationes in Psalmos*. Jerusalem is placed in opposition to Babylon, as in Revelation (and also to Sinai, as in Galatians). While Babylon refers to present life in this world, Jerusalem alludes to future life. Then will the boundaries of time be overcome, and God will be praised forever, *in saecula saeculorum*. In his commentary on Psalm 64. 2, for instance, Augustine begins by referring to the etymologies of Babylon and Jerusalem.[55] The one means "confusion," (Heb. *bilbul*) and the other "visio pacis" (Heb. *yr'e shalom*). The major problem facing the relationship between these two opposite entities is the fact that they are inextricably intertwined throughout history: "Permixtae sunt... usque in finem saeculi."

---

[49] *Hom. in Ier.* 9, on Jer 11.2; *Com. in Ioh.* 10.18: "It is Jesus, God's logos, which enters into the soul, called Jerusalem." See also the triple allegorical interpretation of Jerusalem by the fourth-century Origenist, Didymos the Blind, in his *Commentary on Zacharias,* this text is quoted by H. de Lubac, *Exégèse médiévale: les quatre sens de l'Ecriture*, I/2 (Paris 1959), 645. See also Dom O. Rousseau, "Quelques textes patristiques sur la Jérusalem céleste," *La vie spirituelle* 85 (1952): 378–88.

[50] Medieval references in De Lubac, *Exégèse médiévale*, 646.

[51] See for instance Godefroy of Saint Victor, *Glossa in Ex.*, 20.2, quoted by De Lubac, *Exégèse médiévale*, 646.

[52] See Thraede, above n 47, 752–54.

[53] Augustine, *Enarrationes in Psalmos*, 93.24.

[54] See J. van Oort, *Jerusalem and Babylon: a Study of Augustine's City of God and the Sources of his Doctrine of the Two Cities* (Leiden 1988). For the *Fortleben* of the idea, see E. Gilson, *Métamorphoses de la Cité de Dieu,* (Louvain and Paris 1952).

[55] I quote according to M. Simonetti, ed., tr., Sant' Agostino, *Commento ai Salmi* (Fondazione Lorenzo Valla: Mondatori 1988), 182ff. A similar conception of the heavenly Jerusalem as delivering us from the confusion and slavery of the present life is found in Eusebius, *Demonstratio Evangelica* IV, *in finem*.

Jerusalem represents the love of God, while Babylon signifies the love of the world: "Duas istas civitates faciunt duo amores: Ierusalem facit amor Dei; Babyloniam facit amor saeculi." Hence the criterion for anyone to recognize his own identity: ask yourself what you love, and you'll know where you belong. Such an understanding of Jerusalem, then, denies any localization of the city: Jerusalem is everywhere, or more precisely in the hearts of those who love God.

The full-fledged spiritual interpretation of Jerusalem, with multiple levels of meaning, is found first in the writings of John Cassian in the fifth century. For him, Jerusalem could be understood as referring to the human soul: "Si Hierusalem aut Sion animam hominis uelimus accipere secundum illud: lauda Hierusalem dominum: lauda deum tuum Sion." Jerusalem, he goes on, can be understood in four ways, according to the four senses of Scriptures. According to history *(secundum historiam),* it is the city of the Jews, the earthly Jerusalem. According to allegory *(secundum allegoriam),* it represents the Church and Christ. According to anagogy *(secundum anagogem),* it is "that city of God which is the mother of us all." Finally, Jerusalem is identical to the human soul when understood according to tropology *(secundum tropologiam).*[56] Jerusalem thus becomes the most privileged symbol. *In nuce,* this name includes all the Old Testament, the city of God, the mystery of the *Virgo singularis,* the total presentation of Christian mystery.[57]

Throughout the Middle Ages, these various senses of Jerusalem will appear among different writers, from the Venerable Bede and Hrabanus to Nicolas of Lyra, for whom Jerusalem is the best example illustrating the fourfold sense of Scripture. Such conceptions of the spiritual meaning of Jerusalem should be understood in the tradition of its fourfold meaning stemming from Cassian. Thus, for instance, in Nicolas of Lyra, or in Hugh of Fouilloy's *De claustro animae,* a treatise in forty-three chapters on the four senses of Jerusalem: historical, ethical, anagogical, and mystical.[58]

Cassian's *Collationes* was one of the most influential books in the formative period of monastic spirituality. No wonder, then, that Jerusalem was one of the preferred symbols of contemplative life in medieval literature. More precisely, it would seem that the use of Jerusalem in medieval Christian spiritual and mystical literature stood at the intersection between two traditions, that of Cassian and that of Augustine. It is the combination of these two that permits the emergence and development of Jerusalem as the natural symbol of the contempla-

---

[56] See J. Cassian, *Collationes* 14.8; (SC 54, ed. E. Pichery, 190). Cf. E.A. Matter, *The Voice of My Beloved: the Song of Songs in Western Medieval Christianity* (Philadelphia 1990), 54.

[57] Similar opposition between the free Jerusalem, mother of the Christians and earthly Jerusalem, mother of the Jews, in Marius Victorinus, *Com. Gal.* 19.22, referred to by Thraede, above n. 47, 755.

[58] Book 4; references in H. de Lubac, *Exégèse médiévale* I/2, 646; De Lubac points out that the second and fourth senses are mixed up in Hugh's text.

tion of the divine glory shared by angels and those living the monastic *vita angelica.*

The most obvious author for the medieval spiritual meaning of Jerusalem, however, remains Bernard of Clairvaux. The following quotation is representative of his understanding of Jerusalem:

> You have two from heaven, both Jesus the Bridegroom and the Bride Jerusalem ... . When the holy Emmanuel brought to earth the teaching of heavenly discipline, when the visible image and beautiful appearance of that heavenly Jerusalem which is our mother became known as revealed to us in and through Christ.[59]

For Bernard, the monastery was a training camp for the heavenly Jerusalem.[60] He intended to model the Church after the heavenly Jerusalem.[61] Around 1129, in a famous letter to Alexander, bishop of Lincoln, which has become the *locus classicus* of the new religious sensitivity, Bernard specifically identifies Clairvaux with the heavenly Jerusalem: "Et, si vultis scire, Clara Vallis est. Ipsa est Ierusalem, ea quae in coelis est, tota mentis devotione, et conversationis imitatione, et cognatione quadam spiritus sociata." Bernard was referring to Philip, a monk from England who, on his way to Jerusalem, had made a stop in Clairvaux. Bernard convinced him that his monastery was the new and true Jerusalem, and that there was no need for him to continue on his exhausting voyage.[62] His conception of spiritual pilgrimage is developed in his writing "on conversion."[63] The monastery was not only conceived as a *paradeisos,* but also as a new Jerusalem, the heavenly city of peace, already in the Patristic tradition.

For Bernard, then, the cloister of Clairvaux is a Jerusalem in anticipation. The monk dwells in Jerusalem: this name refers to those who in this world lead the religious life: by a virtuous and orderly life, they seek to imitate the way of life of the Jerusalem above.

> Puto enim hoc loco prophetam Ierusalem nomine designasse illos, qui in hoc saeculo vitam ducunt religiosam, mores supernae illius Ierusalem conversatione honesta et ordinata pro viribus imitantes; et non veluti hi, qui de Babylone sunt.... Mea autem, qui videor monachus et Ierosolymita, peccata certe occulta sunt ... .[64]

---

[59] *SSC* 27.7. This text is discussed by B. McGinn, *The Growth of Mysticism* (New York 1994), 178–79. See also Auffarth, "Himmliches und irdisches Jerusalem," *ZfR* 2 (1993), 111–12.

[60] McGinn, above n. 57, 182.

[61] H.-W. Goetz, "Bernard et Norbert [de Xanten]: eschatologie et Réforme," *Bernard de Clairvaux: histoire, mentalités, spiritualités* (= *Oeuvres complètes,* vol. 1; [Paris 1992]), 514.

[62] Bernard, *Letter* 64; PL 182, 169–70 (*Writings,* 281–82). See discussion of this famous text, inter alia, in H.-W. Goetz, "Bernard et Norbert, 505–25, esp. 518. Another of his letters, also discussed by Goetz, reflects his preference for the spiritual over the earthly Jerusalem. In 1124, he wrote to Geoffroi, bishop of Chartres: "I do not know whether Norbert will go to Jerusalem, as you ask me ... ."

[63] See Bernard, "On Conversion," in Bernard of Clairvaux, *Works* (Classics of Western Spirituality; New York 1987), 65–97.

[64] Sermon 55.2, PL 183,1045c-d. Cf. for instance J. Leclercq, O.S.B., *The Love of Learning*

In the second half of the twelfth century, the school of Saint Victor provided other instances of a similar conception of Jerusalem. Explaining the parable of the Good Samaritan, for instance, Richard of Saint Victor not only saw Christ in the Samaritan, and fallen man in the traveler attacked by thieves (both interpretations going back to Patristic literature), but also argued that the city of Jerusalem which the traveler left, represents contemplation; while Jericho symbolizes fallen man's misery; the descent from Jerusalem to Jericho itself representing sin.[65]

Dom Jean Leclercq, the great scholar of medieval monastic spirituality, has edited an anonymous sermon, probably written in the eleventh century by a disciple of Jean of Fécamp.[66] This text, written with profound enthusiasm, makes generous use of quotations from the Psalms and appears to reflect widely-shared images. It begins by praising the frequent recollection of Jerusalem as a spiritual exercise of great value: "Ciuitatis et regis Hierusalem frequens recordatio dulcis est nobis consolatio, religiosae exercitationis grata occasio, onerosae sarcinae nostrae necessaria subleuatio." I wish to call attention here to the direct link between the representation of a place (even if only a metaphorical, ideal one) and religious meditation, or, as the text has it, an exercise. This would be recognized by Ignatius Loyola, who, in his *Spiritual Exercises,* would emphasize the need to identify a place with oneself in order to meditate on the mysteries of Christ's earthly life. This trend in Ignatian spirituality clearly reflects medieval patterns of thought, especially after the Crusades.

The pairing of Jerusalem/Babylon was not limited to Latin and ecclesiastical literature. Its important influence upon European culture is reflected by its presence in the earliest strata of Italian vernacular literature of the *duecento*. Such texts may reflect Joachite influence. Giacomino of Verona, for instance, writes, in Veronese:

Ierusalem celeste	questa terra s'apella
città de l'alto Deu	nova, preclara e bella
dond e Cristo segno ...	
... contraria de quella	ke per nomo se clama,

---

and the Desire for God: A Study of Monastic Culture (New York 1961), 54. To be sure, this was not a new trend; as is well-known, opposition to Holy Land pilgrimages began in the fourth century, together with the development of pilgrimages. The *locus classicus* is that of Gregory of Nyssa, who had himself visited the Holy Land on ecclesiastical business, and who argued in one of his letters (Letter 2) that Cappadocia was as good a place as Palestine for leading a spiritual life. This text is discussed, within the context of a Patristic discussion of pilgrimage, by B. Biton-Ashkelony, *Pilgrimage: Perceptions and Reactions in the Patristic and Monastic Literature of the 4th-6th cent.*, (Ph.D. diss., Hebrew University of Jerusalem, 1996).

[65] *Liber exceptionum* 12.5, quoted by J. Châtillon, *DS* 13:601. See also on Hugh of Saint Victor, P. Dinzelbacher, *Christliche Mystik im Abendland* (Paderborn 1994), 141.

[66] J. Leclercq, "Une élévation sur les gloires de Jérusalem," *RSR* 40 (1951–1952): 326–34.

città de gran pressura   Babilonia la magna
un la qual Lucifer. ...[67]

Similar perceptions of Jerusalem are found in the *Libro delle tre Scritture* of the poet Bonsevin de la Riva, one of Dante's precursors:

... quella città soprana   si è pur d'or lucente
Le plaze delectevre   le mure resplendante
... Oi De, splendor purissimo   in la città celesta ...
... Oi De, com pò godher   lo just in paradisò ...[68]

In something that can be described as a pendulum movement in the *longue durée,* the image of a golden Jerusalem, indeed, was to cross the centuries (and religious boundaries) as well as the continents. From the song *Urbs beata Ierusalem, dicta pacis visio,* known to have been written for Vespers in the eighth century, continuing in a straight line to the Victorian hymns on "Jerusalem the Golden," and from these to the Hebrew song of Naomi Shemer, which become one of the main symbolic and cultural expressions of Israeli triumphalism in 1967.

Bernard of Clairvaux, Richard of Saint Victor, Joachim of Fiore, and Giacomino of Verona have been adduced here as examples of the understanding of Jerusalem as a symbol of spiritual life. Throughout the Middle Ages, and up to the early modern period, the heavenly Jerusalem represents for this trend of thought the ultimate goal of the pilgrim on his way to a spiritual vision. The total transformation of the symbol, with the complete disappearance of any reference to the earthly Jerusalem, was accomplished in spiritual writings such as those of Bonaventure in the thirteenth century. He speaks of Saint Francis, in his insatiable thirst for peace, as a citizen of the heavenly Jerusalem, which the soul reaches when it enters into itself.[69] At the dawn of the modern times, the Spanish mystics continued this trend. Bernardino of Laredo, for instance, published his *Ascent to Mount Sion* in 1535. The work's historical importance stems from Teresa of Avila's predilection for it. The "ascent to Mount Zion" had become totally metaphorical:

> So that the ascent of Mount Sion is the same as the ascent to Jerusalem ... . And this temporal Jerusalem denotes for us the eternal and sovereign city for which God created us and to which we shall not go unless we ascend from the knowledge of ourselves to the following of Christ.[70]

The message has undergone a radical spiritualization, the earthly Jerusalem has disappeared from sight, and the whole pilgrimage to the holy city is a journey of the soul:

---

[67] G. Contini, ed., *Poeti del duecento*, I (Milan and Naples 1960), 625.

[68] G. Contini, ed., *Le opere volgari di Bonsevin de la Riva* (Roma 1961), 154.

[69] Bonaventure, *The Soul's Journey to God*, tr. E. Cousins (Classics of Western Spirituality; New York 1978), 51, 90.

[70] E. A. Peers, *The Ascent to Mount Sion* (New York 1951), 66. See the edition of the *Subida* by J. B. Gomis, *Misticos Franciscanos Espanoles*, vol. 2 (Madrid 1948).

The fire of the Lord is in Zion, since contemplative souls possess it in this life, and finally are perfected in Jerusalem, since such souls as these, who here begin to love, and persevere in love, grow in love continually as they proceed along the road of this exile, then are led ... into the Jerusalem which is above, where in that fire which had its beginning in ths exile of ours burns without intermission ...[71]

In the late Middle Ages, we can follow the development of new, radical beliefs in a kind of pilgrimage. This can be described as internal and quite atopic, a pilgrimage accomplished not in space, with no need of dangerous and expensive travel to a foreign land, not even in a conveniently miniaturized space at home, but within the soul itself. The traditional images of Holy Land pilgrimage are reinterpreted metaphorically, and the earthly pilgrims are a figure of the march toward the spiritual Jerusalem. Such an idea is found, for instance, in the sermons of Bernardino of Siena, probably the most influential spiritual force in Italy of the first half of the fifteenth century. Toward the end of Chaucer's *Canterbury Tales*, it is also reflected in the words of the country priest, who views Canterbury as the Holy Land for everybody, since earthly pilgrimages are but the image of the spiritual march toward Jerusalem.[72]

I have dealt briefly above with two different phenomena: the imaginary visit to Holy Land shrines at their local replicas, and the tradition of a heavenly Jerusalem, up to the development of spiritual pilgrimages to Jerusalem in the later Middle Ages. I have argued that these two phenomena are related. Various "spiritual pilgrimages," which began to be printed as early as the first half of the fifteenth century, were meant as spiritual guides for those who could not afford the expense of the pilgrimage itself or were unwilling to suffer its vagaries. In a sense, Christian spirituality was thus rediscovering themes already found in late antique Patristic spiritual and monastic literature. The Christian was defined anew as *homo viator*.

Such patterns of thought reflect, in a sense, a return to some fundamental Augustinian attitudes. No wonder, then, if in the fifteenth century Nicolas of Cusa was able "to transpose these themes of spiritual experience to the level of philosophical and theological reflection, and to elaborate a mystical synthesis."[73] For him, it is not only man who can be defined as *viator*. Rather, it is the whole life of the Church on earth that should be understood as a pilgrimage in the footsteps of Jesus Christ.

We can perhaps describe schematically the dialectical evolution of pilgrimage ideas in the following way: the holy places gave birth to the development of pilgrimage in early Christianity. At a later stage, translations of these holy places

---

[71] Ibid., 70, 71.
[72] E. Delaruelle, "Le pèlerinage intérieur au XVe siècle," in his *La piété populaire au moyen-âge* (Turin 1975), 555–561.
[73] Ibid., 558.

brought them to European cities. Finally, the pilgrimage to the local replica of the holy place was transformed into a spiritual pilgrimage.

Apocalyptic spirituality permits the actualization and vivification of perceptions often muted or neutralized in mainstream Christian tradition. The great Calabrian visionary from the twelfth century, Joachim de Fiore, is said to have experienced a conversion to the interior life precisely during a pilgrimage to the Holy Land as a young man. He was to make great use of the name of Jerusalem in his *Liber Figurarum*. The most puzzling pair of figures in this book is perhaps the antithesis of Jerusalem/Ecclesia and Babylon/Rome. Note that the Roman Church, for Joachim, is always Jerusalem, never Rome. While Babylon is the realm of the devil, the heavenly kingdom of God is symbolized by Jerusalem. The theme of the figures is the pilgrimage of the faithful people of God. "The sons of Jerusalem are pilgrims sojourning in the midst of Babylon...." The *Liber Concordiae* starts from the concept of the earthly pilgrimage and throughout makes much use of the figures of pilgrimage and journeying.[74] At the end of history, there will be a third apotheosis of Jerusalem, after the reign of David in the earthly Jerusalem and the pontificate of Pope Sylvester in Rome.

In his *Eternal Gospel,* Joachim goes into a detailed description of the heavenly Jerusalem as described in Revelation 21, seeing a precise symbolism in its various components, such as the different precious stones from which it is built. He insists on the fact that in the heavenly Jerusalem there is no Temple built by men, since the Father and the Son are themselves the only Temple of the Spirit.

In the fourth century, Eusebius and Jerome had pointed out the traditional etymology of Jerusalem, *Yerushalaim,* as referring to a vision of peace, *visio pacis* in Jerome's words. This interpretation was picked up by Augustine and Isidore of Seville.[75] Through their mediation, this traditional etymology had become prominent in medieval texts.[76] The last avatar of the perception of the earthly Jerusalem, in the later Middle Ages and at the time of the Renaissance, reflects a new dimension given to the mystical *visio pacis*. A purely spiritual vision, it also became the best metaphor of an eschatological dream of peace upon earth among religions and civilizations.

In his *De pace fidei*, Nicolas of Cusa dreams of a religious treaty agreed upon in heaven, i.e., in the only rational region, by wise Christians, Jews, and Muslims. Given full powers, they then meet in Jerusalem, the common religious center, in order to receive in the name of all the single faith, and they establish upon it per-

---

[74] As pointed out by M. Reeves and B. Hirsch-Reich, in their magisterial study of the theme, *The Figurae of Joachim of Fiore* (Oxford 1972), 184–91.

[75] See above, Augustine integrates this etymology of Jerusalem into his thought about war and peace; see for instance *Enarr. in Psalmos*, Ps. 64: 4: "Vincet pax et finietur bellum."

[76] See for instance Haymon from Auxerre: "Jerusalem quae interpretatur visio pacis, significat sanctam Ecclesiam Deum mente videntem...."

petual peace, "in order that in this peace, the Creator of all things be glorified in all *saecula*. Amen."[77]

The development of ethnological curiosity, also vis-à-vis "Turks" (i.e., Muslims) and Jews, together with the sorrow generated by religious strife throughout Europe, encouraged a renewal of utopian thought. Jerusalem provided here a ready-made symbol, understood by all. Tomaso Campanella, another visionary from Calabria (this time a Dominican), at the beginning of the seventeenth century dreamed of a new kind of *recuperatio Terrae Sanctae,* which would be the utmost expression of the *renovatio seaculi:* "The Church was born in Jerusalem, and it is to Jerusalem that it will return, after having conquered the whole world." The former presence of the Crusaders in Jerusalem is perceived by Campanella as a step toward the instauration in that city of the messianic kingdom: Jerusalem, indeed, is the Holy City, where Jews, Christians, and Muslims can become united in communion.[78]

A similar mixture of mysticism and politics linked to Jerusalem is found also in the thought of the sixteenth-century Jesuit Guillaume Postel, an Orientalist who became the first holder of the Chair of Hebrew at the Collège de France, and one of the great "illuminés" of the Renaissance. For Postel, Jerusalem, true mother of the universe, is the *figura* of the building of the third Temple, a Temple to serve the whole earth and permit the spiritual rebirth of humankind in the final kingdom of Jesus Christ and the restitution of all things, the *apokatastasis pantôn* dear to the Stoics and to Origen:

> Ceste unité unique, et du tout différente de toutes celles qui ont esté, ou sont, ou jamais seront au monde inférieur, est la personele Jérusalem, de laquelle David escript: Yerusalaim sehubeerah lah yiheddow, Jerusalem cujus associatio aut participatio pro ipsa fit una cum eo. Nos pieds sont establis en tes portes, o Jerusalem. Jerusalem qui es edifiée comme une cité, mais non pas une cité, ains une personne, de laquelle l'accompaignement est pour elle avec un luy, qui en est le chef. Or est il du tout certein et necessaire qu'entre toutes et sur toutes les congregations, polices, estats ou eglises du monde, il y en aye une tele qu'elle soit du tout excellente et differente de tout aultre ... car oultre l'estre un corps mystique ou civil et politique, elle est personele et vive union come chascune aultre mere ou vierge ou femme du monde... C'est donc la finale victoire d'une seule et unike colombe et espouse ... .[79]

---

[77] Nicolas of Cusa, *De pace fidei*, 19. With the dawn of the modern times, such "interfaith dialogues," as they are now being called, or rather "polylogues," became more common. The most famous example of the genre, perhaps, is Jean Bodin's *Heptahemeres,* written in 1596.

[78] A. Dupront, *Du sacré* (Paris 1987), 301–303.

[79] G. Postel, *Le thrésor des prophéties de l'univers*, ed. F. Secret (Archives internationales d'histoire des idées 27; La Haye 1969, 157–59. On Venice as the New Jerusalem (and the New Rome) for Guillaume Postel, see M. Leathers Kuntz, "The Myth of Venice in the Thought of Guillaume Postel," in *Supplementum Festivum: Studies in Honor of P. O. Kristeller*, eds. J. Hankins et al. (Binghamton, N.Y 1987), 503–23, esp. 512: "Esse vero Jerusalem translatam Venetias ab sacrorum inviolabilitatem patet."

One could go on quoting Postel's lucubrations on messianic Jerusalem – for him both a political and spiritual entity. His naiveté and messianic patterns of thought reflect a recurrent trend in religious modern attitudes, with which we are unfortunately too familiar. We are here far from another early modern rein-terpretation of Jerusalem, Pico della Mirandola's *De dignitate hominis,* in which the heavenly Jerusalem is the goal of a spiritual flight kindled by the Socratic delirium described in Plato's *Phaedrus,* a flight that takes the mystical philos-opher far from this world ruled by Satan.[80]

In these pages, I have sought to focus on medieval mental representations of Jerusalem, and to suggest some main lines of their development and transforma-tion processes. As we have seen, these processes are dialectical in the sense that they fuel one another. The heavenly or spiritual Jerusalem lies at the base of Holy Land pilgrimages and crusades, while pilgrimages to the earthly city, in their turn, permit the development of "new Jerusalems" throughout Europe. Eventually, it is such *memoriae* of Jerusalem which permit a constant passage between earthly and heavenly Jerusalem in the "imaginaire médiéval." The spiritualization of Jerusalem and its "multiplications" are two sides of the Chris-tian "uprooting" of Jerusalem, reflecting a fundamental ambivalence in Chris-tian attitudes to the Holy City. In the religious history of Europe, Jerusalem is no longer located "toward the Far East," as it had been for the Palestinian martyr Pamphilus. Jerusalem is both in heaven and at home.

---

[80] I quote according to P. de la Mirandola, *Oeuvres philosophiques* (Paris 1993): 28–29.

Sources

Previous versions of the following chapters have appeared as follows, and appear here with the agreement of the various publishers:

Chapter 1, = "Le radicalisme religieux du christianisme ancien", in A. Le Boulluec and E. Patlagean, eds., *Retours aux Ecritures* (Bibliothèque de l' Ecole Pratique des Hautes Etudes, Ve Section; Louvain 1993), 347–374, and in English in *Israel Oriental Studies* 14 (1994), 173–193.

Chapter 3, in L. Perrone, ed., *Discorsi di verita: paganesimo, giudaismo e cristianesimo a confronto nel "Contro Celso" di Origene* (Studia Ephemeridis Augustinianum; Rome 1998), 81–94.

Chapter 4, in H. Cancik, H. Lichtenberger and P. Schäfer, eds., *Geschichte-Tradition-Reflexion: Festschrift Martin Hengel* (Tübingen 1996), vol. II, 339–368

Chapter 5, in J. Assmann, ed., *Die Einführung des inneren Menschen* (Studien zum Verstehen fremder Religionen, 6; Gütersloh 1993), 168–182.

Chapter 6, in G. Stanton and G. Stroumsa, eds., *Tolerance and Intolerance in Early Judaism and Christiantiy* (Cambridge 1998), 172–184.

Chapter 7, *Numen* 36 (1989), 16–41.

Chapter 8, in O. Limor and G. Stroumsa, eds., *Contra Judaeos Ancient and Medieval Polemics between Christians and Jews* (Texts and Studies in Mediaeval and Early Modern Judaism; Tübingen 1995), 1–26.

Chapter 10, *History of Religions* 30 (1990), 25–50.

Chapter 14, = "Gnostische Gerechtigkeit und Antinomismus: Epiphanes' Über die Gerechtigkeit", in A. Assmann, B. Janowski and M. Welker, eds., *Gerechtigkeit: Richten und Retten in der abendländischen Tradition und ihren altorientalischen Ursprüngen* (Paderborn 1998), 149–161.

Chapter 15, in A. Kofsky and G. Stroumsa, eds., *Sharing the Sacred: Religious Contacts and Conflicts in the Holy Land, 1st to 15th Century* (Jerusalem 1998). 97–108.

Chapter 17, in A. I. Baumgarten, J. Assmann, and G. G. Stroumsa, eds., *Self, Soul and Body in Religious Experience* (SHR 78; Leiden 1998), 198–208.

Ancient Literature

General Index

Abelard 132
Abimelech 201, 219
Abyssinians 150
Achilles 43
Adam 79, 92, 224, 234, 253, 295
Adversus Iudaeos literature 134, 137–140, 143, 144, 153, 155
Aelia Capitolina, see Jerusalem
affirmation 106
Africa 102, 107, 177
ahl al-kitab 149
Ahura Mazda 265
ainigma 220
akitu 159
al-Shâm 258
Alaric 298
alethes logos 47–52
Alexander 40, 61
Alexandria/Alexandrian tradition 44, 49, 73, 126, 141, 146
alien wisdom 41
allegory 36, 42, 49, 306–307
alphabet 54, 262
ambiguity 10–18
Amesha Spenta 265
anachoretes 224
analogy 307
Anastasis (church in Jerusalem) 5, 114, 122, 130, 296, 299–302
ancestral traditions, *patroi nomoi* 2, 36
anchorites 236, 263
Andrew *Salos* 230
androgyneity 234
Andromeda and Perseus 124
angel/angels 153, 196, 212, 214–216, 234, 236–241, 264, 287–291, 308
aniconic religion 50, 51
Anomias 166
anthropomorphism 261, 262, 267

Anthony, St. 126
anti-Judaism 12, 18, 132–156
anti-Pharisaic polemics 89
Antinomianism 5, 246–257
antisemitism 132–156
apatheia 222, 231, 233, 237, 238
apocalypticism 10, 17, 18, 21, 22, 94, 95, 196, 212, 225, 264, 305, 312
apocryphal writings 31, 33, 34, 43, 263, 266, 295
Apollo 186, 192, 197
apologetic literature 19, 41, 177, 189
Arabic 129
Arabs 3, 58, 72, 72–78, 120, 126, 127, 129
arahant 241
Araspas 283
Archontics 263-265
Arculf 301
Arianism 77, 128
Aristotelianism 183
Armenians 39, 57, 150
Artemidorus 226
Ascalon 120, 124
asceticism/ascetics 18, 26, 71, 74, 92, 94, 127, 172, 180, 181, 192, 210, 222, 236, 238, 239, 255, 260, 264, 266, 267
Asclepius 208
Aspabetus 128
atheism 42, 45, 47
Athens and Jerusalem 104
attendant (*paredros*) 192
Audi 264
Audians 76, 258–267
auditor 283
Augustine 28, 36, 39, 41, 298
avelei Sion 121

Ba'al Shem Tov 240
Babylonians 41

Modern Authors

Delaruelle, E. 311
Delcor, M. 272
Delehaye, H. 198, 211, 242
Delumeau, J. 19, 158
Demandt, A. 137
Déroche, V. 139, 228, 230, 235,*240
Derrett, M. 74
des Places, S.J., E. 63, 196, 217
Descamps, A. 249
Deschner, K-H. 19
Desjardins, M. 14
Despland, M. 48
Destro, A. 202
Deubner, L. 193, 194, 195, 211
Devos, P. 113
Devoti, D. 211
Devreesse, R. 120
Dewey, A. J. 269
Diels 250
Dierkens, T. 209
Dihle, A. 24, 61, 65, 73, 74, 75, 82, 173, 246, 248, 286
Dillon, J. M. 92, 169, 248
Dinzelbacher, P. 309
Dirksen, A. H. 158
Dodds, E. R. 55, 87, 173, 175, 180, 206
Doresse, J. 219
Dörrie, H. 44, 46, 61, 63
Douglas, M. 280, 281
Doutreleau, L. 182
Downey, G. 124, 124
Draguet, R. 263
Drioton, E. 267
Droge, A. J. 108
du Bierzo, U. 114
Dulaey, M. 209, 223, 224
Dumont, L. 21, 171
Duncan, J. 74
Dundes, A. 111
Dupont Sommer, A. 276
Dupont, J. 277
Dupron, A. 313
Duval, Y.M. 186

Edwards, D. 10
Efroymson, D. 144
Eisenstadt, S. N. 151, 171
Eisler, R. 14

Eitrem, S. 191, 198, 219
Eliade, M. 100, 193, 195
Emonds, H. 158
Eph'al, I. 77
Esbroek, M. van 295
Evans, C.A. 137

Faber, R. 52
Faraone, Ch. A. 191, 219
Fascher, E. 61, 117
Fauth, W. 290
Fedotov, G.P. 229
Fédou, M. 45
Feldman, L. H. 134, 135
Ferwerda, R. 283, 284, 288
Festinger, L. 23
Festugière, A.-J. 56, 87, 119, 175, 180, 183, 197, 208, 209, 233, 234, 235, 242
Fiaccadori, G. 73
Filippini, F. 301
Filoramo, G. 218
Finkelstein, L. 129
Finkenstein, A. 138
Fleischner, E. 144
Florowsky, G. 177
Flusin, B. 125, 211
Flusser, D. 87, 88, 107, 114, 161, 248, 276
Fonti, M. 301
Forsyth, N. 217
Fortes, M. 115
Fossum, J. 32
Foucault, M. 9, 170, 171
Fowden, G. 80, 125, 181, 192, 195
Fox, L. R. 18, 153, 171, 180, 205, 210, 211, 214, 215, 219, 224
Frazer 194
Fredouille, J.-C. 103, 105
Fredriksen, P. 89, 173, 291, 295
Frend, W. H. C. 100, 113
Frerichs, E. S. 113, 136, 152
Freud, S. 23, 24
Freyne, S. 136
Friedlander, G. 26
Friedman, M. 8
Funkenstein, A. 140
Gager, J. G. 23, 117, 119, 132, 134, 138, 145, 150, 155, 185

Wissenschaftliche Untersuchungen zum Neuen Testament

Alphabetical Index of the First and Second Series

Feldmeier, Reinhard: Die Krisis des Gottessohnes. 1987. *Volume II/21.*
– Die Christen als Fremde. 1992. *Volume 64.*
Feldmeier, Reinhard and *Ulrich Heckel* (Ed.): Die Heiden. 1994. *Volume 70.*
Fletcher-Louis, Crispin H.T.: Luke-Acts: Angels, Christology and Soteriology. 1997. *Volume II/94.*
Forbes, Christopher Brian: Prophecy and Inspired Speech in Early Christianity and its Hellenistic Environment. 1995. *Volume II/75.*
Fornberg, Tord: see *Fridrichsen, Anton.*
Fossum, Jarl E.: The Name of God and the Angel of the Lord. 1985. *Volume 36.*
Frenschkowski, Marco: Offenbarung und Epiphanie. Volume 1 1995. *Volume II/79* – Volume 2 1997. *Volume II/80.*
Frey, Jörg: Eugen Drewermann und die biblische Exegese. 1995. *Volume II/71.*
– Die johanneische Eschatologie. Volume I. 1997. *Volume 96.* – Volume II. 1998. *Volume 110.*
Fridrichsen, Anton: Exegetical Writings. Ed. by C.C. Caragounis and T. Fornberg. 1994. *Volume 76.*
Garlington, Don B.: 'The Obedience of Faith'. 1991. *Volume II/38.*
– Faith, Obedience, and Perseverance. 1994. *Volume 79.*
Garnet, Paul: Salvation and Atonement in the Qumran Scrolls. 1977. *Volume II/3.*
Gese, Michael: Das Vermächtnis des Apostels. 1997. *Volume II/99.*
Gräßer, Erich: Der Alte Bund im Neuen. 1985. *Volume 35.*
Green, Joel B.: The Death of Jesus. 1988. *Volume II/33.*
Gundry Volf, Judith M.: Paul and Perseverance. 1990. *Volume II/37.*
Hafemann, Scott J.: Suffering and the Spirit. 1986. *Volume II/19.*
– Paul, Moses, and the History of Israel. 1995. *Volume 81.*
Hartman, Lars: Text-Centered New Testament Studies. Ed. by D. Hellholm. 1997. *Volume 102.*
Heckel, Theo K.: Der Innere Mensch. 1993. *Volume II/53.*
Heckel, Ulrich: Kraft in Schwachheit. 1993. *Volume II/56.*
– see *Feldmeier, Reinhard.*
– see *Hengel, Martin.*
Heiligenthal, Roman: Werke als Zeichen. 1983. *Volume II/9.*
Hellholm, D.: see *Hartman, Lars.*
Hemer, Colin J.: The Book of Acts in the Setting of Hellenistic History. 1989. *Volume 49.*
Hengel, Martin: Judentum und Hellenismus. 1969, [3]1988. *Volume 10.*

– Die johanneische Frage. 1993. *Volume 67.*
– Judaica et Hellenistica. Volume 1. 1996. *Volume 90.* – Volume 2. 1999. *Volume 109.*
Hengel, Martin and *Ulrich Heckel* (Ed.): Paulus und das antike Judentum. 1991. *Volume 58.*
Hengel, Martin and *Hermut Löhr* (Ed.): Schriftauslegung im antiken Judentum und im Urchristentum. 1994. *Volume 73.*
Hengel, Martin and *Anna Maria Schwemer:* Paulus zwischen Damaskus und Antiochien. 1998. *Volume 108.*
Hengel, Martin and *Anna Maria Schwemer* (Ed.): Königsherrschaft Gottes und himmlischer Kult. 1991. *Volume 55.*
– Die Septuaginta. 1994. *Volume 72.*
Herrenbrück, Fritz: Jesus und die Zöllner. 1990. *Volume II/41.*
Herzer, Jens: Paulus oder Petrus? 1998. *Volume 103.*
Hoegen-Rohls, Christina: Der nachösterliche Johannes. 1996. *Volume II/84.*
Hofius, Otfried: Katapausis. 1970. *Volume 11.*
– Der Vorhang vor dem Thron Gottes. 1972. *Volume 14.*
– Der Christushymnus Philipper 2,6-11. 1976, [2]1991. *Volume 17.*
– Paulusstudien. 1989, [2]1994. *Volume 51.*
Hofius, Otfried and *Hans-Christian Kammler:* Johannesstudien. 1996. *Volume 88.*
Holtz, Traugott: Geschichte und Theologie des Urchristentums. 1991. *Volume 57.*
Hommel, Hildebrecht: Sebasmata. Volume 1 1983. *Volume 31* – Volume 2 1984. *Volume 32.*
Hvalvik, Reidar: The Struggle for Scripture and Covenant. 1996. *Volume II/82.*
Kähler, Christoph: Jesu Gleichnisse als Poesie und Therapie. 1995. *Volume 78.*
Kammler, Hans-Christian: see *Hofius, Otfried.*
Kamlah, Ehrhard: Die Form der katalogischen Paränese im Neuen Testament. 1964. *Volume 7.*
Kieffer, René and *Jan Bergman (Ed.):* La Main de Dieu / Die Hand Gottes. 1997. *Volume 94.*
Kim, Seyoon: The Origin of Paul's Gospel. 1981, [2]1984. *Volume II/4.*
– „The ‚Son of Man'" as the Son of God. 1983. *Volume 30.*
Kleinknecht, Karl Th.: Der leidende Gerechtfertigte. 1984, [2]1988. *Volume II/13.*
Klinghardt, Matthias: Gesetz und Volk Gottes. 1988. *Volume II/32.*
Köhler, Wolf-Dietrich: Rezeption des Matthäusevangeliums in der Zeit vor Irenäus. 1987. *Volume II/24.*

Korn, Manfred: Die Geschichte Jesu in veränderter Zeit. 1993. *Volume II/51.*

Koskenniemi, Erkki: Apollonios von Tyana in der neutestamentlichen Exegese. 1994. *Volume II/61.*

Kraus, Wolfgang: Das Volk Gottes. 1996. *Volume 85.*
– see *Walter, Nikolaus.*

Kuhn, Karl G.: Achtzehngebet und Vaterunser und der Reim. 1950. *Volume 1.*

Laansma, Jon: I Will Give You Rest. 1997. *Volume II/98.*

Lampe, Peter: Die stadtrömischen Christen in den ersten beiden Jahrhunderten. 1987, ²1989. *Volume II/18.*

Lau, Andrew: Manifest in Flesh. 1996. *Volume II/86.*

Lichtenberger, Hermann: see *Avemarie, Friedrich.*

Lieu, Samuel N.C.: Manichaeism in the Later Roman Empire and Medieval China. ²1992. *Volume 63.*

Loader, William R.G.: Jesus' Attitude Towards the Law. 1997. *Volume II/97.*

Löhr, Gebhard: Verherrlichung Gottes durch Philosophie. 1997. *Volume 97.*

Löhr, Hermut: see *Hengel, Martin.*

Löhr, Winrich Alfried: Basilides und seine Schule. 1995. *Volume 83.*

Luomanen, Petri: Entering the Kingdom of Heaven. 1998. *Volume II/101.*

Maier, Gerhard: Mensch und freier Wille. 1971. *Volume 12.*
– Die Johannesoffenbarung und die Kirche. 1981. *Volume 25.*

Markschies, Christoph: Valentinus Gnosticus? 1992. *Volume 65.*

Marshall, Peter: Enmity in Corinth: Social Conventions in Paul's Relations with the Corinthians. 1987. *Volume II/23.*

McDonough, Sean M.: YHWH at Patmos: Rev. 1:4 in its Hellenistic and Early Jewish Setting. 1999. *Volume II/107.*

Meade, David G.: Pseudonymity and Canon. 1986. *Volume 39.*

Meadors, Edward P.: Jesus the Messianic Herald of Salvation. 1995. *Volume II/72.*

Meißner, Stefan: Die Heimholung des Ketzers. 1996. *Volume II/87.*

Mell, Ulrich: Die „anderen" Winzer. 1994. *Volume 77.*

Mengel, Berthold: Studien zum Philipperbrief. 1982. *Volume II/8.*

Merkel, Helmut: Die Widersprüche zwischen den Evangelien. 1971. *Volume 13.*

Merklein, Helmut: Studien zu Jesus und Paulus. Volume 1 1987. *Volume 43.* – Volume 2 1998. *Volume 105.*

Metzler, Karin: Der griechische Begriff des Verzeihens. 1991. *Volume II/44.*

Metzner, Rainer: Die Rezeption des Matthäusevangeliums im 1. Petrusbrief. 1995. *Volume II/74.*

Mittmann-Richert, Ulrike: Magnifikat und Benediktus. 1996. *Volume II/90.*

Mußner, Franz: Jesus von Nazareth im Umfeld Israels und der Urkirche. Ed. by M. Theobald. 1998. *Volume 111.*

Niebuhr, Karl-Wilhelm: Gesetz und Paränese. 1987. *Volume II/28.*
– Heidenapostel aus Israel. 1992. *Volume 62.*

Nissen, Andreas: Gott und der Nächste im antiken Judentum. 1974. *Volume 15.*

Noormann, Rolf: Irenäus als Paulusinterpret. 1994. *Volume II/66.*

Obermann, Andreas: Die christologische Erfüllung der Schrift im Johannesevangelium. 1996. *Volume II/83.*

Okure, Teresa: The Johannine Approach to Mission. 1988. *Volume II/31.*

Paulsen, Henning: Studien zur Literatur und Geschichte des frühen Christentums. Ed. by Ute E. Eisen. 1997. *Volume 99.*

Park, Eung Chun: The Mission Discourse in Matthew's Interpretation. 1995. *Volume II/81.*

Philonenko, Marc (Ed.): Le Trône de Dieu. 1993. *Volume 69.*

Pilhofer, Peter: Presbyteron Kreitton. 1990. *Volume II/39.*
– Philippi. Volume 1 1995. *Volume 87.*

Pöhlmann, Wolfgang: Der Verlorene Sohn und das Haus. 1993. *Volume 68.*

Pokorný, Petr und *Josef B. Souček:* Bibelauslegung als Theologie. 1997. *Volume 100.*

Prieur, Alexander: Die Verkündigung der Gottesherrschaft. 1996. *Volume II/89.*

Probst, Hermann: Paulus und der Brief. 1991. *Volume II/45.*

Räisänen, Heikki: Paul and the Law. 1983, ²1987. *Volume 29.*

Rehkopf, Friedrich: Die lukanische Sonderquelle. 1959. *Volume 5.*

Rein, Matthias: Die Heilung des Blindgeborenen (Joh 9). 1995. *Volume II/73.*

Reinmuth, Eckart: Pseudo-Philo und Lukas. 1994. *Volume 74.*

Reiser, Marius: Syntax und Stil des Markusevangeliums. 1984. *Volume II/11.*

Richards, E. Randolph: The Secretary in the Letters of Paul. 1991. *Volume II/42.*

Riesner, Rainer: Jesus als Lehrer. 1981, ³1988. *Volume II/7.*
– Die Frühzeit des Apostels Paulus. 1994. *Volume 71.*

Rissi, Mathias: Die Theologie des Hebräerbriefs. 1987. *Volume 41.*

Röhser, Günter: Metaphorik und Personifikation der Sünde. 1987. *Volume II/25.*

Rose, Christian: Die Wolke der Zeugen. 1994. *Volume II/60.*

Rüger, Hans Peter: Die Weisheitsschrift aus der Kairoer Geniza. 1991. *Volume 53.*

Sänger, Dieter: Antikes Judentum und die Mysterien. 1980. *Volume II/5.*

– Die Verkündigung des Gekreuzigten und Israel. 1994. *Volume 75.*

– see *Burchard, Chr.*

Salzmann, Jorg Christian: Lehren und Ermahnen. 1994. *Volume II/59.*

Sandnes, Karl Olav: Paul – One of the Prophets? 1991. *Volume II/43.*

Sato, Migaku: Q und Prophetie. 1988. *Volume II/29.*

Schaper, Joachim: Eschatology in the Greek Psalter. 1995. *Volume II/76.*

Schimanowski, Gottfried: Weisheit und Messias. 1985. *Volume II/17.*

Schlichting, Günter: Ein jüdisches Leben Jesu. 1982. *Volume 24.*

Schnabel, Eckhard J.: Law and Wisdom from Ben Sira to Paul. 1985. *Volume II/16.*

Schutter, William L.: Hermeneutic and Composition in I Peter. 1989. *Volume II/30.*

Schwartz, Daniel R.: Studies in the Jewish Background of Christianity. 1992. *Volume 60.*

Schwemer, Anna Maria: see *Hengel, Martin*

Scott, James M.: Adoption as Sons of God. 1992. *Volume II/48.*

– Paul and the Nations. 1995. *Volume 84.*

Siegert, Folker: Drei hellenistisch-jüdische Predigten. Teil I 1980. *Volume 20 –* Teil II 1992. *Volume 61.*

– Nag-Hammadi-Register. 1982. *Volume 26.*

– Argumentation bei Paulus. 1985. *Volume 34.*

– Philon von Alexandrien. 1988. *Volume 46.*

Simon, Marcel: Le christianisme antique et son contexte religieux I/II. 1981. *Volume 23.*

Snodgrass, Klyne: The Parable of the Wicked Tenants. 1983. *Volume 27.*

Söding, Thomas: Das Wort vom Kreuz. 1997. *Volume 93.*

– see *Thüsing, Wilhelm.*

Sommer, Urs: Die Passionsgeschichte des Markusevangeliums. 1993. *Volume II/58.*

Souček, Josef B.: see *Pokorný, Petr.*

Spangenberg, Volker: Herrlichkeit des Neuen Bundes. 1993. *Volume II/55.*

Speyer, Wolfgang: Frühes Christentum im antiken Strahlungsfeld. 1989. *Volume 50.*

Stadelmann, Helge: Ben Sira als Schriftgelehrter. 1980. *Volume II/6.*

Stettler, Hanna: Die Christologie der Pastoralbriefe. 1998. *Volume II/105.*

Strobel, August: Die Stunde der Wahrheit. 1980. *Volume 21.*

Stroumsa, Guy G.: Barbarian Philosophy. 1999. *Volume 112.*

Stuckenbruck, Loren T.: Angel Veneration and Christology. 1995. *Volume II/70.*

Stuhlmacher, Peter (Ed.): Das Evangelium und die Evangelien. 1983. *Volume 28.*

Sung, Chong-Hyon: Vergebung der Sünden. 1993. *Volume II/57.*

Tajra, Harry W.: The Trial of St. Paul. 1989. *Volume II/35.*

– The Martyrdom of St.Paul. 1994. *Volume II/67.*

Theißen, Gerd: Studien zur Soziologie des Urchristentums. 1979, [3]1989. *Volume 19.*

Theobald, Michael: see *Mußner, Franz.*

Thornton, Claus-Jürgen: Der Zeuge des Zeugen. 1991. *Volume 56.*

Thüsing, Wilhelm: Studien zur neutestamentlichen Theologie. Ed. by Thomas Söding. 1995. *Volume 82.*

Treloar, Geoffrey R.: Lightfoot the Historian. 1998. *Volume II/103.*

Tsuji, Manabu: Glaube zwischen Vollkommenheit und Verweltlichung. 1997. *Volume II/93*

Twelftree, Graham H.: Jesus the Exorcist. 1993. *Volume II/54.*

Visotzky, Burton L.: Fathers of the World. 1995. *Volume 80.*

Wagener, Ulrike: Die Ordnung des „Hauses Gottes". 1994. *Volume II/65.*

Walter, Nikolaus: Praeparatio Evangelica. Ed. by Wolfgang Kraus and Florian Wilk. 1997. *Volume 98.*

Wander, Bernd: Gottesfürchtige und Sympathisanten. 1998. *Volume 104.*

Watts, Rikki: Isaiah's New Exodus and Mark. 1997. *Volume II/88.*

Wedderburn, A.J.M.: Baptism and Resurrection. 1987. *Volume 44.*

Wegner, Uwe: Der Hauptmann von Kafarnaum. 1985. *Volume II/14.*

Welck, Christian: Erzählte ‚Zeichen'. 1994. *Volume II/69.*

Wilk, Florian: see *Walter, Nikolaus.*

Wilson, Walter T.: Love without Pretense. 1991. *Volume II/46.*

Zimmermann, Alfred E.: Die urchristlichen Lehrer. 1984, [2]1988. *Volume II/12.*

Zimmermann, Johannes: Messianische Texte aus Qumran. 1998. *Volume II/104.*

For a complete catalogue please write to the publisher Mohr Siebeck, P.O.Box 2040, D–72010 Tübingen, Germany. Up-to-date information on the internet at http://www.mohr.de